TOWARD A NEW CENTRAL EUROPE
A SYMPOSIUM ON THE PROBLEMS OF
THE DANUBIAN NATIONS

PROBLEMS BEHIND THE IRON CURTAIN SERIES

No. 7.

Toward a New Central Europe

A SYMPOSIUM ON THE PROBLEMS OF THE DANUBIAN NATIONS

EDITED AND WITH AN INTRODUCTION BY

FRANCIS S. WAGNER

DANUBIAN PRESS, INC.

ASTOR PARK, FLORIDA

1970

Library of Congress Catalog Card Number: 79-104329

REPRINT BY HUNYADI M M K
HAMILTON, ONTARIO
1991

Manufactured in the United States of America
By Classic Printing Corporation
Cleveland, Ohio 44102

Contents

PART II

FEDERALISM IN CENTRAL EUROPE

Foreword

THE present volume is a collection of articles, essays, documents and statistical data selected from the first six issues (1963-1969) of *Studies for a New Central Europe*, a review devoted to the reorganizational problems and tasks of that area. Besides these, two heretofore unpublished papers have been added to the collection. Namely, Alexander Gallus' "Cultural Pluralism and the Study of Complex Societies in Anthropology," and Edward Chaszar's "The Place of East Central Europe in Western Civilization."

The main purpose of our periodical as well as of its issuing body, The Mid-European Research Institute, New York, N. Y., is to revaluate past and present affairs of Central Europe in order to find a proper solution to its problems: a lasting peace based on justice and equality with the full cooperation of all nations concerned. A growing number of experts grouped around the review and its sponsoring institution have worked incessantly toward achieving this objective. From the very outset their activities have been centered on that goal and without exception they have arrived at the conclusion that in order to avoid past and present errors a system of neutralization and federalization should be established in the Danubian area ranging from Germany to Russia. This common goal has been scrutinized from different viewpoints by authors of various ethnic groups. As a result, almost each and every article reflects as a recurrent feature the urgent need for founding a neutral, federated Central Europe.

The scope of inquiry covers quite a broad field. Part I (International Relations) tries to elucidate foreign policy constellations by examining Central Europe's relations with the East and West with a view toward creating a Buffer Zone situated between Germany and Russia. Part II (Federalism in Central Europe) attempts to clarify some specific factors of a regional arrangement. Part III (The Nationality Question) highlights ethnic conditions with particular emphasis on Czechoslovakia and Rumania. The concluding chapter, Part IV (Economic Problems), considers economic conditions and policies, and the Appendix includes many interesting maps as well as statistical data.

I find myself ill-equipped to say how grateful I am to those who assisted and guided me in the development of this volume. I am happy to record my considerable debt to Mr. Eugene Padányi-Gulyás for having brought this project to my attention and for his subsequent encouragement and advice. My gratitude goes also to the Danubian Press, Inc., Astor Park, Florida, for publishing our enterprise. My daughter, Christina Maria T. Wagner, gave unstinted cooperation in editing and assisted with excellent proofreading. My thanks are also due to Mrs. Edith Talbot Kardos for her generous help in the initial phase of editing.

It is worth mentioning that an all-important volume is already in preparation entitled *A Hundred Years of the Danubian Nations, 1867-1967; A Statistical Handbook* which is to be issued by the Mid-European Research Institute. Members of this Institute have long felt the need for such a work which can help pave the way for a federative solution. This is why the present volume is dedicated and why the aforesaid statistical compendium will be dedicated to those who are able and willing to promote this grand design.

During the whole editorial process I have been keenly aware that uniformity in such a work of widespread collaboration could be achieved only through forcible reconciliation of conflicting views. No attempts have been made to achieve this undesirable goal. All contributors to this volume have been at complete liberty to express their opinions and have not been influenced to any extent in any regard. The views expressed in this book by individual contributors are, therefore, not necessarily those of the Editor. On the contrary, in several instances the Editor's opinion has been in sharp conflict with views represented by individual authors, particularly when historical backgrounds of certain Slavic problems have been depicted. Needless to say, every author assumes full responsibility for his article.

In working on this project I have become increasingly aware of the difficulties involved in materialization of the principles relating to the reorganization of the heart of the Old World. But we shall all the more welcome any suggestion furthering those ideas and any objective criticisms by experts in the fields of the political and social sciences, history, as well as international law. Due to the complexity of the topics in our volume, I felt compelled, in place of a standard Introduction, to depict in historical perspective the most characteristic features of Central Europe which I hope will enable us to arrive at an understanding and interpretation of the complicated reorganizational problems.

Washington, D. C.

September 1, 1969.   *Francis S. Wagner*

Our Contributors

PÁL AUER, Dr., International Lawyer, Paris, France; Honorary Secretary of the League for the Self-Determination of the Peoples.

RICHARD K. BARTONIEK, Economist, Vienna, Austria.

FRITZ BOCK, Dr., Minister of Commerce, Republic of Austria, Vienna.

STJEPAN BUC, Political scientist, Buenos Aires, Argentina; Former member of the Yugoslav Parliament.

EDWARD CHASZAR, Political scientist, George Washington University, Washington, D. C.

TIBOR ECKHARDT, Dr., Hungary's Chief Delegate to the League of Nations, 1934-1935.

JOSEPH GALGANOVICZ, Lecturer on East Central European questions.

ALEXANDER GALLUS, Ph. D., Past President of the Australian Anthropologic Society, Melbourne, Australia; Editor, Studies for a New Central Europe.

MILAN HODZA, Dr., d. 1943 in London; Slovak statesman; Prime Minister of Czechoslovakia prior to the Munich four-power agreement, 1938.

STAN IONESCU, President of the Union Naciones Danubianas.

WENZEL JAKSCH, † Leader of the German Social Democrats in Czechoslovakia; Member of the German Bundestag.

BÉLA TALBOT KARDOS, Dr., Economist, librarian, writer, Washington, D.C.

GEORGE KÉLER, Executive Secretary of the Cooperative Wholesale Comm., Stockholm, Sweden.

JOSEPH M. KIRSCHBAUM, Dr., University professor, Toronto, Canada.

FERENC KOSZORUS, Military historian, Washington, D. C., Former Colonel on the Royal Hungarian General Staff.

EDMUND I. LAZAR, Political scientist, Vienna, Austria.

MIROSLAV LAZAROVITCH, Economist, New York, N. Y.

CARLILE AYLMER MACARTNEY, Professor of history, All Souls College, Oxford, Gt. Brit.

ADAM MAKKAI, Ph. D., Professor of linguistics, University of Illinois, Chicago, Ill.

JOSEPH MATL, Ph. D., University professor and Chairman of the Slavic Institute of Graz, Austria.

F. O. MIKSCHE, Political scientist, Paris, France.

JOSEPH OSTROVSKY, Dr., former lawyer, Kosice, Czechoslovakia.

BÉLA PADÁNYI-GULYÁS, Former member of the Hungarian National Assembly.

EUGENE PADÁNYI-GULYÁS, Former member of the Hungarian Parliament; Chairman of the Editorial Board, **Studies for a New Central Europe.**

G. H. SIKORSKY, Political scientist, Montreal, Canada.

ISTVÁN SZENTPÁLY, Dr., Lawyer, New York, N.Y.

GYULA TASSONYI, Dr., International lawyer, Zurich, Switzerland.

ALBERT WASS, University professor, writer; President, The Danubian Press, Inc., Astor Park, Florida, USA.

FRANCIS S. WAGNER, Ph. D., Staff Member, Library of Congress; Head, Hungarian Consulate General, Czechoslovakia, 1946-1948; Historian, editor of the present volume. His biographical data are included in **Who's Who in the South and Southwest, 1969-1970;** in the **Directory of American Scholars, 1969; Dictionary of International Biography** (London, 1970).

Introduction to the History of Central Europe

FRANCIS S. WAGNER

Highlights of Political Development

THE peoples in the Danubian area situated between Germany and Russia have always led an eventful life. They witnessed historic turning points long before their conversion to Christianity prior and around the millenium. It is worth mentioning that their conversion to Christianity was the first significant step in laying down the foundations of a Central Europe. During this period, roughly between the middle of the 8th and the end of the 11th centuries, Central Europe, historically speaking, took the final shape it was to maintain in the coming centuries. The characteristically Central European feature for the first time in history was reflected in the area's foreign policy constellations as promoted by its leading dynasties: the Czech Premyslides, the Hungarian Árpáds, and the Polish Piasts. Their dynastic policies indeed aimed at the founding of an independent Central Europe, and there were moments when the realization of that design seemed to be imminent. But their dreams could not come true. They went too far to the East, as in Poland's case, or else failure came about as a result of the lack of cooperation of internal forces or of some unfavorable interference by the West or the Oriental hordes of the Tartar invasion (1241-1242) and the Turkish yoke.

For the sake of objectivity, it should be remembered that there was one workable scheme emanating from a German source which could have been acceptable to both Germany and the other nations of Central Europe. But the premature death of Otto III (980-1002) prevented its realization. Emperor Otto III under the influence of his tutor Gerbert of Aurillac, who later became Pope Sylvester II (999-1003), tried to reestablish a Roman Empire extending not only over the West but including also all the Slavs, Hungarians, and other ethnic elements east of the Oder and Leitha rivers. This projected

1

empire would have revived the classical Roman Empire as envisaged by Constantine the Great. Despite the new turn of events, the notion of organizing a strong Central European power never died. It was resurrected in the 13th and 14th centuries by the rulers of the Luxemburg and Anjou dynasties, especially Louis the Great, King of Hungary and of Poland (1342-1382). Jiri z Podebrad, King of Bohemia (1458-1471), and Matthias (I) Corvinus, King of 'Hungary (1440?-1490) understood very well the true mission in Central Europe and made serious efforts to create a federation in that part of the Danube Valley. In the center of these efforts stayed Hungary, Bohemia, and Poland. The advantage of those countries of belonging to a federation was appreciated by their ruling circles when after the death of Jiri z Podebrad and Matthias Corvinus, their countries, along with Poland came to be ruled by the descendants of Jagello, Vladislav II (1471-1516) and Louis (1516-1526). Known as the Jagellon Federal Union, this federation which was later reinforced when Vladislav II was made King of Hungary in 1490, came into direct contact with Central Europe and it had every chance for further development. But it was wrecked by religious disunion on one side and by the military victories of the Ottoman troops on the other.

For centuries to come, the idea of the Holy Roman Empire was the most devastating single factor which stood in the way of making a well-organized Central Europe. This ideal dates back to Charlemagne, king of the Franks, who was crowned emperor of the West, in Rome, in 800, and was continuous until its end under Francis 1 of Austria, in 1806. The concept of the Holy Roman Empire was too Western oriented and ignored the interests of the vast regions east of the Leitha, Oder and Neisse rivers, that is, roughly the present-day Soviet orbit in East Central Europe. This imperial idea has been partly responsible for the Western prejudice which has ever since looked down on the nations of East Central Europe and the Balkan Peninsula as inferior to them.

As I have mentioned previously, the national dynasties of Bohemia, Hungary, and Poland failed to erect a durable, federative political structure in the heart of Europe. Afterwards the Habsburgs proceeded to build up their own Empire the heart of which were the Alpine lands west of the Leitha, Oder and Neisse rivers. The ideal of the Habsburgs stemmed from the centuries-old imperial idea and leaned far to the West. This one-sided orientation prevented them from devoting sufficient attention and energy to Poland which for centuries has been the common target of the Russian Rurik and the Prussian Hohenzollern dynasties. Hungary and Croatia also remained outside of their particular sphere of interests and were left alone in resisting the Turks.

I have already referred to the Habsburg idea of mission which looked exceedingly westward and, therefore, was unable to cope with the new situation. The Habsburgs reacted positively to the Turkish menace only after their own capital, Vienna, was besieged by the enemy for a short while. The mobilized the whole of Christian Europe to liberate Vienna in 1683. And, after the liberation of their Eastern territories from Turkish rule, they introduced, chiefly during the second half of the 18th century, a new settlement policy. As a result, many compact German (not Austrian) colonies were established everywhere east of the Leitha. These newly created German settlements were designed to secure the German character of the westward-looking Habsburg Empire and to keep the rebellious Hungary and other non-German ethnic regions under their firm control. These German settlements later posed a serious problem for the governments of East Central Europe especially during the Hitler regime. Later, under the Kremlin's pressure and the Potsdam agreement (1945), local governments were compelled to expel these German minorities, and did so using inhumane methods. This transfer of German minorities from the Danubian states and the so-called exchange of population between Czechoslovakia and Hungary proved to be one of the most shameful chapters in the history of the nationality question. Instead of severely punishing all Nazi collaborators, German minorities were held collectively responsible for war crimes and expelled from their native countries into Austria and the German occupational zones.

In the 19th century little was done to improve Central Europe's political stature. The old imperial idea survived in the form of Gesamtmonarchie at least until the historic Battle of Königgraetz in 1866 where Austria was defeated by Bismarck's Prussia and thus became a vassal state in foreign affairs of the German Reich up to its disintegration in 1918.

The Uprising of 1848-1849 clearly showed that non-German elements (Slavs, Hungarians, Rumanians) were not ready at that time to even discuss their common problems, with the exception of a few exchanges of views in the post-Revolutionary period when nothing could have been done effectively anyhow in order to rearrange their coexistence. Yet, one lesson could successfully be drawn from the Uprising and from the defeat at Königgraetz: namely, that a federation-like union between Austria and Hungary in the form of the 1867 Compromise could be successfully established. But this form of coexistence included two nations only: Austrian-Germans and Hungarians. By all means, it was a giant step forward and the dynasty finally gave up its outmoded doctrine of the medieval imperial idea. This dual Monarchy existed for half a century and collapsed only as a result of its war partnership with Hohenzollern Germany. The unsolved nationality questions constituted only a secondary cause relating to the disintegration of the Habsburg Monarchy. The broadening of the Compromise to include Slavs and

Rumanians in a future federative system was under discussion and only the outbreak of the First World War put a stop to it. At the last moment, Karl I, Emperor of Austria (1916-1918) made an important effort to save the Monarchy from disintegration but failed. His Manifesto was designed to meet President Wilson's requirements: the Poles were to go their own way, and the rest to form a federal state in which each nation was to formulate its own constitution on its own ethnic territory.[1]

The destruction of the Habsburg Monarchy was against the real interests of the nations of that area. Without the interference of the victorious powers it would have been possible to reorganize the Empire in a democratic way as a republic of all nations concerned which would have blocked the way of the expansion of the Third Reich and of the Bolshevik Russia. In addition, the tragic foreign policies of the French-led Little Entente completely poisoned the atmosphere and prevented the regrouping of the Danubian nations to protect their own interests in the coming struggle. Instead of reorganizing Central Europe as a whole, the great powers created a series of small states which were unable to resist any outside influence coming from either Hitler's Germany or Stalin's Russia.

This system of small states created from the ruins of the Habsburg Empire produced constant crises in Europe and in world politics and led finally to the Munich four-power agreement of 1938 and the outbreak of World War II. And as the aftermath of the War, the right of self-determination was again denied to the Danubian nations.

The postwar treaties repeated the tragic errors of the first Paris treaties with one essential exception: since 1945 not France but the USSR has been the sole leading power taking charge of reorganizing Central and Eastern Europe. Dealing with the newly created situations, Clayton Fritchey, a noted columnist of the Evening Star shares the opinion of the majority of diplomatic historians in stating[2] that "It is hardly a secret that the United States, in looking the other way over Czechoslovakia and Hungary, recognized Russia's hegemony in eastern and central Europe." General Charles de Gaulle[3] went even farther that "the armed intervention by the Soviet Union in Czechoslovakia shows that the Moscow Government has not freed itself from the policy of blocs that was imposed on Europe by the effect of the Yalta agreements..."

Undoubtedly, since the end of World War II all efforts starting with Yugoslavia's split with the USSR in June, 1948, through the East German Uprising in 1953, and the Polish and Hungarian events in 1956, through the present-day Czechoslovak crisis and the Rumanian attitude toward the Kremlin have sufficiently proven that there have been popular movements in that area to free the peoples from the bonds which were imposed on them by balance-seeking great power politics. All these popular efforts have clearly pointed to one direction: to the establishment of a Central Europe free from the influence of East-West rivalry.

Cultural Background

The making of present-day Central and Eastern Europe started with their conversion to Christianity between the 8th and 11th centuries. Systematic attempts at Christianization of the Slovenes were begun after 743 by the Bavarians who had forced the Slovene Duke Borut to submit to them. The missions were directed by the bishops of Salzburg, and many Irish monks.[4] It was not until nearly five hundred years later that the conversion of the Slovenes and the incorporation of their territory into Christian Western Europe were finally completed.[5] The Slavs of Great Moravia, Czechs, and Slovaks, after an early conversion to Byzantine Christianity, were ultimately drawn into the orbit of Rome. Poland received the Roman religion from the Czechs at the marriage of its first historical ruler, Miesco I (962-992), to a Czech princess.[6] Byzantine Christianity was introduced into Moravia by Saint Cyril and Saint Methodius in the second half of the 9th century. But Svatopluk, ruler of Great Moravia (870-894) put an end to Byzantine (Slavonic) liturgy.[7]

In the last quarter of the 10th century and decades afterwards there took place the conversion of the Hungarians to Christianity. The chief architect of their conversion to Rome was Stephen I (Saint), first king of Hungary (d. 1038) who promoted the Western branch of Christian civilization. By this he strengthened the Hungarian state so efficiently that it has since been able to withstand all disasters caused by a series of foreign interventions. The conversion of Hungarians to Western Christianity and the founding of their Christian state had dual significance. First of all, it eliminated the remnants of Byzantine Christianity from Central Europe. Secondly, the founding of the Hungarian state separated the two groups of the Slavs, the Western and the Eastern (or Northern and Southern), and thereby helped preserve Western Christianity among the Czechs, Slovaks, Poles, Croats, and Slovenes. According to the Czech Frantisek Palacky (1798-1876), the establishment of Hungary was a cataclysm for the Slavs because it separated the Slavic tribes forever.[8] The Russian Vladimir Ivanovich Lamanskii (1833-1914) argued quite contrary to Palacky's standpoint. According to Lamanskii, the newly founded Hungarian state was the only effective obstacle for centuries to come against Germany's Drang nach Osten. Accordingly, only the Hungarians were able to prevent the complete

Germanization of the Slavs in the Danube area. Indeed, the Hungarian state was a bastion of Westernization, and to a great extent it also defended the region against the German expansion more effectively than any other nation in this part of Europe. Its first king, Stephen I, laid down the foundations of medieval Hungary, some elements of which survived even in later centuries. From the point of view of Christian civilization, the most essential principle of Stephen's reign was his unique conviction that a "unilingual country with the same, homogeneous manners and customs is weak and fragile.9) This unique principle of nationality policy preferred the multilingual state over the unilingual one and this was in line with the needs of the young Christian state which badly needed more and more foreign-born priests, missionaries, teachers and other learned men to build up a new civilization, new socio-economic structure, and political system on a Christian foundation. This then unique nationality policy was also intended to keep under control the influential Hungarian pagan groups which frequently revolted against foreign-born elements upon seeing the latter in high-ranking positions.10)

The introduction of two different forms of Christianity deepened the already existing gap among the Slavs. Czechs, Poles, Slovaks, Croats and Slovenes finally accep⁺ed Western Christianity while all other branches of the Slavs—Russians, Bulgarians, and Serbs, etc.— became associated with the Byzantine form of Christendom. This religious division of the Slavs became distinguished outwardly as well, since the Roman Church used Latin speech and liturgy while Byzantine Christianity used Slavonic speech and liturgy. The distinction between these two forms of Christianity extended far beyond the language of liturgy and church organization. It entered the fields of political development, cultural philosophy and national characteristics. While Western-oriented Slavs took part for centuries in each and every cultural movement that the West produced, the Slavs of the Byzantine sphere remained willfully impervious to them. It is interesting to note that Russians, Bulgarians, and to a lesser extent, Serbs, were not affected by such important movements as the Renaissance with its focal point: humanism; the Reformation; Counter Reformation; the Enlightenment; and democracy. It is of utmost significance that all these anthropocentric and humanistic movements could not penetrate regions situated east of the Habsburg Empire. As a consequence, the peoples living east of the Empire were not in a position to get acquainted with the freedom concept of the West, and the Byzantine cultural sphere to this day is unable to understand the notion of individual freedoms so deeply rooted in the Western, especially Anglo-American, philosophy of life. Summarizing, we can say that those nations of Central and Eastern Europe which were converted to the Roman Church were throroughly influenced by Western learning while the Byzantine Christian nations could not enjoy the blessings of Western civilization.

The spiritual and cultural progress of the Danubian nations was affected by those two spheres of civilization which had centers in Rome, Paris, several cities in Germany and Austria, Italy, and Byzantium. Their cultural ideas and customs deeply affected the national entity of those nations. Their cultural efforts resulted in a long-lasting coexistence between the religious and national elements. Literary activities were based for centuries upon the Bible and the first products of their literary languages were the Bible translations. Until after the middle of the 18th century, the national consciousness of a nation in the Danubian area was formed and cultivated by the frequent use and application of the Holy Scriptures. The symbiosis of religion with patriotism was so natural in that age that the motto of "bulwark of Christianity (or of Western civilization)" against anti-Christian Turkish imperialism became a common heritage, a widespread phrase for peoples from the Balkan Peninsula up to the boundaries of Western Europe. The formative influence of the Christian faith remained so strong that until about the French Revolution it governed not only the domains of philosophy, belles-lettres, and all of the humanities, but it permeated even scientific activities.

With the exception of Bulgaria and to a lesser extent, Serbia, no Russian intellectual influence penetrated deeply and lastingly the cultural life of Central and Eastern Europe until after the revolutions of 1905 and 1917. The systematic Russian cultural effect started only in 1945. In comparing the occupational policies of the Ottoman Empire with that of the USSR, we arrive at the following conclusion. While the Turkish were almost exclusively interested in economic and military exploitations of the oppressed nations, the USSR from the outset exerted its influence in all possible directions, in all human activities. Since the end of the last war, the USSR has forcibly tried in occupied countries to eradicate Western-based tradicional values of patriotism, the philosophy of life, and most of all the freedom idea, through promoting dialectical materialism in thinking and injecting Moscow-centered socialist patriotism and proletarian internationalism into everyday life. The chief criterion of this policy has been the forced idolizing of everything which is the product of Soviet-Russian communism and labeled with the trade-mark Made in Russia. This consistent and ruthlessly applied politics has been chiefly responsible for all revolts aiming at the overthrow of the establishment in the Danubian regions. In these revolts the traditional Western philosophy of life and its freedom concept settled deeply in the minds of East Germans, Hungarians, Poles, Czechs, Slovaks, Southern Slavs, and Rumanians clashed with the Kremlin-represented Byzantine and caesaropapistic heritage.

Conclusion

In order to better understand present situations we must unearth their roots in past history. To see them in totality we must view them not in isolation but in their full historical context. In other words, when viewing present-day topics in historical perspective, we are able to draw very important lessons from them. In so doing we see as evident that some history-making forces of the past have almost totally disappeared on the scene and failed to play any role any more. Let us refer to three such main factors of the past: Pan-Germanism; Pan-Slavism, and; the idea of the nation-state. It is now crystal clear that because of the inhuman acts of Nazism and the catastrophic defeat of Hitler's Germany, the old-fashioned Pan-Germanism has lost its attraction for the Germans. The same can be said about the attraction of Pan-Slavism for the Slavs. The "idea vzajomnosti" (Slavic reciprocity) as a consequence of Russia's ruthless expansionism has also lost its impetus. Most recently, the Soviet-led Communist invasion of Czechoslovakia in August 1968 and its subsequent occupation were a deadly blow to the historic idea of Slavic solidarity and caused the disillusioned Czechs, once the standard-bearers of pro-Russian Pan-Slavism, to return to the heritage of their outstanding political philosopher, Karel Havlicek-Borovsky (1821-1856). Havlicek-Borovsky, after completing his extensive tour of Russia, became so much disillusioned with the Russian way of life that he categorically stated: "I am Czech and I am never Slav . . . The power of the Austrian Empire is the best guarantee of our (Czech) nationality . . ." [11]

The third factor, the idea of the nation-state, not long ago so powerful and closely interwoven with the threads of Pan-Germanism and Pan-Slavism, is dead. It seems to be a historically proven fact that there never has been and there is not now a Czechoslovak nation or a Yugoslav nation, but instead the reality of several ethnically distinct entities such as Czechs, Slovaks; or Serbs, Croats, and Slovenes, etc. This is perhaps the greatest lesson we can draw from current events. Indeed, we are now witnessing the historic process of correcting an old blunder when before our eyes in both countries the system of federation is replacing the artificial, rigid and imperialistic concept of Ceskoslovensky národ (Czechoslovak nation) and Jugoslavenski národ (Yugoslav nation).

The existence of and the right to self-determination of smaller nations cannot be denied any more. Ironically enough, the Communist Dr. Gustáv Husák is doing the same which was done 30 years ago by Dr. Jozef Tiso, then President of the Republic of Slovakia. Both their conflicting ideologies stemmed from the same ideological roots, according to which the Czechs and the Slovaks are ethnically distinct nations. Similar distinctions are being made in Tito's Yugoslavia. Their leaders correctly diagnosed that some kind of federalization is the right answer to the burning questions of their multinational states. They can now recognize that in the center of the Danube Valley ethnic (language) boundaries are inevitably crossing the state boundaries and the historical conditions prevailing there have never favored the implementation of the nation-state. Obviously, the significance of the above-discussed factors which once played a decisive role was greatly diminished, if not eliminated, for a long period of time. This fact in itself can pave the way toward a federative solution in that multinational region. Besides that, certain other symptoms also point to the possibility of this new solution.

In the post-1945 period, far-reaching political, socioeconomic changes and gigantic industrialization have occurred, all of which have resulted in a never-before-seen social mobility, an entirely new social stratification. The old bourgeois society has been transformed into a socialist nation. It can be said that this new social structure in the countries of Central and Eastern Europe reflects very similar social stratification. This necessarily means that the social and political views and interests of those peoples hold much more in common than ever before. It is an established fact that in the past social dissimilarities prevailing between ethnic groups and nations greatly aggravated nationalistic (racial) tensions and conflicts and, to a lesser degree, even determined the nature of international relations. The new, more homogeneous structure of the society, in my observation and judgment, can be regarded as a positive factor in promoting the idea of federalism.

It is not accidental that the peoples of the Danube area are turning toward the solution of federalism. It was one of the central themes of the Hungarian revolution of 1956, and this is the main stream of public activities in current Czechoslovakia and Yugoslavia. This idea has long been ripe in the minds of the peoples and its materialization is now solely a matter of improved relationships between the small nations and the great powers. If the territories of the Danubian small states can be removed from the arena of great power contests, if the great powers will cease to measure the value of smaller nations as a direct function of quantity (geographical size, number of inhabitants) then the last barrier is eliminated on the road to federalism. After so many centuries of fruitless experimentation, this alone has been left as the sole means of rearranging multinational areas in line with the interests of all the nations concerned.

1) C. A. Macartney: **The Habsburg Empire**, 1790-1918. New York: Macmillan Co., 1969, p. 830.

2) C. Fritchey, "Spheres of Influence in Europe and Asia," **The Evening Star**, Washington, D.C., October 11, 1968, p. A-17.

3) Avram G. Mezerik, **Invasion and Occupation of Czechoslovakia and the UN**; stands of Warsaw Pact invaders, Czechoslovakia in the Security Council and in Prague, positions of Romania, Yugoslavia and European Communist **Parties,** etc. New York: International Review Service, 1968, p. 5.

4) Cf. Francis Dvornik's "Introduction" in Aloysius L. Kuhar's **Slovene Medieval History; Selected Studies.** New York-Washington: Studia Slovenica, 1962, p. IX.

5) Aloysius L. Kuhar, **The Conversion of the Slovenes and the German-Slav Ethnic Boundary in the Eastern Alps.** New York-Washington: League of C.S.A., 1959, p. 213.

6) Roman Dyboski, **Outlines of Polish History.** London: George Allen & Unwin Ltd., 1941. Pp. 15, 17.

7) See Franc Grivec, **Slovanska apostola Sv. Ciril in Metod.** Ljubljana, Izdalo Apostolstvo Sv. Cirila in Metoda. 1927. 180 p., and F. Grivec, **Slovanska blagovestnika Sv. Ciril in Metod,** 863-1963. Celje, Izdala Mohorjeva druzba v Celju, 1963. 241 p.

8) Cf. Frantisek Palacky, **Dejiny narodu ceskeho v Cechach a na Morave.** 1st ed., 1848.

9) "Nam unius linguae, uniusque moris Regnum; imbecille & fragile est." par. 3 of Sancti Stephani primi regis Ungariae, Decretorum Liber Primus. Ad Sanctum Emericum Ducem. De acceptione Exterorum, & nutrimento Hospitum. Caput 6 in **Corpus Juris Hungarici,** Tyrnaviae, Typis Academicis Societatis Jesu, 1751.

10) For details see József Deér, **Die Entstehung des ungarischen Königtums.** Budapest, 1942. 97 p. (Ostmitteleuropaische Bibliothek, no. 38), and J. Deér, **Pogány magyarság, keresztény magyarság.** Budapest, Királyi Magyar Egyetemi Nyomda, 1938. 271 p.

11) Zdenek Solle-Alena Gajanova, **Po stope dejin; Cesi a Slovaci v letech 1848-1938.** Praha, Orbis, 1969, p. 47.

I

INTERNATIONAL
RELATIONS

1. Signs of the Times

Under this heading, between 1963 and 1969, each and every issue of the **Studies for a New Central Europe** carried a timely survey of world affairs geared to the specific situations prevailing in the Danube Valley. These analyses were prepared by the Editors of the journal, primarily by Eugene Padányi-Gulyás, Chairman of the Editorial Board, and Alexander Gallus, Editor. In this volume the last two of those analyses are being republished.

F. S. W.

a) ON AN EAST-WEST SECURITY CONFERENCE

THE necessity of a European Conference aiming at general security, based on regional agreements, was recurrently mentioned by a number of diplomats and foreign ministers, and was expressed in a resolution of the participants of the conference at Karlové Vary in 1967, which is the hundreth anniversary of the Austro-Hungarian Compromise. The peoples who enjoyed a half century long peace following the Compromise, are looking forward with keen interest to a possible new covenant that would establish lasting order in their region.

A reorganized, federally integrated, neutral group of Central European nations seems to be the best way toward their future progress. At the same time, as a significant balancing factor, it would safeguard peace in an area where two world wars started and where eliminating the causes of a possible friction may prevent or localize any future disturbance of international peace.

It is in the interest of both the USSR and the Western Powers, that such a neutralized and federated zone of independent nations be established between the Germans and the Russians. Therefore we suggest that a Consultative Conference be arranged to discuss the possibilities and preconditions of such an arrangement, on the basis of a plebiscite under the supervision of the United Nations. The purpose of the suggested Consultative Conference would be to prepare recommendations for a future European Security Conference.

The peoples of this region are anxious to preserve the benefits acquired in the last decades. They are proud of the industrialization of their countries, achieved by the sacrifices of their workers and engineers who put the common cause before selfish interest. They are ready to go on the still long way leading to social justice for all. They are willing to work for the common goals of an enlightened evolutionary humanism; for a social organization of life on our planet; and for that global peace, which has to be a great, well-planned endeavor rather than bourgeois tranquility. Their dream is a peaceful federation of peoples living in established social order, with no dominating and struggling classes, or nationalities goaded by chauvinistic desire of aggrandizement. They feel, furthermore, that this can only be accomplished in complete freedom. There is a great faith in their minds that once the right of self-determination is granted to them, and based on their past common experiences, they will show new ways for progress by cooperation in a modern world as they did in the past. Between the peoples of Western Europe and the peoples of the Soviets with friendship and good will toward both, they hope to show an example of coordinating different national talents and ambitions to fulfill their common historic role in this area. Rather than merely waiting for the unification of Europe, they are anxious to promote this process with their example by reestablishing that spirit of solidarity which was disturbed and confused only by outdated ultranationalism of past generations. Their different languages, national characteristics and folklore may only make the life of this region more colorful and attractive. They consider it their mutual vocation to demonstrate unity in variety in an age when divergent political forces strive for world domination, with millions of frustrated and suffering people all around the world, living in misery and uncertainty. The dark clouds of threatening Third World War—of a possible first total nuclear war—are gathering on the horizon. "If elephants are fighting, it is the grass that will be crushed"—says an old Indian proverb, and we fear for our people living on a dangerous historic crossroad. All conscientious men striving for lasting peace based on justice, condemning war; desiring to use atomic power exclusively for peaceful purposes; have to reduce the chances of friction and eliminate sources of possible conflicts. Stopping the arms' race; the abolishment of controversial military blocs and the withdrawal of all military forces from all foreign territories;—common goals of all nations interested in peaceful progress—remain, however, in the realm of dreams unless we make practical steps toward more realistic understanding of each other's problems.

Such a practical step would be the further neutralization, the so-called "Helvetization" of East Central Europe, the home of about a hundred million people, whose desire is to live outside the sphere of interest of any major power and to be neutral like Switzerland or Austria. Such a group of independent nations, in some form of federation, would be strong enough to thwart the predominance of any single European power over the common interests of the European family of nations. They have been able to secure this in the past. Their balancing role may facilitate even the slow process toward European unity in the future.

The last hundred years proved without a shade of doubt that the problem of Central Europe remained unsolved. The situation, indeed, is more unstable than ever. This inflammable complex of problems and tensions might be blasted like a powder keg in any major international conflict similar to the cases of Cyprus and Indonesia. This troubled world does not need more crises. Foresight and preventive steps are in the common interest of the major powers and of the peoples concerned.

The area of uncertainty. An atmosphere of general uncertainty and nervousness is increasingly noticeable in Europe, especially in countries located between Western Europe and Russia. A division of the continent into Western, Central and Eastern Europe was created by geography, history and military events and was so acknowledged by President De Gaulle in his speech in the Polish parliament. Though a balance of power—sometimes called a "balance of terror"—seems to exist between the two super-powers, more than a hundred million people living between the Germans and Russians consider their status unstable. They earnestly hope that neither an outbreak nor war will occur. But there was similar hope in 1914 and there are many who still remember that a single shot from a revolver was enough to trigger World War I. World Was II started in the same area twenty-five years later.

Besides the dangerous military situation, there is also no real political peace. Bitter tensions continue among the neighbor states in Central Europe and in their relations to the great powers they feel isolated, dependent, living in a climate of hate and suspicion, where cooperation should prevail. The situation is far from satisfactory. It is ready to explode anew as it did in 1914, 1938-41, and in 1956.

The idea of a Conference on Security. This atmosphere of general uncertainty, viewed in the dark context of the dangerous Far Eastern situation, probably motivated the recent series of public statements urging a "European Security Conference". Delegates of the USSR and other Communist governments and parties at the Karlovy Vary conference in April 1967 declared the urgent need of a European Conference on Security and Cooperation. During the last two years almost all foreign ministers from the Communist countries have taken every opportunity to express this desire. E.g., János Péter, Hungarian Foreign Minister, said on March 11, 1967: "Many West European countries reacted more favorably so far to the proposals of the socialist countries concerning preparations for a conference on European security. After so many dangers and conflicts there now exist the objective prerequisites for the countries and peoples in this part of Europe to develop further their relations to the benefit of the general international situation. Our government strives in the first place to be a constructive factor in the development of the international situation in her immediate surroundings—in the Danubian Valley and in Central Europe."

Following Soviet President Podgorny's visit to Austria in 1968 a communique was also issued strongly emphasizing the necessity of such a conference.

Should not both the Atlantic Treaty and the Warsaw Pact be replaced by a new solution? This would only be possible if a turn for the better takes place in Central Europe and peace and progress are assured by the establishment of a zone of neutrality accepted, acknowledged, and guaranteed by both the Western powers and the Soviet Union.

Past errors and plans for confederation. The many centuries of symbiosis in Central Europe was disrupted several times by outside powers who interfered in the region but had no real understanding of the complex problems of these nations. These foreign powers attempted to use the nations as pawns in their own power struggles in Europe and in their attempts to gain world domination. Such interference in Central Europe was not even in their own best interests as such actions increased their military budgets enormously, and slowed down their own peaceful development.

The only way to achieve lasting peace in the area is to promote the reorganization of the whole region into a greater economic and political unit through a maximum of free cooperation of the nations bound together by geography and history in accordance with the trend of our age rather than by the present treaties and forced alliances created by outside powers.

One economic and political formation—the former Habsburg Empire—functioned over a long period, but was finally disrupted when the rulers became dependent first on an alliance with Germany that led to World War I. The "Little Entente" period was overthrown by the German-Italian venture against Russia (1939-45) that resulted in the Soviet Union's seizing control of Central Europe in 1945. No outside power is strong enough to rule this region permanently without endangering the balance of power and world peace. Such domination always provokes counteraction and counter alliances.

After the ignorant, conceited, and aggressive acts of Clemenceau (1919), Hitler (1938), and Stalin (1944) in East Central Europe, the nations of the Danubian area now recall the plans for a peaceful confederation first formulated by the Hungarian Kossuth (1850), the Rumanian Popovici (1906), the Czechoslovakian Hodza (1936), the Austrian Renner (1946), and many others. They have been impelled to do so by the mistakes made first in 1919 when hundreds of thousands of men and women were made homeless, and millions became second- and third-class citizens. Later—after 1940—again millions were forced to leave their homes and other millions were murdered in the war, in death camps, or perished on the highways and in refugee camps. This still poisons international relations. Peaceful and normal evolution is long overdue in Central Europe. No such normal progress has been made in the last hundred years as evidenced in the Scandinavian countries, in England, and Switzerland where society has succeeded in developing in an orderly way having now the highest standard of living in Europe. In Central Europe revolutions and counterrevolutions have caused catastrophies and misery. One hundred years after the transitory benefits reaped by the Astro-Hungarian Compromise of 1867 concluded after the battle of Koeniggraetz, the nations of this region now hope for a new settlement, a modern Covenant of "Helvetization" to settle their differences institutionally for many future generations. Such a new order of a Central European neutral zone could be based only on self-determination and free self-government.

A new and modern compromise solution needed. Must there be another "Koeniggraetz", another and greater catastrophe to force the great powers to accept a fair compromise in the best interest of all nations concerned? Must Russia wait several more decades before its standard of living is raised to that of Western Europe, let alone that of America? Also, is it necessary that both the USSR and the USA continue their costly arms race that challenges the patience of millions of taxpayers who are now overburdened with heavy military commitments? Would not Germany also fare much better if her neighbors were prospering in a neutral Central European zone strong and healthy along her Eastern borders? Planning for a new expansion eastward at the expense of peace and happiness of those nations who form a natural barrier to the possible "Drang" to the East would be self-destructive.

We have come to the conclusion that the time is ripe for all countries concerned to send their most experienced experts in international and constitutional law, economy, finance, communication, military and nationality problems of Central Europe to meet at a *consultative conference* possibly in Vienna or Geneva. Its purpose would be to work out alternate solutions and make recommendations for a coming European Security Conference. Following this, the governments could further develop the *treaties of neutralization, disengagement, "Helvetization"* of the area involved. Neutral experts could make provisions for plebiscites or special local studies under international control where necessary. The next step would then be a *Summit Conference* of the nations concerned together with major powers to sign the agreements granting and *guaranteeing the neutrality of a New Central Europe* which is the best possible safeguard for a lasting peace and security in the area.

b) TOWARD A THIRD WAY IN A NEW CENTRAL EUROPE

EUROPE is an extremely sensitive area of the world where the use of bare military power will bring neither permanent peace nor a solution to its problems and needs. The Russians will soon realize that the use of a raw force in a highly developed area backfires. The military "blood and iron" method of Napoleon, the Czars, Bismarck, Mussolini, and Hitler harmed in the long run more than they helped their nations and Europe. American and Western policy must also change from their predominantly military counter measures, pacts, and expenditures,—as Richard Nixon recently emphasized—to "preventive diplomacy" and peace planning with "regional peace pacts" and the wholehearted participation of the nations concerned.

Three Alternatives in Europe

The solutions commonly advocated for Europe fall into three categories:

a) *A United Europe.* This is presently politically unrealistic, at least for the foreseeable future and so long as the Soviet Union is a nuclear superpower. Moscow would never give its consent to a politically, economically, and militarily unified Europe that included East Central Europe "from the Atlantic to the Urals." Such a unity exists only culturally, based on deep historical sentiments of the European nations. But politically, a *United States of Europe* is still unrealistic, a fantastic dream like that of Coudenhove-Kalergi's *Paneuropa* proposed between the two world wars to which some statesmen like Briand, Seipel, and Masaryk gave lip service but which proved to be a political illusion. Now, the *European Movement* invites its friends and adherents to almost yearly conferences with its program devoted to "European unification." The main speaker of the last conference, held January 19-20, 1968, in Rome, was the German professor, Walter Hallstein, who emphasized the idea of "Europe as a whole." Another organization, *Action Européene Federalist* held its congress November 18-19, 1967, in Brussels with the participation of Jean Rey, Professor Hendrik Brungmans, Dr. Dieter Roser, Vice President of the German *Europa-Union*, and others. The 17th congress of the latter organization met on March 4-5, 1968, in Cologne. But Jerzy Jankowski, a Polish journalist and editor of *Poland in Europe* who attended these congresses summarized their net results as follows: "The regimes in power in Eastern Europe are hostile to the United Europe idea. Thus, what is there left to say at the congresses besides repeating cheap formulas about an 'entire Europe' and platonic compliments to the peoples of the 'Second Europe'?"[1]

b) The present *Two Europes* organized militarily by NATO and the Warsaw Pact countries would permanently fix the present East and West Europe side by side. This would be hell to those nations caught unwillingly between the two superpowers: the masters of NATO and the Warsaw Pact. This present *status quo* would leave the German problem unsolved, the Berlin Wall and the Iron Curtain permanently established, the Cold War, intermittently intensified, especially now after the occupation of Czechoslovakia and as it was previously, after 1948 and 1956. The greater the increase of military power on both sides of the Iron Curtain, the more unbearable will life be for the 150-180 millions who live between Russia and Germany. Such enormous military expenses incurred by both America and the USSR are also an unnecessary burden on their economies that unbalance their budgets, foreign payments, and hinder finding solutions to their problems at home. Both America and England are willing to withdraw from Europe but as long as the *Two Europes* exist, a military de-escalation in Europe remains a dream. At whose expense were the 650,000 Soviet troops deployed in Czechoslovakia and now rocket bases established there? The NATO forces, America, Germany and also Yugoslavia immediately reacted by increasing their military expenditures, ordering more expensive rockets, tanks and jet bombers. Cannot lessons be learned from Hitler's military failures? The present trend only lays the base for a Third World War which could not be contained in Europe.

c) We submit our realistic solution as a *Third Way:*
THREE EUROPES. 1. Western Europe with its nucleus, the Common Market. 2. East Europe which is practically Soviet Russia. 3. Central Europe, a neutralized buffer zone between Russia and Germany.

French President De Gaulle was realistic when he reminded the world in a speech at the Warsaw parliament, that politically there are *Three Europes:* Western, Central and East Europe. While a *United Europe* is a utopian dream, the present *Two Europes* a hell, *Three Europes* would be to the advantage of all nations—and is politically realistic. It would be in the interest of the nuclear power too, including the Soviet Union.

For Peace and Military De-escalation:
a Neutral Buffer Zone is needed in Europe

It is vain to exhort the leaders of the Kremlin to move their troops out of Hungary, Czechoslovakia, and East Berlin so long as the British-American troops remain and are even strengthened on the other side of the Iron Curtain. Russia was invaded several times since Napoleon and it understandably feels the need of protection against what it calls "German revenge" or other aggression. The present "revenge" of West Germany serves as an admirable bogeyman

MAP 1

PROPOSED NEUTRALIZED BUFFER ZONE WITH MILITARY DISENGAGEMENT

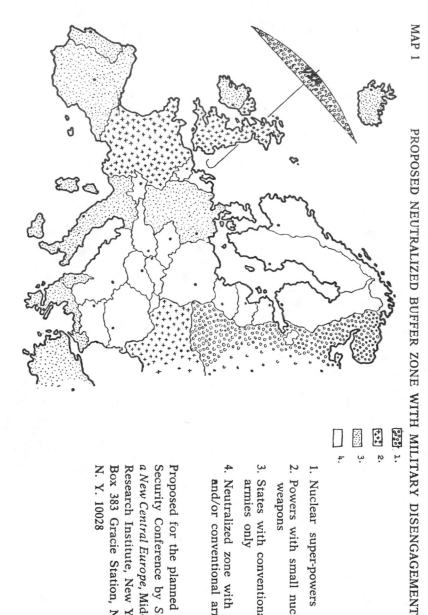

1.

2.

3.

4.

1. Nuclear super-powers

2. Powers with small nuclear weapons

3. States with conventional armies only

4. Neutralized zone with militia and/or conventional armies.

Proposed for the planned East-West Security Conference by *Studies for a New Central Europe*, Mid-European Research Institute, New York, New York, P. O. Box 383 Gracie Station, New York, N. Y. 10028 to keep the Warsaw Pact group in line. Therefore a neutral buffer zone between the Russians and Germans would release the Soviet Union from this fear and enable the Kremlin to concentrate against a possible invasion from China. If a Central European neutral zone were guaranteed by the Great Powers and, as in Austria's case, by some other 60 states, the security of Russia's western frontiers would be unquestionable. Moscow's obsession must be removed by a proposal made through diplomatic channels to neutralize the zone from Finland down through the Danubian countries. Such an agreement would make the motivation written into the recent Soviet-Czechoslovak treaty obsolete. Article 1 of the treaty "ensures the security of the countries of the socialist community against the increasing revanchist strivings of the West German militarist forces." Neutralization would serve the security of the Soviet Union, Poland, and Czechoslovakia as well. It would open the way for a military de-escalation. The neutralization of Austria in the State Treaty of 1955 was one of the wisest steps taken in decades. The Kremlin now has less trouble with Austria than with the non-neutralized Hungary, Rumania, or Czechoslovakia. Neutral Sweden and Finland are better neighbors than Rumania. It will of course be in the best interest of the nations in such a neutralized buffer zone to have good economic and cultural relations with Russia. With their military expenditures reduced, peoples of the zone will attain a higher level of existence.

The idea of a Neutralized Buffer Zone gains momentum

Fifteen years ago many questioned the usefulness of such a neutralized buffer zone between the great powers. Western diplomacy was reluctant in giving consent to neutralize Austria. Only after more than 280 fruitless four-power conferences did it yield. It was the Austrian Chancellor Raab who succeeded in negotiating the matter with Molotov in Moscow. The final Memorandum[2]) contained the "international obligation that Austria will maintain neutrality of the *same type as maintained by Switzerland.*" This was the key. The neutralization of Austria was a step forward. Following this, the withdrawal of troops from Hungary could have been negotiated immediately on the same platform and formula. But Western diplomacy did not see this opportunity. When the Hungarian Revolution broke out in 1956, the government of Imre Nagy proclaimed neutrality. This was not backed by Western diplomacy, and the military intervention of the USSR followed. However, the Hungarian uprising marked the first defeat of Communism in Central Europe and its repercussions in the West undermined the prestige of Communist parties everywhere.

Recently, Western observers in Prague have reported increased interest among Czechs and Slovaks in the concept of a neutralized zone. Dan Morgan, correspondent for the *Washington Post* wrote from Prague on September 14, 1968:

"The Czechoslovak central authorities have completed a candid, confidential report in which they had to acknowledge an increase in a *detectable interest in neutrality for Czechoslavakia.* The invasion episode has also raised a significant doubt about the role of the Czechoslovak army, which, although one of the best in Europe, was not ordered to resist the Warsaw Pact onslaught."

At the tenth anniversary of Imre Nagy's execution, the Prague *Literárni Listy* (June 13, 1968) published a eulogy of Nagy emphasizing his demand for Socialist neutralism. The growing interest in neutralization in Central Europe is also stated in a note sent by Czechoslovakia to the Polish government on September 13, 1968:

"An allegation made in the Polish party paper *Trybuna Ludu,* that the Czechoslovakian National Assembly's Foreign Affairs Committee had advocated neutrality of Czechoslovakia—was absolutely false."

The note, however, acknowledged that the Committee did discuss neutrality but at the insistence of the government came to the conclusion that "a proclamation of neutrality would not bring about a solution." This confidential report proves that a plebiscite in Czechoslovakia would favor neutralization by a large majority. A Hungarian journalist, Tibor Pethő, spokesman for the Government, wrote even before the Czechóslavak invasion:

"Czechs, Slovaks, Hungarians have lived together close to each other for centuries. The common experiences of this long togetherness taught us many things. We gathered ample experiences concerning antagonisms and hatreds; also the advantages of friendship and cooperation ... by eliminating the influence of foreign powers which tried to divide and confuse the people in the Danube basin either by methods of the Habsburgs or by those of Hitler ... We trust in a federalist reorganization." (*Magyar Hirek,* June 29, 1968)

János Péter, Hungarian Foreign Minister, gave the following report to the Parliament (July, 1968):

"Diminution of the dangers in Europe is in the common interest of all continents. For further clarification of the situation in Europe it is necessary to increase the number of existing bilateral agreements, and also that of the *regional agreements.* Only from the mosaics of these can the future peace of Europe be composed. Together with our neighbors we are working for a *well-organized cooperation of Central European and Danubian Basin countries* with different systems economically, culturally and politically, in the interest of the peace and security of Europe."

Western Powers and a Buffer Zone

Franz Joseph Strauss, West German Minister, who has influence on German foreign policy matters, stated in one of his lectures:

"If the *Eastern satellites can be formed into a buffer Europe,* if the mistrust in Germany which derives from the prejudices and experiences of the past can be allayed step by step, if this policy turns the pages of history and liquidates the legacy of the Second World War, then much will have been gained."[3]

Dr. Lujo Toncic-Sorinj, Foreign Minister of the Federal Republic of Austria, expressed his firm conviction more than once, that close cooperation among the peoples of the Danubian region is only a matter of time owing to the natural historical elements at work which will prevail against difficulties created from the outside. Even Otto Winzer, Foreign Minister for East Germany told the National Assembly on August 9, 1968 that "under European security we must understand a *regional system* based on international agreements."

It was the British Prime Minister Eden at the Geneva Conference of Heads of Government who proposed the establishment of a buffer zone on July 18, 1955:

We would be ready to discuss and try to reach agreement as to the total of forces and armaments on each side in Germany and the countries neighboring Germany. To do this it would be necessary to join in a system of reciprocal control to supervise the agreements effectively."

A mutual withdrawal of forces 250 miles on each side was proposed. It is regretable that other events in world politics diverted attention from following up this idea or that of George Kennan on mutual disengagement. See also the study of E. Chaszar: *"The Possibility of a Neutralized Zone in Central Europe."*[4]

The Secretary-General of the United Nations, U Thant, advocated a "vigorous and articulate *Third Force"* between the great powers. We agree with *Nelson Rockefeller:* "The historic choice fast rushing upon us, then, is no less than this: either the free nations of the world will take the lead in adopting the federal concept to their relations or, one by one, we may be driven into the retreat of the perilous isolationism, political, economic and intellectual, so ardently sought by the Soviet policy to divide and conquer."[5]

Richard Nixon recommended a regional buffer zone in his campaign speech at Eatonville, N. J. on October 19, 1968:

". . . regional pacts that can prevent a local conflict from escalating into world war. The regional pact thus becomes *a buffer* separating the distant great powers from immediate threat—and the danger of a local conflict escalating into world war is thereby reduced. A *regional* pact would provide a *buffer* between the United States and the Soviet Union in future flareups."

Dangers to be averted by "preventive diplomacy"

Austrian Chancellor Klaus was told in Moscow during his visit of March 14—21, 1967 that Austria would be breaking the obligations of permanent neutrality if she joined the European Common Market and this would be a *casus belli*. On the other hand, Klaus was told that Austria would be supported if she strengthened her neutrality and her relations with the other Central European states. Austria was also encouraged to call a Conference on European Security to be held in Vienna.

Today many dangers exist in the Central European raea besides a new Anschluss. Because of the unsolved situation, the possibility of widespear protest movements, e.g., in Vienna, East or West Berlin, like those in Paris and France in May-June, 1968, cannot be excluded. Because of the closeness of the Soviet nuclear superpower, De Gaulle's methods would be dangerous. The Soviet forces would step in to "help restore democratic order" in Vienna, Berlin, East or West Germany. If thousands of German citizens were killed in such actions as were Hungarians in 1956, the West German army, supported by fifty million West Germans would certainly step in. Such action could start a Third World War.

Could anyone predict what would happen if the dictator Tito should die without having an able successor to hold the multinational and insecure Yugoslavia together? Is there secure peace or safety in the Rumanian situation? Therefore, it would be wise for the U. S. State Department to nominate a committee of experts on Central Europe to prepare a detailed plan for a neutralized buffer zone between Russia and Germany to be proposed to a European Conference on Security. Although America won two world wars militarily, they were lost diplomatically at the peace conferences because of insufficient preparation of realistic peace plans. Clemenceau, Stalin, Molotov, etc. dominated the conferences because they had plans. Should not Western "preventive diplomacy" possess as carefully elaborated peace plans as the Chiefs of Staff who have their alternative military plans for possible dangers?

1) Jerzy Jankowski: Problems of Eastern Europe at the Three European Congresses. **The Central European Federalist.** New York. 1968. No. 1, p. 17-22.

2) Memorandum on the results of negotiations between Austria and the Soviet Union. Moscow, April 15, 1955. See **Documents on American Foreign Relations.** Vol. 1955, p. 121.

3) Franz Joseph Strauss, **The Grand Design.** Praeger. New York. 1966.

4) Published in this volume.

5) Nelson Rockefeller: **The Future of Federalism.** (Paperback, 1968.)

2. TOWARD A CONSTRUCTIVE IDEOLOGY AND POLICY IN A NEW CENTRAL EUROPE

EUGENE PADANYI-GULYAS

AN historic course began half a century ago. In retrospect, it can be generally characterized as a disintegration of post-feudal empires. First, Czarism was overthrown in Russia, then the Hohenzollern German empire collapsed and the Hapsburg monarchy fell apart. The latter was engineered by the Western powers in accordance with the wartime objective expressed in the political writings of the Czech Edvard Benes.[1] Twenty years later, with Germany's rise to greater power, he had to emigrate a second time. Thirty years later, in 1948 under heavy political pressure of the Soviet Union, Benes became helpless, embittered and died a disappointed man. Czechoslovakia's case is not extraordinary, but typical of the fate of small states in Central Europe. The results of political disintegration were fatal.

October 1968 was the date set to celebrate "fifty years of independence" for Czechoslovakia, Greater Rumania, and Yugoslavia. Flags, posters, books, pamphlets, commemorative speeches and festivals had been readied for the occasion. Then the invasion of Czechoslovakia by Soviet and four other Warsaw Pact countries demonstrated to the whole world that independence does not and did not exist in the Central European area. Between 1920 and 1938 Edvard Benes formed the Little Entente as a satellite system directed against Hungary, Austria and Germany, based on French military power, loans and diplomacy. With Hitler's rise, however, Czechoslovakia broke into two parts, both becoming satellites of Germany together with the other Central European small states. Before his return from his second exile Benes concluded a pact with Stalin and Molotov in Moscow, in 1943, and ousted more than three million Germans from Czechoslovakia. This pact led to such reliance on the Soviet Union that his whole country became its satellite and Jan Masaryk, son of Czechoslovakia's first president, committed suicide or, as it is said, was murdered. Hundreds of Czech and Slovak leaders emigrated for a second, or some for a third time.

No matter how great the efforts of small states in Central Europe were to achieve parliamentary democracy, economic development, cultural improvement, the faulty international political system engulfed the leading politicians together with thousands, even millions of families. The suicides, executions, imprisonment, repeated emigration of national leaders during these fifty years are proof that the "independence" of these small states was and is an illusion—with one exception. The only independent country in Central Europe at present is the *neutral and federal Austria* whose neutrality was guaranteed by the great powers together with sixty other states.

After 1918 a few transitional years of democratic parliamentarian experimentation followed the disintegration of the empire. Then came military dictatorships and police states first from the extreme right and then from the extreme left, Hitler and Stalin. Some anomalies occurred at a number of elections in the twenties and thirties; but in the forties and after no elections at all were held worth this name. There was no freedom from the military powers and their "spheres of influence" centered first in Berlin, then in Moscow. The development of new technology, means of transportation and industrialization continued throughout the last decades although they greatly lagged behind the West. But the advantages of industrial development were counterbalanced by loss of religious freedom, Marxist dominated churches, the muzzling of writers and other intellectuals, Marxist-Leninist dictatorial monopolization of the press and all other means of communication, and by a generally low level of subsistance. "Building Marxist Socialism" did not mean building homes for the people. The elementary need for shelter, housing is still one of the sorest spots in the economy of all satellite states and also in the Soviet Union.

The Germany of the Kaiser and Hitler was replaced by a divided Germany and a divided Berlin with its Wall, and the long Iron Curtain behind which the population seethes. Discontent with the "dictatorship of the proletariat" broke out in the uprisings of 1953, 1956 and now in Czechoslovakia. "In our Czechoslovakia of yesterday," writes the Prague *Literarni Listy* of March 28, 1968, "people were driven to trials like cattle to the slaughter house, their heads covered with sacks. Hands and legs tied, they were beaten up till they lost consciousness. Teeth knocked out, skin branded with red-hot iron happened to many. Who will guarantee that such things shall not reoccur?" The Slovak Alexander Dubcek, newly elected First Secretary of the Czechoslovak Communist Party, demanded equal rights for the Slovaks with the Czechs. The federalization of Czechoslovakia was decided upon. But then Hungarians, Ukranians, Germans in Czechoslovakia also demanded equal rights.

Between the two world wars, the League of Nations became submerged in troubled international waters and the first promising idea of international jurisdiction went down with it. Hundreds of national leaders were persecuted and killed by the so-called "liberators of the people." Ironically this was only the start of persecuting and killing tens of thousands of the same people who were supposed to be liberated. Famine, starvation, executions, concentration camps, purges, genocide, class war, "liberation wars,"—all kinds of wars followed. Freedom of expression, freedom of gathering, freedom of religion, or in one word: *freedom* was destroyed or so manipulated that the result was equivalent to its destruction. The relative peace of the world guaranteed by a shaky balance of power was replaced bu a "balance of terror" with its nuclear detergent. It is clear now, Security would achieve better results than theoretical decisions of the that other diplomatic ways must be found. A Conference on European United Nations. This organization, with the "veto paragraph" in its charter and with its membership of questionable good-standing, without an international police force and due to big-power rivalries, has repeatedly proved itself incapable of solving major problems—with a special impotence in Central European affairs. Cold war methods with their inefficient practices will bring no solutions either.

But, while looking for new ways, we have to admit that a century ago the theory of Marxism could be, and actually was attractive to a good many dissatisfied people. What might have been attractive to the leaders of suppressed peoples of Russia 50 years ago, or of China 30 years ago, did not, however, mean progress for the people of Czechoslovakia 20 years ago, although Marxist-Leninism took over. Our question is: how was it possible that political parties proclaiming class struggle could attract millions in countries where the standard of living was high? How could union leaders with princely incomes and trade union members with adequate social security and pension systems organize Marxist parties all over the civilized world, to take part in coalition governments only to overthrow them? How is it still possible that professors and their textbooks favor Marxism as a progressive movement in countries where a high level of industrialization was accomplished without the people being deprived of decent housing; where reforms in agriculture were achieved without reducing its productivity, and illiteracy was cured by an educational system that did not require the killing of ten millions in revolutions —"cultural" or other. How could the Marxist political parties in the past be so successful in spite of terror, "dictatorship of the proletariat," Iron Curtain, Berlin Wall, censorship, "socialist realism" in art and literature against the will of the majority or the real desire expressed by their conscientious writers? The answer to these questions seems to be essentially that it was possible because of their *international* organization. Calling their movement international meant real progress in a time when other political parties restricted themselves to one nation, not to mention those parties which were even more restricted to the goals and problems of chauvinistic groups within a nation. By organizing their movement internationally, both the Communists and Social Democrats showed foresight in the past decades during and after the dissolution of empires in all continents. Their theoreticians saw the inevitable trend toward international global cooperation many years before Pierre Teilhard de Chardin, whose philosophy emphasized "social infolding," "universal solidarity" and "coordinated planetary systems" toward which the formidable creative power of evolution forces mankind to fare.

It is, however, also a fact that Marxist political parties tried to restrict their international movement to "the worker's class" or "the proletariat," to "the present clumsy and incomplete application of a totalization"—to use Teilhard's words. Today Marxists fulminate against the kind of capitalism which does not exist anymore. Their "international" methods became antiquated.

It is shortsighted to use all the discoveries made available by technical progress for political aggrandizement or economic exploitation of others, by a superpower striving for world domination. An immeasurable amount of material wealth and uncounted millions of innocent lives were sacrificed on the altar of this false god. To ask for more destruction, to call for a global "class struggle" instead of a global struggle against ignorance and poverty seems utterly outdated. An international movement works better when its program is replaced by updated goals and is adjusted to changed demands. A truly internationally organized political movement to achieve the common goals of mankind in an evolutionary progress is right. To try to achieve today's goals with narrow-minded nationalism and chauvinism or with class prejudices of yesterday is doomed to failure.

A New Era of Political Integration and Constructiveness

Construction rather than destruction, integration rather than division, evolution rather than revolution is the idea of our day. These ideas are in the air. The desire for change is very real. But to find the right words expressing the new trend is not easy.

It was four years before Alexander Dubcek, first Secretary of the Czechoslovak Communist Party, started his democratic reforms, when the Alliance of Czechoslovak Democratic Associations called for *positive* constructive movements. The program was significant. It's title is less fortunate.[2] Searching for "nobler and deeper causes," for "new types of international action," Henry Owen refers to a Warsaw philosopher's concept[3] which would eventually replace past national slogans: that of "Community"—and which is, indeed, comprehensive and attractive.

Before looking for more words or slogans, however, and assuming that the nations of a reintegrated, "Helvetisized" new Central Europe will sooner or later be in the position of defining their own policies, let us review the goals of such a movement. After the Hungarian uprising in 1956 and the recent "democratization" movement in Czechoslovakia, one thing seems clear: the people living in this area are looking for a *realistic Third Way* in foreign policy, economy and in ideology, different from that of their neighbors to the East or West.

Their *foreign policy* should be based on the demand, that the zone between Russia and Germany be *militarily neutral, like Austria or Switzerland* and the neutrality of this zone should be *internationally guaranteed.* This was the idea expressed by the Hungarian freedom fighters in 1956 and by the prime minister of their short-lived free government, Imre Nagy, who died a martyr for it.

One cannot, indeed, expect that more martyrs pronounce this demand; consequently we must not wait till the heads of the existing satellite governments declare their independence from the Warsaw Pact. Such a declaration was made on behalf of all the so-called "satellites" by the only free government behind the Iron Curtain and was sealed by the blood of the Hungarian martyrs. The people in the whole region remember this. On the tenth anniversary of Imre Nagy's execution the "Literarni Listy"—the periodical of the Federation of the Writers in Czechoslovakia—reminded its readers of the merits of this great leader, whose ideas on neutrality were premature in his time, but acceptable today.[4]

The wisdom of establishing a neutral zone is obvious. This is the only way for both the American and Russian armies finally to disengage and to pull back to their respective homelands. After this movement—long awaited by taxpayers of both countries—no Warsaw or NATO military pacts can be justified, nor will they be necessary. Eighty to a hundred million people in the "Helvetisized" area will take care of their own affairs and will be ready to safeguard the peace of the region which means a very significant guarantee of the peace of whole Europe. This will be also the time for the major nuclear powers to adjust the objectives of their foreign policies to a realistic assessment of their own capabilities.

The *economy* of the "Helvetisized" region would probably be neither Communist nor Capitalist. As judged today, the region might have a *mixed economy.* De-etatization of state enterprises and cooperatives are already on the way, but state and federal economic planning would continue. This practice is accepted also in the West.[5] Mining, heavy industry, railway, postal service and other means of communication would be state or federally owned enterprises with self-management. Many economic organizations for cooperation of states already exist. Besides the COMECON and its committees, there are specialized agencies for cooperation in transportation, electrification, finances, etc. These would be fully developed, but without the membership of any outside major powers, whose presence only would distort the balance and harmony of the Central European community. Terms of trade and contracts would be concluded on an equal basis toward the East and West. The principle of "participation on all levels"—demanded by the Yugoslav, Czech, Slovak and Hungarian workers and students—would prevent unhealthy dictatorship of any of the inflated capital cities and would pave the road toward equality of the member nations to real democracy without over-centralization.

Thanks to its guaranteed neutrality, the economy of a New Central Europe might be an example of prosperity without giving large sums for massive military budgets that would achieve nothing constructive; an example of continuous full employment without depriving workers of a decent standard of living, good housing, cars and traveling. Considering the world-wide need for *construction* of homes, roads, power plants, dams and factories; for an updated international system of transportation and communication; for re-building the dilapidated cities and for building new cities according to the global trend of healthy urbanization—it appears, that *making peace profitable* is within the reach of mankind. The existing giants in their struggle for world domination have failed to give an example of the prosperity described above. The third way of neutral countries may lead us to it.

Third Way in Ideology

The *ideology* of a New Central Europe may also pioneer an interesting third way. Like standing on an ice block with the right foot and on a red-hot plate with the left, one would not feel an average temperature; a neutralized, "Helvetisized" zone between Germany and Russia very probably would have its own way of thinking, its own philosophy. Historic and recent experiences of these people are quite unique. An ideology, different of that of their neighbors, would be a natural consequence. Considering the ideological bank-ruptcy and confusion around the world, it is time to have some fresh ideas.

Since the world wars, nations and their best men: writers, thinkers, statesmen are labouring on the problem of how to find the path of peaceful, normal, healthy life of mankind, leading away from extremities. It seems now, that neither the promises of the "rugged individualism," nor those of Marxist collectivism resulting in an omnipotent state are any longer attractive.

One of the most interesting and honest statements in this respect, while admitting the seeming success of the Russian Revolution, attributes it to the fact, that a number of basisc Christian principles were used for Communist propaganda all through its fifty years of history. These principles: the solidarity and brotherhood of all men, the brotherly love of the poor, the freedom and peace on earth, however, were emphasized though sometimes betrayed by Christendom throughout the centuries; and the crisis of Communism today originated from its own rebellious intellectuals, who discovered that these great principles were betrayed by Communism too. Thus the search for a new way starts again.[6]

Millions in Central Europe have learned at their own expense, that *in concordia parvae res crescunt, in discordia maximaeque dilabuntur* — little things may grow united, great ones diminish in discord. The feeling of their solidarity, of their natural community of destiny, was recently expressed more than once. This is the force behind their struggle for independence from the outside powers and for intensified cooperation among themselves. The chimera of world domination makes them anxious to separate their way from those who are still pursuing this costly dream. Solidarity, masters in their own home, not domination by others, is their dream.

To start with such a joint venture in this region means that, while preserving the national characters of the respective peoples —their language, their culture, their pride of accomplishment throughout history—their energy will be united to build a new home for themselves according to a plan which would accomodate them at the best contemporary standards. This new home has to be large enough, so that its household could be well organized. Agricultural and industrial production modernized; the best use of the labor force and the forces of nature; tariff-free distribution of goods and smooth flow of traffic on the super high- and railways, on improved waterways and in the air; free exchange of ideas through all channels of modern communication; good schools, good instructions for arts and sciences, open for everyone—this is what a "Helvetisized," intergrated New Central Europe means. If an industrialist in Prague invests a new product, he could sell it to between seventy and a hundred million customers. A new song recorded by Slovaks, Ruthenians or Rumanians could soon be popular also in Vienna or Belgrade. A poem, a book, or a newspaper printed in Budapest, in Zagreb, or in Kolozsvár could reach readers or subscribers anywhere in a territory of about one million square kilometers. Free trade, free competition, mutual respect and support of every effort in pursuing the common goal are prerequisites for the progress of the inhabitants of the region.

Such endeavor is unthinkable without effective political changes and international guarantees. To construct the new home according to old-fashioned blueprints by means of narrow-minded policy of mini-states based on jealousy and chauvinism, or on internationally organized movements aimed at destruction, dictatorship or world domination is impossible. Neither can it be designed by the limited vision and controlled imagination of some dusty old principles of "socialist realism." Therefore a *Constructive Central European Internationale* is needed, with national parties in the individual countries,

31

to carry a joint program among the different peoples. To avoid many difficulties arising from too many small parties campaigning and possibly forming inefficient coalition governments, it was suggested that in a "Helvetisized" New Central Europe a two-party system is desirable. It would perhaps be premature to go into such details as to restrict the number of parties in different states of so many different nationalities. But it seems, that one of the two or more national political parties in every member state should be organized between the states, campaigning on similar platforms and directed by principles and guidelines established at periodic congresses of a Constructive Central European Internationale. This term is used partly for want of a better; but partly because we believe that construction is a concept best characterizing the epoch to come. At the risk of repetition, we must point to the fact, that after a long period of destruction, disintegration, separation by national or tariff boundaries, by Iron Curtains and by walls in Berlin or elsewhere—the time has come for integration and construction. Construction, in the basic sense of this word, of homes for crowded or homeless families. Construction of an integrated New Central Europe for the people of this troubled region. Construction of a better world on our planet for all men of good will.

After all, a good example to prove the possibility of close co-operation and effective government of peoples of different languages, nationalities and religious affiliations is long overdue. Similar problems are waiting for solution in all Europe, in Asia, in Africa, in many places across the world. Our globe, as a whole, presents the same problem today. We have to start somewhere. Why not in a region, where such a new beginning would be only one more in a long series ... maybe better than any of the previous ones. An inspiring example for all.

1) Edward Benes: Détruisez l'Autriche-Hongrie", Paris, 1917.

2) Positive Anticommunism" (Studies for a New Central Europe, Vol. I. No. 3, p. 41).

3) "Foreign Policy Premises for the Next Administration" by Henry Owen, chairman, Policy Planning Council, Department of State USA ("Foreign Affairs", July, 1968).

4) Oswald Machatka in the May, 1958 issue of the "Literární Listy", Prague.

5) Otto Schlecht, chief of the policy division of the West German Economics Ministry: "The ad hoc economy, the economy of the light hand, is dead. We have a new economic system now—a tailored economy. We have learned a lot."

6) P. Werenfried van Atraaten in the "Ostpriesterhilfe" (10-11, 1968). See also the Fourth Dialog of Marxists and Christians (Marianske-Lazne-Marienbad Czechoslovakia, 1968).

3. Neutralization of a Buffer Zone Between Germany and Russia

THE POSSIBILITY OF A NEUTRALIZED ZONE IN CENTRAL EUROPE

EDWARD CHASZAR

NEUTRALITY, pronounced dead on many occasions by statesmen and jurists alike, and condemned from various sides now as "criminal," now as "immoral," has shown a remarkable ability to survive in international relations. Despite the fact that during the initial phase of the Cold War the concept was frowned upon by both of the super-powers, neutrality in foreign politics experienced a sudden revival. Even "legal neutrality" gained ground instead of losing.

If the trend continues, the often proposed neutral zone in Central Europe may yet become a reality in the foreseeable future. With the establishment of a neutral belt in Central Europe—so some of its advocates assert—this territory would cease to serve as a bone of contention between the East and the West; rather, it would become an area of reconciliation between the two.

What are the prospect of a "neutral zone in Central Europe" today? What would be its significance for the area concerned, for the contending forces of the East and West and for the world at large?

In order to answer these questions, at least tentatively, it will be well first to clear up the confusion surrounding the terms "neutrality" and "neutralism," and then proceed to a discussion of the proposals concerning Central Europe, usually connected with the problem of "disengagement."

Neutrality, neutralization, and neutralism

Historically speaking, "neutrality" in international law refers to non-participation in war, coupled with impartial behavior toward the belligerents. It imposes certain rights and duties both on the neutral and on the warring states. The latter, in particular, are bound to

33

respect the territorial integrity of neutrals. Neutrality also assumes the legality of war as an instrument of national policy. When, with the establishment of the League of Nations, and later the United Nations, war began to be looked upon as "illegal," the place of neutrality in international law turned questionable. In theory—at least—the concept of collective security and neutrality cannot co-exist. In practice, however, both the League and the United Nations had left several loopholes for war nad neutrality, consequently the rules governing the latter are still considered applicable in international law.[1]

A distinction has to be made between "neutrality" and "neutralization."

Neutrality is a policy adopted by a State unilaterally in face of a particular war and for no specified period. Thus, Ireland and Sweden during World War II had chosen to remain outside the conflict. In fact, because of her particular situation, Sweden has been able to stay out of war for 150 years and she is considered a "traditional neutral." She was a member of the League of Nations, and joined also the United Nations.

Neutralization is the outcome of international agreement. Belgium, for example, was neutralized by the Powers in 1831 on their own initiative and without her request. Her supposedly "permanent neutrality" lasted until World War I. Switzerland, "permanently neutral" by international agreement at her own request ever since the Congress of Vienna (1815), in a classic example. Once a member of the League of Nations, Switzerland now holds that her neutrality is incompatible with membership in the United Nations. Nevertheless, like Sweden, she is a member of many non-political and non-military international organizations.

More recent examples of neutralization are Austria (1955) and Laos (1962). Both are members of the United Nations. Austria also is a member of the European Free Trade Association and of the Council of Europe, in spite of strong criticism from the Communist side.[2]

Neutralism, as distinct from neutrality, refers to a foreign policy of non-alignment in international relations. It is sometimes compared with the policy of "no entangling alliances," pursued by the U.S.A. until World War I. By adhering to this policy, and occasionally formalizing it in the legal sense through declarations of neutrality, the U.S.A aimed at maintaining freedom of trade with all nations whether in peace or war, without renouncing the right to make war when that was in her interest.

"Neutralists" today claim that although they refuse to join military or political alliances sponsored by the Great Powers, they are in no sense isolationists. On the contrary, the profess to have an active interest in world affairs ("positive neutralism"), and interpose themselves between the opposing sides in the Cold War in order to promote world peace which they need for their own national development.[3])

Notwithstanding the fact that "neutralism" or "nonalignment" is now an accepted feature of international relations, a neutralist country does not enjoy a special status in international law, nor any corresponding special legal rights or duties. This is recognized even by Soviet legal writers who had sought during the last decade to confer some kind of legal respectability and protection on the "policy of neutralism."[4])

Another difference between "neutrality" and "neutralism" is that while the first term always implies a foreign policy of nonalignment for the neutral country, the pursuit of neutralism in itself does not necessarily lead to legal neutrality, nor is it sufficient to establish a neutral status. Success to do so depends on a number of additional factors, such as geographic position, military significance, relation to the Great Powers, and most important, mutual interest of the latter in guaranteeing neutral status.

These factors, it appears today, are in favor of a neutral zone in Central Europe, and render the reconsideration of its establishment timely.

Disengagement and Neutral Zone Between East and West

During the first decade of the Cold War, putting their faith in the principle of collective action against aggression, both the U.S.A. and the Soviet Union maintained a rather rigid, negative attitude toward neutrality and neutralism. The first one to reverse her position was the Soviet Union. As part of the "New Look" in foreign policy after Stalin's death, seeking diplomatic support to balance U.S. nuclear superiority, Soviet diplomacy came to look upon neutrality as a "progressive" course of action under given circumstances, and finally recognized its positive value. International lawyers in the Soviet Union quickly adapted themselves to the new situation, restored the legitimacy of neutrality and accepted its compatibility with the U.N. Charter.[5])

Starting at the Berlin Conference of Foreign Ministers in early 1954, the Soviet government began to put forward periodic proposals for the neutralization of Germany and Austria as a solution of the problem of European security. Subsequently, in April 1955 a Memorandum was signed in Moscow by the representatives of Austria and the Soviet Union, and in May of the same year, after a declaration of Swiss-type neutrality stipulated in the Memorandum, Austria obtained neutral status guaranteed by the Four Powers. In exchange for restoring full independence to Austria, championed for long by the Western powers, these latter had to accept the fact of an extended neutral wedge between the Northern and Southern members of NATO.

As the events of 1956 in Hungary proved, the Soviet Union was not ready as yet to let one of her satellites assume neutral status. Not even the compromise plan, elaborated by State Minister István Bibó in the government of Imre Nagy, which envisaged Hungary's continued adherence to a socialist system, but stipulated the country's withdrawal from the Warsaw Pact, was acceptable to Moscow. The Soviet attitude was expressed by the spokesman of the restored Soviet-backed Communist regime in Hungary, Foreign Minister Imre Horváth, who said: "We approve of the neutrality of certain capitalist countries since it ... means standing apart from the conquerors and those ready to go to war, (while) the neutrality of a Socialist country represents an underhanded attack on the cause of peace and Socialism and its betrayal.6)

The heightened East-West tension which resulted from the events in Hungary and from the Suez affair in 1956 lent urgency to the question of *disengagement*. Officially, U.S. diplomacy, still ingrained with the fear of further Soviet expansion, was wary of such proposals. The best-known of these was the Rapacki Plan (named after the Foreign Minister of Poland), originally presented to the General Assembly of the United Nations in October 1957, and somewhat modified later. It proposed (1) The establishment of a denuclearized zone in Central Europe, to include Poland, Czechoslovakia, the German Democratic Republic, and the German Federal Republic, (2) The creation of an inspection system to keep the zone free of nuclear weapons.

The Rapacki Plan was offered in the conviction that the establishment of a denuclearized zone in Central Europe could lead to an improvement in East-West relations and facilitate further discussion of disarmament, as well as the solution of some outstanding problems. Unofficially there were more far-reaching suggestions from American and British sides both before and after the Rapacki Plan.

Writing in 1956, George Kennan, former top U.S. diplomat and Soviet expert, suggested the acceptance of realities imposed on Eastern Europe by the Soviet Union. At the same time he thought that the gradual evolution of the present regimes toward increased independence and greater responsibilities to domestic opinion was possible, provided that such evolution was not conceived by the West as a military or ideological issue. For this reason Kennan was of the opinion that the dividing line between American and Russian military power in Central Europe ought to be de-emphasized, and the neutral zone that stood between the two ought to be increased, preferably including a unified neutral Germany. In his own words:

"I think it ... a good thing rather than a bad thing that Sweden has never joined the Atlantic Pact, that Switzerland has preserved in every respect her traditional neutrality, that Austria has been effectively neutralized, and that Yugoslavia is not wholly committed either to West or to East. I would wish that this neutral zone might be widened, rather than narrowed. While I realize that the concept of neutrality can be, and has been, exploited for Communist purposes, I don't think that should deter us from recognizing the real advantages it may hold."7)

In 1958, Denis Healey, British Labor leader and spokesman for defense affairs, put forward a model plan for a neutral belt in the middle of Europe. In his thinking the neutralization of Germany alone, suggested by Winston Churchill, and later by Nikita Khrushchev, would be unwise. Healey also opposed the neutralization of Europe as a whole. For him the neutral belt would include the German Federal Republic on the Western side, and East Germany, Poland, Czechoslovakia, and Hungary on the Soviet side; and then, in addition, "as many other states as you could get in by bargaining. It might be, for example, that you could bring in Denmark against Rumania, and so on. But you would have to guarantee some physical foothold on the continent for the West as a base for military sanctions against a possible military violation of the neutral zone by the Soviet Union."8)

According to Healey's plan countries in the neutral belt would be permitted to maintain conventional (i.e. non-nuclear) armed forces —subject to international inspection—to defend their borders against a possible attack. More than any other plan this one also goes into a discussion of the reasons why the Soviet Union might, indeed, go along with the creation of a neutral zone.

Neutralization reconsidered

Ten years had passed since the proposals traced above were made public. Since then a new balance, a "balance of terror," has been reached by the U.S.A. and the Soviet Union, which renders war between the two prohibitive. The Cold War, even though some of the conditions which caused it are still present, has since become history. Suspicion, nevertheless, still lingers on both sides. "Positive anti-Communists" hold that peaceful coexistence is a mere Soviet strategy to build up economic and military power and then to bury the West. Russia, repeatedly invaved and devastated in the course of history, entertains similar fears vis-a-vis the West, and tries to protect herself by a string of buffer-states streching from the Baltic to the Black Sea.

As of late, however, the maintenance of the Soviet protective system has been a costly operation both in tangible and intangible terms. Military and economically the East European countries are now less an asset than a liability for the Soviet Union. At the same time a nem menace is rising for Russia from the direction of China.

By creating a neutral zone liabilities could be written off, and the Soviet Union could devote more attention to her internal and Far-Eastern problems. The unnatural trade barrier which divides Europe could be eliminated by permitting the countries of the neutral zone to trade freely with both sides. Their middle-man role would likely result in increased prosperity. The neutral status, while prohibiting diplomatic and military alignment with the Great Powers, would not exclude the possibility of forming a larger federation of some sort by the common agreement of the neutral states.

In fact, the neutral zone might serve as a logical first step toward the creation of a Central European community, which then could act as a balancer between Western and Eastern Europe, a role unfulfilled and missing since the disintegration of the Austro-Hungarian Monarchy.

A number of future problems regarding the neutral zone, such as its step by step establishment, the rights and duties of its components, their exact relations to the East and West, including economic relations, would have to be examined seriously and in detail.

It is commonly recognized that the European situation, most of all the question of Germany, has been in an *impasse* for too long a period. Another attempt by the Great Powers at the solution of the problem may not be far off.

The creation of a neutral belt in Central Europe, it is submitted here, should be seriously considered again in the light of the changed world situation. The merits of the old proposals should be re-evaluated and, if necessary, new plans should be drafted to serve as possible alternatives for the settlement of the European question. To the students of Central European affairs would fall the task of criticizing the old and elaborating the new plans for eventual use by the interested parties.

1) A good summary on Neutrality can be found in Gerhard von Glahn, **Law Among Nations** (New York: Macmillan, 1965), Chapter 32. For a detailed treatment of present-day problems see Titus Komarnicki, **The Place of Neutrality in the Modern System of International Law,** and Charles M. Chaumont, **Nations Unies et Neutralité,** both published in **Recueil des Cours** of the Hague Academie de Droit International, vol. 80 and 89, respectively (Leyde: Sythoff, 1953 and 1957).

2) On this point see Gyula Hajdu, **A semlegesség** (Budapest: Közgazdasági és Jogi Könyvkiadó, 1958), pp. 261-262. The Austrian point of view regarding participation in the U.N. is presented by Alfred Verdross in "Die dauernde Neutralitaet Österreichs und die Organisation der Vereinten Nationen," **Juristische Blaetter,** July 5, 1955.

3) Examples are given and evaluated in Cecil V. Crabb, Jr., **The Elephants and the Grass: A Study of Nonalignment** (New York: Praeger, 1955), pp. 79-91.

4) See for example the statements made at the VIIth Congress of the International Association of Democratic Lawyers, Sofia, 1960, in **Legal Aspects of Neutrality** (Brussels: I.A.D.L., 1961?), in particular the statement of the Soviet participant L. Modjoryan, pp. 111-112.

5) For a detailed discussion read George Ginsburg's "Neutrality and Neutralism and the Tactics of Soviet Diplomacy" in **American Slavic and East European Review**, December 1960, p. 539 ff. This penetrating article is based on Soviet sources.

6) **East Europe**, July 1957, p. 47. Quoted by Ginsburg, p. 559.

7) George F. Kennan, "The Future of Soviet Communism." **The New Leader**, June 18, 1956, p. 6.

8) Denis Healey, **A Neutral Belt in Europe?** (London: Fabian Society, 1958), p. ? rinted in part in Paul F. Power's **Neutralism and Disengagement** (New Yo. .ribner, 1964). This convenient research anthology also contains excerpts of the Kennan articlé, and one version of the Rapacki Plan. Good case studies on neutralism and neutrality may be found in Peter H. Lyon's **Neutralism** (Leicester: Leicester University Press, 1963).

AUSTRIAN NEUTRALITY AND EUROPEAN INTEGRATION

FRITZ BOCK

FOREIGN affairs in Austria are the subject of deeply rooted public discussions. They even play a part in the election campaign, although elections belong chiefly to internal politics.

For instance, the problem of European integration played a leading part in the election campaign of 1962.

The reason why problems of foreign affairs are subject of ever growing attention lies in the fact that they concern more immediately than ever before, the interests of nations and persons alike.

Economics play a leading part in the sphere of foreign affairs and this arouses the interest of the entire population in them.

Integration policy is an miportant—one could say the most important—part of foreign affairs.

The forming of economic territories stretches itself deeply into the economic policy of a state and determines—not only in the case of Austria—the economic welfare of its inhabitants. Consequently the citizens show—very naturally— a growing interest in the substance, treatment and effect of Austria's foreign affairs.

The first question is, can a neutral state have a foreign policy at all? This question can indeed be a subject of discussion. One must ask oneself, whether neutrality in itself doesn't demand staying away from foreign affairs, from the outset and on principle? The answer to this question is easy: It is evident, that these problems play a part also in the neutral countries. A neutral country must build up its foreign policy entirely by its own decisions. It would be a mistake to imagine that the neutrality policy of all these states is similar. To give you an example: Austria is a member of the European Council since 1956, whilst Switzerland refused at first to join the Council, referring the refusal to reasons of neutrality. They joined only in 1963. Austria is also member of the United Nations, whereas Switzerland —for reasons of neutrality policy—has not asked to be received amongst the United Nations. It is equally possible, that a neutral state shold have common interests, whereas another of these neutrals could disregard it.

Such an example is the attitude of Sweden towards its Finnish neighbor. Neutrality is an international obligation undertaken by each state on its own, as regards standards and holdings, and is fashioned by each state in the regional frame of political structure. This is the case in Austria, although it declared in the memorandum of Moscow, that it wished to fashion its neutrality policy after the Swiss pattern. Nevertheless the aforementioned fact of Austria's membership in the European Council and the United Nations illustrates the fact that the administration and the extent of neutral policy doesn't accept general rules applicable to each neutral country in the same measure.

The paragraph of the Austrian Constitution regarding its permanent neutrality, fixes the fact expressly, that Austria takes no part in any military alliance; this determinates the basis of its obligation of neutrality unequivocally. To remain away from military organizations and to forbid the forming of military bases in Austria, are the obligations Austria took upon herself for safeguarding its own neutrality. That the Austrian foreign policy takes no part in the East-West conflicts and doesn't let itself be influenced by these in the natural outcome of its neutrality policy.

It is equally evident, that Austria cannot neglect certain aspects of its own supremacy like certain states belonging to some coalition, as any such step would render the fulfillment of her obligations regarding neutrality difficult and might even make it impossible.

Sometimes the wish is voiced, that Austria should prepare codes which would contain all the obligations originating from neutrality, where one could at all times look up these obligations and see if one has not infringed upon them. One cannot sufficiently warn against this. Naturally, neutrality demands certain bearings, however, the contents and the extent of these can and should not be cast into a code.

To give an example: If the United Nations invites a neutral country to send a military or sanitary contingent to an area endangered by some conflict, the neutral country cannot refuse to comply with this request. Or if a neutral country is requested to send one of his citizens to act as President in an international court of arbitration, this country cannot back out of this, all the more, because its neutrality renders it particularly suited for this job. However, a neutral country can only decide to vote for certain sanctions and take part in the execution of these sanctions from case to case and in accordance with the circumstances of each case and only if an international forum competent to act in the case, asks for it.

We must perceive, that the drafting of a fixed code regarding the attitude of neutrality, is not possible. Because it is impossible to enumerate all those problems at the decision of which the board of directors must consider the neutral policy balance.

Besides, experience teaches that each case needs a special decision.

It is an open question, how far the manifestations of already known symptoms can serve as examples for deciding on the timely problems.

Consequently, it would be very much mistaken, if a government would impede the fulfillment of its policy of neutrality by publicizing its difficulties and giving rise to a suspicion, that aforesaid government doesn't quite agree with the upholding of neutrality.

Finally, it wold be equally mistaken to comment on obligations of neutrality which do not exist.

For instance: economy and its territories do not belong to the framework of neutral policy. *There is no neutral economy.* Neutrality has got nothing to say about the way any country runs its internal economy and how it tries to direct it rightly.

The neutral state must be independent of the balance of neutral policy when it decides on the best way of running its economy in peace or war.

With these comments, we have reached the middle of the Austrian (European) integration policy. The contract which Austria wishes to enter into with the European Economic Community, is entirely based on economy. It can only extend to economic interests. Amongst other goals, it aims to secure the future of Austrian export-import. The fact, that this treaty would be contracted with a state whose aims do not conform with neutrality, does not play any part in the case, just as the fact that Austria has economic contracts with other non-neutral states—is also a matter of indifference. We must verify that, to secure economic prosperity—and this is the aim of the treaty with the European Market—is the preliminary condition of our country. In peacetime, nothing can endanger a country more than economic need. If we prevent this, we render a considerable service to supremity. Supremity is the preliminary condition of neutrality—this stands beyond question. Seen from this angle, we can say that the treaty which we are trying to conclude—inside the bounds of neutrality—with the European Economic Community, will—by helping the economic welfare of Austria—become a considerable pillar of Austrian neutrality. The existence of Austrian foreign policy is determined by its neutral state, this obliges it to conform itself to the attitude of the surrounding states and this presumes "a priori" the rulings of its policy. There is an Austrian neutral policy, but as it must take into consideration its neutrality, it is not always that simple.

If we draw the line between international neutrality and political neutrality, we get the same valuation. This line of demarcation, in the case of Austria, is very sharply partitioned. Austria is—on the basis of its social system—in every respect a member of the Western world. The line of demarcation between neutrality and non-commitment is often insufficiently marked and is often in danger of becoming blurred. Let us remember the notions of certain individuals, who imagine that Austria should have closer ties with those Communist countries whose conceptions are not quite conform with those of Moscow. It would be a disastrous mistake if Austria would accept these conceptions.

Although our foreign politics, notwithstanding the fact that Austria belongs to the Western sphere, cannot be entirely guided by the foreign policy of the West, it can equally not take part in the political conceptions of the Communist countries, even though these countries don't always agree with Moscow and Peking in some questions. Not even in case afore-mentioned countries would—at some date—accept a policy opposed to Communism. Austria's foreign policy must preserve its independence and individuality. Lastly, a few words about the efficiency of Austrian foreign policy. Needless to say, that the efficiency of small countries must by nature, be a limited one. It would be a mistake to overestimate the possibilities of this efficiency. Austrian policy cannot afford this. However, even between these limited possibilities, the foreign politics of small countries have important duties to fulfill. These small states can—even considering their limited powers—achieve a great deal, particularly if their governments can reckon on the approval of the entire population. This is particularly the case in Austria, whose two-party system has been thoroughly rooted since 1945. It is indisputable, that Austria's foreign policy can only achieve efficiency if the government can refer to the approval of both parties.

Any government that could rely only on a party with small majority in Parliament, would lose a great deal of its international credit and could hardly achieve any results in international life.

If Austria wishes to be effective, it must possess the confidence of both parties—and not *only* because Constitution (unanimous Cabinet decision) prescribes it. Because of this—as long as it is possible—and so far it has proved possible without exception—the Austrian foreign policy must have the approval of both parties.

If ever there arises a fundamental and insuperable opposition, then it might become unavoidable to appeal to the nation through new elections. In this case, the nation would have to bear the responsibility. If, as a result of the elections, the government would be victorious, it would gain a new mandate. But as this process would—for the time being—invalidate the government's power of action, it would be desirable to find the common platform of Austrian foreign policy without having to recur to new elections. It has been so up to now and it is to be hoped that it will remain so in the near future.

IDEAS OF AN AUSTRIAN ON THE COEXISTENCE OF NATIONS IN THE DANUBIAN AND CARPATHIAN BASINS

JOSEF MATL

I WOULD like to start with my own experiences in my homeland on the German-Slovenian-Hungarian boundary line in Styria, then still a part of the Austro-Hungarian Monarchy. Here the river Mur abandons the German-inhabited foreland of the Eastern Alps and enters upon the Hungarian Pannonian Plains near Radkersburg. Here Styrian Germans, Slovenes, and Hungarians have lived peacefully with each other through many centuries, intermarried, and entered into many associations in connection with their daily work. As members of the same community, they lived through the same political and social ecents; for instance, through the Napoleonic wars, the emancipation of the peasant population, etc.

Furthermore, I am able to draw on later experiences when during many journeys I had the opportunity to acquaint myself with the countries of the Danubian and of the Carpathian Basins and with the Balkan Peninsula as well. Again, as an officer in the army in two world wars I came into close contact with the representatives of many nationalities. And last but not least, I have at hand the substance of decades of scholarly work to draw upon which have put me in touch with the cultural problems of these nations, especially the Slavs.

My experience in my homeland, on the German-Slovenian-Hungarian ethnic boundary, seems to underscore some typical features characteristic of the coexistence of nations in this region.

These stand out at once when contrasted with similar traits in the body of my subsequent knowledge of human and spiritual processes in the Danubian Basin. These features are: the factor of *peaceful symbiosis* and the factor of *peaceful ethnical shifts* along a flowing, plastic ethnical boundary, a gradual transition and flow or assimilation of Germans, Slovenes, Croats, Serbs, Slovaks into the Magyar ethnic group; and of Slovenes, Croats, Czechs, and Magyars into a German ethnic majority. Assimilation on this level is a socio-psychical and biologic process of integration connected with intermarriage and social or cultural ascent. These are phenomena of a natural process of assimilation—the German, Slavonian, or Magyar ethnic majority absorbing minority elements ("Germanization," "Slavonization," "Magyarization")—which is completely void of any trace of propaganda. One has only to analyze the family names in Graz, Vienna, Klagenfurt, Budapest, Zagreb, Prague, assessing origins and present national loyalty feelings. We are under the influence of life-processes of biologic origin, which only became controversial during the nationalistic era of the second half of the 19th century and the first decades of the 20th. The new development of nationalism poisoned the natural relations of the different ethnic groups. The outcome of this was that to belong to a certain individual group,—to have ethnical stability or plasticity,—provided new values with pejorative or meliorative meaning. I myself have witnessed in my homeland—and the same applies to the Czechs, Hungarians, Carniolians— that peaceful symbiosis became at once shattered as soon as a mutual campaign of national hate began to spread in the form of nationalistic power-propaganda.

The main instrument for this propaganda was the so-called "Nazional Freiheitliche Intelligenz" (Intelligentsia Fighting For National Independence), whose faith in nationality was only a substitute for lost religious beliefs.

Symbiosis became disrupted to such an extent that when, for example, the house of a German settler in the "Windischen Bücheln" (a Slavonic region) caught fire, his Slavonian neighbours, under the influence of nationalistic instigations, would no longer come to his aid. Or to quote another instance: during the Second World War, completely alien national-socialistic functionaries evicted Slovenian settlers, those who had been friendly with the Germans in the past, who possessed war medals from the Austrians and whose sons were fighting in the German *Wehrmacht*. These settlers were forced to leave their properties in 24 hours. These are only isolated examples of individual tragedies suffered by members of national groups; but these instances are multiplied into thousands and hundreds of thousands since 1918, and during and after the Second World War. There is ample documentary evidence for all this. Only the actors changed. The acts themselves followed the same pattern everywhere: whether Germans, Magyars, or Slavonians acted against each other; or whether national leaders of various creeds, or Communist leaders filled with class hatred made the decisions. Only the methods of destruction changed from country to country.

The "national question," with tensions between ethnic groups was entirely unknown until the first decades of the 19th century; that is, until the beginning of the era characterized by the idea of the "national state."

If wee look closely at this symbiotic coexistence which lasted for several centuries, we find a host of subsidiary phenomena—the integration of different ethnic entities; the enclaves; and the formation of social strata, which, however, developed as national strata. We find, for instance, in Carniola and in the Slovenian Lower Styria that the merhant class in the cities was predominantly German; as was the greater part of the higher and middle civil servant positions until the second half of the 19th century.

In Hungary, the townsfolk and artisan classes were non-Magyar in their origins; however, the civil servants and the gentry were predominantly Magyar. These latter were the protagonists of the Magyar "national state" in a country which before 1918 was confronted wiht a near majority of non-Magyar ethnic groups: Slovaks, Germans, Serbs, Ruthenians, and Rumanians. In Bohemia, the industrially and culturally advanced city population was in the 19th century still strongly German, but there already existed a nationalistically-minded Czech city population and intelligentsia.

Given all this, we can understand the roots of the *characteristic dualistic consciousness* or awareness of belonging both to a state and simultaneously to a different ethnic group or "nation." This dualism developed with the growth of national sentiment in the 19th century and the broadening and progress of education became a characteristic phenomenon in the Danubian and Carpathian Basin under the Habsburgs. It was a diversely stratified, dual consciousness of integration. There have been thousands of cases in which a person was completely at ease professing himself to be a good Croat or Slovene or Czech and a good Austrian patriot. This was especially the case with civil servants and the officers of the army. Such individual duality of loyalties was, however, not restricted to the Habsburg Monarchy. It still persisted, though to a lesser degree, during the era of national states created after 1918. Consciousness of nationality remained solely on the level of the life-functions of a given ethnic group—i.e., language, custom, tradition, a primary sentiment and cultural consciousness—as long as this consciousness did not become contaminated by chauvinistic and imperialistic catchwords. That these circumstances were completely beyond comprehension of a Frenchman, an Englishman, or an American, was clearly shown when prisoners of war were questioned after 1945. English, American, or French investigating officers took the answer of the defendant, that he was a German from Hungary, or from Yugoslavia or from Rumania, as a Nazi provocation. They were capable of thinking only in terms of a national state, where the respective loyalties of "state" and "nation" were felt to be identical.

It is clear that the idea of the national state as a focus of power and the simultaneous endeavours to invest right and power in Hungary only in the Magyar population; in Czechoslovakia only in the Czechs; in Carinthia only in the Germans; and in Yugoslavia only in the Slovenes, Croats, Serbs and Macedonians; in other words this nationalistic idea of the power state—as widely held and practiced in the policies of Hungary before 1918 and in all the new states after 1918,—must be regarded today as a residuum of chauvinistic intoxication. *In the present stage of the world situation, all this appears nonsensical and anachronistic.* It is anachronistic in the same manner as a restoration of the German "Drang nach Osten" appears today to be anachronistic; or a Magyar claim would be to hold sole control in the Carpathian and the Danubian Basins; or the Pan-Slavonic "Drang nach Westen"; or a restoration of the Habsburg Monarchy. All these belong to the past. Such illusory claims are only an impossible drawback to any attempt to rebuild a feasible symbiosis in East Central Europe, especially in the Carpathian Basin. Our value-judgments are no longer connected with national statistical figures but with human security and the inviolability of the law and with the spiritual and moral responsibility of the individual self.

As long as the members of the emigrant groups retain their fascination with such intoxicating psychic complexes of power as are incorporated in the practice of the "national state," and stubbornly petrify it along with an openly asserted or latently understood aim assimilating the other ethnic national groups, e.g., Pan Croat, Pan Serb, or Pan Magyar ideas; they will eliminate themselves from any new attempts at reorganization. It is becoming increasingly clear that the platform of the Austrian Social Democratic Party as promulgated in Brünn dealing with a solution of ethnical problems in the Danubian and Carpathian Basins, and also the so-called Renner Program, with the idea of a national register are still the politically most feasible solutions for a symbiosis of discrete ethnic units into a supranational state. It was a tragedy caused by the interplay of historical forces that this solution could not be realized. I profess myself to be a partisan to this solution, although ideologically and politically I do not stand on their platform. So much for the general description of the problem.

In the Austrian Republic of today the situation is the following: the older generation of the so-called "nationalists" still entertains feelings of superiority, especially in the frontier-regions in Styria, and in particular in Carniola, when facing the Slovenian minority. It does not come to light openly as before, but only in a latent way, when handling practical questions of the cultural autonomy of the Austrian Slovenian minority; e.g., the question of schools. They take a peaceful national and cultural assimilation of this minority as granted and as necessary. This is true, above all, in Carniola, where both groups display an aggressive attitude: a radically-minded German national group and a radical Slovene national group with Titoistic sympathies.

In Burgenland the Croat question did not create acute national tension as in the above-mentioned case. Symbiosis in satisfactory because the Croats are able to live their national life in their hamlets undisturbed. They have their own schools and are well integrated into the general economic life of the state with connections to Vienna. In the Western and Northern States these questions simply do not crop up. In general it can be stated that the remnants of the former civil servant and officer classes of the late Austro-Hungariar Monarchy, who still retain memories relating to peaceful coexistence of the individual ethnic units within the state, are dwindling in numbers from year to year, dying out slowly, and no longer posses political significance. Only a small faction of "Monarchists" tries to keep up the "tradition," but they have no political weight in the realm of public opinion. The new aims of the "welfare state" have disintegrated historical tradition. The younger Austrian generation does not care about problems of coexistence of different ethnic units in the Danubian Basin as these problems no longer exist in the practical affairs of their everyday life. They have adjusted themselves to the problems of their homeland— the minute Austria. The Iron Curtain is seen as a grim reality, as an existing boundary between two politically and economically different systems. Otherwise, interest is focused on Western Europe and on the United States of America.

There is no longer the faintest awareness of possible new opportunities for future cooperation and symbiosis with the adjacent Slavs and Magyars in the Danubian and Carpathian Basins. The same applies to children of emigrants now growing up in Austria, whose parents, (Germans, Slavs or Magyars) were born in the Eastern Bloc countries. Any contacts still maintained with their country of origin are strictly on a family level.

What can be done? We must emphasize in education and in journalism the *common* foundations of evolution in the Danubian and Carpathian Basins, thus building our cousciousness of history on the facts of symbiosis while giving due regard to the perpetuation of particular ethnic traditions in language, music, and customs. We should not repeatedly probe into old wounds which nations of this region have suffered from each other during a century of overheated national antagonisms—German-Czech, German-Magyar, Magyar-Slav, German-Slovene. We should avoid creating new resentments. History, above all, must be taught from a European and Central European viewpoint, and not with a chauvinistic German, Magyar, Czech, or Slovene bias. It is one's duty to clarify historically and rationally, what truth, peace and national justice mean to a whole region.

Perhaps the day will come, when instead of present dual state and political systems and ideologies, there will again emerge a new community of European nations within a European federation. I can fully appreciate the psychology of a crusading spirit so much cherished by emigré groups. Whether there is any hope of success in it when measured against the world situation of today is another question entirely. I, unfortunately have become somewhat sceptical; perhaps because the supporters of the crusade for a "Christian Western World and its Human Liberties" have completely overlooked the deep demoralization inherent in this Christian West and the Western World as a whole caused by the totalitarian traits of a society saturated with luxury and well-being, and are therefore at a loss to notice the weakening of the sacrificial and fighting spirit and of the will to sacrifice self.

THREE NEGLECTED DOCUMENTS ON SELF-DETERMINATION AND NEUTRALITY

MIROSLAV LAZAROVICH

THE Moscow *Pravda* of September 26, 1968 tried to justify the invasion of Czechoslovakia by saying:
"The accupation troops are conducting a struggle for the principle of self determination of the peoples of Czechoslovakia, for their inalienable right themselves to decide their own fate." It continues: "Former ideas of sovereignty and national independence could not and will not inhibit the USSR from forceful intervention against 'counter-revolutionaries' in Communist countries and against the revival of neo-Nazism in West Germany."

This statement is in stark opposition to Lenin's principle announced on November 8, 1917, when Poland, the Baltic states and a great part of the Ukraine were under German occupation. At tnat time, the second All-Russian Congress of Soviets of Workers', Soldiers·, and Peasants' Deputies, at the request of Lenin, accepted the following "Decree on *Peace*":[1)

"The Workers' and Peasants' Government created by the Revolution of 24-25 October (6-7 Nov.) and based on the Soviets of Workers', Soldiers', and Peasants' deputies, proposes to all belligerent peoples and their governments the immediate opening of negotiations for a *just and democratic peace.*

By such a peace the Government understands an immediate peace *without annexations* (i.e. *without seizure of foreign territory, without the forcible incorporation of foreign nationalities)* and without indemnities.

By annexation or seizure of foreign territory the Government understands, in accordance with the sense of justice of democracy in general, and of the laboring classes in particular, the *incorporation into a large or powerful State of a small or weak nationality, without the definitely, clearly, and voluntarily expressed consent and desire of this nationality,* regardless of when this *forcible incorporation* took place, regardless also of the degree of development or backwardness of the nation *forcibly annexed or forcibly retained within the frontiers* of the given State, and, finally, regardless of whether this nation is located in Europe or in distant lands beyond the seas.

If any nation whatsoever is retained as part of a given State *by force,* if, despite its expressed desire—whether expressed in the decision of *political parties,* or by *rebellions* or *insurrections* against national oppression *it has not the right of choosing free—the troops of the annexing or, generally, the more powerful nation being completely withdrawn and without any pressure being brought to bear— the constitutional forms of its national existence, then its incorporation is an annexation, that is, seizure and coercion.*

The Government considers it the greatest crime against humanity to continue this war for the sake of dividing among the powerful and wealthy nations the weaker nationalities which they have conquered."

This practically forgotten Leninist document clearly condemns such military intervention by which the Red Army tried to prohibit self-determination in Hungary and Czechoslovakia and menaces Rumania, Yugoslavia, etc.

Creating a Central European neutral zone would make the Soviet Union secure against aggression and the "danger of revival of neo-Nazism or German revanchism."

It is an historic fact that Russia was invaded from the West several times since Napoleon's adventure. The peoples of Russia are therefore, understandably entitled to absolute *guarantees against a repetition of an invasion* of their country. If they are honestly convinced that the great German nation, perhaps in alliance with other nations, may present a danger, the have the right to ask guarantes. If all the great powers, including the nuclear powers, should guarantee a broad neutral zone between Russia and Germany and, like Austria, sixty nations would sign a neutralization act, this guarantee would serve effectively to allay the fears of the Kremlin. It would make the expensive keeping of foreign armed forces unnecessary in this zone and Anglo-American forces could leave the European continent. This would lead to a real détente, mutual disengagement with international guarantees under the United Nations. The NATO could then be transformed from a military alliance into a peaceful partnership which, together with the USSR, would guarantee the neutrality of the Central European zone. Nothing else would serve so well to prevent aggression.

Rumanian and Hungarian Governments in Favor of Neutrality — 1939

Documents on German Foreign Policy (London 1949—1953. Series D. 1936-1945. Vol. VIII. p. 305, 317, 319) contains the text of the Rumanian government's plan for neutrality which the Rumanian foreign minister, Grigore Gafencu, formulated. (See also his "Prelude to the Russian Campaign." Mules. 1945). The plan was launched by Rumania in November 1939, after preliminary talks with statesmen of the Balkan countries. The Rumanian official plan contained the following points:

1.) The members of the neutral bloc would declare themselves neutral in conflicts of war.

2.) They would sign a nonaggression pact with each other.

3.) They would be obligated to a politically benevolent neutrality if a member of the bloc became a victim of aggression.
4.) Along the common frontiers military units would be demobilized.
5.) Mutual consultations would be held to protect the interest of the neutral countries.
6.) Foreign ministers of the neutral countries would form a council.

The initial reaction of the other governments including that of the Hungarian Pál Teleki favored this plan which the Italian foreign minister, Ciano, also supported. But later Hitler told Ciano that "although the interest of Germany is to maintain the neutrality of the Southeastern and Balkan states, the establishment of a permanent bloc of neutral countries may lead to the crystallization of a situation which may hinder further plans." Therefore, Nazi Germany prohibited the further discussion of this plan for neutrality.

Professor Sándor Szilassy has recently had access to the papers of John F. Montgomery, American ambassador to Hungary between 1933 and 1940. The ambassador recorded that Pál Teleki, several times Prime Minister of Hungary, was also in favor of a neutralization of Central Europe. But caught between the struggle of great powers, he committed suicide on April 3, 1941. (See the article "Hungarian Efforts for Neutrality in 1939," *Uj Látóhatár* (New Horizon) Munich, July-August, 1968 pp. 317-328.)

Neutrality Once Favored by the Hungarian Communist Party

Under the title "Documents from the history of the Party" the official newspaper of the Hungarian Communist Party, *Népszabadság*, (Budapest, Nov. 23, 1968) published recollections of the period following September 1939 when diplomatic relations had been established for a short time between Hungary and the Soviet Union. The article says:

"It would have been possib'e for Hungary to declare a *policy neutrality* in order to avoid the war of the imperialists. The Communist Party, reorganized at that time, tried to influence developments in this direction."

Imre Nagy, Moscow-trained nationalist Communist leader and twice Minister President of Hungary, reaffirmed in October 1956, the demand for neutrality. Why does not the Hungarian Communist Party demand political neutrality now as it had once recommended for Hungary? Or in absence of the Soviet troops would it favor neutrality again?

1) Kluchnikov and Sabanin, vol. II, p. 88. Soviet Documents of Foreign Policy. Selected and edited by Jane Degras. Vol. I. 1917-1924, Vol. II. 1925-1932. Issued under the auspices of the Royal Institute of International Affairs. Oxford University Press. London, New York, Toronto. 1951.

4. Central Europe in East-West Relations

BRITAIN AND EASTERN EUROPE

C. A. MACARTNEY

FOR well-nigh two centuries—ever since it began to take an active interest in the area—British policy towards central and eastern Europe has been constant in its objectives, while varying with the changing conditions in the ways by which it has sought to achieve them. It has constantly opposed, as dangerous to its own interests, the establishment in this quarter of Europe, of a single, over-strong and expansive Power. At the end of the 18th century, when British states-men first preoccupied themselves carefully with the "Eastern ques-tion," the danger presented itself in the form of Russia's expansive urge towards the warm waters, which was held to constitute a threat to Britain's naval communications, and this aspect of it remained the dominant one throughout most of the 19th century, more than ever, after the opening of the Suez Canal. But it was not a policy directed against Russia as such, but only against that Power which happened at the time to look the dangerous one. Round the turn of the 19-20th centuries, when Germany appeared on the scene, united, martial and aggressive, and seeking to acquire a dangerous influence over Turkey, Britain came to terms with Russia and entered a system of alliances for containing Germany. And meanwhile the scope of the problem had widened from the mere defence of the Straits. The immediate occasion of France's and Britain's entry into World War II was Germany's attack on Poland, which Britain had guaranteed, and the reasons for the guarantee policy are nowhere more clearly stated than in a memorandum by the Foreign Office, composed in the summer of 1939, which submitted that it was essential to prevent Hitler from "expanding easterwards, and obtaining control of the resources of Central and Eastern Europe," which would enable him "to turn upon the Western countries with overwhelming force."

Britain has, then, always held it to be her interest that this area should be held by a Power or Powers strong enough to maintain its own real independence, but not strong enough itself to be aggressive. It was because the Ottoman Empire answered this definition in the

19th century that Britain regularly tried to prop up its rule, in spite of the inhumanity of a regime which often caused British Liberal opinion to dissent from the official policy, as cynical and even immoral. It was just the same considerations that caused Britain also consistently to support the Austro-Hungarian Monarchy, although there was much also in the structure of the Monarchy which British progressives disliked. In 1848 there was strong popular feeling among us against the Austrian regime, and very lively sympathy for Hungary, and our Foreign Secretary, Lord Palmerston, fully shared both feelings, but while willing, as he said, to do everything possible for the Hungarians, he refused to do anything for Hungary, because he held that Austria in the absence of Hungary would be too weak to fulfill her role of barrier against Russia and factor in the European balance of power, and that Hungary without Austria would be too weak to take her place. For the same reasons, Britain hesitated long in the First World War (as did France and the U.S.A.) before consenting to a policy which aimed at the break-up of Austria-Hungary, and only agreed to that policy in the Spring of 1918, under the pressure of extreme military necessity and after it had appeared that the Monarchy had surrendered its independence so far under the Spa Agreement that she would thence forward be a mere satellite of Germany's.

But the enthusiasm for the idea of national self-determination was by that time very strong, and the Foreign Office had argued that if Eastern Europe was reorganised on a basis of independent national states, those States would "prove an efficient barrier against Russian preponderance in Europe and German extension towards the Near East, because they would be happy and contended in the realisation of their national aspirations, and strong as regards their economic future." The solution would thus combine expediency with morality.

The event, of course, proved that the authors of this memorandum had been over-optimistic. They had underestimated the complexities of ethnic conditions in Eastern Europe. It proved impossible, at that stage, to make all the peoples of the area happy and contented at the same time, still less, economically secure. In fact, they remained miserable and disunited, and Germany, Italy and Russia ate them up one by one.

What is the lesson to be drawn from the history of the last forty years? Certainly not, that object of British policy, from Pitt to Chamberlain, was mistaken. On the contrary, everything that has happened since 1945 has merely emphasized how much happier and more secure the whole civilised world would feel—leaving the happiness of the peoples themselves out of account—if Eastern Europe were freed from the grip of Power capable of exploiting its resources and using it as a base for aggression. All our interests demand that this great and vital area should be its own master, and should be strong enough to defend its independence (and by strength I do not necessarily mean military strength; the good-will of the world which Switzerland enjoys has been a far greater protection to her than her own armies could ever have been). But how should East Europe be organized—if ever the chance comes to organize it anew—to fulfill these requirements? It seems to me that we must consider the history of the years between the two world wars dispassionately, picking out to preserve what stood the test in them and ruthlessly discarding what was shown to be mistaken.

It would surely be hopeless to try to go back behind the principle of national freedom. The peoples which have once tasted it will never again be content without it. National freedom is the basis on which Eastern Europe must rest.

But it must be national freedom for all: a complete equality. There were times in the past when a State could justify the supremacy of one national element in it, because its peoples were really at different stages in their social, political and economic development. That differentiation has largely passed—that has been one of the benefits brought by those years to the future, at whatever cost to the present in terms of human welfare and justice. Today, total equality is the only firm basis, and to it all sentimental or historical considerations, however humanly justifiable, need to be sacrificed, no matter whether their title-deeds are a thousand years old, or forty.

Equality between all, and freedom for all. But freedom does not necessarily mean complete, self-degrading autarchy, in the sense that each people should exercise all the attributes of sovereignty which West European thinkers of the 17th and 18th centuries chose to attach to that word. The solution for an area such as Eastern Europe, if not for Europe as a whole, is surely that of a multinational community, in which all its peoples can participate freely in their common interests, while retaining their complete self-government in such matters as concern themselves alone. It will be a difficult thing to create, but if the difficulties are great, so is the need, since everything else has failed; and so will be the reward.

AMERICAN INTERESTS AND OBLIGATIONS
IN THE DANUBIAN BASIN

ALBERT WASS

WHEN we talk about the interests and obligations of a nation, our concept of the nation is that of a corporate unit of human society. It does not, therefore, include the self-centered interests and obligations of private individuals, but includes only the interests and obligations of the corporate body called a nation.

It must be made clear, however, that nations are subject to the same ethical and economic rules as are the private individuals, and in the event that these rules are disregarded, the nation as a unit must suffer the same consequences. The laws of cause and effect apply to the corporate body of the nation in the same way they apply to the individual, and the chain reactions of this law must similarly apply.

The present political and economic situation of our globe proves beyond cavil the validity of this thesis. Under the influence of hate, prejudice, misunderstandings and ignorance, some of the bigger nations have used their power to destroy well-adjusted and well-balanced geographical and economic units throughout the world. This has resulted in confusion, misery and permanent unrest.

No matter how powerful these nations might be, sooner or later they will have to suffer from the consequences of the situations which they have created. Some of these nations are already doing so. Our globe is shrinking day by day, under the new concepts of science which are forcing the human race into a closer coexistence, in which every nation, small or large, must share the mutual responsibilities of the globe. No nation, no matter how powerful, can exclude itself any more from the community of mankind. Any nation that expects to keep a leading position within this community must realize all its interests and all its obligations. Otherwise it will not be able to maintain its position on this globe.

The United States of America is still today the most powerful nation in the community of the nations. This great country must also make a clear accounting of its assets and liabilities, its interests and obligations, within and outside of its frontiers.

This study will deal only with a small fragment of these interests and obligations; namely, with those concerning the Danubian Basin. The problems involving that part of the globe may seem to many Americans as far distant and unimportant. Nevertheless, it would be a vital mistake to disregard them. For, as has been pointed out previously, the rapid shrinking of our globe through the advancements of science not only eliminates the distances, but also increases the effects of political and economic blunders which have been caused either by ignorance or negligence, or both.

Through the evolution of history, nations have established themselves under the influence of geographical necessities. Along with the advancement of mankind, these geographical units gave place to economic units as the basic principle on which political units were built.

The first successful economic unit in the Danubian Basin was the Hungarian Kingdom, which brought peace, culture and prosperity to that part of the world from the 11th to the 16th century when the dynamic expansion of the Ottoman Empire destroyed this unit, condemning the entire population of the Danube Basin to an extreme misery that lasted for two centuries. The economic balance was restored only two hundred years later by the Habsburg Empire, while the political balance has never completely recovered since, except perhaps for a few decades between 1865 and 1910. These forty-five years of comparative political freedom and high economic upswing are regarded by many historians as the "Golden Age" of the Danube Basin.

Disregarding here the political handicaps of the system, the Austro-Hungarian Monarchy seems to be the most successful economic unit the Danube Basin has ever experienced.

After World War I, the political aspirations of certain nationalistic groups, prejudice and ignorance on the part of the victors, dismantled this economic unit, and created a number of small countries supposedly based on the Wilsonian doctrine of self-determination, but in reality forcing more than eight million people under the chauvinistic oppression of neighboring nations. Such an unhealthy atmosphere of hate and mutual distrust followed that any effort of readjustment and reconciliation was made impossible. Not until the brutalities of the Russian occupation and the sufferings caused by an inhuman totalitarian regime had moulded the people of different tongues into brothers again, could the idea of a peaceful Danubian unity be launched again successfully.

Today the Danubian Basin is ready for such readjustment and reconciliation, and it is only a question of time when the totalitarian system they endure will be brushed off, giving place to the will of the people. When this time comes, and the Danubian Basin, as a new economic and perhaps political unit emerges on the scene, it will be extremely important which way they turn, and who will be the one that reaches out to them with the first hand.

Once in possession of its independence, there seem to be three possibilities for the Danubian Basin to seek economic contacts. One is Western Europe, the second is Russia and the third possibility is the United States of America.

Due to the fact that the main productivity of the Danubian Basin is still in the field of agriculture, it seems natural that Western Europe will try hard to draw this new potential into the orbit of its Common Market. However, due to present affiliation and contacts, Russia will have a good chance, too, in keeping the already existing economic ties, especially if Russia happens to go through the same political process at the same time and emerges on the scene as a free federation of politically independent republics.

In either case, we must underline the fact that there is more in the potential of the Danubian Basin than a mere exchange of agricultural products for industrial products. First, it represents a still not fully discovered and evaluated source of various important raw materials, such as oil, uranium and many others. Second, it has the political potential of more than fifty million people, which can shift the balance of power on the European scene from one side to another, or can keep the powers well balanced by its neutrality. This neutrality, however, will occur only in the third case; namely, if the hand that reaches out first to help the Danubian Basin is that of the United States of America.

There is no possibility within the framework of this article to enter into all the details of the manifold economic benefits that could mutually arise from such a relationship between the United States and the Danubian Basin. However, it cannot be doubted by any clear-thinking economist that American aid to the development of this most neglected part of Europe would not only open up almost unlimited possibilities for the inhabitants of that region, but at the same time it could also supply the American industry with new markets and raw materials.

Therefore, an active American interest in the Danubian Basin would be fully justified and not based on negative qualities alone. If either Germany or Russia should happen to be the nation which pulls this new potential factor into its sphere, this would also mean an increase of their political influence and again upset the balance of power in Europe.

While speaking of economic prospects, we must not forget those of a political nature. The Danubian Basin has always been referred to as the "Power keg of Europe." The reason for this combustive quality was not its economic, but its political structure. The only way to eliminate the danger of future frictions is to find a solution that solves these political problems with justice and fairness to every nationality involved. Every sign indicates that such a solution is not only possible, but is being worked out in careful detail, and only awaits the end of today's totalitarian oppression in order to become a reality. How much help America gives to the realization of these vitally important solutions will greatly influence any further relations.

As was mentioned in the beginning, there are not only interests, but also obligations involved. During the last fifty year's the United States reached twice deep into the lives of the people of the Danubian Basin. First, they helped create a series of small countries unable to survive on their own, and which as a result, were free prey to any neighbor having political power and aspirations. Hitler's Germany could never have grown into such a power if the problems of the Danubian Basins had been solved with wisdom and good will after World War I.

As a result of the situation created by the Versailles treaties, the nations of the Danubian Basin were forced into World War II against their will. Leaflets which were dropped by American airplanes and American broadcasts promised independence and free elections were the people of the Danubian Basin to surrender to the Russian Army. These promises were never kept, just as twelve years later during the Hungarian uprising the promises made to the people behind the Iron Curtain were not backed up by the American government. All this adds up to a huge moral obligation which the United States of America owes the Danubian nations, and to forget about these obligations would not only be a dark page in American history, but would also result in an increasing distrust in the integrity of the American government and the system it represents. It would be ridiculous to assume that powerful nations could not be harmed by distrust in the hearts of millions, a distrust which has been created by its policies.

In World War I America helped destroy the economic and political balance of the Danubian Basin. In World War II America aided the Communist conspiracy in taking possession of the Danubian Basin and forcing Danubian nations under such brutal oppression as they have never before experienced in history. These facts cannot be and must not be disregarded.

America's future relations with Central and Southeastern Europe depend on the fulfillment of these obligations.

Austrians, Hungarians, Croatians, Slovaks, Serbs, Bulgarians, and Rumanians have always maintained an admiration for America, for its political system, its way of life, its economy. In spite of all the latest disappointments, this admiration still exists. But it is entirely up to the United States whether or not this asset will be turned in the future a harmonious and productive relationship and built into a bulwark of world peace.

CROATIA
AND CENTRAL EUROPE

STJEPAN BUC

THE geopolitical situation of a people is not created by supernatural forces: it is formed in the same way as the people themselves. The task of science is not only to explain the ethnogenesis of the respective collective organism, but also to answer the questions how this collective community of people could maintain its area, and what were the dangers menacing its existence which had to be mastered?

The aim of our article is to explore the character of the Croatian people, one of the oldest peoples of Europe, their biological and historical peculiarities, and their attitude to their neighbors in the Central European area.

Where is "Central Europe"?

In spite of some difficulties in finding a definition that would be of general value, it is not altogether impossible, to my mind, to answer this question in a satisfactory manner. We can fix the limits of our continent rather easily, but the definition of "Central Europe" is difficult because no natural geographical frontier exists. E.g., if we consider the area of "Atlantic Europe" there is at least one quite clear border: it is contained in the very definition of the term. This is not the case regarding Central Europe. Nevertheless, this concept is still used, particularly in German political literature. If we glance at the map of Europe, we must admit that the "Pannonian Plain" belongs to the heart of the continent and that the Carpathian Mountains from such a wall in the East that they can in no way be overlooked. Budapest is almost centrally located between the Rhine and the Carpathian Mountains, while the area between the rivers Drava and Drina constitutes an access to the warmer sea. Although geographers are of various opinions regarding the eastern boundary, we must, nevertheless, take it for granted that one should not go eastward beyond the Carpathian Mountains.[1] Furthermore, the history of this area during the last thousand years can in no way be understood without considering the "Pannonian Plain" as a part of Central Europe. German political literature very often uses the name "East Central Europe" today. This causes more confusion because the basic idea itself is not yet clarified.

The former deputy to the German Reichstag, Friedrich Naumann, created the term "Mitteleuropa" and popularized it.[2] For Naumann it was a matter of political conception; by the term "Central Europe" he referred to the "Central Powers" of that time: Germany and the Dual Monarchy. But he did not stop at the Rhine; he supposed that France should also be included in his "Central Europe." He stressed, however, that the last wars drew France away from "Central Europe." Naumann's error consisted in the fact that he wished for the information of one state comprising all those empires. There is no doubt that through the destruction of these two empires in World War I, Europe also was 'eo ipso' destroyed—thanks to extra-European forces. This, too, proves that "Central Europe" is the kernel of Europe in general. The catastrophe caused by it is evident from the fact that the boundaries of Asia have been extended to the Trieste-Lübeck line and have reached Berlin.

We are of the opinion that this delineation of the boundaries by Naumann—regarding the area itself—is comparatively the most realistic, because it is based today, as at the time of Naumann, on a concrete and historical foundation that could not be destroyed by political catastrophes of two world wars. On the contrary, it seems to bid defiance to all dramatic events that have ruined Europe. Hence, the idea that the area of "Central Europe" is the territory of the former so-called Central Powers (Germany and the Dual Monarchy) is based on the fact that peoples of Western culture inhabit it and that it is situated before the gates of the eastern world: it is a kind of "antimurale occidentis."

Croatia belongs to this area

The surprising ignorance of sociology in East European history has had harmful results regarding the interpretation of Croation history. Even worse, however, are the quite false political conclusions generated by this ignorance. The catastrophic consequences can be best illustrated if one realizes that the present unsound political structure of Central Europe represents one focus of the current world crisis, and that, this results from the above-mentioned ignorance concerning the nature of the peoples of the Indogermanic-Slavic linguistic group. Old Byzantine fairy tales about a fictitious ethnic "Slavic unity" (continuously accepted and carried on also by the romanticism of the 18th and 19th centuries) resulted in the fabrication of those artificial states in the first half of the present century. Not only different peoples and hostile races strangers to each other were forced into such states, but actually two different worlds—the East and the

West—were supposed to unify. Such was the case of the Croatian people who became one of the victims of the false doctrine of so-called "Slavic unity." They were forced into an artificial states—i.e., Yugoslavia—which they never considered their home country, but rather a prison. The fundamental error made was that a European, Western people *were* isolated from *their* organic, natural connection with Europe—let us say, from Central Europe—and *were* forced to be part of an Asiatic-Byzantine power, such as Yugoslavia, as far as its ethnic and cultural aspects are concerned.3)

The well-known Austrian sociologist, Johannes Peisker, 50 years ago referred to an important fact, and according to him this fact is clearly proven by history: "All so-called Slave States of which we have sufficient information turn out to be either Germanic or Atlantic foundations."4) One should keep this statement in mind if one wishes to deal with the historical life of the peoples of the Slavic linguistic group. It would be preferable to correct the denomination "Germanic or Atlantic" to "Germanic or Nordic," for the latter fits better into the geographical and historical aspect. The Croatian state was founded by Illyrian-Gothic elements, while the Serbian state was established by the Turkish (Cumanes).

Hence, the ethnogenesis of the Croats is to a certain degree similar to that of the French: what the Illyrians are in tre Croatian case, the Celts (Galli) are in the French case; what the Goths are for the Croats, the Franks are for the French. The enormous excavations in Croatia, particularly in Bosnia and Dalmatia (from the time of the Roman Empire: "Illyricum Superior" or "Dalmatian Romana," between the rivers Sava and Drina and the Adriatic Sea) are rich with remnants of the Illyrian and Gothic culture, which again prove the above-mentioned ethnogenesis. We would like to mention an important fact: these discoveries reach eastward, mainly to the line which follows the river Drina before its mouth into the Sava, along its upper bed, and from here inclines toward the Adriatic Sea until it reaches it at the little coastal town of Budva. This line forms the most exact and the oldest boundary of Europe: it divided—and divides also today—West and East in that part of our Continent, between the Pannonian Plain and the Adriatic Sea.5) Eastwards is the Turkish-Byzantine, westwards the European world.

Not only the settlements of these areas, but also their historical developments are fundamentally different. The administration of Caesar was divided along this line which cut the Imperium Romanum into eastern and western halves between the sons of Theodoric toward the end of the 4th century. On this same line the Empire burst asunder in the following century, while the former western part became an area in which new states were formed. But the boundary persisted as a perpetual "memento" of the division of peoples and worlds; only a few "emigrés" succeeded in fleeing to the

West at the time of the Turkish domination. Finally, the Christian Church split up on the same line into the Roman and Byzantine churches. Eugene Pittard, one of the best experts of the anthropology of the Balkan peoples, is quite right in asking whether these splits were not separations of quite different ethnic elements that could not live under the same roof.6) This fact cannot be explained otherwise.

A modern sociologist termed the nature of the Illyrians and their importance to the Western world as follows: "... The Celts, Illyrians and Venets (the latter were probably only a tribe of the Illyrians) deserve the merit that the Occident has preserved its name to a greater extent, and that it became European to a greater degree ... The Celts, Illyrians and Venets have prepared Central and Western Europe to be the proper bulks of Europe and the bearers of the Occidental culture.7) The bulk of the Illyrians—we have mentioned already—were living on a Croatian soil; this is confirmed not only by the name of the area (Illyricum), but most of all, by excavations. The Illyrian settlements were followed in the 5th century by a second wave of settlement by Gothic tribes, likewise from the North. They intermixed without any difficulty and constituted a oneness in a similar way of life and in one language.8)

Defense against the East

What it all means to live on the limits o fthe Eastern world is known only by those peoples of Western culture who themselves have experienced it through the centuries. We Croats and the Hungarians experienced it more than sufficiently in the past as well as today. That is why these peoples appreciate the necessity of European ties more than those who are not immediate neighbors to the Eastern world. We know quite well from experience what the modern phrase "coexistence" means for us. God protect us from such a "coexistence!"

Striving for power is generally characteristic of human beings. But if two do the same, it is yet not the same. As the eastern individual is quite different in his nature and character, so will he act and react differently. The Ukrainian psychologist, Professor Yaniv, has characterized the peoples of the two worlds from a psychological point of view as follows:9) "Considering the division of the inner impetus in the human being such as: the intellect, willpower and emotion, the last factor is very much developed in the East; to a certain extent, of course, at the expense of the former two." The Western man—according to Prof. Yaniv—is differently constituted than the Easterner: the intellect and the willpower of the Westerner is less passionate, he is better balanced, more capable of controlling his feelings because he can temper his passion. If we should define the word "freedom," we may state that "freedom" is nothing more than the ability of controlling ourselves. It refers not only to the political, but also to the individual-psychological aspect. Whoever is not able to master himself, to control his emotion, is not a free man but a servant to his passions. And the striving for power, the lust for domination in the East is uncontrolled. The average Western man has only a vague idea of this. He is e.g., dazed, seeing how the authoritative factors of the East decide various important problems. The Westerner simply cannot understand it because all this results from the psychological constitution of the Easterners; it is the emanation of their nature and character. They have a different vocabulary[10] and, likewise, a different logic. The historians, e.g., have proved that the term "democracy" in Byzantium meant something quite different from what it means to us. "Democracy" means for them what "anarchy" means for the Westerners. What in the West is generally termed "democracy", that is dictatorship in the East; what is "peace" for them, that is "a peace of cemetery"; their "coexistence" translated for us means that burglary is to be voluntarily acknowledged by the legitimate owner as a just action of the burglar. Different logic, different moral conceptions; hence, a different philosophy and different ethics. The doctrine of Marx has become—jus to mention it—empty slogans in the East, something that has nothing in common with the original teachings of Marx. When I was studying sociology at the University of Zürich I very often had a good opportunity to meet Ilja Uljanov Lenin in a little library. A few weeks before he moved to Sweden I explained to him that according to the doctrine of Marx the development of his native country was in no way ripe for the introduction of socialism. Lenin answered me by quoting the verses from Faust by Goethe, in which Mephisto says to the student: "...Grey is, my dear friend, all theory ."; at the same time he added: "Facts are accomplished with the fist." For the Easterner, science is nothing more than a "maidservant of politics." With special regard to the culture in the East, the task of science is not the truth, not what exists, but what should be. Lenin explained also that "ethical" is only that which will serve the proletarian to seize power; in other words, what will serve the interest of a certain clique.

It would not be correct, however, to classify the Eastern man and his world as something generally inferior. That world is simply different from ours. Because of these essential differences we simply do not wish to be under the rule of that world. We just cannot endure its domination. We prefer to enjoy our right of self-determination and we wish to live freely in our own state.

Most Croats are of the opinion that they never have received anything good from the East. Byzantium destroyed our state and was eager to enlarge its power beyond this line westward. Of course, the spontaneous resistance of the people was so powerful and the Byzantine Empire so weak that it did not succeed. In the course of time when our state legitimized itself under the Croat name, this resistance became even stronger. Charlemagne was obliged to wage war with

Byzantium because of Dalmatia, as he considered that the entire Croatian area legally belonged to the West. Not sooner than 923, the Patriarch of Constantinople was obliged to give up all claim to the jurisdiction in Dalmatia in favor of the Pope, this jurisdiction being mere theory anyway.

We have cognizance of only one case in the long Croatian history till 1918 when measures were taken there to force Croatia into the eastern camp. It happened in 878 under Prince Sedeslav. But he lost at this very moment, not only his throne, but also his life.

With the decay of this unnatural state on the Bosporus, pressure became weaker, too. But in place of it there had arisen in our immediate neighborhood, beyond the Drina boundary, another aggressor that endangers our existence up to this date: Serbia.

Serbian history bears a likeness to Muscovite history. The Serbian and the Muscovite alike are imbued with similar eastern qualities, at least among their leading class. They are a relatively young people; their history may be traced back not more than 1,000 years.

W. O. Kluchevskij stresses the following regarding the Russians: the history of Russia is the history of a country that is being colonized. As far as we are able to trace back. We may observe the same phenomenon in Serbian history: their rulers try to make Serbia a country by means of colonization. The Nemanjides have endeavored to do it through 200 years but—as Jirecek himself has stated—they have not succeeded in attaining their end. After the collapse of the "Dushan-empire," the church, established by the son of Nemanja, Save, resumed the function of the state. It is very interesting to cast a glance at the nature of this excellent political method whereby the church was the bearer of the colonizing idea in foreign areas. We would like to deal with this at least in brief.

In his book, "The Life of St. Sava"[11], Bishop Nikolav Velimirovic deals also with the motives that led Sava to go on a pilgrimage to Nicaea (Asia Minor) to get approbation for the establishment of the church. At that time the Emperor and the Patriarch both had fled to Nicaea, having been endangered by the crusaders. Sava tried to explain to them how dangerous Catholicism was to the East, and how necessary it was to set up a bulwark against it. Velimirovic writes on it as follows: "Impressed deeply by Sava's lucid explanations, both the Emperor and the Patriarch gladly accepted his proposal as a very reasonable and timely one" (p. 110). In such a way Sava returned as an archbishop from Nicaea (1219) and started the organization of his instrument. While the administration of the Eastern Church in its interior matters reached westward to the Drina, the first step of Sava was to nominate two bishops west of this line; that is, on the purely Catholic area of southern Dalmatia, Ston, and the Bay of Cattaro. The episcopates could not be, of course, maintained for a longer time, but the establishment of the Sava-Church created not only a bulwark against the West, but far more: an outpost for future Eastern expansion in all directions. At the Drina watershed two forces appeared, East and West, that were opposed to each other more than ever before. The renowned Serbian historian, Stojan Novakovic (together with professor Jagic who was the publisher of "Archiv für Slavische Philologie" at that time) writes on this theme as follows: "The Greek Orthodoxy and the Serbians joined in one indivisible unity, and by the stubborness of the patriotic Serbians this new united power could not but cause a struggle: the quite different Catholic civilization of their Croat brothers had become repugnant to the Serbians. A new abyss arose between the Greek Orthodox Serbians and the Catholic Croats resulting in the fact that the two people—although speaking the same language—had formed two kinds of civilization with two quite different literatures without the hope of any sound union in the future. There were two different cultures, the Byzantine and the Roman one, and both decided to wage a bloody war to the death.12) The prominent historian, however, committed an error when—according to the "Slavic romanticism" of that time—he believed that the Serbians and the Croats are two groups of one people. They never were one people, they are not now either, and cannot ever be one people.

On the contrary—owing to the social development in the whole world—they constitute today two entirely different nations, that cannot live together in one state even if they had a common racial basis.13) The unnatural "union" disproved by history alienated these two peoples even more in 1918. The horrible Communist dictatorship is at present the unique means of preserving this conglomerate. Its downfall would call forth at the very moment the decay of Yugoslavia and its disappearance from the map of Europe.

Croatia Belongs to Central Europe

Because of her origin, development, culture, and entire nature Croatia belongs to the Central European area. Conversely, Croatia does not belong to the East nor to the Balkans. Separated from the Western world by treachery and violence, and thank to the fabricated "Slavic Union" that never really existed, Croatia was handed over to a traditionally aggressive Eastern foreign rule. The Croats were not only deprived of their right of self-determination, but at the same time they were exposed to the danger of completely disappearing from the surface of the earth as a cultural entity. May we, at the same time, refer to the Hungarian example, because our situation is best illustrated by it. The Croats and the Hungarians are peoples of Western culture; their struggle against the Eastern aggression is reflected in the honorary titles conferred on them by the Popes: "Fortissima propugnacula fidei et antemurale christianitatis." Croats and Hungarians alike have endured Serbian imperialism under Communist dictatorship, which has proved that the Serbs are madly aggressive. When the Patriarch of Pec Arsenije Crnoevic in 1690, after the debacle of the imperial liberation armies in the southwest, was compelled to take refuge with his people across the Danube. He reserved the right for himself that the refugees would return to their fatherland as soon as possible. Rascia, Serbia were liberated, but the refugees did not come back to their native country. They remained in Hungary, where a Serbian cultural center also developed. Its influence on the later cultural development of the old mother country was quite significant. And what happened later on? The former refugees, who at the beginning were welcomed as guests by the Hungarians, finally became "occupants and conquerors" striving succesfully to annex the ethnic-historical area of Hungary to Serbia. While the German portion of the population was simply annihilated and the remainder expelled, the "Black" (as the Serbs are called there) were moved into this area from the Balkans to colonize this strip of land. The Hungarian part of the population was left where it was; but anyone who knows the nature of the intruders can in no way have illusions what the fate of those who have remained there will be. We would like to mention here some facts illustrating the true nature of the Serb invaders, through pseudo-scientific researches made in the so-called "museum" (in Novi Sad and in Belgrade alike) the Serbs tried to prove that the area had been "Serbian" from time immemorial, and that it has now returned again to its motherland. A few years ago there was news spread in the world, according to which the territory called "Vojvodina"—that came under the rule of the Serbian "People's Republic" and was also enlarged by a portion of Croatia, Slavonia or Sriem—constitutes 51% of Serbian population. I mention this in order to characterize the diabolic methods of colonialism that have come to an end even in Africa and now in that part of Central Europe were put in high gear by the dictator in Belgrade and used against non-Serbian peoples. And this practice happens publicly before the whole world. The same methods are applied also in Bosnia. As already mentioned, Bosnia never had anything in common with Serbia. In its southern area—the Herzegovina—there was an intrusion from Rascia, but the intruders were chased away. During the Turkish occupation, several refugees succeeded in escaping beyond the Drina-line, thus forming the present Serbian minority in Herzegovina. In its insatiable lust for Slavic expansion, Belgrade was eager to denationalize this area. The Bosnian Mohammedans belong to the indigenous population of he country because they are of Illyrian-Gothic origin. The Serbian imperialist's first endeavor was to strip off the nationality of this population; that is why one million people are registered after their confession of faith as "Musulmans" (Moslems). By the same terroristic methods the Croat people are prevented from confessing their Croat nationality. As is generally known, the Serb occupants plan to declare these people at a given moment as "Serbians." This is how Central Europe is being "Balkanized." The former Central Powers constituted a real "Cordon Sanitaire" against this Slavic evil, but this bulwark was destroyed by two world wars and by their consequences. The enemy, however, does not stop at our boundaries. After having reached the Trieste-Lübeck line he continues to march westward. He aims at "Balkanizing" not only Europe, but also the entire West at last.

1) Encyclopedia Italiana. Vol. XIV, p. 645.

2) Friedrich Naumann: Mitteleuropa. Berlin, 1915.

3) This happened later in Yalta to the whole of Central Europe which was given away to be a part of the Soviet orbit. (Editor's remark).

4) Johannes Peisker: "The expansion of the Slavs" in "Cambridge Medieval History," Vol. II. 1913.

5) The term "Illyricum" included also an enlarged area, of course, only for a shorter time. The proper ethnic Illyricum is important because it later became the basis for the ethnic-historical area of the Croatian people. The Drina boundary constituted its eastern limits. See: J. Lucinus "De regno Dalmatiae et Croatiae." Amsterdam, 1666; he quotes the definition of 'Paladii Fusci Patavini Lib. I.,' by stating: "Illyricum auctore Plinio terminus habet . . . ab Ortu (East!) Dirinonem flumen quod et Drinum dicitur." Hence it also included Dalmatia, Istria, Pannonic Croatia, Slavonia (with Sirmium, Sriem, and Bosnia, and (contemporary) Herzegovina.

6) Eugene Pittard, Les peuples des Balcans, Paris-Neuchatel, 1916, p. 44.

7) Wilhelm Schmidt, Rassen und Völker in Vorgeschichte und Geschichte des Abendlandes", Luzern, 1946, II, p. 300.
Luzern, 1946, II. p. 300.

8) Thom. Archidiac, Historia Salonitana, Cap. VII.: "Permixti ergo sunt populi isti et facti sunt gens una, vita moribusque consimiles, unius loquele."

9) Yaniv: Ukrainian Quarterly, Vol. 1. (1950).

10) See "Wordmanship. Semantics as a Communist Weapon", by Stephan T. Possony, Director of International Studies, Hoover Institution, Stanford, California (Printing Office, Division of Public Documents).

11) Libertyville, Ill., U.S.A., 1957.

12) Vol. 33, p. 445.

13) See W. Schmidt's above-cited book, p. 15.

WHAT HAS TO BE DONE

STAN IONESCU

HUNGARY, like Rumania, has been absorbed by the Soviet Union. It is futile to speak of the governmental structure of our countries; the state, self-determination, sovereignty, and boundaries are a mere illusion when faced with cold reality. The fact that our countries are represented abroad just as Poland and the Ukraine are, is meaningless. Westerners know as well as the Soviets and Chinese do that when they speak of "the sovereign states of the East" they speak of lies. Nevertheless, all have become used to living with lies in the name of peaceful coexistence, which in itself is nothing less than communization of the world. According to Soviet thinking, the objective truth is a "bourgeois" concept; the only valid principles being those which are conceived by the albighty Party.

For the last 500 years, Russia has been spreading, enveloping neighboring European and Asiatic peoples with her political and military might. At present, she is persistently exerting her influence upon distant lands such as British Guinea, Cuba and the Congo.

Between 1920 and 1961 Russia totally annexed. while the free world stood passively by, thirteen countries, 551,400 sq. km. and 18,533,000 people.

During the same time, she occupied de facto 12 more countries comprised of 2,641,000 sq. km. and 98,608,000 inhabitants. This conquest is virtually acknowledged by the Western world.

Russia has for 41 years occupied and kept under her arbitrary rule 3,192,800 sq. km. of foreign territory and 117,181.000 human beings of various ethnic and religious groups.

A long list of historians and politicians, from Custin to Gafencu—such as Renan, Michelet, Napoleon himself, Gonzague de Raynold, Bedell Smith—wrote treatises on the actions and influence of Russian imperialism. The single object guiding the political thought of Western Europe up until 1914 was the restriction of this imperialism.

The Paris peace treaties dissolved the Turkish, the German and the Austro-Hungarian empires which had created a natural and political barrier in the road to further Russian advancement. The principles upon which the treaties were founded were the results of typically Western ideals which many nations adopted; but which, however, did not take into consideration the reality of the relentlessness of Russian imperialism.

The Rumanian historians, Nicolae Balcescu and Andrei Popovici, as well as our great poet, Mihail Eminescu, pointed out this mortal danger but our nationalism prevented us from recognizing the rapidly approaching catas'rophe. Marshal Antonescu was righ when he said that borders of Rumania are defended at Stalingrad. The political leaders of our nations from the Baltic to Cairo had accepted as the basis of their political strivings those principles created by French and Italian theoreticians whose countries were not threatened by Russia.

In the name of these priciples—principles that did not take into account the realities in Eastern Europe—tens of millions of people died in wars (which were actually civil wars), destroying a tremendous amount of material goods and creating the political chaos which today governs the world.

The three ruined empires should have been replaced by other political organizations strong and effective enough to stop the Russian pressure. As it happened, the void created in 1918 was easily filled by Russia.

The politicians who committed these mistakes in 1918 were a good match for those of 1941 to 1945, characterized by the same makeshift decisions, the same blind passions, the same ignorance. Our century is ruled by Russian imperialism. Those Westerners who divided the world at conferences of Casablanca and Teheran, Yalta and Potsdam, did not want to think of this danger, and the Western statesmen participating at these conferences pawned the fate of their own nations under the influence of passions that did not take into consideration the true interest of their countries. This line of political thought refused to see the ever-advancing Russian imperialism and its methods of infiltration, a form of which today is Communism and Sovietization of the whole world. For these mistakes, approaching betrayal, the whole world is still paying.

The idea of imperialism is as old as the world itself. It originated from the material needs and the military organization of nomadic tribes. With the birth of the first political units as we understand them today, it started to be modernized. The first imperialism arose in Asia, ten thousand years before the Christian era. The Russians inherited imperialism as an instinctive tendency, and inherited its political methods from the Mongolians who ruled them for three centuries. The Asian imperialisms were followed by others. The world was ruled in succession by Roman, Arab, Spanish, French, British and German imperialisms; and finally, the most cruel and best organized the Russian imperialism of today. All of them had some things in common:

strong central power and centralized management which were internally supported by the military, while the same military might spread itself over their defenseless neighbors. The final goal of imperialism is always unlimited control over the whole world.

In time those peoples who have been crushed by the imperialists' power rise again. They free themselves of the central governing power and create new and independent countries. This is a common occurrence today among the Asian and African peoples. However, the new world may survive only if it finds unity, and its is Russia which feels responsible for the guidance and unification of the world under her leadership.

The Russians, who know history, are aware that the captured peoples are going to rebel because they are more enlightened and are used to thinking freely. To prevent the inevitable historical trend and the movement toward national independence they introduced the Marxist political and economic system which strengthens the rule of the central power and strengthens discipline and economic potential. Under a liberal and democratic system Russial would lose not only satellites like Rumania, but also Turkestan, Mongolia and the Ukraine.

Soviet imperialism is nourished by certain characterestics of the Russian people. These are the desire to dominate and the instinct to take advantage of others and in the traditions of the ruling class the drive for power is restless. The ruling class is molded of the same material whether called Peter the Great, Catherine or Khrushchev. They resemble each other in that they are in constant rivalry with the ruling classes preceding and succeeding them. They are compelled to conquer. Dictators don't like to live unfinished business for their successors. They believe that only they themselves are capable of completing such, and of conquering the world. Khrushchev's haste can thus be explained.

There is no alternative for the free nations but to unite completely and lastingly. This is the only possible means for averting the fatal consequences of Russian imperialism. The choice is not between Russian and American imperialism, but between Russian imperialism and the unificition of all the countries of the free world. This new world organization of the free countries cannot be realized through the United Nations of today, as it was not possible through the League of Nations. It can only be achieved through the economic and military unification of the free world.

The economic and military unification of Europe is now being realized. Within the free peoples of Europe, a loyalty to Europe has replaced the loyalty to national politics in a short time.

The liberation of our people will be accomplished by themselves. The European union which is the first step towards the unification of the free world will undoubtedly weaken and impede Russian imperialism. To imperialism—any imperialism—ceasing to move ahead means defeat. There is no alternative but to press ahead or draw back. The present Soviet might lacks the moral strength and sense of justice which are the only prerequisites justified to rule the world. The Soviet Union is too weak to embody these ideals or to battle them. The satellite nations are restless, their sufferings cannot be assuaged by Khrushchev's promises. Across the concrete and barbed wire barricades from the rebellion of the satellites and the free thinking of the Europeans a united feeling of danger and hope has grown. The Soviet imperialists' efforts are helpless in the face of this unifying spirit.

Therefore, in exile, it is our duty:

a) To pool our internal strength in the cultural fields and to support by our propaganda with all our strength the European unification—and beyond all that, the unification of the whole free world. The European economic unification has been accomplished against the wishes of Soviet imperialism and the local Communist parties representing it. Europe's political unification is in the process of being realized. Three hundred million people, better educated, more productive and more optimistic people than the Russians; well-armed and supported by the military potential of the United States already represent a victory over Soviet imperialism. The Soviet state-capitalism has lost the battle against democratic capitalism and economic neo-liberalism. The economic system of the free world has defeated Marxism, unnerving the Soviets.

b) Through our radio propaganda we have to keep alive the hope for liberation in our countries. Our publications must reach our countries. Many of our countrymen feel deserted and we must fight against this feeling.

c) We emigrants must declare that we already consider our countries united into a single body, without reservation, clearly indicating our desire to make our union part of a United Europe.

d) After the solemn declaration of the union of the peoples of the Danubian Basin, a government in exile must be created. This would be disturbing to some in the West who are in political contact with the satellite nations; nevertheless, we should not be deterred because we have to use every possible means in the successful propaganda battle with the Soviet Union that will keep alive the hope in our countrymen under her rule. Inactivity on our part would dim those hopes.

The exile government of the Danubian Union could be acknowledged by all those nations which have no diplomatic relations with the Soviet Union or any of the satellites, regardless of the fact that certain nations and their leaders are opposed to this thought. They may continue their sinful actions by which they support Soviet imperialism, under the delusion that the Soviet Union will only be satisfied if our countries remain under her occupation.

e) Official publications by this government in exile would prompt a shift in the political thought of the emigrants, from nationalistic to European sentiments. The purpose of our vigorous nationalism is the preservation of our moral and spiritual values, which are the roots of our culture. Civilization and progress are defined by national culture and ethnics not boundaries.

f) Our publications have to support the reunification of Germany. A Christian and democratic Germany will bring about the unification of Europe. Her ideals are our ideals. At the same time Germany is the center of military preparedness in Europe. The Soviet Union, as all imperialistic powers, has respect for opposing might only. Germany is fighting for the political union of Western Europe and, therefore, constitutes a greater power for bringing it about than the Soviet Union.

g) We must not forget cooperation among the religions, and the participation of the Catholic Church in our work up to now. In our battle the Roman Catholic Church has been one of our most loyal and unselfish allies. The spiritual power of the Christians led by the Vatican, together with the great ideals of the unification of the Christian religions is, along with the military might of a United Europe, its greatest strength.

SCANNING THE HORIZON:
WORLD POLITICS AND CENTRAL EUROPE

TIBOR ECKHARDT

IN the present phase of occidental decadence it appears as *the most ponderous fact that coexistence with a major evil, called communism, has become the permanent political goal of the West.* It is hard for us, whose homelands have been overrun by the red flood, to acquiesce in this unpalatable situation. It is of interest therefore to scan the horizon for eventual signs and symptoms of some favorable change emerging from the twilight which has descended on the free West.

As far as my old country, Hungary, is concerned, the recent overall trend was correctly grasped by Max Frankel, when he stated (New York Times, January 18, 1965) "that Hungary is the best example of how far de-Stalinization can proceed without much significant de-satellization." At Khrushchev's initiative, in recent years, the personal life of the average Hungarian has unquestionably improved. But the change is superficial, not basic, and can be reversed anytime at Moscow's orders. For Soviet control of the Hungarian state apparatus has not been relaxed, in fact, Hungary's dependence on the Soviets has been expanded through Comecon in the economic field. Moscow is also pressing for a strengthening of the Warsaw Pact's military ties. Anyway, the passing of time in Soviet servitude cannot be considered by us with indifference, for in several connections irreparable damage is being done meanwhile to the entire structure of the Hungarian nation. The almost total collectivization of the farmland has ruined rural life beyond recognition and has brought it down to the lowest proletarian level. Even more appalling is the decline of the birthrate. Abandoned by the West and utterly hopeless, the Hungarian youth refuses to raise a family. Decimated by staggering losses during two world wars, followed by persecution, revolutions and deportation, the Hungarian nation is on the way of losing position in the Carpathian Basin. The fate of the Hungarians in Transylvania is the worst. Almost for half a century, they have been living under foreign domination, aggravated since 1945 by Communist persecution. How long can the old oak survive this tempest?

Such is the truth, and Hungarians back home and in the Free World must face adversity without wishful thinking. For unless some unexpected turnabout occurs, Russian domination in the Valley of the Danube may be continued for quite a while. Not as if the Soviets were stronger than the Free World, but because *will-power is a more effective force than physical power in the shaping of human history.* 1956, Hungary's Fight for Freedom, was the last opportunity when without going to war, the West could have achieved the liberation of at least Central Europe. Since then, the Western will to resist has been further weakened and the intent to coexist with Communism has been strengthened. *By now we have passed beyond the point of no return.*

A few aspects of this situation deserve to be scrutinized:

1) The Marxist World Revolution has lost in Russia some of its messianic urge, but it has not given up its main purpose: domination of the entire world. Everywhere in the Free World, we still find Communist planning and incitement in the background of the subversive movements, and this applies to South Vietnam just as much as to Harlem in New York. These destructive influences do not create the threat of an atomic war, but they cause a continuous erosion in the Western positions, usually ending in retreat. Lacking in initiative, the West has lost its recuperative power and is pursuing a purely defensive strategy. United action by the International Communist forces against the opulent West is giving way gradually to diverse aggressive initiatives by the "have not-s" which serve Soviet or Chinese national aggrandizement, known in the past as imperialism. Wishful thinkers rejoice over the split between the Soviets and Red China. I wonder if extreme nationalism added to Communist messianism will improve the security of the West. In 1939, the Ribbentrop-Molotov agreement seemed even less probable than an eventual alliance between the two Communist super-powers would appear to be today.

2) With the hasty withdrawal of Western colonialism from most of its positions, Communist imperialism is now penetrating into the vacuums thus created. Unable and unprepared to solve their own tangled problems particularly under a democratic form of government, several new would-be nations have become ripe for the imposition of the Communist discipline which, in its brutal way, replaces intolerable anarchy with the Communist straightjacket. Former colonials have very little reason to stand for capitalism which meant to them foreign interference into their lives. Ties with China may seem welcome to some of them, since the Chinese do not belong to the white race. American policy, still under the influence of its colonial memories, often has been promoting prematurely the acceptance of the democratic form of government, increasing the confusion of the former colonies unprepared for democracy. No human society is able to endure permanent disorder. *In Asia and in Africa a number of doors*

have been thus thrown wide-open for penetration by the Communists.
Due to the human mass controlled by China with an iron fist, and
also to their capacity for modern development, the awakening of the
Chinese people as a Communist great power has started a new
chapter in the history of mankind. More than a decade ago, Admiral
Radford, then Chairman of the American Joint Chiefs of Staff, recognized the rising menace and favored American Aid to be given to
France in the war against the Viet Cong. He predicted that if America
allowed enough time and leisure to Red China to develop an armanent
industry as up to date as that of the Soviet's without a war America
would be licked. Chinese revolutionary exaggerations have saved the
world until now from that catastrophe. But China is learning her
lesson and is catching up rapidly in production of the atom-arm also.
China's pressure on her extended common border with the Soviets is
growing and this may explain the greater reserve of the Soviets
observed lately in their foreign policy toward the West.

3) The history of the first half of our century consists mainly
of the Civil War of Europe fought in two installments and ended with
the post-war French-German Treaty of Cooperation. "United Europe,"
of course, is still a long way off, for even if the present free zone
of Europe becomes united, without its Eastern half Europe remains
incomplete. The Common Market, however, a long step in the right
direction, already acts as a magnet toward the nations locked up
behind the Iron Curtain. There can be little doubt that once the
seven states of the European Free Trade Area join the six of the
Common Market, their joint power of attraction will prove to be
stronger than the Soviet endeavour to keep them isolated and in
bondage.

During the period of gradual unification *some temporary solutions, probably in line with neutralism, will have to be worked out for
Central and Eastern Europe.* There is no chance for the lasting maintenance of the present division of Europe, for the great German
people cannot accept partition as the final solution of Germany's fate.
The reunification of Germany, however, only becomes feasible, if
Europe is being united. The lamentable fate of Hungary is thus
strictly tied up with the problems of European unification. There is
no separate Hungarian question, but there exists a burning problem
of Central and East European emancipation from under Soviet rule
of which the Hungarian question forms a part, including the rectifica-
tion of the mistaken Paris peace treaties. In 1956, the Hungarian
youth presented to the world such a glorious example of its self-
sacrificing love of freedom, that at the first opportunity, when the
present structure of partioned Europe is corrected, the sun of freedom will rise again over the blood-soaked Hungarian soil.

A thorny problem retarding the final organization of United Europe
is *the uncertainty about where does Great Britain belong?* Obviously,

the agricultural production of the British Commonwealth cannot be fitted into the much too limited European Common Market, particularly since the United States demands similar easy terms for her agricultural exports. Furthermore, up to 1966, according to the Rome Agreement, each member-state in the Common Market retained its right of veto. Premature inclusion of Britain would thus lend her a much too strong bargaining position for satisfying British special interests. After 1966, however, decisions could be made in the Common Market by a majority vote. According to the existing powerful trend, British foreign trade will be increasingly directed meanwhile toward the successful Common Market. The time can be foreseen, when Britain will prefer to renounce her preferential tariffs with the Commonwealth in order to allow her to join the more profitable Common Market.

4) In spite of the United States atomic superiority, *the monopoly of American political leadership is nearing its end in the Free World.* With generous American aid not only prosperity but also self-reliance were restored to the Old Continent. By winning the war America won friends and much prestige in the world which she has been losing in later years by thumbing the peace problems. Lavish spending of foreign aid will not help; *peace cannot be bought, it must be deserved.*

It is an unfortunate coincidence that America is being now confronted with arduous tasks in the international field while internally she is passing through an awkward phase of her democratic institutions. Just as has happened in France, two hundred years of wear and tear have used up much of the energies and values on which inspired political leadership could be based, able to solve the present global problems of unparalleled magnitude. The running of the democratic political machine in America has become excessively time-, money- and energy-consuming. Initiative in international affairs has been thoughtlessly replaced by tardy appeasement; image making substituted for policy making; and the favor of public opinion sought on the lowest common denominator. The "wall of shame" was erected in Berlin and President Kennedy drifted to the brink of the precipice, with no other choice left for him in Cuba than the deadly threat with the atom-bomb. Led by the New York Times, powerful media of communications tried to condition American public opinion for accomodation with a leftist world opinion arbitrarily made up by those media. Public life was being paralyzed by a philosophy which calls itself "liberal"—but favors Marxism, particularly in its British form of "Fabianism."

Healthy reaction has quite obviously started against this decadence denounced in America. An honest order is just as important in a nation's life as is freedom and the American political order may not differ from the moral order bestowed upon us by our Creator. There is nothing wrong with the American people, they are resilient and well-intentioned. The want of success in the postwar era was caused in America in every instance by the failure of political leadership.

5) There is much conflict in the present world, not only between the two, ideologically opposed camps, but also within each camp because of national divergencies. This has helped to reduce the danger of an atomic war. Leninism-Stalinism has failed to achieve its basic goal: a monolithic world empire built up around the Kremlin. At Yalta, Stalin may have agreed with Roosevelt to partition Europe into two spheres of influence. Nevertheless, Western Europe is only losely tied to America, while in Eastern Europe nationalisms and their self-centered policies are moving towards polycentrism, away from Muscovite dictation. The breakdown of the "two power world" concept has lessened the danger of a major war which appeared very real as long as only two super-powers were confronted day by day with their inescapable conflicts, entrenched in rigid positions with no room for maneuver.

There still exists, however, among American Leftists—some of them indeed in high positions,—a nostalgia for Roosevelt's two-power world concept, which by now appears foredoomed for:

a) Red China systematically and inevitably is building up an Asian Empire of her own.

b) Whatever difficulties may still be encountered, the unification of the European Continent is making progress. That powerful unit will have to be welcomed as a "partner" by the United States of America in a not too distant future in order to help hold the balance against upcoming Red China.

c) Great Britain, even if led by the Labour Party, has not become resigned to the role of a second-rate power. She may have lost much of her prewar political and economic influence, but she has retained the know-how in political matters and has not forfeited her ability as a trader. Britain is prepared to make her presence felt as a middleman, throwing her weight on the side of one or the other superpower as her interests, particularly security, demand.

Several power-political units have thus emerged onto the international scene, which provide more flexibility in the international situation than had existed shortly after the World War's end. Possibilities for diplomatic maneuver have improved and the danger of atomic war has been reduced. Even if the West appears to be unwilling to exploit its superiority, the balance of power at least can certainly be maintained. The danger of a third World War could only be roused by a tragic slackening of Western preparedness, or by some senseless aggression by Red China. Such abnormities however, I prefer to eliminate from my computation.

6) Although the Communist regimes in Central and Eastern Europe are becoming gradually stabilized, I do not doubt that every-

day life may further improve as years go by and experience demands. A regime is most cruel when it feels insecure. Every revolution slows down in time and even the pitiless Chinese Communists will lose momentum, though it may take considerable time. A return to brutal Stalinism is most improbable in Russia just as much as in the captive countries, for the people almost unanimously would resist that relapse. Nor can Soviet colonial exploitation under Comecon auspices be continued indefinitely. The subservient János Kádár accepts this Soviet abuse; trade with the Soviets cost the Hungarian people 263 million dollars in a single year (1962) if compared with free market prices. But national resistance against Soviet colonialism has successfully been launched by Rumania already and it is bound to spread and become general behind the Iron Curtain. The captive nations—each in its own way—are seeking ways and means leading to emancipation from colonial rule.

It seems important to note that geographically and politically also, Hungary's road toward the Free World leads through Vienna. In the Moscow Protocol on Austria (October, 1943) the Soviet Union agreed that after the cessation of hostilities Austria would renew her prewar connections with the neighboring states. This stipulation is still valid and could be used to better advantage. Hungary does not have to rely on Red China, if and when she decides to loosen her economic ties with the Soviets.

Communism has failed in our time not only politically and economically, but morally also, as an incurable evil. Resistance to that malignancy must continue unhesitatingly. But our struggle must be intelligent, above all, mindful of the international situation which may bring success or defeat. The main lesson to be drawn from the present state of world affairs can be condensed in a single sentence: *the road to take by European captive nations is evolution, not revolution.* This is particularly true as far as Hungary is concerned.

FORGOTTEN SENTIMENTS:
THE BRITISH LABOUR PARTY AND CENTRAL EUROPE

ALEXANDER GALLUS

(To the attention of Prime Minister Wilson of Great Britain)

IT is perhaps of some interest now that a Socialist Government has again entered the scene in Britain to recall the policy, aims and views of the Labour Party during and after the First World War, as they materialized in a concern for peace and for a pacified Central Europe.

*The main personality to study, of course, is Arthur Henderson.*1) The mounting tensions of the immediate pre-war years, saw the British Labour movement in affiliation with the Socialist Internationale. The Bureau of the Congress of the Internationale sat in meeting in Brussels, when on the 25th of August the Austrian declaration of war against Serbia, was made. But the Bureau still considered organizing an international policy to prevent war, because—according to the theoretical international solidarity of the working classes—they did not consider the possibility of members of the working-class movement being thrown into murderous battles against each other.

"It was still hoped—says Hamilton—that such a meeting would serve to keep the socialists of the world firm in resistance to any threat to world peace on the part of their individual national Governments, in accordance with the solemn undertakings to which they were collectively committed." On the evening of the same day, in Brussels, at a public meeting, Belgian, German, French and British delegates passionately denounced war.

But the participants did not reckon with the national sentiments, which by then, were already aroused. On the 31st of June, Jaures, the French Socialist leader (and one of the speakers in Brussels), was murdered. In Britain, however, at a mass meeting in Trafalgar Square and at various other meetings, the following resolution was adopted by Labor: "We protest against any step taken by the Government of this country to support Russia, either directly or in consequence of an understanding with France, as being not only offensive to the political traditions of the country, *but disastrous to Europe.*2) And declare, as we have no interest, direct or indirect, in the threatened quarrels, which may result from the action of Servia, the Government of Great Britain should rigidly decline to engage in war but should confine itself to efforts to bring about peace as speedily as possible."

During the war, Henderson became a member of the War Cabinet and saw the war through conscientiously. But as the possibility of peace drew near, his views became markedly differentiated from those of his colleagues. He wholeheartedly endorsed the speech of Wilson (June 22, 1917), that there should be a peace of *reconciliation* and not one of force. (Peace without victory.) So his long struggle against imperialistic peace begins. This struggle, though hardly mentioned today, still should be remembered by those who became victims of measures which he wanted to avoid. The revolution in Russia freed Henderson and his movement from the embarrassment of having to work together with the Czarist regime and made it possible for him to reformulate a set of ideals for the common struggle and an ideal peace. In summer 1917, he visited Russia which made his views on a future peace and its terms clear.

He was much impressed by a statement of the new Russian Government on its war aims, *which were neither imperialistic nor annexionalistic,* two aspects of a possible future peace he especially feared. Thus the prospect of a democratic Russia and the entrance of Wilson's America into the war filled Henderson with hope for a democratic and just termination of the war which would be able to settle or to solve important questions raised by the defeat of the Central Powers, *in a spirit of human solidarity.*

In order to dispel uncertainties, the Russians suggested calling together in Stockholm an International Socialist Conference for the definition of war aims. Henderson, in various addresses given in Russia, already anticipated the League of Nations: "There should be *a family of free natoins, with full opportunity to work out their own salvation,* competing only in science, education and social reconstruction ... The free democracies of the world must unitedly work for the great change, for militarism and war are the brutal negation of our highest ideals ... These were the ideals in which we believed in 1914, and we *cannot desert them in 1917,* for they have been made sacred to us by the blood of our sons."

The Prime Minister, Lloyd George, first endorsed the conference, but later under the influence of his Cabinet Ministers, withdrew the official support of the Government. Nevertheless, his telegram, showing his original frame of mind, is of interest: "Re-establishment of a general peace, *should not tend towards either domination over other nations or seizure of their national possessions, or violent usurpation of their territories."* "... it should be a peace without annexation or indemnation and based on rights of nations to decide their own affairs ..."

These formulations which originated with the new Russian Government were acceptable to him "provided that by these phrases it was not intended that French and British should be bound to restore to Turkey, or German mis-government populations in Africa or Mesopotamia which they have rescued from it and also that it was understood that provinces which have been torn from France by German militarism should be restored to her." In plain terms, the reservations voiced by Lloyd George refer to the annexation of German colonies and the "revanche" so dear to France.

It was understood that delegations from the German and Austrian Socialist Parties should attend.

Unfortunately, the conference did not materialize, because Lloyd George withdrew his support. When the Bolsheviks took over in Russia, even the Russian support vaned. But Henderson's aims were set as he left the War Cabinet. Henderson wanted victory expressed in selfless and "democratic" terms and his views were accepted officially by the Labour Party. He was promptly declared a "defeatist" by the nationalist press, but for Henderson, war was a horror and only justifiable it it had a *noble purpose*. "The common people" so he said "the democracy, did nothing to create the conditions out of which the war came; but the common people have done everything to realize the ideals for which we entered the war."

He convened a special Labour Conference to formulate the war aims of the Labour Party, independently of the War Cabinet. This conference established as its aims:

1. Just territorial settlements.
2. Self-determination.
3. An international organization to prevent war. (League of Nations as a Supra-National Authority.)

In February 1918, a Conference of Allied Socialist Parties adopted, in essence, the English formulations. Henderson again spoke up: "We do not seek victory of a militarist or diplomatic nature. *We seek a triumph for high principles and noble ideals. We are not influenced by imperialistic ambitions or selfish nationalistic interests.* We seek a victory, but it must be a *victory for international moral and spiritual forces, finding its expression in a peace, upon the unalienable rights of common humanity.*"

But as the end of war drew near the victory seemed secured, Henderson's hopes to influence events faded. Clemenceau, the British War Cabinet, W. M. Hughes of Australia, moved in the direction of a "Peace of Revenge and Power Policy."

This trend could no longer be halted, not even by an International World Conference of Socialist and Labor Parties, which was convened by Henderson in Berne on January 26, 1919 (Armistice was signed on November 11th, 1918).

In Britain new elections were fought with the above background that made it easy to misrepresent the public image of Henderson and his party. Charges such as: "Pro-German," "Defeatist," "Bolshevik," and the creation of a new party, the National Democrats, all had their effect and the election was lost. Henderson clearly saw the consequences of his stand, but remained faithful to his principles.

He canvassed for a just settlement, one animated *by the spirit of reconciliation and not of revenge. A settlement must not be imposed,* but must be arrived at by mutual understanding to be able to safeguard the future. He claimed direct representation for Labor in the planning of the terms of peace. The party platform stated: " ... the democratic diplomacy which found expression in the war aims of Labour, has been one of the most powerful factors in winning the war, and must be the most powerful factor in the rebuilding of the world. The Peace which Labour demands is a *Peace of International Conciliation.* It declares absolutely against secret diplomacy and any form of economic war ..." Labour appeals to all, "who are determined that the fruits of victory shall not be wasted in the interest of riches or of reaction."

Hamilton strongly criticised the attitude of Lloyd George. "Lloyd George had got to have a party and a majority. He could have secured both for a reasonable and decent programme: for *peace based on undertakings given to young German Republic and to the people of Great Britain in the pre-Armistice negotiations* ... Had he stood by the outlook he had professed to the Trade Unions at the Laxton Hall in January 1918, he could have won the peace. Instead he chose, almost wanted, to lose it..... He could have mobilised sane emotions, as easily as he mobilised insane.... The Prime Minister could, if he had so chose have gone to Versailles armed against short-sighted nationalism. As it was, he went as the slave of angry passions, he had himself created and in the upshot, had to make the demands of others an excuse for what his own cooler judgement by then saw to be a fatal course. Yet along this fatal course it was he who led in 1918."

As a result the negotiations became "a Peace Conference of the hoary old type, at which the victors divide the spoils and squabble among themselves over the division."

The joint executives of the Labour Movement in Britain declared that the Peace Treaty is fundamentally defective "in that it accepts and indeed is based upon the very political principles, which were the ultimate cause of the war. The Treaty involves the violation of the principles embodied in Labour and Socialist Conference decisions; it also violates the understanding on which the Armistice was signed, and is therefore a repudiation of the spirit and letter of the declarations of President Wilson, Mr. Lloyd George and other Allied statesmen."

Here we may leave the struggle of Henderson against an inhuman peace and take a glimpse at the sentiments of the rank and file of the

Labour Movement, as expressed in a pamphlet by Charles Roden and Dorothy Frances Buxton (The World after the War, first published in 1920).

Setting aside the decided leanings of the authors towards the Bolshevik Movement, which influenced their criticism of the new settlements in Europe, specially as the decisions taken were partly connected with the desire to create a "cordon sanitaire" against revolutionary tendencies, we note here the general tone of their attitude. Already Chapter 2 has a significant title: "The Balcanisation of Europe." " . . . on the ruins of Germany, Austria-Hungary and Russia, a bewildering transformation had taken or was taking place . . . All the distraction and confusion which had made the Balkans synonym for political unrest and danger had now been reproducer, with tragic exactness over a far greater area, and has begun to affect the life of peoples more advanced in civilization and more accustomed to order and culture. The Central Region of Europe was included, in a very real sense, within the frontiers of the Balkans, now moved Northwards and Westwards, to the Baltic, the Oder and the Rhine . . ."

The former enemy states were economically crippled and the idea of "Public Right" was completely disregarded. "It is true that the sovereignty of certain states—those regarded by Paris as hostile—was very strictly limited, but this did not mean that the rights of the small states were equal to those of the great, or that the strong were controlled for the sake of the weak."

"Public Right" in this sense could only be secured *by some genuine form of super-national Government, representing the interests of all the states and capable of being called to account by the humblest of them.* The new League of Nations did not constitute such a Government. *It was the Allied and Associated Powers under a new name."*

"As for the principle of "nationality" it received a notable application in the setting up of new states, nominally based upon ethnical considerations. *But if old injustices were removed, new ones were created. The national principle was applied where it was advantageous to the Allies from a military point of view, where it promoted the interests of powerful capitalist groups, or where it could be invoked to punish an enemy.* In other cases it was violated."

"The test of a genuine national settlement may be put in the form of a question — *Does it leave behind it grievances so considerable that men will look forward toward some future rearrangement by war?"* "Judged by this test, the policy of the allies conspicuously failed. Poland, Czechoslovakia, Rumania, Yugoslavia displayed many of the characteristics of the imperial states out of whose wreck they had arisen, and whose violation of nationality had always been regarded as a menace to peace. Mr. Morgenthau, the former American Ambassador at Constantinople, early pointed out, that these new States . . . were "spreading themselves out, quarrelling, weakening themselves in the process, and trying to swallow up peoples of different races and aspirations."

"Czechoslovakia included 3½ million Germans, and large blocks of Ukrainian and Hungarian population. Its very name was invented to justify the incorporation in it of the Slovak race, which though ethnically allied to the Czechs, had not demanded to be united with them, and at one stage set up an independent republic in opposition to the Government of Prague. Yugoslavia beside being troubled by the internal dissensions of Serbs, Croats, Slovens and Montenegrins and the chronic resistance of her Albanian subjects, had to hold down a large Macedonian population, whose sympathies lay with Bulgaria and who had been assigned to Bulgaria by a treaty with Serbia herself in February 1912. Rumania included Bulgarian, Ukrainian, German, Hungarian and Serb populations."

To exemplify the chaotic conditions under which the solutions of the Peace Treaty were decided, the authors of the pamphlet point out the fate of Hungary. "As soon as the armistice with that country was concluded, in November 1918, its neighbors, Czecoslovakia, Rumania and Yugoslavia were encouraged to invade it. The two former overstepped the limit of their "nationality" claims and entirely ignored the remonstrances of the "Big Four" sitting in Paris. Rumania did so with some reason, for the Bucharest Foreign Office held to in its pigeon holes the Secret Treaty of August 1916, promising to Rumania a territory which included great blocks of Hungarian population. When Hungary set up a "Bolshevist" Government, the neighboring states were not only allowed to retain what they had taken (including virtually all the mineral resources of Hungary), but were encouraged to the total overthrow of the Red Army of Béla Kun. Yugoslavia alone refused to join in the attack." They had enough on their hands without this. "They had been in armed conflict with the Italians over the question of Dalmatia; they had fought an other Ally, Rumania, over the Bánát and Temesvár, and they had on their hands a third quarrel with the Austrians over their Northern frontier. There had been repeated encounters over the Austria-German towns of Klagenfurt and Marburg, the former of which had been occupied by the South Slavs on direct opposition to Allied orders."

"The actual armed conflicts must be pictured against a background of discontent and misery too widespread and confused to be summed up in any brief description." "The real bearing of the proposal of a League of Nations on the peace settlement can only by appreciated in conjunction with the other provisions of the treaties. These transfer whole populations against their will to alien forms of government, and consign the enemy peoples to a state of economic servitude ... Now the immediate task of the League ... is to guarantee the stability of these *essentially unstable conditions*. This is the most important of the reasons which influenced America in her refusal (November

1919) to be bound by any of the more substantial obligations of the covenant." Any League endeavouring to implement the above task, would become a "great militarist organization destitute of the healing spirit of reconciliation which alone can make it an instrument of progress." "The political system of Europe, in so far as any such system was emerging at all, was the old 'Balance of Power' in new form." ●

"The territory of the *beaten group* was amputated on all *hands,* large blocks of German, Austrian, Hungarian and Bulgarian population being handed over the rule of their enemies. Of the economic provisions ... it is enough to say that they had the effect of ruining the enemy states as commercial rivals. Large quantities of their agricultural stock and railway material, and the main part of their merchant shipping were handed over to the victors. Their industry was deprived of its main sources of supply." A further effect of the Peace Treaties was "the denial to the beaten states of reciprocity in commerce, and of the equality of trade conditions among all the nations consenting to the peace which was promised to them by the third of President Wilson's Fourteen Points." "Finally the Peace Treaties imposed an overwhelming financial burden upon the defeated countries." "The Armistice Agreement of November 11, 1918 was made upon the basis of President Wilson's Fourteen Points." It was on the faith of this agreement that Germany laid down her arms." "The Peace Treaty violated every one of the principles on the faith of which Germany laid down her arms; and it was not long before the "Fourteen Points" were openly repudiated by the Allied press." "... the (economic) blockade was the most powerful weapon they had for enforcing of terms contrary to the Armistice Agreement." "Perhaps, however, the aspect of Allied policy which is destined to leave the deepest impression on posterity is its *betrayal of the principle of nationality.* No principle was more loudly and continuously professed during the war." "The right of national self determination was violated. The right of peoples to decide their own destiny, first raised as an inspiring war-cry, has sunk to the position of a rather stale joke." This principle was violated by secret agreements. "Similar agreements were probably made among the enemy Governments. The difference was that these Governments did not propose the same lofty ideals. The Allied statesmen have hardly completed the series of speeches in which proclaimed the disinterested purposes of the War, before they had begun to wave a network of secret engagements, wholly incompatible with these purposes. It was the disastrous series of secret *agreements* which prevented every attempt at peace on the basis of self-determination and public right."

Thus "Wilsonism" failed to materialize, and the statesmen did not realize that: *"wrongs done to Germany or Russia, to Hungary or Bulgaria, were merged in the greater injury to humanity, including, of course, the injury to ourselves.* They were not great enough to call a halt in the process of destruction, in order to preserve or reconstruct *the indispensable basis for the civilization of the future."* If the sense of responsibility towards the interests of other peoples is not again restored "we shall drift back into the same attitude of indifference to the interests of other peoples and to our relations with them, which helped to render this War possible and which will contribute, if we revert to it, towards the making of other wars in the future."

I feel that these excerpts will suffice to prove the trend of opinion of an important sector of the British public, which was critical toward the reorganization of Europe on a basis completely alien to the humanistic ideals born in America and represented by Wilson.

It is now a truism, that this analysis of the situation created after World War I, has in its essence withstood the test of time. The Second World War was largely the consequence of the faults made in the Peace Treaties after the First World War, and especially of the failure of the statesmen in coming to a satisfactory and humanistic solution of the ethnic difficulties in Central and Eastern Europe. These difficulties are still unsolved. A new settlement, if past mistakes should be avoided, must be based on some simple and *commonsense* principles. These are:

1. The solution must be agreed upon by all concerned and not imposed by force.

2. The solution must be based on the right of self-determination for all ethnic units in the area.

3. The solution must lead to the optimum human well-being of the inhabitants of the area and not serve the well-being of a selected few, or the interests of power outside the area.

4. A reorganization of the area is the sole concern of its inhabitants and cannot be based on any outside interference whatsoever.

5. The solution must lead to a new political form of peaceful cooperation within the area, which will make it possible for the present state boundaries—which dissect ethnic boundaries—to become the concern of administrative reorganization, and that the administrative units thus constructed, will not in future block the free cultural and ethnic development of national or ethnic units, which not so long ago have cohabited the area without harming each other, in an intricate pattern of neighborly, side by side settlements.

---

1) **Arthur Henderson; a biography,** 1938. By M. A. Hamilton.
2) All italics by A. G.

THE SECOND PHASE OF GERMAN FOREIGN POLICY IN EASTERN EUROPE

WENZEL JAKSCH

"It is not premature to think of a Unified Europe".
John F. Kennedy in Berlin.

"In order to eliminate the partition of Germany, we, in the Federal Republic, are ready, to bear the burden of substantial financial sacrifices, if summoned to do so".
Federal President Dr. Henry Lübke, before the Congress in Lima.

"We are ready to do some spending for reunification".
Federal Chancellor Dr. Ludwig Erhard, in the Sportpalast of Berlin. (Jan. 13, 1965)

IN the five years, 1965-70, the course of the foreign policy of the Federal Republic of Germany, will proceed through the rapids of a labile world situation. More than ever before in the past will German statecraft face up to a challenge to spell out new, formidable developments in the East as well as in the West, in the language of its own activity. She will be able to find support in the extraordinary efficiency of her economy and in the goodwill of her people, matured in adversity.

Facing the world with an open mind, permeates our cultural life and characterises the young generation. This trait will favourably promote the development of a foreign policy rich in ideas. Foreign policy will be further benefited by a substantial increase in experience about Europe, which accumulated through our handling of the tragic problems of Eastern Germans, who have been forced from their homeland, and through our readiness to take part in the integration of the European West.

We will not lack the benefits of availability by a reliable staff of expert civil service employees. But there is one subject which has not been touched since the time of Otto von Bismarck, and which should be revived. That is *the art of a synthetic view of Eastern and Western*

developments, as seen from the level of legitimate German interests.
Searching for the driving forces which should give life to a successful home- and foreign policy, we cannot fail to notice a lack of intellectual leadership and an atmosphere of moral confusion which
ostensibly prevails, at least on the surface of the West German scene.
Maybe, it is unavoidable, being the consequence of a simple rule of
physics, that the swing of the pendulum far out in one direction must
be followed by a swing equally far in the other direction. So it was
perhaps a must, that after years of an inflated ego, years of self criticism and self-analysis had to come. The leaning towards exaggera-
tion, lurking in the character of our nation, must have had its fill
during the last decades, in both directions. But then, the process of
disillusion, according to common sense, should not be pushed to its
furthest consequence of self-dissolution.

At any rate, it is unfortunate that the ideological controversey
with the near past has suffered a sectarian distortion which led to
an interpretation of the phenamena of German fascism as the falling
into sin of a whole nation and its government. Such simplifications
may only furnish easy proof for the false deduction that the Germans
are the only sinners in a world of the just. This frame of mind, now
dominant at certain universities, overlooks, with a culpably unscientific approach, the international character of totalitarian process and
the appalling growth of inhumanity in our century. A sentence by
Brentano's should be remembered here, who said, that practically
there does not exist any grade of lowness which cannot be imposed
onto men under a dictatorial regime. From such a vista it seems to
be our highest moral duty to hinder the building up of new dictatorships and not to nurse the self-righteousness of a new, as yet untried,
generation, growing up as it were on the ruins of already fallen
dictatorships. *Recent history seen in the light of a false diagnosis by
our intellectual leaders.* must by necessity blunt the moral persuasion
and penetrating power of our newly born German democracy. New
strength can only be gained from self-analysis, if it gives back to our
people as well a legitimate portion of self-assertion. And if it lives
up to the task of leading our youth not only toward a necessary,
critical observation of its past, but also and mainly, toward an improved way of building up our future.

As long as the dominant intellectual and cultural leaders of a free
Germany will fail in this, uneasiness will grow, when facing the static
and seemingly frozen situation in the question of a partitioned Germany. Periodic outcries, clamoring for incentives, resulting in more
paperwork will not soothe this uneasiness. Of course, symbolic ges-
tures, to put into relief a fact of injustice, are necessary, too, as long
as a real elimination of the problem proves to be impossible. Pointing
out the Wall of Berlin to visitors is important. To remind the Allied
that they have contractual duties is important as well. More: a con-

tinuous moral pressure on the powers who have brought about the state of partition, in order that they might enter into discussions about the ways and means of terminating it, is an essential manifestation of our firm determination to bring about German unity. But more important still is an honest endeavor to come to mutual understanding within the ranks of our nation itself about the possibilities of self-help. Such a theme, of course, does not give good material for conventional stylistic exercise. The main ingredients of a discussion about existing situations of injustice are morally founded convictions, and a living sense of what is right.

The first thing to be acquired in this respect is to overcome in the Federal Republic in foreign relations a certain form of thinking in terms of being the *object of happenings*. I mean a habitual looking out for the opinion of foreign powers, which became accepted in the years after the total capitulation of Germany. A country which is registered as the second greatest economic power of the free world, does not have to ask every day afresh, what the East and the West are intending to do with her. In the same way the predilection to quote foreign displeasure in the course of controversies within our own ranks, must find at last its limits in a shouldering of responsibilities by our German democracy itself.

A thriving nation of 75 millions truly represent a level of achievement and volition, even in a state of forced partition, which cannot be overlooked, when building up peace for Europe. A faith of the leaders in the *independent importance of the German cause* is a necessary precondition of a change from thinking in terms of seeing ourselves in the situation of an object to *subject-thinking* in public opinion, without which we will never attain any success in our striving for unification and the formulation of a just peace.

The necessity is really in the air to come to an understanding about the extent of possible elbowroom when acting in our own cause. Every available experience of this period after the war points toward the fact, that a free Germany should build up its role in a world of to-morrow, as an *economic power* and as a *factor for integration*. Translating this sentence into the language of policy-making, it means that the well-known good qualities of our nation have to be infused into the task of forming constructive aims for German foreign policy.

Perhaps we are allowed to enumerate our good qualities from time to time. The so often quoted "economic wonder" of West Germany was not only the result of a still unaffected ethical attitude toward work in Germany or simply the result of the principles of market-economy. Not denying these vectors, their worth, we still are allowed to insist that a more than average preparedness of the German nation toward organizational activity has been in a gratifyingly high measure a satisfying match for the requirements of the permanent industrial revolution of our times. Under the circumstances of competition as brought about by modern technology, the reliance on *partial rationalisation*, which economises the use of the available human working-force, is no more enough. Much more depends on *full rationalisation*, that is an integration of the economy as a whole, resulting in reduction of the cost factor.

It is not to be denied that in the Federal Republic we have successfully solved the problem of a balanced functioning of economic processes and factors of production, when seen especially in the light of the economic and social integration of a mass of 13½ million refugees, who were evicted from Central Germany and when contrasting our own state with the chronic bottlenecks (and disproportionalities) in the economy of the Eastern Bloc nations.

The experiences and institutions of resettling, the program of building homes for the masses, the industrialisation of the flat country, the exigencies of planning for agriculture, and the developments undertaken in the territories of the Zone-boundaries, all these constitute for our Federal Republic *a whole arsenal of tools for social integration*, which in the same time makes extraordinary achievements possible in our economy as well.

We should not wonder therefore that the economic and financial capacities of West Germany have been called upon from many quarters. We cannot deny that there exists a real danger of splitting up our productive power too much. We have permitted that the principle be forced upon us, that aid for development should be given without strings attached, without referring to premises of political nature and satisfying human rights. There are countries which de facto burden the readiness of the Federal Republic to help, with continuous threats about their willingness to acknowledge the Zonal Regime of Pankow. (This of course is true, in spite of the attitude of Bonn, which would not suffer to make this well-known fact officially conscious). It seems so natural to ask whether one should not eradicate the embarrassment right at its source, instead of following up its repercussions all over the world. Complicated questions cannot be answered simply. At any rate perhaps it is an idea worth considering to actuate a frontal breakthrough on the petrified front lines of our Eastern European policy-making with the aid of a concentrated use of the economic potential of the Federal German Republic.

This idea is discussed here without, however, claiming that universal remedy has been found. Nevertheless, it seems to open up profitable vistas when analysing the economically integrated areas of Eastern as well as Western Europe, and of Soviet Russia, also their mutual relationships, which have merited hitherto little attention. The problems to be solved are an intricate maze, which has economic and political connotations. The opinions of specialists only are not enough to find our way. Naturally, when planning our future decisions in policy-making for Eastern Europe, we have to take into consideration all available intelligence, from both sides of the Iron Curtain. Such procedure will have the interesting result that optimistic opinions, voiced about *evolutionary possibilities inherent in the Eastern Bloc*, emanate from Western experts who are now facing the new generation of technocrats and economic managers in the captive countries. But opinions of specialists which stand behind the logic of present article as well, are by no means misled by the illusion that the notion of a partnership between Western and Eastern Europe will at once elicit on echo of assent from the governments of the Warsaw Pact. It is much more likely to meet first with an outbreak of sentiments betraying genuine suspicion and artificial scorn. But if we are convinced that our action lies on the line of historical necessity, then we can entertain full faith in the efficacy of positive ideas.

Creative initiative is the best method for clearing the air in ethnopsychic relations. Surely it is a task, which should not be underrated, if we propose here to extend a helping hand to our Eastern neighbours, with the result of creating again a positive public image of the German nation. Today, as in the past, it is still ritually repeated in the daily propaganda of the Eastern Bloc — insofar as it emanates from Moscow, Warsaw or Prague — how the Federal Republic constitutes a forum for sinister plots and the focus of a new war. But the inhabitants of these countries are surely well aware of the war-potential of Soviet Russia in order to gain a clear picture about the real hierarchy in the field of armament. Thinking in terms of modern military strategy it is simply unimaginable that even a unified Germany should ever be able to disturb the peace of its neighbours. It should be commonsense to imagine that in case of an atomic war, territories which are densely populated, should become much more vulnerable to attack, than any other state, with a continental expansion and a much lesser density of population.[1]) A sabre-rattling Germany no longer exists.

In Eastern Europe we can expect to find not only hatred but also old sympathies. The Federal Republic is today the broadest surface of communication between the Free World and the Western wing of the Eastern Bloc. She is the brilliantly lit shop-window of the West. Cultural emanations penetrate deep into Eastern European soil, where the vestiges of German language and cultural traditions have not yet been completely effaced. The faithful of the persecuted Eastern Churches see in her a bastion of religious Liberty. For the peasant population which has been pressed into kolkhoses, she represents a land of free farmers. In the consciousness of the elder generation of workers in Eastern Europe (and also in the knowledge of their sons and daughters) there still lingers the memory of the early pioneering role of the Free German Worker's Movement of the past. Up to the first world war party platforms of German Social Democracy had been widely discussed far away in Russia and Siberia. The program of the Austrian Social Democrats on the treatment of nationality inspired Lenin and Stalin to formulate counter proposals. Such intellectual avenues of contact have not been entirely buried. We may see a still existing example in present-day Austria which, as one of the farthest bastions of Western Europe in the Danubian Basin, has become a shining counter-proposition to the ways of the people's republics around her. We do experience now the astounding phenomenon that the strongest sympathies offered to modern Austria emanate from those countries which in 1918 so abruptly turned their backs on her. This phenomenon gives us authority to hope, that a first breakthrough against a partioned Europe will come to pass along the line of the Danube.

More dangerous than the psychological hurdles to be taken in Eastern Europe are misapprehensions in the Federal Republic itself, when confronted with the question of an economically oriented conception of German eastern foreign policy. If regarded only under the aspects of immediate profits the whole conception lies naturally wide open to every criticism of demagogues. Facing many needs in the homeland, it will always be most unpopular to offer, even in the form of credits, millions to foreign countries, which moreover are not of an especially friendly disposition toward us. But the real dilemma to face is the question how we could help peoples and countries of Eastern Europe, without simultaneously fortifying the Communist Governments which rule them? At the present moment we may envisage the expediency of encouraging evolutionary forces within these countries. But against exaggerated hopes for a peaceful disengagement, we may well heed the warning of the Austrian Foreign Minister *Dr. Kreisky* (in his address before the Catholic Academy in Munich, on the 5th of July, 1964) that we cannot buy away from Communist governments their Communist creed by simply offering credits and auspicious trade agreements. But, in spite of this, we still have to look out, living at it were, along the pressure line of opposite systems of ideologies and economic practices, for *pragmatic solutions*. The whole of Western Europe is vitally interested in strengthening within the Eastern Bloc the impetus of evolutionary forces. An evolution completely disjointed from its foundations it, of course, unthinkable. But surely there exist the possibility that new human forces who struggle for recognition will make an option for new alternatives.

The Iron Curtain as far as human insight goes, can be broken neither by the military power of the West, nor by the lowering of its military preparedness. An uncoordinated economic policy of Western Powers toward the Eastern Bloc would only succeed in fortifying the Communist governments without bringing essential relief to the Eastern peoples. Thus it remains only to choose between a static atmosphere of sickly hopes, or the launching of constructive ideas which would spell out new determination of the West toward action.

There should be no difficulty to opt for this device in Free Germany. The nation would have an especial readiness to carry the main load of an initiative against the economic partition of Europe, because it is only through economic sacrifices that we can come nearer to our ultimate goal of German reunification and of a just peace. Naturally, there can be no question of a *"financial Rapallo"* of the Federal Republic, because of considerations which should be treated separately, at greater length. Only if Western Europe as a whole will announce its readiness to answer, step by step, new features of a new evolution within the Eastern Bloc, by offering *a policy of economic partnership*, only then will it be possible for dynamical forces East of the Frontier to come into their own, and focusing onto crearly formulated aims, to attack the forces of stagnation.

1) Putting the chances of survival in relation to the density of population, we come to the following picture of inhabitants as per square kilometer: France 87, West Germany 232, CSSR 109, Poland 98, Soviet Russia 10, Red China 75, U.S.A. (without Alaska and Hawaii) 19.

THE HUNGARIAN FREEDOM FIGHT
AND THE ENTRY OF THE SOVIET ARMY

ISTVÁN SZENTPÁLY

THERE are always secrets, mysteries, false reports about historical events. The traditional state-interest with its carefully guarded
official secretiveness prevents the exposure of the driving forces behind facts. The searcher has often nothing to go upon, except the
careful work of analysis, the uniting of the links in the chain of cause
and effect. This system leads mostly to an explanation the event itself
does not offer.

The Hungarian Freedom Fight and Revolution of 1956, is also
full of questions which have not been answered so far.

1.) There is no answer to the question of what caused the alleviation of political terror shortly before the Polish and Hungarian
events?

2.) For instance, what caused the dismounting of the technical
sealing of the frontier, the wire obstacles, mine-fields, the watch-
towers—the demolishing of the Iron Curtain on the Hungarian-
Austrian frontier?

3.) Why was Mátyás Rákosi removed from the forefront of politics
in Hungary?

4.) How did it happen, that the invading Soviet troops got
mobilized weeks and days before the outbreak of the Revolution, so
that on October 23, they could invade the country?

5.) What is behind the fact that the Soviet troops thought themselves in Suez when they sighted the Danube?

6.) What was the moving force of the Soviet diplomatic decisions
which followed each other rapidly in those days and which culminated—as the greatest surprise—in the concluding of the Austrian
State Agreement they had so violently opposed until then?

To these questions one could add many more—diplomatic activity,
the constrained framing of the "atmosphere of Geneva," the anti-
Stalin drive and a whole string of measures inside of Hungary which
could facilitate the movements of a large army inside the country.

On the 6th of November, 1956, in the days of the crushing of the Freedom Fight, Soviet Brigadier General K. Grebenyik, commanding officer of Budapest, put his signature on posters and leaflets. The first of those orders sought to explain the presence of the invading troops and their opposition to the Revolution thus:

"The Soviet troops have temporarily entered Budapest on request from the Revolutionary *Workers* and Peasants' Government, to give brotherly aid to the Hungarian people in their struggle to protect the fruits of their socialist efforts, to crush the counter-revolution, to avert the Fascist danger etc., etc."

This order was no surprise, nor was it new, it only repeated what we had heard on the radio on October 24, 1956 at 9 a.m. in Budapest:

"Counter-revolutionary bands have caused a serious situation by their base armed attack during the night. The bandits have entered plants and public buildings. The government did not reckon with this bloody, treacherous attack and has appealed to the Warsaw Pact—for help from the Soviet troops located in Hungary. These have responded favorably to the request of the Government and are taking part in the restoration of order."

This news release had appeared in all major international papers. It was underlined by the fact of the Government having asked for help from the Soviet army and had thus given a legal aspect to the presence and intervention of the troops. Between the measures of the Government on the 24th and the Order of the Day by Grebenyik on Nov. 6, there is a vast and important difference. The measures of Oct. 24 limited the help to the local garrisons of Soviet troops, the order of Nov. 6, already mentions "entering troops" to execute the order of intervention. It is remarkable that the garrisoned troops hardly responded, though their forces would have been sufficient to crush the unprepared and unarmed revolution. The evaluation of the Hungarian Revolution had achieved an international importance. From this point of view, it is particularly important to confront the facts with the mental attitude and to recognize the reality of the situation.

☆ ☆ ☆

On the 24th of October 1956 at dawn, I started from my home in Szentendre—23 kilometers from the capital—on a bycicle to Budapest to see personally how things were regarding the Revolution. Halfway there, I met an acquaintance on the highway, which was jammed with excited people. He (P.M.J.) was trying to reach his home on a battered, muddy motorcycle. He told me that he had left Záhony (on the Soviet frontier) in the afternoon of the previous day. "The troops are pouring in, I couldn't get ahead of them up to Szolnok."

We couldn't as yet evaluate the importance of this information; I only drew the conclusion that the Soviet troops would crush the

Hungarian Revolution and one could not romance about the effective development of affairs. I didn't keep this opinion to myself; I mentioned it to my friends and acquaintances without getting much reaction. I reflected long on the words of the acquaintance I had met. The fact of troops streaming into our country before the outbreak of the Revolution shows that these troops marched in irrespectively of the Revolution, with some other intention.

During the first week of the Revolution, I bicycled in every day to Budapest. I saw Soviet tanks and small units, they did not seem to have any inimical intentions. They seemed to say: If you don't hurt us, we won't hurt you! But at certain points, further away, one could distinctly hear shooting across Budapest.

On the 26th of October, I visited a friend—a doctor—in the Pharmaceutical Institute on Üllői út. To my astonishment, I saw a first-aid station in a corner of the building and just as I passed, two young students were leading in a wounded Russian soldier. His left arm was shot through. As they removed his coat, some Rumanian money fell out of his pocket. "How did you get these "lei," I asked him. He told us, that he started with his unit from Temesvár, Rumania, on October 19. They thought that the Suez Canal was their destination. His words corroborated everything my acquaintance on the motorcycle had said earlier. It was evident, that there was no connection between the invasion of the Soviet Army and the spontaneous outbreak of the Revolution. It was visible that the silence surrounding the invasion was hiding some secret Soviet intention. Otherwise why would the proclamation on October 24 only have mentioned the mobilization of the units garrisoned in Hungary and not openly admitted that the troops in the neighboring countries—such as Rumania—were already marching in to suppress the Revolution.

In the first days of November, 1956, I arrived in Salzburg, Austria. This town and its surroundings were the headquarters of the fleeing Hungarians streaming into Austria. There was a separate camp where those were quartered who had arrived with arms and had to be treated as prisoners of war. I interceded on their behalf with the "Landeshauptmann" of Salzburg, Dr. Joseph Klaus (later Primer Minister of Austria), who immediately intervened at my request that those unjustly held as "prisoners of war" should be freed. Through the news I collected from among these I enlarged my information regarding the Soviet invasion and got a full picture of the entire affair. I heard that some of the units of the invading Soviet Army had left their headquarters as early as October 12 and entered Hungary according to a previously well-prepared plan. Their starting points were: Kiev, Sofia, Bucharest, Uzhorod, Temesvár, etc. Their forces had 15 divisions. To these were added other units. The Soviet troops were armed for war and differed on this point entirely from the garrisoned troops. Many of them thought that the Danube was the Suez Canal. In Salzburg the editors and staff of the paper, "Salzburger Nachrichten," helped me to continue my data-collecting activity. The entire archives of the paper were at my disposal and thus I was able to put the results of my research into regular files. I discovered from the large European newspapers, that the Soviets had made preparations for moving units in the first days of October. The chief concentration place for these maneuvers was around the "Bagdad States." News of similar activities came also from the Polish and East German frontiers. I did not find any concrete details about their movements in Hungary—this could only be heard on the Hungarian revolutionary radio—but these mostly agreed with other disturbing items of news. Today, seen from a distance of 10 years, the facts registered at the time have not changed their importance. On the contrary, they have gained stronger illumination by being coupled with newer details.

On November 23, 1961, on CBS Walter Cronkite interviewed General Eisenhower. We watched the interview. "It began this way," said Eisenhower, "that everyone got a little confused, you know this anyhow—and when the large Soviet Army invaded Hungary with the tank units, there was nothing one could do about it, the tragedy just happened." In 1964 an American book called *Diplomat Among Warriors* by Robert Murphy, came on the book market. Murphy was Deputy Secretary of State in Washington in 1956, so that his information was of the utmost value. He says in his book, that nobody expected the Revolution and nobody had any plan how to act: neither the USA, nor Moscow, nor Tito, nor the Hungarian authorities. The American Legation in Budapest had no Minister. Mr. Christian M. Ravndalt had been sent to Ecuador in July 1956. His successor, Mr. E. T. Wailes, serving in the South African Union, only arrived in Budapest on the 2nd of November. Several members of the Government blamed the State Department and the USIA for having been taken so unaware of the impending danger. Murphy only heard of the Soviet troops entry into Hungary across the Carpathian passes on October 28, Sunday at 3 a.m. He writes: "The invasion by Soviet troops of Hungary was the greatest international entanglement since the Korean War 6 years ago. It was even more dangerous, because of the possibility of direct contact between the American and the Red Army in Europe." Murphy affirms that the units of the Red Army took action on October 24 and that further units entered the country in the next few days. In the November and December issues of the newspapers "Kanadai Magyarság" and "Amerikai Magyar Élet", Alexander Szücs mentions the events under the title: "The frontier station at Záhony during the Revolution". Szücs was at the time stationmaster in Záhony. He relates that during the Revolution, owing to the general strike, the Soviet could not convey troops by rail. However more and more crossed the frontier daily and marched into Hungary. This announcements received small credit at the time.

☆ ☆ ☆

It is beyond question that the Soviet mobilization was not caused by the Revolution in Hungary and that her military movements began much before the outbreak of the Revolution. The arms and equipment of the mobilized Soviet army were not meant to subdue an unarmed revolution but were intended for far more subtle aims. It ought not to be difficult to find the plan of these aims. One cannot fail to connect the Soviet march into Hungary with the similar military movements in the Bagdad States and other European countries. Such movements were accompanied not only by many plans, preparations and problems of transportation but also by diplomatic arrangements. It we study the Soviet case, diaries of 1956 and prior to 1956, we can find carefully prepared military and diplomatic regulations, each one of which proves the Soviet plans of action. In this article we naturally must concentrate on the Hungarian events, but if someone takes the trouble to study the events in Poland and the character of the Soviet movements there, he will surely discover similarities to the situations in Hungary.

The Soviets Preparation for Mobilization in Hungary

After the 2nd World War, when the Soviet's political situation seemed to be consolidated in Hungary, the occupation troops retired to certain camps, so that after 1947 the Hungarians, particularly the people in Budapest had little contact with them. It was the more astonishing to note that in 1956 this situation suddenly changed. The capital and its immediate surroundings observed that the military occupation had not ceased. Trucks filled with Soviet soldiers raced about everywhere. Already in the spring of 1956, the population on the Soviet-Hungarian frontier noticed the arrival of mechanized units which, as it was later proved, were intended to inspect the load capacity of the bridges and underpasses and roads. In 1956 on the 10th of May to everyone's surprise the dismantling of the Iron Curtain began on the Austrian frontier. Wire obstacles and mines were removed. In August 1956 strict orders were issued for the economical use of gasoline and oil. Most bus lines were closed. Private cars had to be given up, railways restricted. Railroad officials declared at the time that large transports had arrived from the Soviet Union. It became known that the "headquarters" would be located on the Danube island of Szentendre, north of Budapest. Ono could watch the preparations from the opposite shore. At many places bridges that had been situated on the branch of the Danube were moved over to the island. On the right shore underground cables were laid towards the north, in the direction of the mountains. According to unconfirmed reports the Soviets planned to install rockets there.

On the first of December 1957 I got a letter from Germany:

"I took part in the autumn of 1956 in maneuvers at about 120 kilometers from Kiskúnfélegyháza, Bugacpuszta on the line to Kalocsa. This was the manipulation with atomic arms produced by the Soviet army. They were perfectly managed. All of the Hungarian units were elite troops numbering 32,000 men. The attacking troops stood between the town—Kiskúnfélegyháza and the Danube. 12 kilometers further back the defending forces stood. Both had all the arms that existed in the Hungarian army. The nucleus consisted of an extra Soviet unit. The attack began on October 3 at dawn and lasted 4 1/2 days, till the attacking forces reached the Danube. I took part personally in finding the territory where, the atomic explosion took place —7 kilometers to the west of Bugacháza. The maneuvers ended when the attacking forces reached the Danube line. Crossing the Danube was accomplished by technical units on 3 bridges and 11 heavy ferries."

Such a maneuver in itself does not mean much, but it belongs to the completion of the entire picture.

I must add my personal experience. From the end of July and continuing over a period of about 30 days, every night towards midnight air units coming from the direction of Czechoslovakia and going to the south flew en masse over my house which was on the ridge of a hill. I heard later, from workmen in the airport, that these machines were transporting munitions to Egypt. There were as many as several thousand. It is known that at the time of the Suez conflict the Israeli army captured an entire arsenal. This arsenal was certainly connected with the above-mentioned activity.

More interesting even are the diplomatic steps taken to secure success to the armed forces. The most spectacular was the Austrian State Treaty. This was surely in connection with the military plan. Till the treaty, Austria was divided into 4 zones and required strong Western units. It had now to be made into a "military vacuum." Together with the Western forces, the Soviet forces had to leave. This sacrifice was cheap by Soviet reckoning because it opened the way across the Austrian military vacuum.

The dismantling of the Iron Curtain served the same purpose and corroborated Eisenhower's and Murphy's communications. They do not deny that they feared an armed conflict which would have happened—according to Eisenhower—had America made a military move. The Soviet secured its position not only to the West but in all directions and regulated all its pending alliances by, among other instances, restoring the friendship with Tito and Japan.

Political Aims of the Soviet Back of the Mobilization

In 1956 the events in Suez ranked first in importance in the political world. The aim of the Soviet Union was the creation of an Arab Soviet state.. If this would have succeeded, it would have entirely changed the Near and Far Eastern political balance. Its advance toward the West was intended to secure the plans for Suez. The Soviets' military advance meant such a menace to the West that it was generally supposed that no opposition would be attempted. The menace to the West was strengthened as a result of Austria's disarmament. Both Eisenhower and Murphy corroborate this. But we cannot agree with Eisenhower where he says that the Hungarian Revolution could not have happened at a worse time than when the West was occupied with Suez. We think, on the contrary, that by sacrificing herself, Hungary through having disrupted the entire railroad system, having obscured the political plans of the Soviets, and having frustrated their aims was an asset in preventing the Western assault by the Soviet Army. This was quite sufficient to enable the French-English intervention to develop itself with full force and by this initial success to upset the entire Soviet plan and oblige them to accept a compromise. Without the Hungarian Revolution the Soviet would have reached the Austrian frontier unopposed, and if this would not have been sufficient to stop the French-English intervention, it might have resulted in an international conflict, in which case—according to American judgment war would have been inevitable.

We have answered the questions posed at the beginning of this article with the following explanations. The alleviation of the Rákosi terror served the purpose of creating a peaceful atmosphere in which the advancing Soviet troops could move and the dismantling of the Iron Curtain opened the way towards Austria. The Austrian Treaty likewise served these same purposes.

The Hungarian Revolution acted as a bomb. Soviet plans were disrupted by the astonishment created by the Revolution. The Western radio stations gave the impression that America might have had a hand in it. The news of the Revolution awakened dissatifaction in other vassal states, thereby preventing many military moves of the Soviets. The Kremlin even thought of giving up Hungary to save the rest of its satellites. When they found out that nobody stood behind Hungary they turned all their might and fury against a country that stood disarmed and helpless.

The Revolution is an unpaid debt weighing on the Western conscience. The Russian people would honestly like to erase the memory of those days. Time will never let it be forgotten. And when nations get back their rights only then will the debt of the West be paid.

THE POET YEVTUSHENKO AND PEACE IN CENTRAL EUROPE

G. H. SIKORSKY

AN interesting poem written by the well-known Russian poet, Yevtushenko has been published in translation in several East European literary reviews.

Does the Russian want war?

Ask the wheatlands, the willow and the linden tree,
But first of all, the soldiers
In whose soil they are rooted,
And ask youth.

I think not for a small stretch of land
Did so many suffer death but in order
That madness should not further threaten
The peoples of the earth.

When the trees in Paris, New York and elsewhere
Whisper and murmur in the night
Ask in your dreams:
"Does the Russian want war?"

Though he is a good soldier and knows how to fight,
who wants the miserable death of our earth?
Ask the mothers, the wives.
They know.

What Should We Ask and of Whom?

The question Yevtushenko asks is also platonic or merely poetic. The answer to "Do people want war?" (including the Russians) is obviously a universal NO. Unfortunately, the wheatlands, the willows and linden trees would not understand nor could they answer any questions. Certainly, mothers, wives, youth and soldiers could be asked but let us add workers, peasants, writers, teachers, scientists, intellectuals, engineers, all the people and not only the Russians but their *neighbors* to the West, South and East; the Czechs, Slovaks, Rumanians, Hungarians, Poles, Mohammedans and the Israelites. Instead of useless platonic questions let us ask politically realistic, useful questions, from the Central European nations and great powers. E.g., ask the Central European nations concerned if they want to continue the uncertainties of the post-war world with its Iron Curtain, Berlin wall, and nuclear powers directly facing each other in Central Europe where World War III could break out at any time. Or do they want military disengagement, the army of each nation stationed in its own country and an internationally guaranteed neutral Swiss-type buffer zone between such hostile powers as Russia and Germany. The present military expenses could be greatly reduced both in the NATO and Warsaw Pact countries. These pacts could even be dissolved and replaced by international agreements between the nuclear powers guaranteeing the neutral zone and promoting mutual disarmament. This would raise the present low standard and, in a few decades, raise the per capita income to the Swiss or even the American level.

Useful steps have recently been taken toward international agreements: atomic tests have been banned from the atmosphere and the proliferation of nuclear weapons has also been recently forbidden in an agreement. Let the search for international agreements continue.

An Historic Precedent

Almost all the agreements reached at the Congress of Vienna in 1815 have become outmoded. One exception wah the *neutralization of Switzerland* between three neighboring powers. Thereby Switzerland became a haven, a model country for the peaceful co-existence of several nationalities.

Specifically, we urge a Conference on European Security and/or a plebiscite of all East and Central European nations under UN supervision on the following questions:

1. Are they in favor of neutrality like Switzerland and Austria or do they want to continue living under the domination of far greater powers?

2. Do they want peaceful co-existence of all nationalities in the multi-national area of Central Europe along the Swiss pattern or should one nation possess privileges above the others (minorities) in the so-called "national states"?

Yevtushenko's Invitation To Central Europe—

The Russian poet visited Cuba and the United States a few years ago. Why not visit Central Europe now and ask these questions from the Slovaks, Hungarians, Czechs, Rumanians, Croatians, Serbians?

The Soviet Union and the Western powers took the first step toward an effective peace when they signed the Austrian State Treaty of 1955. The benefits of a neutralized zone in Central Europe should be obvious to all. We trust that Yevtushenko and all Central and East European intellectuals and politicians will recognize this vitally important idea. Rather than posing poetic or theoretical questions, practical ones that lead to peace, security and a reduction of armaments should be asked. Instead of propaganda poems writers have the obligation to listen for the true interest of the nations concerned, and express it. On the other hand, the statesman of those nations possessing nuclear power can do much more in the interest of peace than increase their military potential.

THE PLACE OF EAST CENTRAL EUROPE
IN WESTERN CIVILIZATION

EDWARD CHASZAR

THE study of European history, when elevated to a sufficiently high level, demonstrates the unity of European culture, from which the Western or Atlantic Civilization has developed.1)The history of Europe is one of ideas, and basicly, of Christian ideas. In it the nations of East Central Europe have had an uninterrupted, active, and productive participation for ten centuries both in times of their national independence and in times of submergence in one or another of the great empires that have held sway.

The present article will be a brief survey of the interaction of ideas between East Central Europe and the rest of the continent. It will touch on the main currents of European culture, and indicate the major directions along which the people of this particular region have made their lasting contributions to the political, religious, and cultural history of Europe.

Political history: A search for regional unity—

It is mainly on the plane of history that the nations of East Central Europe can be considered as a unit. The same is hardly possible on the social, economic, or geographic level, so diverse were its developments in those fields, so separated and subdivided is the land by geographic features. Yet, when one candidly examines the history of these nations by rising to a level higher than their domestic problems, one can detect a common direction: a continuous effort to achieve some sort of East Central European political unity.

The formula by which this unity was sought has been ever changing, and developing along the requirements of the times. Attempts of expanding dynastic rule by conquest and marriage (Piasts, Premyslides, Matthias Corvinus) alternated with federation-like arrangements, which included the granting of autonomy, equal rights, and privileges to the associated lands, to their Estates and the Church. The state system of Louis the Great of Anjou (1342-1382), bordering on the Adriatic, the Black Sea, and the Baltic, and expanding further to the North-east under his daughter, Hedvig (Jadwiga), commanded general respect and praise in Europe. In a different grouping, the system was revived and continued first by the Luxemburgs, then by the Habsburgs. When, after a long period of adversity, the dynastic arrangements failed to satisfy the peoples concerned, 19th century liberalism produced Kossuth, and later Masaryk in East Central Europe.

Lajos Kossuth, the great liberal statesman and politician, who led Hungary's unsuccessful fight for national independence in 1848—49 against the absolutism of Vienna, foresaw the need of multi-national co-operation and elaborated a plan for a Confederation of the Danubian States, based on self-government. (Forced into exile after the defeat of 1849, which was caused by Russian intervention, Kossuth toured the United States and delivered a brilliant speech to Congress in 1852. With a prophetic vision he outlined the future imperialist expansion of Russia and predicted that 100 years hence the U.S.A. would also be threatened by the Russian danger.) Fifty years after Kossuth's proposals, Thomas G. Masaryk, the founder of modern Czechoslovakia, well-known political philosopher and statesman, worked out plans to solve the complicated question of nationalities in the Dual Monarchy. In his work, *The Problem of Small Nations in the European Crisis* (1915), he advocated a regional solution on the Swiss model.[2]

Parallel with the unceasing, but as yet unsuccessful search for a lasting political unity, the history of East Central Europe reveals a constant struggle against any forceful or oppressive association with the great expansive political systems of both the West and East. Witness the opposition of Bohemia and Hungary to the designs of the Holy Roman Empire; the opposition of Poland, Moldavia, and Hungary to the Mongolian invasions; the struggle of Wallachia, Serbia, Hungary, and Croatia against the Ottoman Turks, and so on through the period of the Habsburg and Tsarist Empires to the totalitarian aggressions of the 20th century.

History of religion: Making a common cause with Europe

The early religious history of East Central Europe reflects the great endeavors of the dissemination and defense of Christian faith. This was the age of universalism in Europe, to which the first contributors were the wise rulers who introduced their peoples to Christianity between the 9th and 11th centuries. Their line opens with St. Vaclav, Duke of Bohemia, continues with St. Stephen of Hungary, his son Emeric, Mieszko I and Boleslaw I of Poland, St. Vladimir, Great Prince of Kiew, and closes with St. Ladislas of Hungary. Conversion made these lands an integral part of European evolution. By the time the Ottoman rule came to the region, its cultural development within the European community was already high.

The advanced early constitutional developments, culminating in events like the promulgation of the "Golden Bull" in Hungary (1222), comparable to the Magna Charta, were slowed down more than once by foreign invasions, occupations, and partitions. Yet, the age of the Crusades could still produce Andrew II of the Magyar Arpad House to lead a Crusade to the Holy Land in 1217, and later two Jagiello kings, Wladislas I and Louis II, to die on the battlefield against the Turks. John Hunyadi, Regent of Hungary between 1446 and 1452, earned the name "Defender of Christianity" by inflicting heavy blows upon the same enemy. His brilliant victory at Nándorfehérvár (Belgrade), which halted the advance of the Ottoman world for a considerable time, was commemorated by the tolling of bells at noon in the churches of Europe—a custom still observed, although its origin is forgotten. The decline of Islam in Europe was hastened by the decisive military exploits of Poland's last great ruler, Jan Sobieski (1674-1696).

The ferment of the age of Reformation and Counter-Reformation was not confined to the field of religion alone. It introduced new political and social doctrines as well, and proved to be extremely fruitful in the development of the native literary languages of the various nations. Previously the Latin language had monopolized literary life.

The first center of activity in this age was Bohemia, where the teachings of Wycliffe found an ardent exponent in the religious reformer Jan Hus, who preceded Luther by a century. An equally well known intellectual figure was Jan Komensky, or Comenius (1599-1670), the last bishop of the Union of Czech Brethren. A pioneer educational reformer, influenced by the ideas of Francis Bacon, he anticipated the social and educational doctrines of the 19th century. His modern educational methods are explained in his *Didactica Magna*, translated into many languages. Comenius stated knowledge, piety, and morality to be the threefold aim of education; educational opportunities, he declared, should be open to all according to ability rather than sex, social, or financial status. He also advocated the visual method of instruction and published what was probably the first picture textbook.

In Hungary the famous orations and literary works of the great counter-reformer, Cardinal Péter Pázmány, were disseminated widely both in the Latin and Magyar languages. Meanwhile, in Transylvania protestant literature blossomed under the rule of the Bocskays, Bethlens, and Rakoczis. Their well-equipped printing presses turned out translations of English and Dutch works as well as treatises written by Hungarian reformers and scholars. Among others James I of England's book of instructions to his son was translated into Hungarian and widely read in Transylvania. The introductory poem to the translation was by Albert Szenczi-Molnár, an outstanding figure in Hungarian Calvinist literature.

The period of Enlightenment brought religious tolerance to these lands at the end of the 18th century. Then, in the middle of the 19th century, liberalism worked toward an even greater toleration. By the time of the dissolution of the Dual Monarchy the number of "accepted" or "recognized" religions had risen in the Czech lands to six, in Hungary to eight. This favorable development in the field of religious ideas was the result of a long process that had its origin in the 16th century in Transylvania. There the Diet of 1564 promulgated that for the sake of the country's peace, each town or province was to be given free choice of its own religion. Although this did not signify complete religious liberty or tolerance, it was a more democratic solution than one could find anywhere else in Europe in those days. Following this, the Diet of 1571 recognized four "receptae religiones," accepted religions in Transylvania, these being the Catholic, Lutheran, Calvinist, and Unitarian.3)

Arts and Humanities: A cultural give and take

The first great European intellectual movement in which the nations of East Central Europe had full participation was Humanism. The royal courts of Bohemia's Charles IV, Hungary's Louis the Great, Poland's Casimir IV, and many of the major cities became renowned centers of scholarship and art. Cathedrals and castles were built in stately Gothic style. Some of them, like the famous Hradcany castle in Prague, or the Cathedral of Cracow, weathered the troubled ages to follow. Others, like the cathedrals of Pécs and Székesfehérvár in Hungary were destroyed by invaders, who put slender minarets in their place. Naturally, it must not be supposed that Western European styles and fashions reached East Central Europe without any modification. A good example is the so-called "Vistula Gothic" in Poland. This interesting variant of "classic" Gothic introduced the use of walls that could take the functions of the second row of buttresses, thereby eliminating a feature applied by German, French, and English architecture at that time. The Church of the Holy Virgin in Cracow is an outstanding work of art in "Vistula Gothic". In Hungary the churches of Ják and Zsámbék, built in the 13th century, likewise reveal certain modifications of the then dominant Romanesque style.

During the humanist period universities were established in Prague (1348), Cracow (1364), and Pécs (1367). These institutions produced and attracted the best scholars, and gradually attained European fame. Kepler, the great German astronomer, studied in Prague (1600) as assistant to the Danish Tycho Brahe, imperial astronomer.

Their famous predecessor and founder of modern astronomy, Copernicus (1473-1543), was educated at the University of Cracow. The celebrated Polish astronomer, once professor of mathematics at the University of Rome, took 27 years of painstaking work to produce his revolutionary astronomical treatise, *De Revolutionibus Orbium Caelestium*. Looked upon at first as heretical, the heliocentric theory of Copernicus, expounded the concept of which some faint foreshadowings had been given by Pythagoras, namely that the sun is the center around which the earth and the planets revolve. Upon the foundations laid by Copernicus, other distinguished astronomers, as Kepler and Galileo, built, until the edifice was completed by Newton. The University of Cracow, modeled on the Paris Sorbonne, became un international center for humanism in the 16th century.

Prior to this a similar development had taken place in Hungary during the Renaissance, after King Matthias Corvinus (1458-1490) married Beatrice of Arragon. Matthias founded the university in Pozsony (Bratislava), patronized literature and the arts, invited Italian artists and scholars to his country. Bonfini and Galeotti wrote his biography and have left picturesque descriptions of his court life. His royal palace at Buda, built in French *flamboyant* Gothic style, housed one of the best libraries of his age. Janus Pannonius, a Hungarian humanist, was widely known in this period for his popular classic poetry.

National literatures and men of letters

The 16th century saw a blossoming of literature in Poland. Clemens Janicki was a noted Latin poet and humanist, while in a later generation Matthew Sarbiewski was acclaimed as the "Christian Horace". The greatest poet of Renaissance Poland was Jan Kochanowski (1530-1584). Through a long development of literature in the Polish language (beginning with a Bible translation by the Jesuit Jacob Wujek), the best known men of letters by the 19th century included Adam Mickiewicz, the great romanticist *(Pan Tadeusz)*, and Henryk Sienkiewicz *(Quo Vadis?)*, who became Poland's first Nobel Prize winner. A generation later he was followed by Wladislaw Reymont *(The Peasants)*.

In the beginning of Czech literature in the native language, Jan Blahoslav (1523-1571), literary critic, musical theoretician, historian, and translator of the New Testament, made great contributions to Czech and European culture. The baroque period, sometimes called the "dark age" of Czech culture, produced the patriotic historian Bohuslav Balbin. The revival of cultural life came at the end of the 18th century. The trend was away from German centralism. Pavel Josef Safarik, philologist-archeologist, and Frantisek Palacky, the historian, were outstanding representatives of this tradition. Palacky produced a comprehensive work, the *History of Bohemia to 1526*. As a scholar and as a leader of the Czech national party he sought the re-establishment of the Czech kingdom which had lost its independence after the Battle of White Mountains (1620). In the period of Romanticism, the poets Karel Erben and Karel Macha, as well as the founder of modern Czech prose, Bozena Nemcova, were the most influential. No Czech writer has ever won such international recognition as the playwright Karel Capek (1890-1938). Strongly influenced by pragmatism, and an admirer of Masaryk's philosophy, Capek was an advocate of reason and a spokesman of the individual against the abuses of collectivism. His contemporary, F. X. Salda, achieved an European reputation as a critic.

In Slovakia the linguist Ludovit Stur (1815—1856) took the first decisive steps toward the establishment of a Slovak literary language. Prose was pioneered by Jan Kalinciak, and by Martin Kukucin, the first important realistic novelist and teacher of later generations of writers. Pavel Orszagh Hviezdoslav (1848-1921), the greatest of Slovak poets, enriched the Slovak cultural horizon also by his excellent translations from European literature.

The first significant lyric poet in the Hungarian language was Bálint Balassa (1551-1594). His contemporary, the epic poet Ivan Gundulic of Ragusa, made lasting contributions to the literature of the South Slavs. In the same period the publication of the New Testament in Transylvania marked the beginning of Rumanian literature. Another important work was the translation of the Bible by the Rumanian bishop Michael Tordasi from the Margar version of Gáspár Heltai. The brothers Zrinyi, Croats by origin, attained fame as poets and patriots. The name of Nicholas Zrinyi was well known in Europe. A political leader and military strategist as well, he eulogized, in Hungarian, the heroic death of his ancestor in the fight against the Turks. His brother, Peter, was active in Croatian literature.

During the 18th century the Hungarian Matthias Bél (1684-1749), linguist, geographer, and historian, and his contemporary, Dimitri Cantemir in Moldavia, contributed significantly to European historiography. The Protestant Bél was accorded recognition by the emperor, and even by the pope. Cantemir was elected member of the Academy of Sciences in Berlin, founded a few years earlier by Leibnitz.

Well into the 19th century the literary center of the Danubian Basin was Budapest, an international city where people of different nationalities made contacts and influenced each other in their cultural work. Ludovit Gaj, promoter of Croat national renaissance, met here with the great Slovak man of letters, Ján Kollár. Here Safarik's first treatises on Slavic philology were published, and the first Serb literary society was established. Books in Cyrillic script were printed by the University Press for Serbia and Bulgaria. The city was also a center of Rumanian studies, and served as a place of publication for the dictionaries and historical works of Samuel Micu, Petru Major, and George Sinkai.

Alexander Petőfi (1823-1849), born of Slovak parents and raised in the Hungarian plains, had lifted Hungarian lyric poetry to heights as yet unattained. His works, and later those of the Montenegrian Petar Petrovic Njegos, the Rumanian playwright Joan Caragiale (*Lost Letter*), the Hungarian playwright Emeric Madách (*The Tragedy of Man*), as well as various South Slav epic collections, were widely translated into European languages. At the turn of the century the prolific novelist Maurice Jókai, the poet Endre Ady of the "Westerners," and Dezső Szabó, founder of the modern populist school, stood out in Hungarian literature.

Top honors in natural sciences

A number of travelers and explorers attained fame as a result of their scientific achievements. László Magyar mapped some of the unexplored regions of Africa. Sir Aurel Stein, of Hungarian descent, was knighted by the King of England for his geographic and archeological explorations of Central Asia. Alexander Csoma de Kőrös, explorer and philologist, set out to investigate the origin of the Magyars in Asia. While there, he spent four years in a Buddhist monastery studying the language and the Buddhist literature, then compiled the first Tibetan-English dictionary and grammar. His scholarly analyses of Buddhist sacred books · are still quoted by orientalists.

The number of East Central European physical scientists who had won international recognition is impressive. The Hungarian mathematicians, Farkas and János Bolyai are known for their epoch-making work on non-Euclidean geometry. The physicist Baron Lorand Eötvös invented the torsion pendulum named after him, and used for the detection of coal and oil strata. In 1861, professor Semmelweiss of the University of Budapest made a very important discovery in bacteriology on the danger of septic poisoning of women in childbed. Two generations lated Dr. Albert Szentgyörgyi received the Nobel Prize for his research on Vitamin C. Six other Hungarians were accorded the same honor: Philip Lenard (1905), Robert Barany (1914), Richard Zsigmondy (1925), George Hevesy (1943) then George Békésy (1961), and Eugene P. Wigner (1963). The scientists Edward Teller, John Neumann, and Prof. Szilárd contributed significantly to the advancement of nuclear physics in the United States.

Dr. Carl F. Cori and his wife, recipients of the Nobel Prize in the field of medicine (1947), were born in Czechoslovakia. Jaroslav Heyrovsky of the same country received the 1959 chemistry award. It will also be recalled that Mendel, the founder of the science of genetics, was an abbot of Brno when he carried out his famous experiments on the crossing of peas. The renowned physicists Mach, Lecher, and Einstein were all connected with the University of Prague. Poland, as mentioned before, had two literary geniuses worthy of the highest award, but even greater acclaim went to the discoverer of polonium and radium, Marie Sklodowska, known by her married name as Mme. Curie. The Curies were showered with honors by the scientific world for their momentous achievements. The greatest of these honors was the 1903 Nobel Prize in physics, which they shared with the French Becquerel. In 1911, Mme. Curie again was awarded the Nobel Prize, this time in chemistry, for isolating pure metallic radium in one of the most difficult operations known to science.

Musical traditions: Rich and original

In the field of music many of the composers, performers, and conductors who hail from East Central Europe, are known by musicians and audiences the world over. It would be difficult to find an opera house that has not performed the charming comic opera, *The Bartered Bride*. It was written by Bedrich Smetana, the founder of modern Czech music. The *Slavonic Dances* of Anton Dvorak took the public by storm. His Fifth Symphony in E minor *(The New World)* is one of the most popular symphonies in the United States.

Few only know that hidden in the German-sounding names of Franz Liszt and Franz Lehár are two persons who were born in Hungary. Liszt, the great pianist and composer of 19th century Romanticism, dedicated his popular Hungarian Rhapsodies to his native country. In a much lighter vein, Lehár composed delightful operettas. The melodies of his *Merry Widow* are still being sung in the remotest corners of the globe. The truly Magyar musical tradition of Hungary is represented by Zoltán Kodály and Béla Bartók, neither of whom needs any introduction. Their unique musical compositions and their wonderful collection of some 30,000 folksongs in the East Central European area remain monuments to their greatness both as composers and folklorists.

The name that represents Poland among the celebrated European composers is that of Chopin, enchanter of generations of music lovers, while Paderewski, the most famous pianist of the world at the turn of the century, leads the scores of performing artists. Today the names of Arthur Rubinstein and Wanda Landowska are no less well known. The Rumanian composer Enesco, the Hungarian pianist-composer Ernest Dohnányi and the conductor Eugene Ormandy, as well as Jan Kubelik and George Szell from Czechoslovakia, Leopold Stokowski from Poland, are only a few more of the outstanding persons who represent today a rich and honored musical tradition in the West.

Conclusion

Were it possible to enumerate here all the excellent graphic artists whose works had found their way into the best exhibition halls and museums of Europe, Jan Matejko and Mihály Munkácsi, painters, and Ivan Mestrovic, sculptor, would probably head the list. Developments in the field of fine arts were no exception to those in other areas of human endeavor, and even a brief survey, as the one presented in this article, offers ample proof of East Central Europe's valuable participation in all the great political, religious, intellectual, and cultural movements of the West: Humanism, Reformation, Counter-Reformation, Enlightenment, Classicism, Romanticism, as well as the movements of the modern age. The passing of this region behind the "Iron Curtain" has deprived the fertile Western intellectual scene of some of its most productive, colorful, and irreplaceable cultural streams.4) And while the separation of this region from the rest of Europe in the political and economic realms is likely to persist for some time to come, a *détente* between West and East, and a possible neutralization of this zone, might restore the cultural give-and-take which had proven beneficial to both in the centuries past.

1) For an exposition of this view see Arnold Toynbee, **The Study of History**, and John Bowle, **The Unity of European History** (New York, 1950). Also, T. S. Eliot, **Notes Toward the Definition of Culture** (New York, 1949), especially the Appendix: "The Unity of European Culture."

2) Two scholarly works, dealing with the search for political unity in East Central Europe, are recommended in particular. Oscar Halecki, **Borderlands of Western Civilization** (New York, 1952), and Francis Dvornik, **The Making of Central and Eastern Europe** (London, 1949), See also Stephen Gál. ed., **The Danubian Confederation of Louis Kossuth** (Budapest, 1944); Bela T. Kardos, "The Federalist Papers of Louis Kossuth," publ. in this volume.

3) For details see Chapter 7, "Church and State," in **Czechoslovakia**, edited by V. Busek and N. Spulber (New York, 1957), and chapters 5 and 6 in Dominic G. Kosáry, **A History of Hungary** (Cleveland, 1941).

4) For additional information on the cultural history of East Central Europe consult the following sources: Bernadotte E. Schmitt, ed., **Poland** (Berkeley, 1945). Robert J. Kerner, ed., **Czechoslovakia** (Berkeley, 1940). Count Paul Teleki, **The Evolution of Hungary and its Place in European History** (New York, 1923). Walter Kolarz, **Myth and Reality in Eastern Europe** (London, 1946). Stojan Pribichevich, **World Without End: The Saga of Southeastern Europe** (New York, 1939). Julian von Farkas, **Südosteoropa** (Göttingen, 1955). The last three works discuss Yugoslavia, Rumania, and Bulgaria as well. Because of Byzantine influences, the cultural development of the latter three countries has been somewhat different. A survey of their history and an adequate statement of the cultural similarities and differences with the rest of the East Central European region would necessitate a separate article.

II

FEDERALISM
IN CENTRAL EUROPE

II

FEDERALISM
IN CENTRAL EUROPE

FROM KOSSUTH'S
UNKNOWN FEDERALIST PAPERS (1)

BÉLA TALBOT KARDOS

LOUIS KOSSUTH wrote on February 25, 1850 in Brussa, Turkey, an *Address to the People of the United States of America* which was published in Washington D.C. by the newspapers "Union" on October 21, 1851, and the "National Era" in October 1851; also by the "New York Herald" on October 20, 1851. In this Address Kossuth said:

"Citizens of America! To you I declare with honesty that *my final aim is the idea of Federation which would weld Hungarians and the other smaller neighbouring nations into a Union,* to secure the nationality and independence of each and freedom for all; freedom, not power was their desire. The sentiments of sympathy for our sufferings will inspire among the smaller states and races the wish for a fraternal confederation for that which I always urged as the only safe policy and guarantee of freedom for them all."

Main Principles of Federalism and Self-Government(2)
Introduction: Antagonism of Centralization (Etatism)
and Federalism (Self-Government)

Most misunderstanding originates from words ill-defined. I shall try to clarify them.

I have always been an enemy of political centralization which absorbs the independence of all communities, counties, provinces. I opposed it at a time when, in Hungary too, many heads were confused by brilliant theories sanctified by European, especially French biases. I have always been an enemy of centralization because I never could coordinate it with freedom.

This my conviction stands today firmer than ever. And I think there are many good reasons for it if we see what happens in France. even under the form of a Republic.

On the other hand, Habsburg Austria started a godless war against us under the pretext of its centralized system. Subsequent events—and I can say without boasting, I had a large part in them—

forced some constitutional reforms on Austria. But the Viennese government threw off these constitutional guarantees, and being a sworn enemy of freedom, returned to forced centralization, thereby paralyzing liberty which the constitutional forms seemed to give to the peoples concerned.

The French nation is a great nation. Under most varying forms of government it experimented with centralization. Yet under all these different banners, it has never been really free, not under the revolutionary Convent, neither under the Consulate, Emperor, Restauration, Louis Philip, nor at present. Not "suffrage universelle," the general right to vote, could unite centralization with freedom. And I predict that the efforts of the Socialists will also end in illusion, if, after getting into power, they will not abolish centralization by a radical change for federalism.

True Liberty Is Impossible Without Federalism

True liberty I am able to imagine only in the form of *federation*.

This has been my unchanging conviction ever since, knowing my mind, I have had my own way of thinking.

If I was asked—many years ago—when anybody, who had declared the events of 1848-49 to be possible, would probably have been called insane—if I was asked what I thought of Hungary's future, I replied that she has either no future, or if she has, her future is to form with the neighbouring smaller nations a *federation* which shall secure the political liberty and independence of all these smaller nations against the overwhelming weight of any power, and their nationality against absorption.

If I was asked why I am a friend of the county system, I answered: Because I see the idea of *federation* also approachable in the inner organization of my country by planning the county system on a democratic basis.

If I was asked how I think the reconciliation of the nationality disputes, artificially stirred up or naturally awakened, possible, my reply was again: through the idea of *federation*.

This is an old belief of mine—a belief which I did not learn from anybody but derived out of myself, for which I was often derided as a dreamer—the persistence in which is not a concession on account of the present sad condition of my country, but an old conviction of which I have always been an adherent under favorable and adverse circumstances, undauntedly. It was this idea that led me even then, when, in 1841, I proposed the independence of Croatia and stood all alone with that opinion in the whole country.

If, therefore, somebody stands up against me in the name of the federation and calls himself above me, before me, the man of liberty, he has either never understood me or has given no account to himself of his own belief.

116

Small Nations Cannot Maintain Their Independence Without Federation

Small nations can secure their political existence and independence only through a straight federation among themselves. Otherwise their political existence will ever be threatened by the preponderance of larger powers, and their nationality will be exposed to absorption.

This idea of federation is the surest guaranty of liberty everywhere, and for our country and the neighboring peoples it is the only possibility without which the secure existence of their respective states in inconceivable, to such an extent are they surrounded and threatened not only by overwhelmingly large, but by their very nature, also absolutistic powers.

From this situation follows for us and our neighbors in addition to the claims for securing our existence the destination to secure Europe and the civilization of Europe.

Europe felt that she needs a wall of defense against this danger and sought it at the cost of the oppression of so many peoples, in the Austrian Empire. So that the existence of the Austrian Empire is for Europe no longer a guaranty but a danger. This is the fact which cannot be denied, admitting no longer any alternative or choice. The confederation referred to above is an indispensable necessity for Europe.

The idea of confederation was thus designated by divine providence, the finger of which is revealed in the events so strikingly, as the only remedy for Europe. An *Europe will have to atone mercilessly, if she does not obey the admonition of providence.*

Principles and Aims of Federalism

The fundamental principles of the organism of this confederation are the following:

1.) Each confederate state is entirely independent from each and from the whole confederation in all its domestic affairs.

2.) The entire confederation *in solidum* secures the independence and national competence of each confederate state.

3.) It is only natural that the relations of Serbia and Moldavia-Wallachia with the Turkish port(3) being their domestic affair, they are outside of the sphere of the confederation, and the federal government does not only not mingle with them but even offers to secure its friendly intentions toward the Port by a mutual defensive alliance.

4.) The objects of the confederation are:
   a.) Common defense against exterior enemies.
   b.) Common customs.
   c.) Common diplomacy.

5.) The affairs of the confederation are to be governed by a federal council into which each confederate state delegates at least one and, in proportion to its population and territory, at most, four members.

6. The members of the federal council are to be elected by the legislative bodies of the states concerned and may be recalled by them.

7.) The proportion of the contribution to the common defense and the common expenses, according to the population and the size of the territory, is to be fixed in the fundamental covenant of the confederation.

8.) The government of each state is bound to execute the decision of the federal government in its own sphere of authority, and the execution is to be guaranteed by the confederate states *in solidum.*

9.) In the ministry of each state one portfolio will be entrusted with the federal affairs; the federal councilors of the states being in constant official contact with the minister, the latter will represent the federal affairs at the national legislatures of the states concerned.

10.) Envoys to foreign powers are to be appointed and instructed by the federal council, the government of each state being free to have their own affairs represented either by the federal envoy or by a special delegate.

11.) The declaration of war and the conclusion of peace belong to the rights of the federal government.

12.) The seat of the federal government will be a place to be selected in the interior of Hungary, but not in the same place where the seat of Hungary's own government is located. The seat of the federal government is under the direct authority of the federal government, but is to be governed according to Hungarian laws and does not loose its right to representation in the Hungarian legislature. (See footnote on page 128).

13.) The federal council elects its president for one year from among its own members; it also decides itself as to the language of the deliberations and the minutes.

14.) The federal covenant would be subject to revision in every twenty-fifth year, on which occasion each state would be free to withdraw from the confederation or to bind itself to stay.

The above would be the principal feature of the constitution, subject of course, to modification in their form.

Inner Structure of a Member State and Division of Power

After these premises I shall draw up the contours of my construction in a short sketch:

1.) A good political division into counties (cantons) (4) which shall be of equal size as far as possible and properly answer the natural requirements of successful administration.

2.) In this division attention must be paid mainly and above all to the nationalities, so that *people of the same tongue shall be contained in a county (canton) as far as possible.* This division solves the question of the reconciliation of the nationalities, or nothing can solve it, and the various peoples are condemned, mangling one another, to get all under the yoke.

From Kossuth's PRINCIPLES OF A POLITICAL CONSTITUTION WITH REGARD TO THE SOLUTION OF THE NATIONALITY PROBLEM.(5)

Preface

The Disappointing Example of French Centralized Etatism

The example of the French Republic furnished striking proof of a thesis, which I have maintained all of my life. viz. that in order to guarantee both the rights of the individual and the freedom of the people it is not sufficient to just pronounce the sovereignty of the people, if the power of government is too extensive, and in case any assembly whatsoever, though elected by universal suffrage, is constituted as the sole organ of that sovereignty, the said assemly being vested with unrestricted legislative powers, and forming at the same time the only legal barrier against the encroachments by the government on the rights of the individual and on political freedom.

We have seen a President of the French Republic (6) elected by general suffrage, rebel with impunity against the honor, the dignity and the liberty of his country.

We have seen a legislative assembly, likewise elected by universal suffrage, even do away with that same universal suffrage, the source of its own mandate.

We have seen how, through the criminal coagency of these two unrestricted powers not only were all rights, all liberties violated, all guaranties broken, all democratic institutions falsified and perverted, the Republic turned into a falsehood, but also how thereby the nominal existense of that very republic was called in question, so much so that before these all-powered organs of the people's sovereignty republican sentiments and attachments to the Republic had assumed the character of crimes, and that the poor French Republic had been reduced to a point where, as Th. Moore said deploring the fate of his country:

"It is treason to love her, and death to defend her."

Poor France! Here you are in need, not being able to guard yourself against the loss of everything you have gained by so many revolutions, except by resorting to a new revolution!

It is very sad, indeed! But it is quite natural! I have foreseen it,

I have publicly foretold it the very day when reading the constitution of the French Republic I became aware that France, in spite of all those trials, has not yet learned to rid herself of that fatal propensity to *centralize power*, a propensity so flattering to the vanity of glory, but at the same time so injurious to liberty!

Do you expect that a government having at its disposal a numerous standing army which is subject to a rigorous discipline, such as is indispensable for the existence of such an army, disposing of an annual revenue of one and a half milliards, controlling all offices and employments, even those of mayors of communes; having the power to disband the National Guard, to establish martial law in the country, etc. and all this subject only to the condition of not being disapproved by the majority of an assembly who in their turn are covetous of governing and of sharing the advantages, which the government doles out; do you expect that such a government should not have ambitious desires? Do you expect an all-powerful assembly not to take advantage of its absolute power?

But this would directly run counter to human nature—in order to succeed nothing less would be required than a nation of Washingtons! Washingtons, however, are very rare!

However, it may very well be that this unhappy propensity to centralization, sprung from the inexhaustible source of traditional sentiments, originates in the character of the French people, thus being sort of fated; in this case, it is to be regretted rather than found fault with, for the hearts of nations, like those of the individuals, may easily break, but change only with great difficulty; thus France will still have to undergo many trials until she contrives to change that fatal trait in her character.

State Sovereignty Should Not Suppress the Inalienable Rights of the Individual, the Family, the Town and Community, the Autonomy of the Church, the Rights to Nationality and Freedom

I am a Hungarian, knowing the character of my people, whose propensity lies in the opposite direction, whose traditional sentiments, though immutable, rebel against any kind of centralization, I who am not striving the vanity of a conqueror's glory for my country, I, striving only after true liberty and the happines of complete democracy for my country, I loath the centralization of power, I detest the claim to omnipotence both in government and in legislation; I shall never aid the introduction in my country of similar institutions which I consider absolutely incompatible with the inalienable rights of man—by the centralized state. Political freedom cannot be combined with a centralization, diametrically opposed—according to its natural direction—to liberty.

I wish that these rights, this liberty be secure from the encroachments of authority. There follows a rough draft of the principles of political organization, as I should submit it for approbation to the people of my country.

Fundamental principle: *Sovereignty of the people constituted in a democratic republic.*

But the people as a whole this totality of all the citizens of a country, revealing themselves through universal suffrage and the functions of the mandatories elected through that suffrage—will only in matters common to the state as a whole be the sole organ of this sovereignty.

The individual with regard to his personal rights—the family in family matters—the commune in communal matters—and the county in county matters—are likewise the organs of the said sovereignty!

Even the most absolute despot had never dreamt of taking families in the management of their domestic business under his tutelage, merely on the strength of the possibility that they might mismanage their affairs.

Thus the same liberty, the same right must be reserved for the individual, the commune, the province or county.

Men must be free in the exercise of their *individual rights*, free in their domestic affairs, free in the business of the commune, free in that of the county.

The rights of the individual cannot be subjected to the will of the family, of the commune, of the province, of the state; on the contrary, the commune must afford them support and protection against the tyranny of the family, the province against that of the commune, the state against that of the province, and the inviolable principles of the constitution against that of the state; they must also find support and protection in the communes and provinces being entitled to refuse to act as executives of the state's tyranny; finally, the actual responsibility of the public officials must guarantee to every individual, to every family, to every commune, to every province the right of lodging complaints against and claiming damages from any officials whatsoever before the duly constituted tribunals.

The liberty I have just claimed for the individual, I claim likewise for the communes, for the provinces.

I cannot content myself with that homeopathic dose of liberty which consists of being entitled to go periodically to the polls with millions of my fellow citizens—I also want to enjoy individual liberty and a continuous influence on communal and provincial affairs.

Bill of Inalienable Rights

Therefore: The individual rights of man (to be enumerated in the constitution) do not fall within the province of state legislation.

Among these rights are: freedom of thought (of the press), freedom of worship (of religion) and freedom of association.

I hold that it is an inviolable right of the individual to freely associate with others with the view to the development, protection and safeguarding of both their moral and materials interests.

People of the same creed, of the same religious associate—the churches are such free and independent associations that govern themselves at their discretion, according to the principles of their respective cults, of their respective religions. They have nothing to do with the state, and the state has nothing to do with them. (That is liberty.)

The *Right to Nationality* is inalienable,—has nothing to do with the State. Nationalities may freely, like religions, form associations, autonomous bodies irrespective of denominations or political frontiers. They will draw up statues for their associations, and will govern them in accordance with these statutes. The association will have nothing to do kith the State and the State will have nothing to do with it. (Here again we have liberty, here we have social nationality guaranteed by the freedom of association.)

Communities and Towns. Rights of minorities

Let us pass on to the commune.

The commune is free and independent in the administration of communal affairs. The organization of this administration is based on the inviolable principle of universal suffrage, by all those that compose the commune.

The constitution states the required condition of an aggregation of several families to qualify for being considered a commune; it recognizes the inviolability and immutability of universal suffrage, and of the right of every official being recalled by those who elected him; but beyond that, neither the county, nor the government, nor the legislature have the right to interfere with the administration of communal affairs. Consequently every commune stipulates itself *in which language it will be administered.* They draw up their reports, write their correspondence, their petitions addressed to the counties, to the government, to the legislature in the language they have chosen for the communal administration, and they will receive the reply of the county, or the government through the intermediary of the county in the same language. (So much for nationality politics in the commune.)

But the constitution guarantees to the minority the right of lodging a complaint, or of addressing a demand to the commune, and of pleading its cause before the tribunals in its own language, or, what is more, the right of forming into a separate commune, provided it meets the requirements established by the constitution for the formation of a commune. (So much for the protection of the minority against oppression by the majority.)

Among the conditions indispensable for the constitution of a commune is the establishment of at least one primary school maintained and administered by the commune. The language used in this school will be one chosen for the administration of the commune. (So much for the development of the nationality in the commune.)

But the constitution guarantees to the minorities the freedom of educational activities both in the commune and in the associations (as the church, national associations, associations of farmers, manufacturers, trades people, etc.) Everyone has the right to open and maintain schools under the sole protection of the public, and everybody is entitled to avail himself or herself of any schooling that might be had. (So much still for the guaranty of the rights of the individual, and those of minorities.)

As to the primary schools of communes, neither the county, nor the government, nor the legislature have the right of interfering with them; the legislature, however, in view of the common interests of the State may prescribe a *minimum* of public instruction, e.g. every citizen being obliged to defend the country against any aggressor, it is necessary that elementary military instruction (drill and the fundamental maneuvers) should already be given in the communal schools. The communal official in charge of directing the school is responsible to the government, which latter is vested with the right of inspection, which it may, however, exercise only through the county.

So much for the sovereignty of the inhabitants of communes in communal matters.

But the commune and its officials as elected by the inhabitants of the commune are also the performers of the decrees issued by the county, of the orders issued by the government, and of the laws issued by the legislature of the county in all matters reserved to the county, the government, and the legislature respectively. (A true democracy: the people make the laws and the people carry them into effect.)

For the performance of the above duties the respective officials of the commune are responsible to the county and to the government. (So much for the efficiency of the government.)

But the government cannot get into direct touch with the communes; it may send them orders only through the intermediary of the respective county. The rights of the county will be outlined below. (So much for the barrier to protect the communes against oppression by the government.)

The Counties (Cantons)

Let us pass on to the discussion of the counties.

The government establishes the boundaries of the counties, into which the county will be divided.

In so far as geographical conditions permit, the boundaries will be so established with regard to the diverse nationalities that, as far as possible, inhabitants speaking the same language live together in the same county.

The principles, which I have just established for the administration of communal affairs, will in a similar manner apply to the administration of the affairs of the counties.

The counties are composed of the representatives of the communities, who may be recalled at any time and are elected periodically by the inhabitants of the communities on the principle of universal suffrage.

The county-assembly decides in its first session by a vote of majority, which will be the language to be used in the administration of the county for the duration it is in office. It will thereafter carry on its correspondence with the government in the language so chosen. (So much for the national policy in the county.)

Kossuth's paper ends with an apology for the errors he may have unwittingly committed in 1848-49: "I openly confess with full sincerity of the brotherly feelings in my heart if the wishes of the other nationalities escaped my attention, it was because they were not brought to my knowledge. But our co-citizens of other languages may be convinced that the Hungarian nation has long since buried the previous mutual grievances. It offers its hand in brotherhood and is willing to give freely what one brother may offer to the other."

PLAN FOR A DANUBIAN CONFEDERATION

(First published in the Italian review "Alleanza" May 1, 1862.)

Since the undoubtedly peculiar conditions of countries situated between the Carpathians and the Danube, the Black Sea and the Adriatic render the formation of a unified state very difficult, it is desirable that the old historical states in this region should enter into a federation with one another, which might be called "Danubian Confederation." In addition to the affairs of mutual interest, which would be attended to by the federal authorities, the legislation, jurisdiction and administration of each state would be entirely independent. By extensive decentralization and by allowing ample freedom to each community and province, all inhabitants of the federation could develop without hindrance, and each people could occupy the place due to it in the great family of humanity.

The basis of the new order in the Danubian countries would be the free consent of the peoples concerned either by a constitutive assembly or by universal vote. For instance, the inhabitants of Transylvania would decide by general vote whether their country shall be one with Hungary, or whether it shall be politically united and administered separately from Hungary or, finally, whether it shall be only in alliance with Hungary and the other federated states, as an autonomous state, on the basis of complete equality. Concord between the Hungarians and Rumanians, which is my most fervent desire, would secure well-being and freedom to both. I sincerely hope that we shall attain that great object.

Should the oriental question be solved by the independence of the Christian peoples, it would be desirable that Serbia and the other Southern Slav countries also join the Danubian Confederation which would then extend from the Carpathians to the Balkans and consist of Hungary, Transylvania, Rumania, Croatia and the provinces eventually to be appended to Serbia, etc.(7)

For the solutions of such delicate questions as could not be agreed upon by the peoples the mediation or verdict of friendly powers could be requested.

Principles of a Federal Covenant

The covenant of the confederation would be drawn up by a legislative assembly, on the basis of certain principles, some of which I am going to indicate.

1.) Affairs of mutual interest would be the defense of the territory of the confederation, foreign policy, foreign representation, the commercial system including commercial legislation, customs, the principal lines of communication, weights and measures.

2.) All questions concerning the military and naval forces, fortresses and naval ports would be regulated by the authorities of the confederation.

3.) The individual states of the confederation would have no separate representatives at foreign courts, the diplomatic service will be one and common for all states.

4.) Customs affairs will be common, and the revenue of the customs will be divided among the individual states in accordance with the decision reached in this matter by the legislative assembly. Commercial legislation will be common. One currency, one system of weights and measures throughout the whole confederation.

5.) The legislative assembly will likewise decide whether the federal assembly (parliament), which exercises the legislative power, shall consist of one chamber or of two, as in the United States of America. In the latter case, the members of the House of Representatives will be elected in proportion to the number of inhabitants of the individual states. In the Senate, large and small states will be represented by the same number of members, which principle constitutes an excellent guaranty for the smaller states.

6.) The exclusive power will be exercised by a federal council to be elected by the chamber (if there is to be only one) or by both chambers (if there are to be two). The council will direct the foreign policy, too, under the control of the legislature.

7.) The legislative assembly will decide which is to be the official language of the confederation. In the exercise of the executive power every member can use his own mother tongue.

8.) The towns: Budapest, Bucarest, Zagreb and Belgrade, will be the seats of the authorities of the confederation by rotation.

9.) The head of the state, in which the authorities of the confederation will reside according to the above order, will be at the same time the president *ad interim* of the federal council and of the confederation.

10.) Each individual state makes for itself such a constitution as agrees best with its interests, provided, of course, that the principles of that constitution be not in conflict with the principles sanctioned by the confederation.

The Rights of Nationalities and Religious Bodies:

Nationalities like religious denominations, may organize in free associations, irrespective of political frontiers and administrative boundaries.

11.) The relations of the various nationalities and religious denominations would be regulated on the following basis:

a.) Each community decides its official language itself. That language will be used in its oral deliberations, its reports and communications to the chief of the country, its petitions to the government and the diet. Each community decides also as to the language of its instruction in schools.

b.) Each country decides by a majority vote which language shall be used in the administration. The oral deliberations and protocols, as well as the correspondence with the government will be this language.

c.) In the discussions of the parliament, each representative may use at pleasure any of the languages current in the country.

d.) The laws will be promulgated in all languages current in the counties and communities.

e.) In the interest of their nationality the inhabitants of the country can freely unite into large national associations (consortii), organize themselves at will and hold smaller or larger meetings and periodical conferences for the settlement of their religious affairs. They may also elect a national chief, whom they may call Woyvode, Hospodar, or some similar name.

f.) They can entrust the nationality associations with taking measures in regard to their churches and schools, freely electing their prelates, calling them patriarchs, metropolitans as the case may be.

g.) They can enact statutes in regard to their organization and their nationality and religious interests.

h.) The state demands from them only one thing, viz. that their decisions and acts be made public.

Mutual Understanding Between Hungarians, Slavs and Rumanians

I trust that all Danubian countries will accept the above propositions, for they are in accordance with their desires and interests, and secure their future. Thus we should succeed in creating inner harmony between them the first consequence of which would be the fall of the tyrants and the crumbling away of the senile and decayed states which keep them now in bondage and hinder them in their noble endeavours. In the name of Heaven, I entreat the Hungarians, Slavic and Rumanian brethren to throw a veil on the past and to stretch out their hands to each other, rising like one man for their common liberty and fighting all for one and one for all *according to the old example given by the Swiss.* In the name of Heaven, I entreat them to accept the plan, which is not a concession, but a mutual and free confederation. Each nation of the lower Danube, even if it should succeed in gathering around itself its racial relations now belonging elsewhere—could form, in the best case, only a second-rate state, the independence of which would incessantly be in jeopardy, and which state would necessarily be subjected to foreign influences. But if the Hungarians, Southern Slavs and Rumanians accept the above plan, they will form a first-rate, wealthy and powerful state, which will weigh heavily in the balance of Europe.

Unity, concord, fraternity among the Hungarians, Slavs and Rumanians! This is, indeed, my most fervent desire, my most sincere advice! Here is a smiling future for all of them!

(1) The following texts are from a manuscript: **The Federalist Papers of Louis Kossuth** which gives the original explanation and historical background of Kossuth's partly unpublished papers on the Confederation of the Danubian nations. The manuscript of Béla Talbot Kardos was awarded a Gold Medal Award from the Cultural Meeting of Hungarians in America, Cleveland, November, 1962. In the following pages we publish some excerpts of Kossuth's more extensive and detailed plans.

(2) "Main Principles of Federalism and Self Government" was written by Louis Kossuth in Kutahia, Asia Minor, June 15, 1850 in the first year after the collapse of the Hungarian Revolution of 1848-49. The original manuscript is in the archives of the Hungarian National Museum, Budapest, No. 342, Kos-

suth's Papers. It was first published in a little-known Hungarian review printed in Transylvania: "Magyar Kisebbség" (Hungarian Minority (Lugoj-Lugos. 1932, by Dr. Imre Deák, p. 376-392, part of which was translated into English in 1944. It was never published in book form but a few copies of the translation-proof sheets—edited by Stephen Gál remained. Other parts have been translated by Béla T. Kardos.

(3) Kossuth wrote this plan while a guest of the Sultan on Turkish soil. Point 3 is antiquated.

(4) Under "counties" Kossuth understands not only administrative subdivisions of a state but suo jure existing self-governing units resembling Swiss cantons. The word "county" may be replaced by "Canton".

(5) Written in Kutahia, Turkey in 1851 during his exile in Asia Minor. This sketch was published in French translation in the book of Irányi-Chassin: "Histoire politique de la Révolution de Hongrie, 1847-1849" (Paris, 1859, Appendix).

(6) Here Kossuth means Louis Napoleon who misused his name and power in order to become Emperor of France.

(7) When Kossuth conceived this plan, the Turkish empire still included the Northern part of the Balkan Peninsula.

Editor's note: Items 8 and 9 on p. 118 seem to be impractical as they exclude the establishment of a permanent federal government and its offices. Instead of a changing seat of government, in a convenient central location a federal Capitol should be built—Kossuth's plan of 1862 did not include the provinces of Austria, therefore Vienna, Prague etc. are not listed in this paragraph.

FEDERATION IN CENTRAL EUROPE

MILAN HODZA

Milan Hodza (1878-1944) was an eminent Slovak politician, head of the Agrarian Party, member of the Czechoslovak cabinet several times between the two world wars, and finally Prime Minister between 1935 and September 22, 1938. He drew up the "Hodza plan" in 1935/36 to avoid the collapse of Czechoslovakia. His plan, however, which included Hungary, Austria and the Danubian countries that Austria was willing to accept to avoid Anschluss was sabotaged by his opponents.

Hodza early recognized that a system of small pseudo-national states was erroneous because, from time to time, they became pawns of foreign powers.

While in London, after the collapse of Czechoslovakia, Hodza elaborated his plan for a **Federation of Central Europe** in a book published in London and New York in 1942. Unfortunately, he died in 1944, and his opponent, President Benes, again pursued the wrong path away from federalism toward ultra-nationalism and great power politics. By this choice he brought about not only his own ruin but, in 1948, a new tragic turning point for all Central Europe toward Stalinism. The following are some highlights from Mr. Hodza's book.

Preface

WAR events in Central Europe obviously fully vindicate the idea of a solidly organized future co-operation of all those eight states which are placed in complete geographic coherence between Russia, Germany and Italy. According to pre-war statistics, that means a space of about 582,000 square miles, i.e., not very much at variance with the total of the territory of the United Kingdom plus France plus Germany plus Italy, which is about 620,000 square miles.

For the overwhelming majority of Central European nations, and at the end indeed for all of them, it is precisely their present condition which provides the evidence that only understanding and co-operation could ever strengthen their security, and that lack of this co-operation has proved to be a critical point with them.

Some of their neighbours may be less enthusiastic about their federation schemes. Still, one day they will have to realize that the small and middle-sized nations of Central Europe mean about one hundred million people in the aggregate. It certainly would be a futile undertaking to attempt to extinguish the national life of one hundred million people, or to drive them away from their homes.

As for Soviet Russia, one day she may be interested in an independent and strong bloc established between herself and Germany. For Western Europe and its permanent and indelible forces, Central Europe means for them the indispensable continental pivot of European security. It has to become in fact much more than the object of tactical interest in an extraordinary situation. It is rather in the light of a durable political interest that not merely the one or the other Central European country will contribute to the building of a new Europe, but that it is the united potential of all of them which is to be one of the indispensable supports of the peace to come.

Central Europe is going to develop in the course of history into not only a geographic, political, and economic unit. It also has its determined artistic and cultural climate. Warsaw, Poznan, Cracow, old Vienna, Prague, Budapest, and recently also Bucharest, Belgrade, Zagreb, Sofia—they all have the merit of shaping cultural values. By their traditional organic growth and youthful temperament, their peoples have already been recognized as able partners in and co-workers for European civilization. The Central European cultural effort is a worthy completion of an All-European cultural mission. For decades past it has been giving Europe new and fresh impulses and subjects originating in the particularities of its soil and soul. Placed in a vast territory between Berlin and Moscow, the Central European nations will have to play a part in European intellectual and artistic production which can only lay a very great stress on their importance.

A Scheme of Constitution

The freedom and security of individuals are to be guaranteed by the State. The freedom and security of small nations can only be guaranteed by their federation.

Is it, however, not too great a loss for a nation to sacrifice its full sovereignty? Since the Greek scientist and Minister, Politis, had the courage to establish what the position of sovereignties is becoming in the progress of a recent political development, discussing sovereignty is no more a crime. So it may be said that a voluntary agreement of putting sovereignties together and of making them a comparatively strong unit means definitely more to a small nation than the permanent danger of losing its sovereignty with no compensation at all.

It is not important to add to the discussion what federation may imply according to the various theoretical definitions. There may be several forms of it, from an organic but very loose co-operation to a federal state. The important point is rather plain. As any federation means an organized co-operation in order to secure for its members the advantages of a great economic and political unit, it is obvious that authorities have to be set up and machinery devised to provide a common administration and legislation for the Commonwealth as far as concerns those matters which are recognized by the Federation as common.

The Constitution. What is to be the constitution of a Central European Commonwealth?

It is tempting, indeed, when adopting this ambitious title to think of imitating the British model as well. It would be a mistake, however, to look at foreign models. And it would be another and a worse error to neglect the special circumstances in which the British Commonwealth emerged from world history, not to speak of the oceans which divide its constituent parts and necessarily compel them to use the fullest possible autonomy. Constitutions have to rise out of their own soil and out of their own historic, economic, and psychological conditions. Central Europe is undoubtedly a special case. What it may accept from the classic British models is rather the *animus rerum gerendarum.* A spontaneous self-decision and expediency are the primary requisites of legal constructions. Central European co-operation may be enrooted in common purposes. It will be reinforced by very many historic affinities. Its ability to conduct its affairs will be increased by some common features of social and political differentiation as mentioned in the fourth chapter of this book. Spontaneous self-decision offers the basis of a constitution which in a cast-iron framework will have to express the goodwill to co-operate for the sake of national and European security.

So the independent and reconstructed countries will have to set up a Federal Treaty establishing common affairs and the mutual obligations by virtue of which their own constitutions are modified by transmitting the administration of those common affairs to the Federal Government.

Political practice has to reckon with psychological obstacles, and in some cases should accept temporary stages of federation, provided that these stages are not employed as instruments of obstruction but are accepted as steps in an organic evolution.

The Federal President and the Federal Chancellor. The Federation is to be headed by a Federal President elected first by a conference of national Prime Ministers and subsequently by the Federal Congress for a period of one year. The President has to appoint the Federal Chancellor and the members of the Government as well as the chiefs of army administration. He himself is the supreme Chief of the Army. His privilege and duty are to decide upon the resolutions of the Federal Congress if disputed by the Federal Government or by the majority of any national representation.

Customs union; common currency; finances; commercial policy; defense; foreign affairs; federal law; communications; co-operation of trade unions and professional associations. A Central European Federation has to be based upon a customs union admitting interior tariffs for standard articles for a period of not longer than five years. Agricultural produce, the critical item of Central Europe, is to be dealt with by marketing regulations. A common currency has to be established. Defence and international policy are common affairs. This implies that the following affairs should be conducted by a Federal Government:

1.) *Finances*, embracing all affairs connected with common currency as well as with budgeting Federal affairs. The revenue from certain definite taxes is to be reserved for the Federation by Federal Congress and by national legislative bodies. A Federal Bank has to be subordinated to the Federal Finance Minister. Fifty percent of the national Post Office Savings Banks have to be administered by the Federal Bank.

2.) *International Trade* may require planning in some branches of production, in order to avoid over-production and to facilitate marketing policy. Planning requires special agreements with national governments while international trade has to be fully reserved for a Federal Minister of Economics.

3.) A Minister of Federal *Foreign Affairs* has to concentrate the whole of diplomacy and external policy.

4.) A Ministry of Federal *Defence* has to concentrate all branches of military administration.

5.) A Ministry of *Communications* and *Posts* will have to provide for measures designed to align the respective policies of the federated countries. Necessarily, it will have to deal with special Federal means of communication.

6.) and 7.) Special Ministries for *Air* and *Shipping* have to be established.

8.) Considering the fact that the Federation is to be an economic unit, a wide field of *Law* will require a strict co-ordination of the national policies in question. The Ministry of Federal *Law* will also have to deal with Inter-National State's affairs.

The Minority policy of the National States has to be solidly embedded upon the principle of reciprocity. Inter-State arrangements based upon this principle should be compulsory. The respective treaties and their execution have to be put under the protection of the Federal Government and especially under that of its Ministry of Law.

9.) A Federal Ministry of *Co-operation* should foster by every means open to governmental power an effective fellowship of all national professional associations recognized by law. Effective provisions for raising standards of living and for dealing with labour conditions will have to be a prominent joint matter of the Federal Government and the professional organizations.

Federal Ministers with portfolio; National Ministers without portfolio. All federated nations have to be represented in the Federal Government by Ministers of their nationality without special portfolio.

The Federal Government is headed and led by the Federal Chancellor, who is responsible to the Federal President.

The Federal Ministers are appointed by the Federal President on the proposals of the Federal Chancellor to whom the owe responsibility. The Federal Ministers without portfolio are to be proposed and appointed by the respective national governments and they owe responsibility to those governments as well as to the Federal Chancellor.

The Federal Ministers with portfolio have to be assisted by Under-Secretaries of State belonging to all federated nations.

In staffs, nationals of all federated countries have to be appointed in the ratio of population proportion.

Federal Congress. Control over the Federal Government's budgeting and legislation concerning Federal affairs is exercised by the Federal Congress of which the members are appointed by a two-thirds majority in the national parliaments, in the proportion of one member to one million inhabitants.

The function of Federal Ministers is incompatible with Congress membership.

The duration of membership of Congress is identical with that of the respective national parliaments, which, however, are entitled to replace Congress-men at their convenience.

The official language of the Congress is to be decided by a two-thirds majority of its members. For individual speeches, limited to fifteen minutes, each member is entitled to use his own national language. These speeches are to be interpreted simultaneously into the official language by official interpreters appointed by the Congress Presidency.

The Presidency of Congress consists of the President and as many Vice-Presidents as are necessary for the representation of the nationals of all federated countries.

The presence of all members at all sittings is compulsory.

Committees are to be set up for all Federal affairs to prepare legislation and the decisions of Congress.

Members' salaries have to be determined by Congress.

Statute and procedure for the Congress have to be settled with a view to directing its discussions in an objective and dignified way.

The permanent seat of the Federation and its Congress and Government is to be settled by the Congress.

The decisions and legislation of the Congress are definitive. They have to be put into operation by the Federal Government unless the Federal Chancellor re-submits them within a fortnight to the Congress for reconsideration. In the event of Congress's refusing to reconsider its decision within a month, the Federal Chancellor may submit the matter to the Federal President whose finding will be final and definite. The same procedure applies to a decision of Congress when the protest of the two-thirds majority of any national group has been lodged against it.

The Federal constitution set up by Congress has to be endowed and promulgated by the federated parliaments.

Secession; Supreme Court; Citizenship. Secession from the Federation is not admissable unless the constitution be modified accordingly.

A Supreme Court has to decide upon constitutional questions raised by the Federal or any national Government or Ministry.

Citizenship of any national state implies Federal citizenship, valid in all states of the Federation.

The official language of the Federal administration, as far as the internal service of Federal affairs is concerned, is identical with that of Congress. Federal administration in federated countries, however, has to be performed only in the respective national language and only by the respective nationals in Federal services. For Federal staffs and definite categories of employees, knowledge of the official language of the Federation is obligatory from the third year of the Federation onwards.

Fundamental principles aiming at strong unity in common affairs. It must be emphasized that the items put forward in this sketch of the constitution can only point out the leading principles upon which a system of federation law has to be constructed. Setting up these principles, however, may offer full evidence that the suggestion advocated here does not demand a loose co-operation, but a strong union of those national energies in which the freedom and prosperity of Central Europe have to be embedded.

These principles are not in full accordance with precedents such as the British Commonwealth of Nations, or the U.S.A., or Switzerland, nor do they follow the lines laid down by many outstanding Western European authors. All these writers, including a number of experts, have the great merit of tackling the problem with the methods of conscientious scientists. They are constructing a wide, strong and useful basis for discussion. My suggestions, supported by some practical experience, may just be a contribution to the abundant material presented by them.

As to practical precedents, they can have the value of instructive examples only. The mechanical transplanting of constitutions into different circumstances would lead to failure. As I have said, constitutions have to emerge out of the particular historic, political and psychological conditions of those whom they are to serve.

This consideration may explain why a sort of Central European "Real Union" should be preferred to a loose connection similar to the British Commonwealth. Central Europe is a coherent territory on the Continent while the British Commonwealth presents itself as an ocean empire of world dimensions.

Why a Congress of national delegates, not immediately direct elections? None the less, one could hardly suggest even for the geographic unit of Central Europe a parliamentary representation directly elected by the people of the federated countries. Without at present mentioning some politico-psychological handicaps which may disappear after a certain period of closer collaboration, there is good reason for building up the Federal parliament upon national delegations. There is hardly to be found on a comparably small territory a more mixed variety of suffrages and ballots than those of eight pre-war countries of Central Europe. And what suffrages some of them were and are! And what ballots! One might describe some of them rather as ways and means of concealing the people's political opinions and desires than of expressing them. An official arrangement will have strictly to respect national self-government and also in electioneering machinery. But a direct election of Federal M.P.s certainly could not be complicated by a sort of eightfold ballot. We have just to accept these facts and hope that Central Europe will, as soon as possible, get rid of what may involve a diminution of those national democratic forces from which the Federation will have to derive its vitality. In point of fact, Federal Congress will have to consist of national delegates appointed, in due proportion, by the national parliaments and each national state will have to be represented in the Federal Congress by not less than ten and not more than fifteen members.

Parliamentary "wire-pulling" to be avoided. The constitutional position of the Federal executive requires the most careful consideration. If it is made dependent upon the Federal Congress it may be doomed to lose time in that *jeu parlementaire* which can be prevented only by a strong parliamentary democracy gaining its forces from either its tradition or its cast-iron ordered discipline. Both of them require time to come to full strength. An organic evolution of Central Europe will certainly be apt to lead to this ambitious democratic goal. At present, however, federation itself is more important than the range of power of a new parliament. In the difficult first years of its functioning, it could hardly fail to embarrass the indispensable dynamism of the Federal Government. Central Europe may appreciate the fact that the Government of the U.S.A. also enjoys a great measure of independence of Congress and Representatives.

Incompability of Congress membership with posts in Federal administration may offer another guarantee of the disinterested objectivity of Congressmen as far as their attitude towards the Front Bench is concerned.

Federal official language. There is one suggestion to be considered very carefully indeed. This is the urging of a Federal official language and its obligatory knowledge by those employed in Federal administration. This certainly means the obligatory learning of a foreign language. Astonishing as it may seem to anyone belonging to a great nation, it nevertheless seems unavoidable. The army, communications, national trade and also very many ramifications of intellectual work and leadership should never be handicapped by an inconvenience as petty as the necessity to make oneself understood. Oppressed peoples hate learning the language of the oppressor. Free nations, however, seeking national advantages in co-operation, and abandoning for this purpose a measure of their former sovereignty, will assuredly regard a special Federal language not as a nuisance, but as an advantage.

As far as learning languages is concerned, most Central Europeans know at least one world language. Why should they not continue this tradition by getting familiar with that world language, very probably the usual diplomatic language, which their Federation may one day endorse? Languages have to help men in communicating with, not dividing, each other.

Embedding the Federation in deep and wide layers of the national masses. An explanation may be useful to clarify the function of a Ministry of Co-operation. Political systems and federations would prove futile efforts if they were doomed to live on the surface of an administrative and legislative mechanism only. The Central European Federation has to be the bulwark of the racial and social security of its peoples. So the stability of its political organization requires that it should be founded in the deepest strata of the nations which it has to unite for a common work and a common fate. A real federation has to embark upon a precisely organized intrinsic co-operation of the peoples concerned. That means that all national organizations recognized by public law have to set up Federal centres. There they have to meet each other, seeing eye to eye and joining their valuable energies for what is a common purpose. All Chambers of Commerce, Industry, and Agriculture, workers' Trade Unions and all sorts of co-operatives, the professional associations of all vocations, such as the men and women of law, technical and medical services, science, journalism and education—they all have good reason to unite in co-operation. There is hardly a single field of human activity so indifferent as to be ignored by a federation which seeks the support of all the creative forces of those nations which expect it to provide for their moral and economic progress. All these associations are and remain as a matter of course; but to increase their efficiency, to assure for themselves the advantages of great entities, they also will find it useful to launch federations of their own national organizations. Like any human institution, a commonwealth of nations also requires Men apart from Measures. It must not throw the task of and the responsibility for its efficiency upon the shoulders of its Ministers and high officials. It has to be the organized co-operation of the lasting forces of its nations. This is the reason why a responsible federal government has to deal with it. No doubt national forces will frequently endeavor to reach federal co-operation through individual initiative as they have always done. But why not foster a combination of individual effort by governmental power? We will allow no part of public life to fail when an accumulation of the whole national potential has to make the Federation a living organism of creative initiative, of creative force and of creative effect.

Epilogue

Referring to the Turkish victory over Hungary in 1526 and its sequels, a great British historian says: "It has been one of the standing misfortunes of Europe that the Poles, the Czechs and the Magyars have never been able to devise any durable form of political co-operation ... From Bohemia, the richest and most civilized of these three monarchies, Poland was estranged by religion, Hungary by religion, race and language alike ... The conjunction of Hungary and Bohemia ...might have imposed a final limit upon the incursions of the Turk ..."

The British historian refers to the religious conflicts and power policy which separated the two realms and their leaders. The Polish Jagellons were to undertake the task of uniting the forces of half Central Europe, but failed; and it was Habsburg who was going to build up his sway over the nations which were not able to unite their forces to erect upon this union their national freedom.

Yet, in the first period of Habsburg domination up to the end of the seventeenth century, European Christian civilization was safeguarded against Turkish aggression by Danubian Austria, supported at the critical moment by Poland. Now there is no Turkish aggression to be resisted. Now Liberty is to be defended on a larger scale than ever before.

Is it too daring a speculation to suggest that a Central Europe has to be constituted as a vanguard contributing a worthy share to the defense of Liberties by completing the architecture of European security?

DANUBIAN FEDERATION

F. O. MIKSCHE

Statesmen in Favor of a Federal Solution

NO responsible statesman has ever questioned the importance of unity in the Danube Basin for European stability. The following quotations have been selected from the large number of declarations on record:

"The Austrian Monarchy is a combination of ill-assorted States. Such a power is necessarily weak, but it is an adequate bulwark against the barbarians and a necessary one. In the future the Habsburg Empire will stand with its back towards Europe and its front to the East, thus protecting Western civilization from the aggression of Russia."

(Talleyrand to Napoleon, on the 17th October, 1805, before the battle of Austerlitz.)

"What should be put in that space in Europe which is occupied now by the Austrian State, from Tyrol to the Bukovina? New formations in that region would be of a permanently revolutionary character . . ."

(Bismarck, in 1866, on the eve of the Peace of Nikolsburg.)

"If Austria did not exist she would have to be invented. The disintegration of the Austrian State into small republics would be an invitation to German and Russian imperialism."

(Frantisek Palacky, Czech historian, in 1848. Palacky is generally considered in Bohemia to be the 'Father of the Czech nation', but is unfortunately less famous in the West than T. G. Masaryk.)

"The other possible course for the Peace Conference of 1919 would have been to decide that this well-balanced economic territory, with its unified system of money and credit and communications, should remain an entity formed from components enjoying national autonomy within a federal constitution."

(The late Dr. Karl Renner, President of Austria, in the American quarterly review, **Foreign Affairs**, July, 1948.)

"A federation would considerably improve conditions. It would be within the strategic triangle of Europe formed by Budapest, Vienna and Prague. It would combine those nations living in the Danubian Basin formed by the Carpathians, the Sudeten Mountains and the

Alps. Only by solving the Danubian problem can the peace of Europe be established."

(The late Pál Teleki, Prime Minister of Hungary, in a message on the eve of his suicide on the 2nd April, 1941. See **Transylvania**, by L. Cornish, published in Philadelphia in 1947. p. 166.)

"A federalized Central Europe is one of the absolute necessities of a new post-war order. It is the only possible organization which in that region can preserve the principles of national and individual liberty and ordered freedom."

(The late Dr. Milan Hodza, Prime Minister of Czechoslovakia in 1938, in his book: **Federation in Central Europe**, London, 1942.)

"Federalism honestly applied is in the interest of Czechs, and Hungarians, Austrians and Slovaks. It is one of their most vital interests. Benes' and Masaryk's democracy broke down because it was not a Christian democracy but a purely mechanical one."

(Peter Privadok, Secretary General of the Slovak National Council, in **Hungaria**, 11th January, 1952.)

"The second cardinal tragedy was the complete break-up of the Austro-Hungarian Empire by the treaties of St. Germain and Trianon. For centuries this surviving embodiment of the Holy Roman Empire had afforded a common life, with advantages in trade and security, to a large number of peoples none of whom in our own times had the strength or vitality to stand by themselves in the face of pressure from a revivified Germany or Russia."

(Winston Churchill, **The Gathering Storm**, London, 1946.)

"It may be that closer relations among the Danubian States will once again emerge as a stabilizing influence in this part of Europe. The collapse of the Austro-Hungarian Empire was a calamity of peace. If the countries that formed it could one day find some arrangement that would allow them to work together again in happy association, how welcome this would be."

(Anthony Eden, in the **New York Times**, 6th October, 1950.)

"The spirit of federalism, the future organization of the world in political respect, will play an important role. In the same measure it safeguards the natural and healthy life of human communities in bringing about the greatest welfare of all mankind. I wish you great success in your labour and God give you light and assistance."

(Pope Pius XII, to the members of the Congress of World Federalists, held in Rome, April, 1951.)

"In America and elsewhere it was hard to convince people that it would be necessary to break up Austria-Hungary. Austria was generally looked upon as a counterpoise to Germany, as a necessary organization of small peoples and odds and ends of peoples, and as a safeguard against balkanization. I feared that we might achieve nothing if the war ended quickly. If it were protracted we might have more time for propaganda."

(T. G. Masaryk, **The Making of a State**. London, Allen & Unwin, 1929.)

Federalism in Multinational Regions

There have been many changes in the Danube Basin since 1918, but the problems of the area are still basically the same. Experience has shown that small sovereign states soon become fiercely antagonistic in regions where the peoples are intermingled and the political frontiers do not coincide with the ethnical ones; also, they are frequently used as pawns in the game of Great Power rivalry. In a multinational area it is difficult to define the territory of a people, and the inevitable claims and counterclaims between non-cooperating states in such an area lead to irredentism, border disputes, forced assimilation, and the massacre and deportation of thousands of innocent victims—millions in the recent cases of Poland and Czechoslovakia. International anarchy reigns until a Great Power intervenes and "creates order". In the collision between democracy and nationalism the latter, unless checked by federalism, overpowers and destroys the former. Democracy alone is not a sufficient safeguard against excessive nationalism, and may even multiply its evils by misusing majority rule; in fact democracy usually resorts to majority rule in the interest of one people in multinational areas divided into sovereign states, and at the turning point, when the oppressed minorities revolt it becomes a dictatorship. Consequently the nationalistic form of democracy not only destroys the cultural life of the common homeland and plunges millions of its peoples into misery, it also destroys its own political system and opens the way for the intervention of foreign powers. All this was clearly illustrated by the case of Czechoslovakia, which might properly be considered a prototype of such developments. Even democratically-minded Czech statesmen, because of their antifederalist nationalism, agreed with the expulsion of millions of their fellow citizens, an act which violated the basic principles of democracy.

Before 1918 Czechs and Sudeten Germans shared the government of Bohemia, and in Slovakia the Hungarians dominated the Slovaks; after 1919 Czechs secured the dominant positions in both Bohemia and Slovakia, and held them until 1939, when the minorities revolted and Slovakia became independent. After the war, in 1945, the Czechs returned to power and violently expelled the non-Slavic minorities, the principal sufferers being the 3.3 million Sudeten Germans. This expulsion of the most anti-Russian elements of the population made the subsequent seizure of power by the communists, in 1948, much more easy than it would otherwise have been; and led to the shackling of the Czech people in the chains of a new slavery. In Central Europe small sovereign states are and always will be unable to guarantee the rights of national and religious minorities, which can only be secured by sincere acceptance of the principle of federation. The promises of exiled statesmen that this will not be so in the future cannot be trusted; the system is faulty, and even politicians who are liberal and benevolent in outlook are subject to the pressure of nationalistic public opinion and are almost driven to commit injustices, whereas only justice can ensure peace. The freedom and security of small nations can only be guaranteed by their inclusion in a federation which confers common citizenship on all its inhabitants.

It must be emphasized that an attempt to organize a Central European federation on too big a scale would be a mistake which could easily end in frustration and failure. A federation stretching from the Baltic to the Black Sea and the Adriatic could not be expected to have the necessary stability, because the widely differing peoples inhabiting the region—Poles, Latvians, Lithuanians, Czechs, Hungarians, Slovaks, Croats, Serbs, etc.—have no common historical, economic, cultural, psychological or geographical background, but there is reason to believe that something of this sort is in the minds of the Poles. It may be, however, that Poland will one day have serious difficulties—with Germany over the Oder frontier line, and with the Ukrainians over East Galicia. These matters do not concern the peoples of the Danube Basin, but if their countries entered into a federation with Poland they would inevitably become involved in them. Even under the Habsburg Monarchy the Polish provinces were to a great extent isolated, because they were separated from the Danube Basin by the Carpathians, and the two regions had little in common either economically or culturally. Another important reason for not attempting federation on too large a scale in the first place is the probability that a federation which included Poland would not be joined by Austria. For economic reasons Austria, as it was fashioned in 1919, cannot remain independent for very long and must eventually either join a federation or enter into a new Anschluss with Germany, and if the Germans got back to Vienna the political order of the entire Danubian region would be jeopardized, and German pressure on the whole of South Eastern Europe, especially the Balkan Peninsula and Rumania, would become overwhelming. Only the inclusion of Austria in a Danubian federation would avert the danger of such developments, which could not fail to have an adverse effect on relations between Germany and the Western nations, particularly France. There are strong reasons for believing that some Polish politicians are trying to persuade the Americans that a new Anschluss should be tolerated as compensation to Germany for the loss of her Eastern territories; but Germany needs the sparsely inhabited agricultural territories behind the Oder, not Alpine rocks, to relieve the pressure of surplus population in her Western regions and solve the problem of food production, which is the cause of her present excessive dependence on industrial exports.

How Federation Can Be Achieved

The problem of creating a Central European federation can only be solved in one way, by setting up a limited federation in an area where the conditions are favorable, which would act as a nucleus to which neighboring nations would in time adhere. The regions inhabited by the Austrians, Czechs, Hungarians and Slovaks, which are geographically, culturally, psychologically and economically complementary, provide the most favorable conditions for the initial federation. It is a historical fact that these nations united against the Turkish danger in the year 1527, maintained their union until it was destroyed by the Peace Treaties of 1919/20. Both before and after 1919 it was the narrow nationalism and economic selfishness of the ruling political cliques rather than the sentiments of the masses that fostered discord, hatred and oppression; the people were always more disposed to be cooperative than their leaders cared to admit.

There is no irreconcilable antagonism between Hungarians, Slovaks, Austrians and Czechs; *trouble begins only when the Czechs call themselves 'Czechoslovaks'*. It is the support still given by the West to the idea of a Czechoslovak State that complicates the situation in Danubian Europe, and once this support is withdrawn the problem will be much simplified. There are several important reasons why this matter should receive serious consideration. The majority of the Slovaks will never willingly accept their former position or anything resembling it, and without them there can be no Czechoslovakia. The few Slovak emigrants in the West who advocate the idea of a unified Czechoslovakia do not represent the views of the Slovak people, at least 80 per cent of whom are fanatically anti-Czech. For the Hungarians the Czechoslovak State represents Czech hegemony in the Danube Basin, and the Austrians also regard it with great hostility. Czechoslovakia does not fit naturally into the framework of the Danube Basin, and can only be kept in place by force.

Although there can be no question of making political decisions contrary to the freely expressed wishes of the peoples affected, it should not be too readily assumed that public opinion is always right. The results of plebiscites and other devices for measuring opinion are often swayed by passing passions, and decisions made under the stress of emotions are seldom wise or durable. Public opinion is largely the creation of propaganda, and propaganda could do an immense amount of good in the Danubian region, if it aimed at canalizing the will of the peoples toward a natural solution of their problems. If they were able to express an opinion today the majority of Austrians and Hungarians would certainly favor a federal solution; and so would the Slovaks, without whom there can be no Czechoslovak State. *Exiled politicians claim that the entire Czech people favors the Czechoslovak conception, but this is not true, it is only popular in certain intellectual and middle class circles which represent only a tiny minority; the great majority of industrial workers and peasants are, if anything, indifferent.* The reconstruction of Czechoslovakia would merely satisfy the ambitions of a handful of Czech nationalists, and it is to be hoped that no one will assume on their behalf the responsibility for reviving past conflicts in the Danube Basin. Even if the Czechs were solidly in opposition the projected federation would still correspond with the wishes of the great majority of the Danubian peoples, because the Austrians, Hungarians and Slovaks together total 22 million, against only about 6.5 million Czechs.

If the West really wants to remedy its past mistakes it cannot begin too soon.

To sum up: *There are no differences between Austrians on the one hand and either Czechs or Slovaks on the other, and the Hungarian-Czech and Czech-Slovak antagonisms would disappear if the West ceased to support the idea of a Czechoslovak State.* The following problems would then remain to be settled by the Danubian nations:

1.) The frontier question between Slovakia and Hungary. Within the framework of a federation this would be a matter of settling an internal line of demarcation, rather similar to that between two cantons in Switzerland, and it should not be difficult to agree on a division which placed the majority of inhabitants of each nationality under the administration of their compatriots.

2.) The problem of Ruthenia, or the Sub-Carpathian Ukraine. The northern frontier of a Danubian federation can only lie along its natural line, the Carpathians, if Ruthenia is included in the federation. This region belonged to Hungary for a thousand years, and was inhabited by 450,000 Ukrainians, but the Treaties of 1919/20 gave it to Czechoslovakia. A promise of provincial autonomy for Ruthenia within the Czechoslovak State was broken by the Prague government. By agreement between Prague and Moscow, Ruthenia was ceded to the Soviet Union in 1945, and was added to the Ukrainian S.S.R.; the majority of the original inhabitants have since been banished into the interior of the Soviet Empire.

To attach Ruthenia to the Ukraine—either the present Soviet Ukraine or a future independent Ukrainian Republic—is to bring a historically foreign element into the geopolitically clearly defined Danube Basin, and there are other reasons why it should be part of a Danubian Federation. From the Ukrainian point of view Ruthenia lies on the far side of the almost unscaleable Carpathians and is as difficult to administer as, for example, a Spanish province across the Pyrenees would be for France. The region is economically dependent on Hungary, and for hundreds of years the inhabitants lived by felling timber in the Carpathian forests in winter, floating it down the river Theiss (Tisza) to Hungary in the spring, and working at the Hungarian harvest in the summer; it was a disaster for them when their country was separated from Hungary in 1919.

In the broadest sense the solution of the Danubian problem depends on blending the various peoples in suitable proportions in a federation. The proposed association would comprise about twenty-eight million souls, some twelve million of whom would be Slavs

(Czechs, Slovaks and Ruthenians) and sixteen million non-Slavs (Austrians and Hungarians). In such a federation, consisting of five autonomous countries—Austria, Bohemia and Moravia, Hungary, Slovakia and Ruthenia—the Czechs, Slovaks and Ruthenians would be a guarantee against Pan-Germanism, and the Austrians and Hungarians against Pan-Slavism. Only in this way can the Slavic nations of the Danube Basin be prevented from falling victims once more to Pan-Slav ideology, and the Austrians and Hungarians be diverted from Pan-Germanism. Only a solution on these lines can restore the internal equilibrium of this vital part of Europe, and make it once more a stabilizing factor in international politics. The decisions made after the First World War can no longer be regarded as a satisfactory foundation for the future, and the ideas on which they were based should be abandoned. The order which was then created lasted only twenty years, and its collapse was a main cause of the Second World War and the catastrophic world situation of today. It should not be forgotten that Czechoslovakia was an international calamity throughout her existence, and that any policy based on false historical foundations can only cause new calamities.

It remains to be seen whether the West will continue to support the ambitions of a few exiled politicians who may or may not represent the wishes and interests of their peoples. It is not surprising that many Czech politicians find it easier to make political capital out of the Masaryk legend than to follow an entirely new line, but would it not be advisable to eliminate this myth from Western propaganda and make no more use of names which bear a heavy responsibility fir disrupting the unity of the Danubian region? It is difficult to see how the creation of a new Europe can be assisted by the memory of people whose narrow nationalism had such a baneful influence on the course of history. Politicians of Masaryk's type are very often public dangers, for they rouse peoples to revolt and then fail through weakness to guide the forces they have conjured up in a suitable direction. A new spirit is needed, and the entire Central European problem must be settled on a basis of "what is right?" and not "who is right?"

The creation of a Central European Federation would naturally be beset by many difficulties. It would be necessary for Austria to be raised to a more important position than she has occupied since 1919, which would greatly influence the future of the entire Danube Basin. Austria is the only Danubian country which is relatively free, and Vienna is one of the most important advanced posts of the West in Central Europe, but she will only be able to carry on the fight against Bolshevism on the one hand and Pan-Germanism on the other, if she is granted a greater measure of justice than she received under the 1919 Treaty of St. Germain. The Western Powers would be well advised to base their future policy in the Danubian region on Vienna, and not on a few discredited exiled politicians.

The often repeated argument that the partition of Czechoslovakia would increase the dislocation in the Danube Basin is unconvincing if it is remembered that such a partition is an essential prerequisite for the creation of a larger political organization. The restoration of the unity of the Danube Basin would not hinder eventual federation of the whole of Europe, on the contrary, it would facilitate it. From whatever viewpoint the problem is regarded, the establishment of a Danubian Federation appears to be the essential first step which must be taken toward the future political reorganization of Central Europe. If Mr. Eden's words: "The collapse of the Austro-Hungarian Empire was a calamity for peace. If the countries that formed it could one day find some arrangement that would allow them to work together again in happy association, how welcome this would be ..." were seriously meant the present policy must be abandoned and a new one adopted.

Political actions should be judged by their results and not by the nationality of those responsible for them, and usually it is at least a generation before the true nature of these results becomes apparent. Viewed from this distance in time it is obvious that Masaryk's "liberation" led to the Balkanization of Central Europe, and that the Treaties of 1919 created a situation incomparably worse than the one they were supposed to remedy. These may seem to be strange words for a Czech to write, but no better ending could be devised for this study than the wise words of another Czech, the famous historian Frantisek Palacky: "If Austria did not exist she would have to be invented."

MAP 2
THE SOLUTION OF THE DANUBIAN PROBLEM

The proposed solution would associate about 28 million souls, some 12 million of whom would be Slavs (Czechs, Slovaks and Ruthenians) and 16 million non-Slavs (Austrians and Hungarians), in a federation consisting of five autonomous countries — Austria, Bohemia and Moravia, Hungary, Slovakia and Ruthenia. The Slav elements would be a guarantee against Pangermanism, and the non-Slavs against Panslavism.

145

REGIONAL FEDERALISM OR A NEW CATACLYSM

MIROSLAV LAZAROVICH

The Great Central European Dilemma

Comparison of the historical-chronological tables I and II reveals that: 1.) The most outstanding statesmen, political thinkers, poets, representative men of those nations, when free to speak and write, favored development of self-government and close cooperation (confederation or federation) between the Central European nations. 2.) Yet throughout the last hundred and fifty years authoritarian governments, assisted by military intervention of one or more great powers, have blocked the fulfilment of these hopes as expressed by the representative men.

These nations, however, with their limited freedom were not entirely blameless victims of historical tragedies. Some of their leaders were misled into antagonistic camps by powerful nationalistic forces, autocratic rulers and imperialistic powers (Germany, France, Russia, etc.). Such actions distorted their own lives and evoked hypernationalistic, violent or micro-etatistic dreams among their people which were in turn exploited by outside powers.

Historical Periods: Uniting and Dividing Forces

The first great historic fact of Central European existence was the *conversion to Christianity* of all the Danubian and Baltic nations between 800 and 1000 A.D. This common heritage cannot be overlooked even today by any "ideology". Christian kings formed the larger historical units out of many warring tribes. Feudalism, which might be called the age of "feudal confederations" followed between 1000 and 1800 A.D. Defense of the area made the evolution of a warrior class necessary which consisted of the nobility and dynasties.

There were some centuries in which the difference between Western and Eastern Byzantine Christian nations, later the split between Catholics and Protestants, weakened the unity of the Central European area was not developed into a "large Switzerland". Most of the states-the Polish King Jan Sobieski came to the help of the other nations in the Habsburg empire, the Turkish invaders were finally driven out. With the liberation of Vienna in 1683, the whole area—with the exception of the Balkans—was liberated from the Turks. During the Habsburg rule in the 17th and 18th centuries, the multinational empire including the somewhat more constitutional Hungary developed to a higher cultural and economic level than the areas South and East of it.

Historical Evolution and Modern Turning Points

From the end of the 18th century, the Baroque-feudal empire of the Habsburgs committed several fatal mistakes that caused later the dissolution of the empire:

a.) They refused to grant liberal, constitutional self-government to the people and clung too long to the authoritarian police state methods of the *ancien régime*. The continental European dynasties closed their eyes to the new demands of the age.

The important turning point of modern history was 1776, the year of the American Declaration of Independence and that of the publication of Adam Smith's work *The Wealth of Nations*, the Bible of liberalism. Invention of the steam engine a few years previously (1769) signalled the beginning of the "industrial age". 1789 brought both, the French Revolution, and the American *federal* Constitution, a model of federalism and self-government. During the following century, especially those countries with a Protestant majority: England, Holland, the Scandinavian countries, Switzerland, developed a democratic self-government and a modern political life *without revolutions*. Today they enjoy the highest standard of living in Europe.

The dynasties of the Bourbons, Habsburgs, Hohenzollerns and Romanovs opposed modern evolution. They clung desperately and sometimes tyrannically to their baroque authoritarianism, aristocratic and semifeudal political structure which could only be liquidated by wars and revolutions. This process was long and painful, interrupted at times by a return to reactionary totalitarian regimes: Napoleonism, Fascism, Communism that brought the armies of foreign powers to Central Europe. (Table II)

b.) The Habsburgs made the great mistake of forming a military alliance with Germany against Russia in 1879. By this act they bound the peoples of the entire area to Germany in wars with Russia, bringing them into opposition also to the powerful nations of the West, the allies of Russia: France, England and later, America. Subsequently, the Danubian nations were drawn into the foreign great power struggles, into two world wars in which their lands were ravaged, victimized and finally Balkanized against their own will.

c.) Another error of the Habsburg era was that the multi-national area was not developed into a "large Switzerland". Most of the states-

147

men and political thinkers (Table I) favored peaceful cooperation of *many nations* in the form of (con)-federation. Some even prepared elaborate and detailed plans[1] and principles for such a federal organization; e.g., the Hungarian *Kossuth*,[2] *Eötvös* and *Jászi*, the Rumanian *Popovici*,[3] the Austrian *Renner*,[4] the Slovak Hodza and many others (Table I). Even Professor Tomás Masaryk developed a plan to transform the Habsburg empire into a "monarchic Switzerland" up to 1915. The Czech E. Benes published his doctoral thesis in Paris (1908) in which his central theme was a "federalized Austria.[5] But Vienna and especially the Emperor Francis Joseph I withstood all attempts to change the Dual Monarchy into a multi-national federal system. His rigid stand was supported by short-sighted political programs that denied equal rights to *all* nationalities.

Super-nationalist Politicians in Power Are Slow to Accept Federalism

The otherwise liberal Hungarian statesman Lajos Kossuth, as governor, made the mistake of proclaiming, in 1848/49, a centralized and independent Hungarian national state in a multi-national Carpathian area. Later, however, he recognized the error and while in exile, following Russian intervention, he worked out a detailed plan for a confederation of the Danubian nations.

In 1867, one hundred years ago, Hungarian and Austrian statesmen established an interesting system of federation between Austria and Hungary which became a reality and existed for fifty years up to 1918. This was a peaceful half century for Central Europe. It formed a "Common Market" without internal customs, enjoyed an excellent gold-silver currency, freedom of communication over a large area where the railway system and navigation were well developed. The area became culturally and economically superior to the neighboring Balkans and Russia. Its weakness consisted, however, in the predominance of German-Austrians and Hungarians, the refusal to modernize the semifeudal political structure and denial of extending it to the Slavs and other nationalities (Trialism, etc.).

The excellent Nationality Law of 1868 written by Ferenc Deák and József Eötvös in Hungary which was a masterpiece that might have transformed the counties into Swiss-type cantons was sabotaged by succeeding statesman such as Minister presidents Kálmán and István Tisza. In the Austrian part of the Monarchy, the Pan-Germans who relied on the support of nearby Germany, opposed the just demands of the Czechs, Slovenes, Poles and others. Thereby internally weakened, the Dual Monarchy with its fateful alliance with Germany, could not survive World War I. Czarist Russia also fell in 1917. The victorious Western powers, however, yielded to French Minister President Clemenceau's "peace plans" in 1919. Neither Lloyd George[6] nor

Wilson[7] originally favored the destruction and dismemberment of Austria-Hungary. Charles Seymour of Yale University, chief of the Austro-Hungarian Division of the American delegation at the Paris Peace Conference, stated: "The United States and Great Britain would have been glad to create a federation of the Danubian nationalities which, without the vices that had led to the fall of the Habsburgs, might have accomplished the economic integration and preserved the political order, so essential to the tranquillity and prosperity of Southeastern Europe."[8]

The Little Entente Period: 1918-1938

During the last phase of World Was I, after 1917, the Western statesmen accepted solutions presented to them by some Central European politicians who had emigrated to the West. Embittered, these had replaced their former federalist programs with their own national micro-étatism. E. Benes now urged the great powers: "Détruisez l'Autriche-Hongrie" (Destroy Austria-Hungary). This slogan was adopted by the French Premier Clemenceau and became one of the dominant principles of the Paris Peace Conference of 1919. Benes promised that "Czechoslovakia's government would be like that of Switzerland" ("semblable á celui de la Suisse" in his Memoir III). But the promise was not fulfilled when he became leader of the new multi-national state. In a total population of 13 million, Czechs comprised only 6.3 million or 48.4%; with 25% Germans; 16% Slovaks; 9% Hungarians; and the rest divided between the Ruthenians, Poles and others. In Yugoslavia, there were 43% Serbs; in Rumania 67% Rumanians; but in Transylvania there were only 54% Rumanians. Between 1919 and 1938 most politicians in Prague, Belgrade and Bucharest were inclined to overlook the presence of numerous nationalities that, in many parts of the state, formed compact majorities and could not be regarded as second and third class citizens or "minorities" as they were called. The central governments refused to grant them autonomy, not to say federalism "like that of Switzerland" in the newly created states. The danger of allotting millions of other nationalities to the newly created micro-states was foreseen at the Peace Conference for which reason signing of a "Treaty for the Protection of Minorities" was required when accepting, the peace treaties. Some representatives of the newly created states refused to sign it. This "revolt" was led by the Rumanian Bratianu. It was at this point that President Wilson gave his remarkable pronouncement, almost a prophecy on May 31, 1919:

"How can a power like the United States, for example, after the signing of this Treaty, if it contains elements which they do not believe will be permanent, go three thousand miles away across the sea and report to its people that it has made a settlement of the peace of the world? It cannot do so, and yet there underlies all of these trans-

actions, the expectation on the part for example of Rumania and of Czechoslovakia and of Serbia, that if any covenants of this settlement are not observed, the United States will send her armies *to see that they are observed ... In those circumstances is it unreasonable that the United States should insist upon being satisfied that the settlements are correct? Mr. Bratianu suggested that we could not, so to say, invade the sovereignty of Rumania, an ancient sovereignty, and make certain prescriptions with regard to the rights of minorities. But I beg him to observe that he is overlooking the fact that he is asking the sanction of the Allied and Associated Powers for great additions of territory which came to Rumania by the common victory of arms, and that therefore, we are entitled to say: "If we agree to these additions of territory we have the right to insist upon certain guarantees of peace."* (See op. c. footnote 8)

Bratianu was not convinced by Wilson and resigned. Bucharest, not wanting to forfeit new territorial gains, sent another delegate who reluctantly signed both treaties together with the representatives of the other new states. These were organized soon into an alliance known as the Little Entente sponsored by France (1920-38). Yet Bratianu became Minister-President several more times. Although they had accepted the territorial gains, both he and the other statesmen of the Little Entente relegated the treaty on the Protection of Minorities to the archives. In consequence, a flood of petitions were sent to the League of Nations by the various nationalities in Czechoslovakia, Rumania and Yugoslavia.[9] They testified to injustices committed against the millions of national "minorities".

The League of Nations dominated by France proved to be impotent in the field of protecting nationalities.[10] These suffered heavy losses of schools, economic status and language rights, ecclesiastical and other institutions beside the neglect of their vital administrative interests.[11] Failing to be heard in the League of Nations, they turned to their co-nationals beyond their frontiers, e.g., the Hungarians and Germans. After 1927 Hungary (and the Croatians) turned to Italy, while the German minorities turned to the mighty "protector" of the rising Nazi Germány. Hitler used their cause for a pretext to intervene in Central and East European affairs. Following his invasion of Austria, the Danubian nations suddenly became aware of the acute danger facing them. At this point, Professor James Shotwell, of Columbia University, initiated a"Peaceful Change Conference" sponsored by the Carnegie Foundation for International Peace. The conference met in June 1937 in Paris. Many excellent working papers and proposals were submitted favoring a Swiss-type solution for Central Europe (some were presented by the Hungarian Minister President Pál Teleki). But the representatives of the Little Entente continued to resist any peaceful change.

After 1938

The following year, Hitler increased his political pressure on Czechoslovakia in support of the Sudeten Germans. It was too late when President Benes finally offered a "Fourth Plan" on September 5, 1938, to "cantonize the Sudetenland with a system similar to Swiss cantons". It is to be regretted that his plan was not accepted at that time. Hitler and Mussolini were pressing for a Munich conference of the four Great Powers. Here the partition of Czechoslovakia was effected. Subsequently, Hitler's army invaded Central Europe. Then he made a pact with Stalin and Molotov to partition the whole area between Germany and Russia. Within a few years Hitler invaded not only others parts of East Europe but Russia as well. After the Battle of Stalingrad, however, the Red Army with assistance from the West, reversed the course of the war and half of Europe fell to the Soviets, the other half becoming an "Atlantic" sphere of influence.

In the early forties many exiled politicians, i.e. the Czech Benes, the Slovak Hodza, the Hungarian M. Károlyi, the Polish Sikorski and others, worked out again federal regional plans for the post-war years. Before his suicide in April, 1941, the Hungarian Minister President, Pál Teleki, sent messages to his American friends and to his Minister in Washington, that regional federalism in Central and East Europe was absolutely essential.(12) Benes hurried to Moscow in 1943, knowing the consequences of a takeover of Central Europe by Stalin, to make a pact with him. At the insistence of Stalin he discarded all plans for federation and upon his return handed Subcarpathia (Ruthenia) over to Russia as the price demanded for expulsion of the Sudeten Germans and keeping a possible pre-war *status quo*.

Subsequent events, however, exposed Stalin's hunger for much more, namely, a complete takeover of Central Europe. Benes' life ended in tragedy; Pál Teleki, Jan Masaryk committed suicide; Maniu and many others died in prison or were executed; the Rumanian Minister President, Jorga, was killed. The more fortunate politicians escaped to the West. Several million, caught up in the big power struggle, lost their homes, were expelled(13) from their ancestral lands—and the bitter years of the "cold war" began.

Compromise Solutions for Real Peace and Prosperity Demand Some Sacrifice From All Parties

Many knew that perhaps a decade would elapse after the end of World War II before vengeance and hatred would subside sufficiently to seek rational solutions. Now more than two decades have elapsed since the end of hostilities and it is time to bring about a lasting peace to this area without relying on the intervention of foreign military powers. Some sacrifice on the part of all concerned is necessary to move away from untenable positions which military victory had brought about on a transitional basis.

An unjust military position cannot be guaranteed forever. Napoleon came to the conclusion: "It is easier to conquer a territory than to keep it." From the 16th to the 19th centuries a small army with superior weapons was able to conquer large tracts of foreign lands. But England, Spain, Holland, France, the great colonial powers have wisely yielded to the demands of modern times to give up their far-flung conquered territories. The late 19th century efforts toward colonial expansion earned Germany the enmity of England and other powers. Without colonies she now enjoys a greater degree of prosperity than before.

How is revenge to be excluded from Central Europe? The domination of any outside great power in the Central European multinational area causes reaction from other great powers (revenge). On the other hand, when Switzerland was declared neutral in 1815 after Napoleon's unsuccessful attempt to conquer the country, three great powers were effectively divided by a buffer zone consisting of a federated area. Even at the time of Nazism and Fascism, Switzerland retained firmly its status as a neutral, prosperous buffer country.

In Central Europe, the Soviet Union had difficulty first with Yugoslavia (1948-53), then with Hungary (1956) and currently with Rumania, and Czechoslovakia. Because of the unsolved problem of Germany, and remnants of Stalinism, uncertainty and discontent is widespread.

If the area were neutralized, the Soviet Union would have no more difficulties with these nations than it now has with Finland, Sweden and Austria. On the other hand, if the West were asked to sanction the presently dangerous unstable situation in Central Europe and permanently fix the *status quo* at a European Conference on Security, the American Government could well reply with the words of President Wilson quoted above:

"How can a power like the United States after the signing of this treaty, if it contains elements which they do not believe will be permanent, go three thousand miles away across the sea and report to its people that it has made a settlement of peace in the world? Under such circumstances is it unreasonable that the United States should insist upon being satisfied that the settlements are correct?"

One hundred years ago, in 1867, a compromise solution was found in Central Europe, in which both parties of a federalized union brought some sacrifice to gain peace and prosperity. That compromise solution brought fifty years of peace and relative prosperity to Central Europe. Today, a new solution could be worked out that would exclude revenge yet *would coincide with the interests of all Central European nations* beside *that of the interested great powers:* neutralization and "Helvetization" of the are between Germany and Russia. *How long will true self-government and federalism (Helvetization) be hindered by great powers in Central Europe?*

Historical Table I

PLANS AND PRONOUNCEMENTS ON CENTRAL EUROPEAN FEDERALISM PRECEDING IMPORTANT HISTORIC TURNING POINTS

Nationality I. Preceding the Revolution of 1848/49.

French:	Rep. Lherbette, Paris, French National Assembly, July 5, 1848.
Austrians:	Adrian-Werburg, 1841-1847; **Austrian Parliament, Kromeriz,** Nov. 22, 1848; March 6, 1849; **Löhner,** Nov. 1848; Sommaruga, 1848.
Croats:	**Ostrozinski,** Oct. 7-Nov. 5, 1848.
Czechs:	**Czech National Council,** June 7, 1848; **Palacky,** Sept. 1848; Rieger, June 7, 1848.
Hungarians:	**Wesselényi,** 1843, 1849; Kossuth, 1843; **Széchenyi,** 1842, Nov. 27, 1860; F. Deák, 1847.
Poles:	Czartoryski, Jul. Aug. 1830. 1848-1850; Mickievicz, Paris, Feb. 23, 1849; Krasinsky, Apr. 25, 1848; Bystrzonowsky, Oct. 1848.
Rumanians:	**Rumanian National Committee,** May 15-17, 1848; **Barnutiu,** May 16, 1848; Balcescu, May 27, 1849, 1850; Golescu, 1848; Ion Ghica, 1848-1849; Maiorescu, Nov. 16, 1848; Dumitru Bratianu, 1848.
Serb:	Garasanin, 1844.
Slovaks:	**Slovak National Council** of Liptovsky Sv. Mikulás, May 10, 1848; Stur, May 10, 1848; Hodza Sr., May 10, 1848; Safarik, 1848.
Slovene:	Kavcic, 1848.

II. Preceding the establishment of Dualism, 1867

Austrians:	**Beust,** Oct. 1866; Sommaruga, 1867; **Fischhof,** 1861, 1866.
Croats:	Strossmayer, Oct. 15, 1850; Tkalac, June 2, 1848; Sulek, June 1848; Polit-Desancic, 1860-73.
Czech:	**Palacky,** 1865.
Hungarians:	**L. Teleki,** 1849-1861; **Kossuth,** 1850-1865; **F. Deák,** 1850-1876; **Jókai,** 1850-1904; **Eötvös,** 1850-1871; Klapka, 1850, 1861, 1865.
Rumanians:	**Balcescu,** 1849-50; Golescu, 1850.
Serbs:	M. Obrenovic, May, 1859; Stratimirovic, 1865; **Miletic,** 1865-1877.

III. Preceding the Peace Conference of 1919/20.

Austrians:	**Beust,** 7 Nov. 1870/71; **Hohenwart,** Aug. 14, Oct. 23, 1871; Taafe, 1879, 1890; **Fischhof,** 1868-1893; Schuselka, 1871-1886, Fr. Thun, 1898; **Francis Ferdinand** 1905-1914; **Renner,** 1906, 1918; **Emperor Charles-Hussarek,** Oct. 16, 1918; Bauer, 1907; Seipel 1916.
Czechs:	**Palacky,** 1868; **Rieger,** Apr. 1871; **Prazak,** 1871; **Benes,** 1908; **Masaryk,** before 1916; Kramar, 1915.

Croats:	St. Radic, Jan. 5, 1905 and 1918.
Hungarians:	Jászi, 1918; Ady, Nov. 3, 1918; Béla Bartók, Nov. 3, 1918; Zoltán Kodály, Nov. 3, 1918; Babits, Nov. 3, 1918; Kassák, Nov. 3, 1918; D. Kosztolányi, Nov. 3, 1918; Marcel Benedek, Nov. 3, 1918; Schöpflin, Nov. 3, 1918; Rippl-Rónai, Nov. 3, 1918; István Csók, Nov. 3, 1918; R. Vámbéry, Nov. 3, 1918.
Hungarian Communists:	Eugene Varga, later Soviet Chief Economist, Nov. 3, 1918; George Lukács, Marxist aesthetician, Nov. 3, 1918; Lajos Barta, Nov. 3, 1918; Béla Balázs, Nov. 3, 1918; G. Bölöni, Nov. 3, 1918; Fogarasi, Nov. 3, 1918; Andor Gábor, Nov. 3, 1918; Béla Uitz, Nov. 3, 1918.
Rumanians:	Popovici, 1906, 1916, 1918; Stoica, Oct. 26, 1916.
Ruthenians:	Zatkovic, Oct. 26, 1916.
Serbs:	Jasa Tomic, March 1905; Musicky, March 1905; Stojan Protic, Jan. 2, 1909; Savic, 1917.
Slovenes:	Adamic, Oct. 18, 1918.
Englishmen Americans:	Woodrow Wilson, Jan. 8, 1916; Lloyd George, Jan. 5, 1918; General Smuts, Jan. 5, 1918; Stephen Bonsal, April 12, 1919.
Frenchmen:	E. Denis, Oct. 31, 1914.

Organizations:

Common Aims of Independent Mid-European Nations, Oct. 26, 1916.
Ligue pour la Confédération Balcanique. Paris, Jan. 1895.
Interallied Labor and Socialist Conference, Feb. 20, 1918.

IV. Preceding the Peace Conference of 1947.

Americans:	F. D. Roosevelt, Summer, 1941; William Royall Tyler Sr. 1940/41; Dorothy Thompson, 1941; Louis Craig Cornish, 1922, 1925, 1947; Charles Seymour, 1921; J. T. Shotwell, 1945; P. J. Anthony, 1943; Ross J. S. Hoffman, 1944; Sumner Welles, 1944, 1945; C I. Janovsky, 1945.
Englishmen:	Churchill at Teheran, 1943 and War Memoirs; Seton-Watson, Sr. 1943; Seton-Watson Jr., 1943; Macartney, 1939; Phillips Price, Oct. 1943; Christopher Robinson Bart, March 1940; Launcelot Lawton, Jan. 1940; H. A. Procter, May 1940.
Frenchmen:	Tardieu, 1932.
Austrians:	Renner, 1944/46; Coudenhove-Kalergi, 1943.
Czechs:	Ex-president Benes, 1942, London; Necas, 1942; Prchala, Oct. 12, 1945.
Hungarians:	Hantos, 1932; Gratz, 1932; D. Szabó, 1935; Zs. Móricz, 1940; Paul Teleki, 1940; Eckhardt, 1941; Mende, Oct. 1943; Ignotus, Oct. 1943; Rostás, Oct. 1943; Károlyi, Oct. 1943; B. T. Kardos, 1937, 1946; Géza Teleki, 1946; F. Wagner, 1938-.
Poles:	Sikorsky, March 9, 1943; Gross, 1943, 1945; Racinsky, 1946/47.

154

Rumanians:	Gafencu, 1932; Tilea, Nov. 1942; Budeanu, Oct. 1943; Cornea, Oct.
	1943; Cristea, Oct. 1943.
Serbs:	**Gavrilovic**, Oct. 1943.
Slovaks:	Pridavok, 1943; Minister President Hodza, 1935/36, 1942.

V. After the Peace Conference of 1947.

Americans-
Englishmen: Eden, Oct. 6, 1950; Harold McMillan, 1947; S. D. Jackson, Oct. 24, 1951.

Austrians: Coudenhove-Kalergi, July-Aug. 1948; **Renner**, July 1948; **Strausz**-Hupé, Winter, 1950; **R. Wierer**, 1960; Frankenstein, May, 1951.

Albanians: Dosti, April 16, 1951.

Baltic: Sidzikauskas, April 16, 1951; **Pakstas**, April 16, 1951; Blodniak, April 16, 1951.

Bulgarians: Todorov, Feb. 11, 1951; G. Dimitrov, Apr. 16, 1951; Vichegorov, Feb. 11, 1951; Fournadiev, Feb. 11, 1951; Matzankiev, Feb. 11, 1951.

Croats: **Macek**, Feb. 11, 1951, April 16, 1951; B. Radica, Feb. 11, 1951; Jelic, 1951.

Czechs: F. O. **Miksche**, Nov. 1951; **Majer**, Feb. 11, 1951; J. Cerny, 1951; Jar. Hrazsky, 1950; **Ripka**, Nov. 6, 1950, Feb. 11, 1951.

Hungarians: **F. Nagy**, Feb. 11, '51; March '51, Apr. 16, '51, June 21, 22, 1951; B. Varga, Jan. 17, 1951, Apr. 16, 1951; **Jászi**, July-Aug. 1948; **Auer**, Sept. 21, 1948, 1950, 1952; **I. Kertész**, 1947; B. Bessenyey, Jan. 12, '51, Feb. 11, 1951; **Borsody**, Feb. 1949, Sept.-Oct. 1951; Eckhardt, Feb. 11, 1951; **B. T. Kardos**, 1951-1967; Barankovics, April 16, 1951; A. Gellért, Sept. 7, 1951; A. Radvánsky, 1951; Máriaffy, Apr. 1951; Máté, Dec. 18, 1951; Emődy, Sept. 1951; Csicsery-Rónay, June 21, 22, 1951; Kárász, June 21, 22, 1951; Szántó, Feb. 24, 1951; Vince Nagy, Feb. 11, March, Apr. 30, 1951; Pfeiffer, Feb. 11, 1951; Peyer, Feb. 11, 1951; Málnási, 1961/63; Fábián, Feb. 11, 1951; Közi-Horváth, Feb. 11, 1951, June 22, 1951; Kern, Nov. 1949; Géza Teleki, 1951; **B. Szász**, 1929, 1966/67; E. Padányi-Gulyás, 1963; F. Wagner, 1945-.

Poles: Mikolajczyk, April 16, 1951; Seyda, April 16, 1951; Popiol, April 16, 1951.

Rumanians: Popa, Feb. 11, 1951; Costa, Feb. 11, 1951; Ghilezan, Feb. 11, 1951; Visoianu, Feb. 11, April 16, 1951; Radescu, Feb. 11, 1951; Davila, May, 1949, Feb. 11, 1951; Buzesti, May, 1949; Zissu, April 1951; Assan, April 16, 1951; Coste, 1951.

Serbs: Jocic, March, Oct. 1951; Fotic, Feb. 11, 1951; Kosanovic, March, 1951; Pridavok, March, 1948, 1943, Jan. 11, 1952; Pokorny, Dec.

Slovaks: Lettrich, Feb. 11, 1951; Papanek, Feb. 11, 1951; Osusky, Feb. 11, 1951; Pridavok, March, 1948, 1943, Jan. 11, 1952; Pokorny, Dec. 1950; Durcansky, Dec. 1950; Kirschbaum, 1948-1967.

Slovenes: Krek, Feb. 11, 1951, April 16, 1951.
Ukrainian: Korostovec, Spring, 1951.

Organizations:

Slovak National Council, March 1, 1948; Committee of Liberal Exiles, April 16, 1951; **Central-Eastern European Committee,** April 16, 1951; Committee for Eastern European Labor Center in Exile, April 16, 1951; Christian Democratic Union of Central Europe, April 16, 1951; Committee for Eastern and Central Europe of the European Movement, Oct. 1951; **Danubian Club,** London, July-Oct. 1943; **Hungarian Social Democratic Party,** 1943, American Hungarian Reform. Min. Assn. Sept. 10, 1943; **Central European Federal Club,** Oct. 12, Dec. 1945; International Peasant Union, May 8-10, 1950, March 16, 1951; Pope Pius XII, April 1951; **Czech Federalist Democratic Party,** second half of 1951; Hungarian National Council, Feb. 11, 1951; **Memoranda to the Hungarian Peace Delegation of 1946,** 1946/47; American-Hungarian Federation, 1951; Hungarian Peasant Assn. June 21, 22, 1951; Hungarian Smallholders Party, May 8-10, 1950; Liberation Movement of the Voivodina, Oct. 1951; Slovak League of America, May 1951.

Historical Table II

ANTIFEDERALIST, AUTHORITARIAN AND MILITARISTIC ACTIONS
BY GREAT POWERS

that hindered the development of self-government and federalism in
Central Europe.

A. Between 1789 and 1848/49

1789- Suppression of liberal movements by ancien régime police state.

1806-1813: Armed interference in Central and East European countries by **Napoleon.**

1815-1816: **Holy Alliance** created at the **Congress of Vienna** by statesmen of ancien regimes and conservative diplomats. The **status quo** sanctioned by Czar **Alexander I,** King **Friedrich Wilhelm** of Prussia and Emperor **Francis' (Habsburg).**

1810-1848: Era of Chancellor **Metternich,** West-German born statesman; **Sedlnicky,** Austrian police chief (1817-); and Count **Kolowrat,** Austrian Minister of Interior (1825-).

1830-1831: Czar **Nicolas I** and Prince **Pashkievicz,** Russian Chief Commander, suppress the Polish revolution and occupy Warsaw.

1848-1849: Czar **Nicholas I** assists Emperor **Francis Joseph** in suppressing the uprising of Central European nations (Vienna, Prague and Buda-Pest). Governor Kossuth's proclamation of an independent Hungarian national state instead of a confederation of nations for which he later developed a plan in 1850-1865.

B. **Between 1849 and 1867**

1849-1866: Rigid authoritarian governments under Emperor Francis Joseph I; Pillersdorf (1848); Schwarzenberg (1848-1852); A. Bach (1850-1860); and Schmerling (1860-). Centralization was dominant.

C. **Between 1867 and 1918: Dual Federalism of Austria-Hungary**

1871-1879: Count Julius Andrássy opposed extension of federation to the Slavic nations (trialism).

1878: Conferences at San Stefano and Berlin where Balkan affairs were arbitrarily decided. (Bismarck, Andrássy, Gorchakov, Disraeli, etc.)

1875-1890: Hungarian Minister President Coloman Tisza and son, Stephen Tisza, (1900-1918) opposed the demands by other Danubian nations for national autonomy or federalism.

1879: The fatal Zweibund-treaty between the Monarchy and the German empire signed by Andrássy and Bismarck bringing German influence and power policy further into the Danubian, Balkan and Baltic areas; also provoking the Russian-French alliance.

1883-1903: Count Khuen-Hédervára, authoritarian Governor of Croatia.

1885: Bismarck expulses Poles from Prussia.

1888: Wilhelm II; Emperor of Germany, enters his expansionist policies toward the East and Balkans.

1894: Czar Nicholas II enters into a French-Russian Alliance, later prolonged (Aug. 11, 1911).

1897: Meeting of Francis Joseph and Nicholas II in St. Petersburg.

1903: Peter I, King of Serbia, takes over power, asks help from Czar Nicholas II (March 1910).

1906: Serbian Minister President Pashich asks help from Russia.

1908: Austria forces annexation of Bosnia-Hercegovina. Count Aerenthal refuses an international settlement. The Russian Izvolski proposes Russian intervention in Central European and Balkan affairs.

1909: Nikolai Hartwig, Chief of Balkan Division of the Russian Foreign Office, becomes Russian ambassador to Belgrad.

1910: Nikita (Petrovich) assumes title of King of Montenegro.

1911: Aug. 11. Treaty of French-Russian military alliance published.

1912: Aug. 9-16. French Poincaré visits the Russian Czar Nicholas II.

1914: March 10. Military agreement between the Dual Monarchy, Germany and Italy.

1914: July 23. Ultimatum to Serbia after murder of Francis Ferdinand in Sarajevo.

1914: July 25/26. Mobilization in Austria-Hungary and Russia.

1914: Aug. 1. Mobilization in Germany.

D. **Peace of 1919/20 and the following years leading up to World War II**

1919-1920: Peace treaties of St. Germain, Neuilly, and Trianon with Austria, Hungary and Bulgaria masterminded by Minister President Clémenceau, contrary to Wilson's principles of self-determination. Benes,

Bratianu, Pashich "Balkanized" the area into small "national states" with no plebiscites.

1920-1938: Era of the **"Little Entente"** under French leadership.

1920-1938: Czech E. **Benes**, Foreign Minister and later President of Czechoslovakia, developed a centralized state. He did not follow through with his declared intent (1919) of making it "another Switzerland".

1924: Serbian **Pashich** centralized the new state in Belgrade and abolished the federal constitution of the "Kingdom of Serbs, Croats and Slovenes". National and religious minorities were considered second class citizens.

1929: King **Alexander I** and General **Zivkovic** created a military dictatorship in Jugoslavia which brought on the assassination of the king by the Croats.

1920-1940: Rumanian governments headed by General Avarescu, Bratianu, Vaida, Maniu, Iorga, and Goga forced centralization without national autonomies.

1920-1939: Witos, General **Pilsudski**, Beck, Moscicky headed governments in Poland.

1920-1940: Governments under Admiral **Horthy**, especially Minister President Count Bethlen (1921-31) overemphasized irredentism, "revisionism", frontiers, at the expense of social and agrarian reform, industrialization, self-government and good relations with neighboring nations.

1938: March 13. **Hitler** invaded Austria; supported Nazi parties in Hungary, Rumania, Croatia, Slovakia, Sub-Carpathia, etc.

1938: Sept. 29. **Hitler, Mussolini, Chamberlain, Daladier** agreed in Munich to detach the German Sudetenland from Czechoslovakia.

1938: Nov. 2. **Ribbentrop** and **Ciano** determined the frontiers of Slovakia and Hungary in the first Viennese Arbitration Award.

1939: Aug. 23. **Ribbentrop-Molotov** treaty signed in Moscow in the presence of Stalin; partition of Poland and the Baltic states between Germany and the Soviet Union.

1939: Sept. 1. With **Hitler's** invasion of Poland, World War II began.

1940: Aug. 30. Partition of Transylvania by **Ribbentrop** and **Ciano** in the second Viennese Arbitration Award.

1940; Oct. 8. "Training" troops sent to Rumania by **Hitler.**

1941: April 6. Yugoslavia invaded by **Hitler.**

1944: March 19. Hungary occupied by Hitler's army.

1944: Sept. 3. **Red Army** reached the Danube.

E. Peace Treaties of 1947 and Years Following

1941: **American Lend-Lease Act** giving unconditional assistance to **Stalin.**

1945: Conference at **Yalta** dominated by Stalin. The four power zones that later formed the basis of Iron Curtains were established.

1947: **Paris Peace** treaties with Rumania, Hungary and Bulgaria: heavy pressure by **Molotov** under instructions from **Stalin.** Western powers yielded.

1947:	June. Western allied powers moved out of East Europe while the Red Army stayed.
1948:	Stalinist take-over of East European countries: **Rákosi** in Hungary, **Gottwald** in Czechoslovakia, **Gheorghiu-Dej** and **Anna Pauker** in Rumania, **Cyrankiewicz** in Poland, etc.
1948:	**Tito's** break with **Stalin.** Federation with Bulgarian prohibited by **Stalin.**
1956:	Oct.-Nov. Polish and Hungarian uprising. **Khruschev's** military intervention in Budapest.
1959:-	"Liberalization" in Communist regimes. Tendency toward normalizing relations with neighbors; "peace and security" remain an illusion without the consent of interested nations, self-government, neutralization and federation.

(1) A survey of the federal plans before 1918: **Robert A. Kann:** The multinational empire. Nationalism and national reform in the Habsburg monarchy, 1848-1918. New York. 1950. I-II vol. and **Rudolf Schlesinger:** Federalism in Central and Eastern Europe. New York, 1945.

(2) **Talbot Kardos:** From Kosstuh's Unknown Federalist Papers. Publ. in the present volume.

(3) **Aurel Popovici:** Die Vereinigten Staaten von Gross-Oesterreich. Leipzig. 1906.

(4) **Karl Renner:** Der Kampf der Oesterreichischen Nationen um den Staat. Wien. 1902 and 1918.

(5) See chapter "La Lutte pour l'Autriche Fédéral" in **E. Benes,** Le probléme Autrichien et la question Tchéque. Paris, 1908, p. 312.

(6) **Lloyd George:** "Pronouncements in January 1918," and "Memoirs of the Peace Conference." New Haven. Yale Univ. Press. 1939, vol. I, p. 51.

(7) President **Wilson:** Message to Congress January 8, 1918, point 10. Messages to Congress on February 12, 1918, July 4 and September 27, 1918.

(8) **"What really happened at Paris,** Story of the Peace Conference 1918-19". Ed. by Col. E. M. **House** and Charles **Seymour,** New York, Scribner, 1921, p. 214.

(9) The mere titles and subjects of these petitions fill an entire book: H. **Truhart:** Völkerbundpetitionen der Minderheiten. Stuttgart. 1935, p. 180, and several later editions.

(10) **Balogh, Arthur.** L'Action de la Société des Nations en matiére de protection des minorités. Paris, 1937, 186 p.

(11) **Macartney,** Carlile Aylmer: National states and national minorities. London, Oxford Univ. Press. 1934, 553 p.

(12) Teleki's messages were published by Minister John Pelényi in the **Journal of Modern History** (Chicago, June 1964). (See also **Studies** 1966, vol. I, no. 3, p. 36.)

(13) Theodor **Schieder:** The expulsion of the German population from the territory East of the Oder-Neisse line, Czechoslovakia, Rumania, Hungary, Yugoslavia etc. Bonn. 1954-1960. Vol. I-VI.

159

PROBLEMS OF FEDERALISM IN THE DANUBIAN AREA

BÉLA TALBOT KARDOS

Motto: "In the name of God, I invite my Hungarian, Rumanian ad Slav brothers to drop a veil on the past and to hold out their hand towards each other, and to rise as one man in a common struggle for freedom, and to fight all for one and one for all."—Louis Kossuth in the Preface to his *"Plan of a Danubian Confederation,"* 1860.
"A federalized Central Europe is one of the absolute necessities of a new post-war order ... The mistake of Versailles may lie in the fact that these small nations of Central Europe were not authoritatively advised to set up a cooperation which would provide them with the advantages of a great commonwealth able to normalize and stabilize its relations with its neighbors ... This Commonwealth of Central Europe is the suggestion which I am putting forward in this book ... It is the final goal which I have aimed at during my whole political career" ...
Milan Hodza, Prime Minister of Czechoslovakia between 1935-1938 in his book *"Federation in Central Europe."* (London, 1942).

A. Fundamental Considerations.

1.) *The Declaration of Independence of small nations should be followed by a positive decision for free federalization or both independence and liberty will be lost again.*

Many nations have tried to copy the American Declaration of Independence. Lafayette kept a gold framed copy of it in his (French) home. October 1918, Czechoslovakia together with other East European nations promulgated her independence in the historic hall of Philadelphia. Most of the statesmen, however, did not follow the next step which was federalization by acceptance of a well-balanced federal constitution. Without the latter, the freedom and independence of our states would have been lost just as the independence of Czechoslovakia and the other East European states were lost several times. In France the Jacobine revolution proclaimed penalty of death for the advocacy of federalism. As late as 1929 a French citizen appeared before a criminal court at Besancon to defend himself for advocating the federal organization of France (*Le Temps*, June 24, 1929). Yet French democracy was not fully successful with the theory of a centralized national State, "une et indivisible". In the multinational area of Eastern Europe the application of this idea had catastrophical consequences.

Some may even question whether those small states created after the First World War possessed independence at all. Even Czechoslovakia, relatively the most independent among them, was first a French satellite, then broke in two, one an unwilling, the other a more willing satellite of Germany; after 1945 a gradual lapse into Russian dependence followed. With some variation a similar fate befell the other East European nations. It is time to quote the words of Proudhon: "Qui dit liberté, dit fédération, où ne dit rien." (Who says liberty, says federation or does not say anything.)

Switzerland maintained her independence and freedom among the most threatening imperialisms of our day. European politicians realized, under Russian threat, the importance of federal democracy for larger areas, yet they are still unwilling to study either the Swiss or American model more closely. They think the era of federalism can be entered without substantial change in the old pattern of sovereign overcentralized governments.

Bakounine was right when he said: "...aucun Etat centralise, bureaucratique et par-la méme militaire, s'appelant méme république, ne pourra entrer sérieusement et sincérement dans une confédération internationale." (Oevres: Federalism, socialisme. Paris, 1895) (no centralized bureaucratic and militaristic state, even when called a republic, can enter honestly and sincerely an international confederation.)

Some European countries are working for a customs union, but at the same time are loath to give up their own currency systems. The presupposition of federalism is a fresh mentality and some sacrifice of old habits. As it is necessary to give up some of the irresponsible habits of free bachelorhood when entering an honest marriage and family life, so is it with federalism. Father Lincoln, the federalist, was a higher type of man than the free bachelor Edgar Poe. We prefer the settled habits of Tomás Masaryk, senior, to those of his free bachelor son, Jan. Likewise federal democracy is a more settled and higher type of democracy than revolutionary and finally centralized democracy, not to speak about Communist democracy.

2.) *National autonomy granted as a privilege is no final solution because it is injust and impracticable.*

To counterbalance the ominous effects of national centralization, several attempts were made to grant autonomy to certain special areas like Transylvania, Carphato-Ruthenia, or to some nations, e.g. the

Slovaks, Croats and others. The international minority treaty signed by Rumania September, 1919 in St. Germain-en-Laye provided for autonomy to the Transylvanian Szekel and Saxon community. All these attempts were impracticable and therefore dropped or reversed even if their execution was more or less attempted. Moldavia has as much right to autonomy as Transylvania. Why should the Slovaks have more autonomy than the Czech lands? The Hungarian government would be unjust to grant autonomy to Transdanubia and refuse it to the other parts of the state. Autonomy granted within a nationally centralized state to a specified nation has the consequence of creating, beside a dominant nation, a less privileged second-class nation which enjoys some autonomy when all the rest are without it.

All parts of the state have an equal right to the same autonomy. All cultural and educational institutions, all churches and nations must possess it equally which is possible only within a federal system.

3.) *National states in Eastern Europe have been, are and will be unable to guarantee the rights of national and religious minorities without federalization.*

Attempts have been made since the First World War to guarantee the rights of minorities by special international treaties such as those signed in the St. Germain-en-Laye on Sept. 10, 1919. All the former and present peace treaties contain imperative clauses on the rights of minorities. The League of Nations was entrusted to supervise them or other methods of international procedure like arbitration were stipulated as means of safeguarding the rights of freedom.

Wrapped in the cloak of independent national sovereignty, national states refused and continue to refuse to carry out their international obligations. Any legal interest shown by international organizations is regarded and refused as "interference in their domestic affairs".

Some national states have gone so far as to incorporate the rights of national and religious minorities in their constitution. But this was a mere platonic step undertaken with the intention of window-dressing. Their practice has not changed and the suffering minoritites cannot bring their grievances to an impartial court. Even if a national state should provide legal procedure and penal clauses against violators of minority rights, there is no guarantee of unbiassed justice as the national courts in a national state are dominated by one nation.

Promises of emigrant politicians that this will be different in the reestablished national states cannot be trusted. The system in itself is guilty and individual politicians, even if benevolent and liberal, are under the pressure of a nationalist public opinion within a national state. They are almost driven to injustice whereas peace is a byproduct of justice which can be guaranteed only by federalization of the multi-national area. Within the federation each nation and group will be a guarantee to the rights of the others under a supreme federal court consisting of representatives of all member nations.

If we consider how many millions, sometimes one-fifth of the population, have been driven out of their homes, exterminated in gas chambers, properties and institutions confiscated, we may realize the importance of making an end to this national and class-war "bellum omnium contra omnes".

4.) *Bad-neighbor policy is a characteristic of national states; good-neighbor policy is a rule of federalized states.*

A federal state like Switzerland, the USA and Canada are typical examples of good-neighbor policy. On the other hand, the French type of national state wherever applied has brought bad-neighbor policy, perhaps nowhere more tragically than in Eastern Europe (also in the Middle and Far East). Czechoslovakia, Hungary, Rumania, Poland, etc. were on constant bad relations with all their neighbors and were forced into plotting with the enemies of their enemies, i.e. with the enemies of their neighbors and great powers outside of the Danubian area. Against bad-neighbor policy there is no more effectual cure than federalization.

The existing national councils of emigrant politicians should discontinue the fostering of those ideologies which bring them in opposition. At present the antagonism and the germs of a future bad-neighbor policy are present to disrupt the seeming harmony. The ardently awaited "Day of Liberation" may turn into another "Day of Self-Deception" and all the sacrifices made by Americans be frustrated if irrealistic illusions are not replaced by the best political form which is known to political science and experience: federal self-government.

5.) *Recurrent revolutions, counter-revolutions and dictatorships are the unavoided consequences of the establishment of centralized national states. Federalism excludes dictatorship.*

The peculiar type of the French centralized national state has been and is a hot-bed of revolutions and counter-revolutions. The government being concentrated in a few hands, in a cabinet, in a large capital, under the pressure of a large city population and industrial proletariate, is easily captured by a violent group headed by a dictator. In the non-Protestant and multinational area of the European mainland, the polarizations between the extreme conservative right and the violently radical left is so intensive that a moderate two party system is almost impossible in the long run.

The advantage of federalism is that power cannot be seized all at once because it is distributed between the federal and state governments and all local autonomies. President Wilson said about American federalism: "With life everywhere throughout the continent, it is impossible to seize illicit power over the whole people by seizing any central offices. To hold Washington would be as useless to a usurper as to hold Duluth. Self-government cannot be usurped." Likewise if Berne should be captured by a usurper, the Swiss cantons and other local autonomies would continue their normal life. On the other hand we know how many times the Budapest, the Prague or Bucharest central government has been captured by a small violent minority and the whole country was immediately in their hands.

6.) *Incomplete distribution of powers is a source of recurring political crisis in national states.*

In the American and Swiss federal systems, the legislative, executive and judicial branches are well separated. The executive is on a firm footing, elected for four years with option of reelection during which terms he cannot be removed except by impeachment. The executive is not at the whim of nervous parliaments as in France before de Gaulle; neither can he become a dictator of the legislative body as a Napoleon or Mussolini or any of the East European governments have been able to. The executive does not have a vote in the legislative. The members of the legislative bodies are busy with their legislative work and not with plotting how to overthrow the head of the cabinet or its members.

In a politically highly sensitive, polarized and multi-national area, like Eastern Europe, a balanced government or peaceful life of the population is not possible without a complete separation of powers and a firm footing of the executive branch of the government. The Swiss pattern of seven executive federal councillors as a cabinet will serve the purpose better than a single chief executive, as in the USA. It is important that they should be elected and serve for a *definite, fixed period* and as *executive*, not as "the government." According to federal democracy, the government consists of the legislative, executive and judiciary branches together. In this system the possible transgressions of one are corrected by the other two. This system of checks and balances is the safety valve of democracy. The revolutionary democracies in Eastern Europe did not have such safety valves and manometers—consequently the boilers exploded when overheated. Either the legislative body became unruly, continuously ousting the cabinet from office or the cabinet became a "strong government" usually in the person of one man who, as a dictator, made the legislative subservient to him. In consequence of not separating the legislative from the executive, East European revolutionary democracies derailed several times into dictatorships.

Most continental democracies commit the error of calling the executive branch "the government". The Bonn Constitution of the present Federal Republic of Germany declares in paragraph 62: "The Federal Government shall consist of the Federal Chancellor and the Federal Ministers." This contains the seed of dictatorship, especially when this government precedes the legislature which is regulated in later paragraphs. The Swiss and USA Constitution establish first the legislature and the cabinet is called simply the executive though in its own sphere or function it is firmly established without the possibility of becoming a dictator.

7.) *Choice between a revolutionary or federal democracy.*

Revolutionary democracy is the first—so to say—negative stage of democracy. Swiss and American history also had its revolutionary phase but elsewhere in Europe this phase lasted more than one hundred and fifty years owing to the strong resistance of the "ancien regime" with its feudalism and landlordism, national, social and intellectual oppression. Switzerland and America were happy because they succeeded in overthrowing the old regime at an early date and almost at one stroke. Europe, as a whole and especially Eastern Europe was not so successful. Several revolutions were necessary and therefore it had no time to build a more positive and peaceful democracy. As to the positive aims of revolutions, European politicians and thinkers manifested an irrealistic vagueness, from the Communist Marxist "pie in the sky" with a "dwindling of the State", which remained an Utopia, to the Phalansters of Fourier, the dreams of Zola, and the violent syndicalism of Sorel or the Fascism of Mussolini.

Revolutionary democracies end in some form of military dictatorships if the transition to federal democracy is omitted after the overthrow of the old regime. This was omitted in Eastern Europe. European democrats did not grasp the necessity of studying the more mature and positive form of federal democracy in Switzerland or in the U.S.A. although Benes, Clemenceau and Trotsky lived for a period in the U.S.A. Lenin, Mussolini and many emigrants lived in Switzerland but failed to see the positive features of federal democracy. Home they went and built overheated political boilers which had no safety valves and manometers, which eventually blew up. East European politicians were trained mostly in the ideas of revolutionary democracy in Paris and later in Moscow. No wonder that the more mature forms of democracy had very few followers as even the peace conferences promoted the erroneous type of revolutionary democracy (democratorships) in Eastern Europe.

Revolutionary democracy of both the Jacobin and Marxist type is antireligious. Consequently it is at war not only with the churches but with the religious majority of Eastern Europe, the peasantry and family life. Federal democracy, on the other hand, has a free religious basis (Washington, Franklin, Lincoln, Jefferson, Wilson). "The Nation" is not the highest concept because both nation and individuals are seen to be "under God" and under Divine Law.

The significance of this is that above the Nation a higher instance is recognized, be it federal law or universal international law with its roots in the ethical laws of mankind and the golden rule, Revolutionary class-war democracy does not accept such a universal platform but the "nation" or even class interest is regarded as the highest. Consequently, force is regarded as the *ultima ratio* of revolutionary democracies. On the other hand, federal democracy settles disputes and injustices within the frame of a federal constitution.

In revolutionary democracies legislature often surpasses its competence, wiping out the most elementary rights of the individual, even destroying their existence as happened with millions of racial and religious minorities in Eastern Europe. Jefferson said, as quoted by Madison in *The Federalist*, No. 48: "It will be no alleviation, that these powers will be exercised by a plurality of hands, and not by a single one. One hundred and seventy despots would surely be as oppressive as one ... An elective despotism was not the government we fought for; but one which should not only be founded on free principles, but in which the powers of government should be so divided and balanced among several bodies of magistracy, as that no one could transcend their legal limits, without being effectually checked and restrained by the others."

This is not the place to enter into further explanations of the principles of federal democracy. It is our purpose only to draw attention to it in order that more careful study should be given especially to the Swiss and American type of federalism.

8. *Economic and technical backwardness of Eastern Europe*
   is a cause of unbalanced political systems. Federalism
   opens higher standards of living.

Like the house divided against itself, Eastern Europe could not reach the standard of living which according to the present state of techniques and applied science is possible because the shackles of an antiquated regime hindered progress and caused revolutionary tension. When the old regime was removed the economic area was broken up into small national centralized states, divided into opposing camps. Strict visas, severe police methods made economic cooperation, normal communication and even visits between family members impossible or very difficult. Economic life was plagued by nine or more soft currencies with not firm relation between them. Although the natural wealth of the area, its fertile plains, rich minerals, extended forests and other natural resources surpassed those of Switzerland or Scandinavia, the per capita national income has been and is less than one fourth of the Swiss or Scandinavian. The Balkanization of the Danubian area after the First World War froze the possibilities of using interstate natural resources. The present border line between Austria and Hungary crosses the Lake Fertő (Neusiedler See), which is utterly neglected and unutilized, hardly accessible because of marshes. Plans for the regulation of the area cannot be carried out by one state alone. Wide tracts of fertile land could be added to agriculture beside fish ponds and resort places.

The river systems of Eastern Europe are insufficiently developed both as a means of communication and a source of energy. National states in possession of mountainous regions (Carpathians, etc.) did not concern themselves with flood prevention of the lowlands belonging to other states. Interstate cooperation against animal and plant diseases was and is unsystematic, casual.

Long distances communication in Eastern Europe was and is very neglected. Deep freezing and other technical improvements would enable the Vienna or Prague markets to be furnished by fresh fruits and abundant vegetables from as far as Bulgaria. Instead of such far ranging traffic possibilities, international roads and railways are neglected.

9.) *Cultural relations between East European nations is blocked by the chauvinism of national states, and distorted by either nationalistic or Marxist prejudices.*

The genius of East Europeans was expressed in remarkable works of poets and artists, some of which equal the best in Western culture. Yet they are unknown outside of their own small nation. The national states dominated the official intercourse between nations and, almost like the czarist regime in Russia which kept Tolstoy hidden from the world, they distorted the international exchange of cultural goods. Hungarians have had great writers like Jókai, Ady, Juhász, Zs. Móricz, D. Szabó, László Mécs, but very few Rumanians, Croats or Czechs have had the opportunity of knowing them. Likewise, very few Hungarians or Ruthenians know anything about the Croat Michelangelo, Mestrovic. The peasant population of this region possesses a very rich folklore heritage which has been recently explored and partly published, but the interrelations of neighboring areas were neglected. History and other social sciences also suffered because of national and Marxist state interference with the scientific projects of universities and individual scholars.

All the disadvantages of this biased era can be eliminated only by a fresh start in the spirit of federalism of East European nations.

Instead of knowing each other indirectly through the great Western cosmopolitan centers, East European nations should find their free direct cultural intercourse in a spirit of free federalism and free cooperation.

10.) The case of Austria: Anschluss repeated or federalization with Central-Eastern Europe?

In absence of better alternative, Austria may join Germany again within some years, thereby commiting political suicide anew and at the same time putting in motion political crisis in central Europe, high pressure politics of German nationalism toward the East, restlessness in Hungary, Bohemia, Poland, etc. All the great sacrifices of America in occupation cost and ERP Marshall Aid would be thereby lost and the pacification of Central Europe frustrated for the next few generations.

Austria, especially Vienna, got a larger part of her food requirements from Hungary and the lower Danubian countries. Between the two world wars when custom lines and custom duties hindered interstate commerce, the food import came in the following large proportion from Eastern Europe which shrank after the Second World War to insignificant amounts:

Austria's food import before the Second World War (1937)

	wagons		*wagons*
Total food import	111,924	*Total cereal import*	85,642
out of which from:		out of which from:	
Hungary	28,306	Hungary	22,927
Yugoslavia	29,103	Yugoslavia	27,058
Rumania	23,308	Rumania	22,620
Czechoslovakia	6,606	Czechoslovakia	5,959

As may be seen, 87 thousand out of 111 thousand wagons food import of Austria came from the four Danubian countries, and 79 thousand wagons of cereal out of the total import of 86 thousand. The 1937 import is however much lower than the imports in the 1920s or before the First World War when there was no custom line between Austria and Hungary or Bohemia.

On the other hand, Austria's industrial export found a ready market in the Danubian agricultural countries. Its wood, pulp and paper products could be shipped by waterways. All this natural interrelation between mutually interpedendent areas is broken up into uncooperating national states. The late Austrian president Karl Renner, one of the earliest champions of a transformation of Austria-

Hungary into a federal Switzerland on a large scale, complained bitterly in the July 1948 issue of the American quarterly *Foreign Affairs* in an article entitled "Austria, Key to War and Peace", about the wrong decisions of international peace conferences.

The danger of underestimating Austria's self-interest is imminent. As early as the elections in 1950 it showed signs of an increasing tendency toward a second Anschluss. As Mr. Strauss-Hupé said: "Austrian youth of the League (new Independent Party) looked to Berlin... Austria will be in the future even less capable of maintaining her independence than she had been under relatively more benign conditions... There are the two alternatives to Anschluss: Danubian Union, and debated ground: the faint promise of a new solution: European Union."

Present-day nationalists of Austria should consider that within a true federalism which would include all the Danubian areas, Austria could be as prosperous as Switzerland. Within Germany it would be a discontented province and provoke similar consequences to those of an annexation of German Switzerland by Germany. A forgotten statement by Bismarck which should have warned Hitler and should warn all Austrian nationalists against such a step is á propos. The well-known Hungarian author, Maurus Jókai, obtained an interview by Prince Bismarck in 1874. John Ruskin's "Fors Clavigera" reprinted the interview (Letter XLIII) as it was published in the *Pall Mall Gazette*, March 7, 1874: "Small independent States in the East," said Bismarck to Jókai, "would be a misfortune to Europe. Austria and Hungary must realize their mutual interdependence... The notion that Germany has an inclination to annex more land is a myth. God preserve the Germans from such a wish!... Should the Germans of Austria want to be annexed by Germany, I would feel inclined to declare war against them for that wish alone. A German Minister who should conceive the desire to annex part of Austria, would deserve to be hanged"—a punishment the Prince indicated by gesture. "I do not wish to annex even a square foot of fresh territory—not as much as these two pencils would cover."

11.) *The European union in its relation to Eastern Europe.*

Many Austrian and some of the East European statesmen are convinced that the realization of an European Union would automatically solve the problems of the East European nations. If, under the high pressure of Russian imperialism the European Union could not achieve more unity than periodical parliamentary sessions at Strassbourg without true federal legislative and executive powers, what will happen, when the Russian pressure will diminish, recede, or collapse—which is a presupposition of East European new arrangements?

To a true federal customs union, a currency union is the precondition. It is impossible to imagine a federal custom territory with several independent currency systems. Any change in the value of one or the other currency would upset the custom tariff, the price levels and production costs in the different areas of the federal union.

Basic agricultural population and production in Western countries like Germany, Switzerland, England need protection agains the competition of cheaper producing areas. Industrial costs and conditions are so widely differentiated that a sudden transition into a single federal union would cause the collapse of many areas and the economic standard of many millions. Of course, a complete breakdown of the European continent in a Russian *Blitzkrieg* leaving Europe in a devastated condition like Korea would make a European federal Union absolutely imperative. But God forbid such a disaster!

Under present conditions however, it seems more likely that regional economic federations can be worked out successfully. In Eastern Europe before the First World War the larger part of the Danubian area formed an economic union in which the living standard and civilization was higher than outside of this area, in Southeast Europe (the Balkans).

The Rumanians, Serbs and Croats within the federation reached a higher cultural and economic welfare than their brothers living outside of the federation in small independent national states.

Since the First World War, the formerly exclusively agricultural countries have travelled the road of industrialization and therefore their economic level is nearer to each other than before. These nations are still aware of the advantages of a greater economic unit, of one currency, one custom line without internal barriers, without Chinese walls between national states. Consequently, economic federal union in Eastern Europe is not a dream but a realistic possibility based on firm psychological foundation in the life of the millions.

The next step in Europe seems to be the formation of regional unions such as the West-European, the East-European, the Scandinavian, Mediterranean, etc. Above the regional federal unions, the European Union cannot be much more than an organization like the inter-American OAS (Pan-American) cooperation with yearly convened parliaments, coordinated foreign policy, with cultural and economic agreements, compulsory arbitration.

If, however, despite the above reasoning, European Union could be realized as a close federal union with a single currency and custom line, the formation of a federal union in Eastern Europe could still serve a useful purpose. It is the opinion of many East European politicians that it would be more advantageous to enter the European Union not as single small national states and be used by the great

Western Powers as chess men played against each other, but rather as a federation. We came to the conclusion that, positive plans and agreements for the formation of federal union in Eastern Europe should be prepared, ready for some sort of execution as soon as the Russian withdrawal or lessening of pressure would leave a *vacuum juris* in Eastern Europe.

12.) *Growing tendency in favor of East European federalization among statesmen.*

Politicians in exile from Communist countries arrive increasingly at the conclusion that liberty and independence of small nations cannot be maintained without the correlative principle of federalism that was first applied successfully by the Swiss and American fathers of the federal constitution.

The Philadelphia declaration of Feb. 11, 1951 was an outstanding act where many prominent politicians pledged themselves not only to the cause of liberation but the cause of federalization. New study groups are forming to elaborate the principles and application of a close cooperation of the European nations. Scientists and scholars should help prepare a scientific, realistic work with all possible alternatives for a future settlement.

The multi-national pattern of Eastern Europe is not in itself a plague or hindrance to progress. On the contrary, it may be a source of more vitality, beauty, health and cultural competition of the races concerned. The idea of dominion and superiority of one race above the other, or combination of some against the rest is untenable. Neither the state or federal power should be combined with the policy of one special nation. It is difficult for national politicians to leave behind the antiquated pattern of national domination within the boundaries of a state over the rest of the population. Prominent politicians however, even if they once entertained the wrong concept have had their lesson in its ominous results.

In 1948 the Hungarian Louis Kossuth was still spellbound by the French revolutionary idea of a Nation-state. A Serbian deputation from southern Hungary presented to the Hungarian Diet in Pozsony a petition for the recognition of their nation. Kossuth reacted with *hauteur:* "What do you understand by a nation?" he asked the Serbs.

"A group of people which possesses its own language, customs, and enough consciousness of itself to want to preserve them," was the answer.

"A Nations must also have its government," objected Kossuth.

"We do not go so far," returned the Serbian, "One nation can live *under several different governments,* and again *several nations can for a single State.*"

But Kossuth at this time was unable to conceive a nation which was not definable as a state. "In that case, the sword will decide," he ended abruptly.

Later he had bitterly to condone his attitude. Impatience and misunderstanding drove the Danubian nations against each other, becoming an easy prey to renewed absolutism. In exile after his visit in England and America, Kossuth became a federalist democrat, accepted in 1852 a plan for a Danubian confederation which he worked out in the next 10 years together with Serbian, Rumanian and other friends. The motto heading this article is quoted from his paper.[1]

Nevertheless, after the collapse of the Dual Monarchy, the false concept of small Nation-States was implemented by the peace conferences. That Masaryk, Wilson, Lloyd George, Take Jonescu and many others had in mind originally a federal collaboration of the interested nations can be easily proved. But Clemenceau and Benes thought it more "realistic" to establish independent small states. It became a source of infinite trouble and suffering—irredentism on one side, oppression and bitter complaints on the other—which opened the way for violent interference from outside.

Like Kossuth, the other East European statesmen became interested in federalism when in exile. The Czechoslovak minister president, Hodza, published his book "Federation in Central Europe" almost as a testament of his life. Even Benes and many other leading statesmen spoke about federalism but on return to power the principles of federalism were abandoned, new nationalistic injustices were committed by them and thereby collapse was hastened.

We don't question the sincerity of the pronouncements in favor of federalization in Eastern Europe made by statesmen in exile but they seldom realize the change involved which is like changing from bachelorhood to family life. The latter, like federal democracy, calls for more planning than revolutionary democracy or bachelorhood. Up to the present however, there has not been a detailed, scientific investigation and evaluation of the alternative possible solutions for federalism in Eastern Europe, summarizing the geographical, economic, statistical, cultural, ethnographical, legal and historical aspects. The absence of such synthetic, positively realistic, scientific investigation including the constitutional formulation of the federal structure was the main reason for politicians abandoning the idea of federalism on coming into power. This should not be repeated. Scientific investigation should therefore prepare the application of correct federal principles in Eastern Europe.

B. *Special problems of federalization in Eastern Europe*

Even if general principles of federalization are agreed upon, it is still necessary to clarify their application in special areas. Wilson's Peace Points and the Atlantic Charter contain important general principles but in absence of more detailed, specific agreements they were misinterpreted and therefore misapplied. In order to facilitate the application of the principles of federal democracy to specific areas, let us investigate the outstanding problems of Eastern Europe.

1.) *Territorial problems and the extension of federation.*

A considerable divergence of opinion exists among the adherents of federalism concerning the territorial extension of federalization in Eastern Europe. Some are in favor of one single large federation comprising all nations and countries between Russia and Germany from the Baltic countries to Greece. This would be a federation between the Baltic, the Adriatic and the Black Sea and therefore sometimes called Intermaria. The advocate of this solution argue mostly from a military defensive standpoint and have a large federation in mind as a bulwark agains Russian or German aggression.

Considerable numbers of politicians and scientists favor a Danubian Union without Poland and the Baltic countries but including Yugoslavia, Rumania and Bulgaria. Others again advocate a separate Balkan federation. The Danubian and Balkan federation have some historic precedence—one in the former dual Monarchy, the other in the loose Balkan Union before the last war.

Principally the number of participants in a federation is irrelevant. It is somewhat like a game in which the number of participants is not limited. A national or imperialistic state tries to expand its frontiers like monarchs and dynasties in former periods. The spirit of federalism is different. In 1919 Vorarlberg decided by plebiscite to join Switzerland. Switzerland did not accept the decision because it would have spoiled her good-neighbor policy with Austria.

The territorial extension of a federation should be decided on practical *realistic* grounds and not mere sentiments, transitory interests or negative motives alone. Such motives like anti-German or anti-Russian ones should not be the dominant elements.

The crucial point in deciding the territorial extension of the federation is a clarification of its purpose. Is the primary purpose a military defensive one or an economic union, a political-national, cultural or geographical- historical symbiosis?

If our federation is primarily military, its territory may be extended very far. We see that the Atlantic Pact comprises distant countries from Canada to Italy, Greece and Turkey. If the East European federation is to become primarily a military one, then it could be extended to the three oceans.

If, however, our purpose is more limited—for instance nationalistic— it is evident that our federation will be limited by our narrower purpose. For instance, if all the people of Yugoslavia should decide to form a single federation with the Bulgarian, it is evident that this federation could not extend outside the area inhabited by the Southern Slavonic races.

If, however, the purpose for federation is economic, the inter-relation of economic areas must be studied in order to find out the *natural limits* of our federation. In this case we must take into account, which areas form a marketing unit suitable for one customs union; which are the main lines of communication, the direction of trade and traffic; where are the main resources of raw materials and energy of industries and where are their consumers. Each motive should be investigated separately and a synthetic evaluation and appraisal arrived at.

The primary purpose of federalization in Eastern Europe is not military. Military security problems are dealt with on a much higher level than a regional federation. The greatest military powers are out-side of Europe. Eastern Europe will contribute its share to world security when intraregional antagonism will not paralyze its efforts. Otherwise its restlessness will continue to endanger world peace like the Arab-Israel or Pakistan-Kashmir-India antagonisms do. The causes of enmity must be removed and therefore we must look for other means of solution.

The primary object of federalization in Eastern Europe is to pacify the multinational area by spiritualizing the economic and political frontiers between closely interdependent areas. In many areas no correct national boundaries can be drawn. Any line which claims more than a borderline between two cantons or that between Mary-land and Virginia will damage the vital interests of the population. Such an invisible state frontier existed between Austria and Hungary before 1918 with its obvious benefits. Both were independent states with different legal and internal structure, nevertheless absolutely free communication and trade was possible.

Our problem is how to have several partners within the federation instead of only two. But in determining how far the federation could be extended we must investigate which nations and areas form a *close* economic unit and which are conscious of their historic interdependence. If we enlarge the area of a close federation further than real-istic facts warrant, difficulties may arise which cannot be met now. The average Greek or Bulgarian knows nothing of Vilna or Riga, nor do the Baltic states export or import essential goods to or from the Danubian area.

Any map of communication will show the main traffic lines run East-West or West-East like the Danube. Trade and traffic between the North and South have been less significant. The northern lines of the Carpathians cut the area into practically independent economic and historical spheres between which the connecting link is weak. The Danubian are was formed under the historical forces of the Habsburg and Turkish empires. Poland and the Baltic area between the Prussian and Russian antagonism. The nationalities in the Danubian area are biologically interrelated i.e. neighboring nations and areas are interlinked by personal family ties and common historical, cultural heritage. Beside the same historical background, even the peasantry and folklore are mutually interwoven.(2)

All these factors must be carefully considered and scientifically studied before coming to final conclusions. If the centripetal forces are not strong enough, a federation cannot be successfully administered because the legislative bodies would consist of heterogeneous elements without a common platform. The Swiss and American federal unions were also formed out of heterogeneous areas with an intimate knowledge of each other's *common historical background.*

For these reasons it would be best to begin with a Baltic-Polish federation north of the Carpathians, and the Danubian federation which also includes Yugoslavia, Bulgaria and Rumania. Should the latter, however, prefer to form a Balkan federation together with Greece, a difficult problem would arise for the Slovenes, Croatians, Transylvanian Rumanians and the people of the Voivodina: to which federation, the Danubian or Balkan, should they belong? The solution could be found through plebiscites by zones but it would be wiser not to put the question this way thereby risking the partition of areas which should not belong to two different federations. Greece and Albania would fit better in a Mediterranean federation as their trade and interest has few connections with the Danubian basin.

Between the Baltic and Danubian federation the dividing line is clear though the two federations should be like the U.S.A. and Canada —two federations but in friendly alliance. An amalgamation of the two federations may be possible in the future but in Eastern Europe as a starting point, two separate federations are more realistic.

In the following pages we shall give an outline of a Danubian Federal Union for the formation of which the time will be ripe as soon as Russian domination of the area is over. The Polish-Baltic area is less known to the author and to the politicians of Danubian origin.

2.) *Nations contemplated for a Danubian Federal Union.*

The Danubian area in its strict sense plus Bohemia extends over a territory of 1,029,000 square kilometers with a population of 80 million:

	Millions		Millions
Czechs	9.1	Bulgarians	6.7
Slovaks	4.0	Hungarians	12.8
Russians	0.9	Rumanians	17.5
Serbs	7.8	Germans	7.8
Croats	4.3	Macedonians	2.0
Slovenes	1.6	Others	5.5
		Total	80.0

These nations cannot be separated by national frontiers. The bulk of each nation lives in a certain area where it may form 75 to 98 percent of the total population but between the compact areas, large tracts of debated territories became the *Eris apple* for which the solid areas contended. The problem cannot be solved by force or by dictated terms. No politician, nor peace conference has the right to deprive the local population of expressing its natural human right to self-determination. Before a plebiscite is held in those debated areas, the interested population should be asked by plebiscite whether it wants a *national* state frontier which would cut the area up like the Paris peace treaties did, or do they prefer federal state frontiers as between two cantons or two states in Switzerland or in the U.S.A.

During a transitory period, national armed forces should occupy only those territories where one nation forms more than 75 per cent of the total population. The racially mixed and debated areas should be administered by international or neutral armed forces until a decision based on plebiscites is reached. To avoid misunderstandings, more detailed agreements are needed about the areas in question, the right to hold a plebiscite, the successive order in which they should be held and the composition of the neutral board of arbitration disinterested in local feuds. If the principle of federation is agreed on, such local plebiscites will settle the existing differences in the most harmonious way because the line chosen by plebiscite will form but an administrative, almost invisible frontier as existed between Austria and Hungary before 1918.

The problem of nationalism is the most burning one in the field of public education. Further below we recommend a solution according to which cultural affairs may be administered irrespective of state frontiers in the form of cultural autonomy and the State administration is relieved of the heavy burden of State-owned school systems. The Swiss school system of local community schools combined with educational and cultural autonomy is to be preferred to a State dominated school system which indoctrinates ephemeral political ideologies and is tempted to misuse political power in the schools.

Legal protection given to the rights of nationality should have federal sanctions guaranteed by the high authority of a supreme federal court specialized in the defense of national minorities.

3.) *States of the Federation and their subdivision.*

Nations will have their cultural autonomous organization irrespective of state frontiers(see chapter below). Constituent members of the federation should be the following states: Austria, Czechia (Bohemia, Moravia and Silesia), Slovakia, Ruthenia, Hungary, Slovenia, Croatia, Serbia, Transylvania, Rumania, Bulgaria, Macedoni ı.

It is important however, to realize that these states should not be regarded as *national* states, entities where the predominant race has privileges at the expense of others. To avoid this misunderstanding such neutral names as Transylvania, Carpathia, Moravia, Transdanubia would eliminate the application of the erroneous principle *"cuius natio, eius regio"* which is as destructive as the principle of religious intolerance expressed in the Westphalian peace treaty: *"cuius regio, eius religio."* National intolerance and oppression can be banished only by divorcing administrative or state power from a dominant nationality.

For practical and historical reasons the commonly accepted names of states may continue. As the language of the administration will be practically adjusted to the needs and predominant language of the population, the state cannot avoid having a semblance of national character. Even in Switzerland we speak of French and German cantons. The official language should not be overemphasized. It is not the language of administration in which a nation expresses itself but the language of literature, art, social and family life. The language of administration cannot and should not be in opposition to the local language spoken. Like the clever merchant beside good service to his customer tries to speak the language of the latter, so a good administrator in a mixed region will be successful if he accomodates himself to the situation. The contrary would cause national friction and opposition to an unpopular administration.

The usually over-centralized state administrative of Europe should disencumber itself by developing the local autonomies of counties, districts, townships and communities. Successful democracy and federalism is impossible without honest local autonomy at the base. In national states of Eastern Europe the cutting of the minorities by county and district lines into two or three parts to weaken them was a general practice, according to the rule *"divide et impera."* E.g. the Hungarians and Germans north of the Danube were united with the Serbs and Macedonians south of it. Prior to World War I the Saxon and Sekel regions of Transylvania were alloted to districts and counties that possessed compact Rumanian majorities. Such practices caused unnecessary suffering, national friction and bitterness. In a federal system practical administrative viewpoints lead to administrative divisions on practical lines, one of them being that language difficulties of the administration and the population can be better mastered if homogeneous and natural administrative units are formed according to the democratic wishes expressed by the local population.

It is self-evident that borderlines between states or other administrative units should be without customs, passport visas or other hindrances to the normal flow of persons and goods. This does not exclude the right of single states to regulate the permanent residence and employment of persons coming from other states.

4.) *Metrodanubia, capital city of the federation: Bratislava-Pozsony.*

As seat of the federal government no better site could be found than Bratislava-Pressburg-Pozsony, a middle-sized town lying between Austria, Hungary and Czechoslovakia on the shore of the Danube. It is easily accessible, centrally located between the German, Hungarian and Slav elements. In its population all the three are represented. During the Turkish occupation it was the capital of Hungary as now it is the capital of Slovakia and is predestined to play the Washington, D.C. role in the Danubian federation. Eventually, a new name like Metrodanubia or Centrodanubia could be found to replace the older ones.

Beside the legislative, executive and judiciary branches of the federal government, the capital would also have within its boundaries such institutes as a federal university, where the federal employees would receive their higher instruction in federal government. This university would also serve for the exchange of national cultures in the Danubian area, an intellectual clearing house for ideas and plans. A federal museum, archives, library, radio and television, etc. would serve the international relations.

C. *Constitutional and organizational problems.*

1.) *Competence of the federal government: affairs in common.*

The general rule should be to keep the *affairs in common at a minimum.* Especially at the beginning the federal administration should not be overburdened. Let as many affairs as possible remain in the competence of the states. The constitution should specify which affairs should fall within the competence of the federal government. The following are suggested:

1.) Federal currency, federal bank, federal finances and budget.
2.) Federal customs, tariff problems and income therefrom.
3.) Interstate commerce and communication.
4.) The administration and the institutions of Metrodanubia.
5.) Federal Supreme Court.
6.) Foreign Affairs.
7.) Federal Defense Policy.

The last two items, though important, were purposely left at the end. Previously, e.g. in the Danubian Dual Monarchy of the Habsburgs, they were overemphasized and misused as instruments of imperialism. The area between Russia and Germany should be neutralized like Switzerland, though membership in the United Nations would involve international responsibility and share in the United Nations peace keeping activities.

Paragraphs 18-20 of the Swiss Constitution regulating state and federal military powers could be adopted with only slight changes. Military experts should decide which types of armaments should be exclusively in possession of the federal army.

While the affairs in common should be kept at a minimum, the number of those affairs administered by the individual states in *common consent* or special agreement with the others should be at a maximum.

Agriculture, industry, commerce, civil and penal law, police, tax and credit system, census and statistical service, etc. should be left in the competence of the individual states though a *maximum number* of agreements should be concluded between the states. These should be either: 1.) voluntary, 2.) obligatory.

1.) Voluntary agreements may be concluded between two or more states concerning the same methods, procedures or administrative systems, for instance in health or veterinary administration, regulation of cartels, insurance, consumption taxes, power plants, etc.

2.) Agreements may be made compulsory only by the federal legislature and after ratification by two-thirds of the states. Such agreements may be enforced by federal courts.

Among the latter we may mention the unification of statistical methods throughout the whole area of the federation, though the execution would remain within the competence of the individual states. The national income statistics should be prepared also by a unified method under the supervision of the federal government because the quotas of individual states would be determined on the basis of national income statistics.

In this way the competence of the federal government and that of the states would be clearly defined under the safeguarding of the federal courts.

A Bill of Rights for individuals and minorities should be included in the federal constitution and placed under the protection of the federal courts. Neither the federation nor the states should have power to interfere with religion or church affairs. The separation of church and state and their institutions should be complete but in a friendly spirit. Articles 49 to 51 of the Swiss constitution on religious affairs could be adopted with only slight changes.

About the relation of public education to state and federal powers we shall speak later in the chapter about national-cultural autonomies.

2.) *Composition of the federal government.*

Federal government consists of the legislative, executive and judicial powers, well separated and with the necessary checks and balances. Any two of these restrain the third if it goes beyond its competence. The Cabinet would not constitute the "government" but is simply the "executive", separated from the legislature, firmly established for a number of years like the American president. The difference would be that instead of one head there would be seven or nine executives libe the Swiss federation possesses. Members of the Cabinet may participate in the discussions of the legislative bodies but are without vote. They would be chosen for a fixed period of time during which they could not be removed except by impeachment.

a.) *Legislature* would consist of the federal

House of Representatives   (300-400 members)
The Senate .... (33 members)
Legislative committees and subcommittees (see below).

The *federal House of Representatives* would be elected in proportion to the population. Each member state determines its own rules of election. If we count one representative for two hundred thousand of the population the House would consist of 380 members, elected for two years but each year one-third of the total membership changes —if not reelected.

The House of Representatives of the Danubian Federation would be drawn from all nationalities. Though language difficulties may be eliminated by modern techniques it seems necessary to limit the competence of the House to the fundamental rights of parliamentarism i.e., the yearly budget, taxation and federal incomes, finances and the election of the executive Cabinet (Council) members. The enactment of other federal laws would not fall within the competence of the House though it could initiate laws. The laws would be prepared by legislative committees elected and composed by the House of Representatives.

Legislative committees would consist not only of members of the House but experts of the economic and cultural life selected from professional organizations such as the Chambers of Commerce, of Agriculture, Trade Unions, universities and lawyers, etc. With respect to the limited competence of the Danubian federation, *three legislative committees* would suffice: A.) Economic and Financial Committee. B.) Committee for Constitutional and Legal Affairs. C.) Committees for National Cultural Affairs. These legislative committees would form special subcommittees for special tasks assigned, for instance, an Interstate Electrical Power subcommittee. The subcommittees would prepare the special laws and act for the above legislative committees. If accepted by the latter it could go directly to the Senate. This procedure would ensure a due share of influence by the experts during the period of formation of the laws. The House would have the right to *initiate* new laws or *propose* amendments to existing ones but they would not come up for discussion in plenary session. This would simplify and improve the legislative procedure and instead of lobby groups would enable the experts to take part in the preparatory work of legislation. A multinational House of Representatives would be too ponderous to handle all legislation in plenary session.

For enactment of international treaties and all affairs of military concern, and for foreign affairs, i.e., all rights of federal sovereignty, the Senate would have competence.

The *Federal Senate* should fulfill a role similar to that which the American fathers of the Constitution originally assigned to the American Senate, consisting at the time of only 26 members. Beside being the Second or Upper House of Legislature, it is the highest consultative and deciding body in matters of foreign policy, international relations, defense policy and highest sovereign rights. Its membership should be kept small for efficient handling of its affairs and in almost continuous session.

The Senate of the Danubian Federation should consist of about 30 to 40 members representing all regions of the federation, somewhat like the following:

Austrian senators: 5 (1 Upper, 1 Lower Austria, 1 Steiermark, 1 Karnten, 1 Tyrol, 1 Vorarlberg).

Northern Slav senators: 6 (2 Bohemia, 1 Moravia, 1 West Slovakia, 1 East Slovakia, 1 Ruthenia).

Hungarian senators: 6 (2 Trans-Danubia, 1 Central Plain-Lowland, 1 East of the Tisza, 1 North Hungary, 1 Hungarian from Transylvania).

Rumanian senators: 6 (2 Moldavia, 2 Muntenia, 2 Transylvanian-Rumanian).

Southern Slav senators: 9 (1 Slovenia, 2 Croatia, 1 Bosnia-Hercegovina, 2 Serbia, 1 Macedonia, 2 Bulgaria).

Other nationality: 1 (from Voivodina and Banat may be Slav, Hungarian, German, Rumanian, etc.).

Total number of senators: 33.

It should be remembered that senators don't represent nations but *regions* of the federation and act accordingly in the spirit of federation. The composition of the national proportions may be somewhat different from the above tentative proposal, for instance, a Moslem could be chosen from Bosnia, etc. The total number of senators could also be changed even to the double of the above. A lower number is, however, obviously more practical in a multinational area. Instead of doubling the number, vice or assistant senators could be elected who could replace them in case of absence.

The senate nominates the candidates for membership in the Cabinet (Federal Council) which are elected by the House for a fixed period.

b.) *Executive power* is in the hands of the Federal Council which consists of 7 or 9 members elected by the House for 4 years—twice renewable. It would act as the Federal Council (Conseil federal) of the Swiss Constitution (Art. 95-104). The president of the Council is appointed yearly by the House or may rotate.

Full permanent membership in the Council would be given to the states of Austria, Czechia, Hungary, Rumania, Serbia, and Bulgaria. Smaller states would have half membership i.e., chosen for two years only. Members of the Federal Council are responsible for the execution of federal laws, for the branches of federal administration and for all federal institutions. The staff of the federal offices is appointed by a federal council with regard to fair quotas for all nationalities. High appointments are subject to confirmation of the Senate.

c.) *Judicial powers* are represented by the federal courts headed by the Supreme Federal Court which should have the power to annul unconstitutional laws and ordinances. A special section of this would exist for federal protection of minority rights assisted by special institutes for scientific fact finding in the field of minority problems. Such impartial federal authority under the direction of the federal Supreme Court is necessary, and would eliminate or arbitrate doubtful cases by studying them impartially on the spot.

3.) *National corporations for cultural autonomy.*

The relation of educational systems to public power in Eastern Europe became enemy No. 1 of the cultural development of the individual. Before the rise of nationalism, schools were in the hands of the churches. Though education was limited to a proportionately small strata of the population, the educational institutions of the churches did excellent work in this field. After the rise of nationalism, the state system took over the schools. The same nations which as minorities protested against the invasion by the state school system of their own autonomous church schools (Rumanians, Slovaks, Serbians, etc. in old Hungary) applied the same methods of educational étatism when they came into power. Abolition of autonomous church schools was accomplished sometimes at one stroke, as in Yugoslavia in 1921, or gradually as in other states. After the nationalization of the complete school system a second wave of red propaganda swept over the entire system. Pupils, parents and teachers were and are helpless before the state-assisted indoctrination of national and Communist-atheist class war policies.

In a multi-national area it is pernicious to attach the school system to changing political powers. In the national revolutionary states, not even the universities, Academies of Sciences and Arts kept their cultural autonomy. Consequently the independence of scientific research and criticism has vanished in the national and revolutionary states. No Thomas Masaryk or Ady could critizice the hypernationalism or totalitarianism of his own countrymen or politicians in power now.

A completely new arrangement must be found to secure the national and individual cultural rights and autonomies in an East European federation. The *community school* (township) in Switzerland is the basic school type, in which the parents have a deciding share. It is better than the rigid state system which served the purposes of denationalization of the minorities, as was so frequently the case in Eastern Europe. The states should not have more power than to fix the standards of compulsory education, sanitary conditions and the supervision of their execution. The elementary schools should be community owned with the language of the parents' choice.

Schools and educational institutions of each nationality, irrespective of state or administrative frontiers should form a cultural entity: a national corporation for cultural autonomy operating irrespective of state frontiers—similar to a church organization. Officials of the national cultural corporation should be teachers and professors. Therefore the organization would extend into all communities and villages where members of the respective nationalities live. The Austrian Renner was the first to propose such a non-territorial organization of the nations in the Danubian area based on the personal membership of individuals. Between the two world wars, a similar system was established in Estonia called "cultural autonomy" and was quite successful. The existence of such an organization in the Danubian area would mean that neither the state nor the federal government would posses a Ministry of Public Education but only an office to supervise the educational standards. Each nation would have a Minister of Education, the elected president of the national cultural organization whose power would extend across state frontiers to the farthest village where members of the same nationality live.

The national corporations for cultural autonomy should be entrusted with the higher institutions for science, art, radio, television, film, folklore, literature, including the universities, academies of sciences, literary organizations, etc. Each national corporation would possess its own constitution chartered by the federal government on similar grounds. Within this cultural constitution the corporation would possess legislative power over its own cultural affairs, executive power to carry them out. Teachers and professors, artists and writers of the same nationality would possess their own associations within this corporation wherein they would have protection from state interference.

Conclusions and the future

We have shown in the previous pages that the formation of a federation in Eastern Europe is necessary, possible and realistic. Principles couched in general and vague terms like the Wilsonian points, the Atlantic Charter or other pronouncements about liberation of

Eastern Europe are insufficient. A realistic application must be worked out before action is taken. We have therefore given a more detailed proposal for further discussion and clarification. We may be sure that Kossuth, Palacky, Masaryk, Hodza, Radic, President Wilson would approve such pacification by federalist agreements. They would also give hope that, after the present vicious system, instead of renewed outbursts of confused nationalism, a constitutional order of federated nationalism would secure a permanent peace.

There are about five million immigrants having brothers and sisters, parents and relatives in Eastern Europe. These Americans are anxious to see a peaceful system established in their former homeland and look for an elimination of existing antagonism between the representatives of those nations. They know the best form of pacification is *constitutional federal* self-government instead of chaotic *national-revolutionary* democracy or democratorship that ends in violence.

The Passion Week of 1301 saw in Constanza a remarkable event. The emperor, Henry III, went to the pulpit and turning to all sides proclaimed a *Treuga Dei* (God's Peace), forgiving all offenses committed against him and inviting all to do likewise. The national representatives of Eastern Europe could profitably to the same. For God's Peace in our day there is no better platform than federalism (*foedus*, the Latin word meanings peace pact is connected with the word *fides*—faith).

In the eighties of the last century Crown Prince Rudolph, the only son and heir to Emperor Francis Joseph began the publication of a voluminous scientific description of the lands and peoples of the former Dual Monarchy in 18 volumes with the collaboration of best available scholars and writers. What a rich variety of nations, natural resources, mountains and lowlands, culture and possibilities! At the time much was yet undiscovered, petroleum fields and coal mines, electric energy and folklore of the peasantry. In the presence of so much richness, Crown Prince Rudolph committed suicide. Likewise did the whole Danubian area of nations commit political suicide. Its life and hopes for a better future are not lost. After discovery of the main errors, the rebirth may be found, a better life organized in the spirit of free *federal* self-government. Plans in this direction should be further elaborated in a scientific way and possible divergencies eliminated with the help of neutral American, Swiss, Canadian and other aid.

(1) See the author's article: "From Kossuth's Unknown Federalist Papers".

(2) This essay was first published in 1951 in the review **Uj Magyar Ut**, Washington, D.C. Since this year Poland's economic life and resources have been brought in closer contact with the Danubian area, especially with Czecho-

slovakia and Hungary ("Intermetall" etc.). This should be carefully considered. Morphologically, however, Poland and the Baltic States still form a quite distinctively separate area.

The fact that the foreign trade of the East European countries is linked at present up to 30-45 per cent with the Soviet Union, and that the latter furnishes important raw materials ("Friendship"-oil pipe line, iron ore, cotton, etc.), and is also an important buyer of goods, does not involve the necessity that the Soviet Union should be included into a single East European Federation. An independent Danubian Federation will be able to trade on better term with East and West than a fragmented and economically not fully developed area.

Once— it is hoped—also the Soviet Union will be a truly democratic federation, and not a Pan-Russian imperialistic pseudo-federation. In this case friendship and mutual economic relations of the neighboring federation could be as excellent as the economic relations between Canada and the United States.

INITIATIVES TOWARD COOPERATION IN THE
DANUBIAN BASIN IN THE 19TH AND 20TH CENTURIES

PÁL AUER

FEDERATION in the Danubian Basin was first discussed during the revolutionary year of 1848. *Frantisek Palacky*, Czech statesman, in an open letter, suggested the reorganization of the Habsburg Monarchy in line with the principles of Federalization and noted that it would be the only efficient defensive move against German and Russian pressure. Being present at the assembly of Frankfurt, he emphasized his conviction that the Monarchy could not hope to survive unless a federative cooperation is found, and noted that if the Monarchy as a frame of reference would not have been in existence it should have been invented and realized for the benefit of Europe and mankind.

Palacky, by the way, was interested mainly in the fate of people living in Austria; the problems of nationalities in the Hungarian Kingdom were less attractive to him. In his first draft he wanted to federate the Poles, Czechs, Austrian Germans and Illyrians (Southern Slavs). In his second scheme he added the Ruthenians.

The Croatian *Ostrozinski* suggested in a similar way during the fall of 1848, a federative reorganization of the Monarchy. The same year, 1848, saw a recommendation from Poland, *Count Waleryan Krasinski* being responsible for the suggestion of a Western Slav Catholic Federation under the rule of the Habsburgs.

Some years afterwards *Lajos Kossuth* occupied himself, during his exile, with federative ideas. His plan was published in 1862, in the Italian periodical "Alleanze". According to this plan, common decision would have to be reached in matters of foreign relations, military, finances, customs and duties and commmercial legislation. He recommended a Federative Parliament with an executive Federal Council. The capital would have rotated annually between Pest, Bucharest, Zagreb and Belgrade. The Presidency would have gone automatically to the Head of State of that country whose capital city was in the turn of events to become capital of the Federation.

Though he announced that the plan connected with his name was actually the work of *Ferenc Pulszky*, there is no question about

Pulszky, who represented the emigration of Kossuth in London, having not formulated the views of the former Governor of Hungary and of General Klapka.

The Hungarians, Southern Slavs and Rumanians would have built up the federative state, since Kossuth would not have included the Czechs and Austrians. This restriction was partly the cause of the political failure of the scheme. On Kossuth's explanation of his suggestions, Napoleon III replied, that he would have liked best to have the Germans living in three different states and that he regretted their present division in only two, living as they are, in Austria and Germany. He feared that if Kossuth's plan could become a reality, Austria which was left out of it, would have been compelled to join Germany. It is of interest to note, that the spectre of an "Anschluss" already haunted the mind of Napoleon III.

Kossuth addressed the following words to the nations who were to participate in the Federation: "In the name of God the Almighty I entreat my Hungarian, German and Slavonic Brethren, to forget past grievances, to grasp hands, to revolt like one soul, and to fight for the cause of liberty, all for one, and one for all."

The Rumanian *Popovici* also championed a Danubian Federation. In the 19th century another Rumanian writer, *Emanuel Gojdu*, wrote: "I can assure the Hungarian nation, that there is not one Rumanian thinker who is not deeply convinced that Divine Providence, the God of All Nations has decreed his will, that the Hungarian and Rumanian nations have to live in an eternal Alliance. Only then can they hope in a glorious future. A contest between them can only lead to the ruin of both."

Unfortunately, neither the entreaties of Kossuth, nor the allocution of Gojdu have sufficed to move the listeners. What would be the reaction of Gojdu, if confronted with the present genocidal policy of the Rumanian government against the Hungarian minority?

It is of interest to note the views of *István Türr*, the soldier and diplomatist, a friend of Cavour and Kossuth and an intimate of Victor Emmanuel I and Napoleon III. In 1860, his opinions were published in the "Pester Lloyd" and the "Journal des Debats." After discussing a forthcoming congress on European Unity in France, he writes:

"Study Switzerland: The strength of this small country lies in the variety of its composition. The Italian, German and French Cantons know very well, that if they would part, everyone of them would fall victim in a very short time to the aggression of one of their mighty neighbors. Every unit respects the national autonomy and national pecularities of the other federated nation. The same reasons should instinctively impel the different nationalities of the Austrian Empire to move towards a close Confederacy. In the Austrian Empire there are 16 million Slavs, 10 million Germans, 7 million Hungarians and 3 million Rumanians. If these nations could congregate into one political organization, a common state, they could assume the common name of a Danubian Federation."

Until the second decade of the 20th century only scarce mention was made of a possible federative solution of the problems of the Danubian Basin. Only during the First World War, in 1915, did the German Lutheran Pastor *Friedrich Naumann*, who later became a member of the parliament of Weimar, and a candidate for Presidency of the German Republic, but died before the elections, published in his book "Mitteleuropa" and did publicize in many addresses, his plan for a Central European Confederation. It would have worked through common institutions and was to include Germany and the Austro-Hungarian Monarchy.

The author of present essay was asked by Naumann to work out the statutes of an elected Arbitration Court which would have dealt with all disputes arising between members of the Confederation. Naumann did not anticipate the outcome of the war nor the devastating peace treaties.

At the opening of the Austrian Parliament (Reichsrat) on the 30th May, 1917, the Czech delegates demanded a reorganization of the Monarchy into a Federation with a united Bohemia and Slovakia taking part.

It was Archduke Franz Ferdinand, the successor to the throne himself, who previously wanted a reorganization of the Monarchy on the lines of a threefold division instead of the existing dual solution in order to secure to the Slavonic element beside the German and Hungarian participants an equivalent representation. It was, however, exactly the gun of a Southern Slav which made the realization of his ambitious plans tragically impossible. King Charles in his celebrated manifesto of 1918 recommended to his subjects a federalistic solution, though he himself was fully aware that his recommendation was late by "fifty years."

After the end of the First World War, *Oszkár Jászi*, Hungarian minister for minorities, would have liked to form in Hungary a "Switzerland of the East," a Danubian Federation in which all nationalities would have received equal rights and would have been secured equal opportunities of development. But the neighbors of Hungary, who already in the last year of the war had clear ideas of what to expect from the ordinances of the forthcoming peace treaty, turned a completely deaf ear to the suggestions of such a solution. It is well known that the Peace Treaty of Trianon engendered in Hungary an intense movement for redress, whereas in the neighboring states, which enriched themselves at the expense of Hungary, the treaty favored the development of extreme nationalism. Perhaps the only fortunate statute of the treaty was the one which pointed toward a Hungarian-Austrian-Czechoslovakian system of preferences. Unfortunately, all the other ordinances of the treaty led to the birth of such mutual hatred, that the three nations did not live up to the possibilities offered. Instead the Danubian states have built up so many national autarchies, which, especially as the states were small, and not self-sufficient, led to untenable conditions.

In 1920, better to say in the following year, Czechoslovakia, Yugoslavia and Rumania founded a League which became known as the "Little Entente." This League was put onto a permanent footing in 1933. They agreed on a meeting of the Foreign Affairs Secretaries of the three states, which was to take place, from time to time, as resolved. This "permanent council" on ministerial level, could only take unanimous resolutions, so that every one of the three representatives had a veto right. They established a permanent secretariat. The Little Entente occupied itself only with military, it is better to say with diplomatic matters, not with economic questions or any other matter of public interest. The sole purpose of its foundation was to furnish a defense mechanism against an eventual resurgence of territorial demands from the part of a mutilated Hungary. Thus the Little Entente was not a federal body, nor a confederation, but, in its essence, it was a military league. Hungary first tried to take up connections with Yugoslavia and then with Italy, and later it allied itself with the Rome-Berlin axis.

Still back in 1922, the then premier of Bulgaria, *Alexander Stambolijskij*, tried his hand with a Southern Slav Federation, but in vain.

The year 1931 brought the agreement signed by Curtius and Schober which aimed at establishing a customs-union between Austria and Germany. France, naturally, could not remain unmoved. Thus Premier Tardieu found it most convenient to take up a proposition from Budapest which was formulated at a non-official conference.

In 1932, as chairman of the Hungarian Chapter of the Pan-European Union, seeing the success of the policies of Hitler, and having a shrewd guess that the agreement between Curtius and Schober must ultimately lead to an Austrian "Anschluss," and that after the "Anschluss", Hungary will unavoidably slither into a situation of dependence from Germany, I resolved to convene an international conference.

I notified those invited that I do not ask them to attend in the name of the Pan-European Union, because not all of the invited were members of the Union, and that the aim of the conference would be to study whether there is any possibility for the Danubian states to set up amicable cooperation, better said to study what are the premises and methods of such a cooperation. Naturally, I was fully aware that my action was not compatible with the policies of the Hungarian government and so I arranged that no word was breathed about the conference by the newspapers, and I tried by any means to organize the conference in such a way that it remained on a pure study-basis. I was not even certain that those invited would attend. I was rather surprised to get in quick succession letters to the effect that nearly all accepted the invitation. Thus the following made known their intention to attend: from Rumania *Grigore Gafencu,* former Foreign Minister, *Viorel Tilea,* former Minister of the Interior, *Mihail Manoilescu,* former Minister of Finances and *Pillat,* Member of Parliament; from Czechoslovakia *Hubert Ripka,* future Minister of Foreign Trade and *Václav Schuster,* Minister of Finances; from Yugoslavia *S. Franges,* former Minister of Agriculture and *Givotic,* former Consul General; from Austria *Dr. George Günther,* former Minister of Foreign Affairs, *Dr. Heinrich Mataja,* the well-known Member of Parliament of Bosnian descent and *Strakosch-Feldingen,* the famed economist; from my own compatriots, *Gusztáv Gratz,* former Minister of Foreign Affairs, *György Lukács,* former Minister of Education, *Elemér Hantos,* former state secretary in the Ministry of Commerce, *Antal Rainprecht,* Member of Parliament and *Antal Székács,* Chairman of the Chamber of Commerce and Industry in Budapest. In the forthcoming deliberations the following persons also took part besides those already mentioned: *Dr. Basch,* Chairman of the National Bank of Czechoslovakia, *Lazar-Markovic,* former Yugoslavian Minister of Justice, *Moncilo Nincic,* former Yugoslavian Minister of Foreign Affairs, *Feest,* the "Praesidealchef" of the Austrian Chancellery, and from Hungary, *Dr. Tibor Eckhardt,* chief delegate to the League of Nations, and Member of Parliament.

The Conference was convened for the 12th of Feb., 1932. On the previous day, I unexpectedly was telephoned by *Louis de Vienne,* Ambassador of France to Hungary, who complained that in spite of our-amicable relations, I did not notify him of a conference which holds such exceeding interest for his government, and which will take place on the next day. The French Government clearly got word of the conference from either the Rumanian or from the Czech participants. But I was still more surprised that an hour before the conference started, I was telephoned at home by *Antal Mocsony,* the Chief Equerry of the King of Rumania, a person whom I did not know before and who was not invited to the conference, but who now asked for an urgent interview. We met just before the conference and he told me that he was authorized by his sovereign to take part in the conference if feasible, as an observer, for the king, who entertained the greatest interest in the development of friendly relations between the Danubian nations and who regards the conference as an important event.

From the beginning to the end, the consultations were carried through in a most friendly atmosphere. During the banquet on the first night, *Gafencu* delivered a beautiful, poetic address about the necessity of a Danubian cooperation, of the mutual interests of the nations living on the shores of the Middle Danube and of the bewitching charm of the Danubian Basin whose influence we all feel. During the conference it became clear that though we all hoped for the realization of a Danubian Federation or at least of a Confederation in the future, still for the time being our immediate task should be a deepening of economic ties, because time is not yet fully ripe for a solution on the political level. Thus, the same thing happened much later in Western Europe where the six states forming a cooperative body, in spite of their final aim at a political solution, contended themselves presently with the setting up of an economic cooperative organization.

Gusztáv Gratz and *Elemér Hantos*, both eminent political economists, suggested the formation of a standing committee which would be convened from time to time. Thus we founded the "Comité pour le Rapprochement Economique des Pays Danubiens," and I was elected Chairman. The committee was operative until it was blocked by the policies of Hitler. We had sessions in Basel, Vienna and again in Budapest. A periodical was also founded. At the conference which began on the 12th of Feb., 1932, we finalized a draft in order to be submitted to the Governments of the Danubian Basin, which contained as its essence suggestions amounting to a lowering of customs duties between the Danubian countries, the cancelling of import and export restrictions, better to say prohibitions, the introduction of mutual preferences for the industrial goods of Austria and Czechoslovakia on the one hand, and for the agricultural produces of Hungary, Czechoslovakia and Rumania, on the other hand. We further suggested that non-Danubian countries should participate in the implementation of the plan by abolishing their "most favored nation" clauses and by securing unilateral preferences for the agricultural produces of Southeastern Europe. Our aims was first the creation of a unified Danubian economic territory and second, that the Western nations by buying the agricultural products of the Danubian states, should offer a secure market for these commodities against overseas competition through preferential treatment. Naturally, we also hoped that the new situation thus created will eventually lead in the Danubian Basin to peaceful political cooperation, the solution of the question of the minorities, and to a greater independence in relation to Germany.

De Vienne, the French Ambassador, asked on the next day for the submission of our decisions and sent them with special courier to Paris. Tardieu faced by impending elections and in need of a plan for Central Europe, favorable for French policies, but outbalancing the *Curtius-Schober* agreement, saw at once its utility, and at once adopted it. In the West hardly anybody was privy to the intelligence, and it is even today unknown, that the "Tardieu-Plan," which acquired notoriety in its time, was born at an unofficial conference held in Budapest.

The same *Louis de Vienne* who notified his premier of the results of our deliberations, wrote a book in 1937, "Le Guépier de l'Europe

Central." He argued that the only possible solution of the problems of the Central Danubian Region lies in federative ideas, but such a solution has for its premises the abandonment of the rigid negative policies of the Little Entente governments when challenged by the territorial problems of Hungary.

The realization of the Tardieu-Plan was successfully obstructed by the negative attitude of Italy and Germany. The importante of the Plan was anyhow already greatly diminished by the fact that it was only meant to take effect in the economic sphere. The conference of Stresa in 1935, convened on French initiative, closed its deliberations in the same way without results.

The only statesman of the Little Entente who tried in 1935-36, to bridge the differences between the Little Entente and the stipulations of the "Protocols of Rome" was *Milan Hodza*, a former Czechoslovak Premier. But he too had to restrict himself to economic measures and had to be content with modest demands: abolition of increases in customs duties and cancellation of currency restrictions in addition to the favored use of Yugoslav ports instead of German ones. Hodza, by the way, was the only statesman of note, of the Little Entente, who mentioned before the author the possibility of a revision of the Hungarian frontiers. *Tomás Masaryk* was, besides him, the only other person whose statements were such that they allowed the deduction of a similar viewpoint. Hodza, in 1942, turned to the West in a book, where he brought together his views regarding a federative solution. He pointed out the dangers of the Soviet regime and the necessity of support to be given to the democratic governments in Central Europe, and emphasized the important role to be played by the present populations of the Danubian states. According to his solution, federation should be built around a common President and a common Congress, which should be elected by the national parliaments. He recommended a federation of the three states of the Little Entente with Hungary, and Austria and even, perhaps, Poland. The plan, however, ran into difficulties because of the foreign policy of Yugoslavia which, at that time, was hostile toward Italy, and appeared to be influenced by an apprehension against Habsburg restoration in Austria, and a further obstructing factor was present in German pressure upon Rumania.

During the peace negotiations after the Second World War, I was assigned the unpopular role to deliver an address dealing with the question of the Hungarian-Rumanian border. I was asked by the Hungarian Ministry of Foreign Affairs to show my manuscript. I, naturally, complied with the demand. In my draft I pointed out that contemporaneously with a revision of the frontier lines, the organization of a Danubian Federation would be necessary. But this part of my address was cancelled. Immediately after the war, even during the last year of the war, there existed several federative suggestions.

The so called "Intermarium"—group should here be mentioned which wanted to organize into a federation all nations which lived between Germany, Austria and Italy on the one side, and Russia, on the other. The author of present article published on the 20th of Feb., 1946, a letter to the New York Times, which contained the following passages: "The peace treaty to be concluded with Hungary and Rumania will more or less decide the fate of all Danubian countries. At last the preliminary conditions for cooperation among Danubian nations must be created and the possibilities of its evolution must be secured. Peace, calm, a balanced situation, the solution of minority problems, the securing of the existence of Austria who proved to be incapable of living by herself, the advantages of great economic units can be secured in Southeastern Europe only if the anarchy lasting since 1918 among the nations living here, comes to an end and if again some form of cooperation is developed."

"The Great Powers, the Council of Foreign Ministers, or the Security Council of the United Nations Organization should ... take upon themselves the role of advisers and initiators and should give assistance to creating suitable conditions for economic cooperation and its unhampered functioning."

"They ought to stipulate for the gradual winding up of customs duties for economic rationalization and joint sale for their products; for the establishment of a Danubian "Tennessee Valley" scheme, the accord of these countries' foreign policies; the equitable solution of minority problems; the provision for periodical meetings of foreign, finance and economic ministers and bank presidents as well as of meetings of parliamentary delegations. Only thus will it be possible that the treaties should bring the long awaited peace to the harassed Danubian countries."

Though immediately after the revolution of 1917, the Soviet leaders delighted in the use of federative slogans, nevertheless they were not prepared to accept federation within their satellite empire. The Bulgarian *Dimitrov* favored a Danubian, especially Balkan Federation, which was enough for Stalin to liquidate him, thus persisting in the old tradition of divide and rule.

On the 26th of June, 1946, *E. Bevin*, then British foreign secretary received, in Paris, the Hungarian Peace Treaty Delegation. Bevin made some interesting remarks about the Hungarian-Rumanian frontier line and the position of the Hungarian minority in Czechoslovakia, and, then literally stated the following: "I myself as a member of organized labor, am constantly giving priority to economic problems, and I am favoring solutions which are apt to secure to nations an increase in their standard of living. Already during the war I tried to persuade the leaders of the Eastern European Governments then residing in London, as for instance Benes and Sikorski, that they should endeavour to create a customs-union or if not feasible, economic agreements which will enable every nation in Eastern Central Europe to realize its own economic interests."

At present, as the dependence on Russia seems to become somewhat less severe and the Danubian nations are again beginning to hope for a better future, the same problem, or at least the discussion of the problem, regains timeliness. Its importance is now greater than it ever was. It is really a commonplace today that small nations might only then secure their survival and independence, if they are able to become members of a larger formation within which hegemonic aggression is eliminated. Today we live in an era of "interdependence." The hope today of the Danubian nations lies in their membership within an European community. It might be possible, however, that the Soviet Union, once reconciled with the restoration of self-determination in the Danubian countries, will nevertheless uphold the condition, as already done in the case of Austria, that these states should not join any European community. It is further possible that the West European countries will not move to accept these nations in their midst, immediately after the Restoration of Human Rights, or, perhaps, the new configuration of the economic and social structure will need some time to adapt itself to the new situation. In all these cases, a federative cooperation shall by all means become necessary. But even in the event that an integration into the European Community should meet no objections in the course of its realization, even then, within the fold of the European economic and let us hope, political community, the Danubian countries would be able to play, in the form of an integrated economic unit, a much more decisive role than in a state of disorganization, entering the community as separate states.

It is unnecessary to emphasize, that the importance of a federative solution does not stem from economic considerations alone or from the necessity to secure a position in which we would no more become victims of the power politics of great nations, thus securing peace in Europe, but also it is of the highest importance to solve through federation the vexed question of national minorities, especially if the treaty between the states could be supplemented by a more intimate administrative federation. Perhaps all the commonly endured deep sufferings, the lessons of the past, and an equalization of social and economic structures, will at last, in spite of renascent neo-nationalistic tendencies, secure a peaceful and close cooperation of the nationalities within the Danubian Basin.

FEDERALIST ASPIRATIONS IN EAST CENTRAL EUROPE

EDMUND I. LAZAR

THE somewhat fictious theory that before man lived in society he dwelt in a "state of nature" was helpful in explaining the contract theories of the 16th century. Hobbes called this condition the "state of war" in which every man was against every man. The unrestricted individual was driven by competition, diffidence and glory, and his passions were held in check only by force. Thus it was necessary for mankind to enter society in order to end this *Bellum omnia contra omnes.*

Therefore, man transferred part of his sovereign powers to the State and the "state of nature" ceased to exist within the borders of the state. But already Hobbes realized that this was just a partial solution because sovereign states do not obey higher laws and thus they still live in a "state of war". In his words, "though there had never been any time, wherein particular men were in in a condition of warre one against another: yet in all times Kings, and Persons of Sovereign authority, because of their Independency, are in continual jealousies, and in the state and posture of Gladiators; having their weapons pointing, and their eyes fixed on one another; that is, their Forts, Garrisons, and Guns upon the Frontiers of their Kingdoms; and continual Spyes upon their neighbours;; which is a posture of War."[1]

Would it not be accurate to say that the national state, which claims absolute external sovereignty and adheres to no limitation of its power to any international organization or law is motivated by competition, diffidence and glory, and limited merely by force? Hobbes' *jus naturale*, which is the "Liberty . . . to use his power, as he will himself, for the preservation . . . of his own life, and consequently, of doing any thing, which in his own judgment, and reason he shall conceive to be the aptest means thereonto . . ." is actually the sovereign power of the national state.[2]

This "state of nature" in which states live today can have tragic consequences. Through the tremendous technical progress in the 20th century, modern weapons are capable of destroying humanity. But it is also true that "Technical progress which annihilates distance, time, and geographical barriers makes possible a spiritual unity".[3]

However, there is an obvious cleavage between technical development and spiritual development. International solidarity and cooperation are lagging far behind material progress.. The material development has not been accompanied with equal progress in humanistic
culture, social relations and international relations. As Gross formulates it, we have "alongside our twentieth-century weapons ... nineteenth century relations between nations."[4])

There is an obvious need for states to enter the "society of nations", to obey higher laws in order to put and end to international
anarchy. There were many attempts made in this direction. The most
noted ones, the League of Nations and the United Nations, tried to
achieve world society by one bold step, the latter acknowledging the
usefulness of regional organizations. It seems, however, that the
proper architecture of this world society would be to start out by
uniting small nations in regional units, which units then would meet
the contemporary economic, political and cultural needs of the people involved.

What should the method of unification be? There are two major
methods: unification by force, by domination based on power; or
unification by consent, based on equality and cooperation. This latter
one we call federation. We see both methods used on a limited basis
today. Soviet Russia achieved a certain union by conquering the different peoples in her orbit. Nazi Germany used the same method. On
the other hand, Switzerland united different nationalities, peoples of
different religions and tongues in a cohesive union. The founding
fathers of the United States created a stable, strong and successful
union applying federalist principles to the heterogeneous elements of
the large North American continent.

In the microcosmos of the multi-national, multi-state region, we
find the macrocosmic problems of a whole continent, or even those
of world society. Such a multi-national, multi-state region is East
Central Europe and in the microcosmos of this region, the macrocosmic problems of Europe are nearly completely represented.

Definition of Terms

A. Federation

Federation is a process, which aims at the establishment of a federal system, or federal government. This process can be the unification of parts, or the limited dissolution of one unit. Political scientists
defined federation in following ways: By federation, K. C. Wheare
means the "method of dividing powers so that the general and regional
governments are each, within a sphere, coordinate and independent".[5])

The following definition is from a less recent source: "Where several states unite themselves together under a common sovereignty and establish a common central government for the administration of certain affairs of general concern, or where a number of provinces or dependencies are by unilateral act of their common superior transformed into largely autonomous self-governing communities, we have a federal union, or federal state."6)

"The name federal government may be applied to any union of component members where the degree of union between the members surpasses that of mere alliance, however intimate, and where the degree of independence possessed by each member surpasses anything which can fairly come under the head of mere municipal freedom."7)

"In the federal state, the member states have a part, described by the constitution in forming the supreme will of the state. In a federal state, the sovereignty lies in the central government which is separated from the member states".8)

Karve points to the failure of eminent jurists to find a satisfactory definition of federation. He believes that the principle of federalism is not like a principle of an exact science, thus any definition might not stand the test of observation and experience for all time. His careful definition is the following: "Federation is the name wi give to the process by which a widening sense of social solidarity is reconciled with the attachment for local identity, through the provision of dual political organization."9)

B. Federalism

This term could be called also the federal principle or the federal idea. It explains more than just the legalistic and institutional aspects of this political method. Here are the more enlightening definitions of federalism: Lang explains federalism by saying:

"Its aim is diversity within unity and pointing out that federalism's transcendent or universal character penetrates, but does not absorb. The interaction of each federated part creates an organic unity that avoids a chaos of the dynamic parts. There is an interdependence between the particular and the universal. A federal polity is not an aggregate of its component members, it is not the sum of its local and general governments, it is a synthesis which is greater than, and different from the congregation of its parts. Federalism is a means for establishing order without sacrificing freedom among states that refuse to be amalgamated but realize that they must be united. Federalism, however, is more than political mechanics, it is also a symbol of union. Where there is federalism, political bodies have decided to accomplish some purpose in common, to some degree, under a rule of law. Since the federal structure must rest upon connsent as well as a collective purpose, it cannot be imperially imposed. Federalism is sim-

ultaneously a political technique and a social synthesis; it is a method, an ideal, a mechanism and a symbol."[10]

Mogi, the Indian scholar of federalism gives the following interesting definition: "The federal idea is the formation of harmony between plurality and unity on the basis of pragmatic utilitarianism on the ethical basis".[11] Mogi thinks that the federal idea is not confined to the political sphere of the state, but is the general basis of human organization. "The federal idea is the spirit of the pragmatic interdependence of the pluralistic universe and its theory is the basis of human association of any kindn. I may describe the new federative theory as the applied science of that pluralism, which is the guiding principle of the theory on which the harmony between unity and plurality is based, or, in other words, the theory of equilibrium."[12]

Werner Kaegi emphasizes that federalism is not against unity, it is but opposed to the tendency of "Gleichschaltung". He believes it is a unity in which "die Autonomie der Glieder und damit der Eigenart und Vielgestaeltigkeit im Rahmen des Ganzen Raum laest; es ist eine Einheit, in der die Glieder ein recht haben, Ordnung und Weg des ganzen Verbandes irgendwie mitzubestimmen. Diese Verbindung von Selbstbestimmung und Mitbestimmung—die föderative Freiheit— ist für jede föderalistische Ordnung kennzeichnend."[13]

Proudhon, the French socialist, wrote in 1863: "Only federation can solve, in theory and practice the problem of an adjustment between the principles of liberty and authority by leaving everyone his proper sphere his true competence, and his full initiative. Therefore, federalism alone warrants on one hand ineffaceable respect for the citizen as well as for the government, and the other, order, justice, stability".[14] Or, as the Encyclopedia of the Social Sciences formulates it, "Federalism is characterized by a tendency to substitute coordinating for subordinating relationships, or at least to restrict the latter as much as possible. Federalism develops from the theory of social contract. It replaces the Roman idea of domination by force with voluntary agreement, reciprocity, understanding and adjustment. Its basic aspect is pluralistic, its fundamental tendency is harmonization and its regulative principle is solidarity."[15]

If we accept Wheare's reasoning that both general and regional government should be limited to its own sphere and, within that sphere, should be independent of the other,[16] then the theory that the central government has absolute internal sovereignty, would not hold water. Thus it would be safer to say that federalism is the theory or method of equilibrium in a pluralistic society, which voluntarily has united for some common purpose, under the rule of law in a way to preserve and safeguard diversity and the rights of the component parts. Politically, this union is more than a league or a confederation, internally it grants more than just municipal autonomy to its diverse parts.

The knowledge of the federal theory can be helpful, and the lack of its proper understanding — as we will see — was sometimes the major stumbling block on the road towards the East Central European aspirations for a federal union. But even more important is to understand what are the basic preconditions which are necessary to such plans. These preconditions can be the only foundations on which a federation can be built, and in our case, without these foundations all attempts of unity in this troubled and explosive area, which is so richly endowed by nature's gifts, have little or no chance of success.

C. Preconditions to Federal Plans in the Middle Zone

The first precondition for a successful federation of the small East and Central European nations is a new kind of tolerant nationalism. Political nationalism has to be forgotten. Tolerance is of the essence of true nationalism, because respect for my national sentiment presupposes respect for yours. But political nationalism in its tolerance makes exclusive what should be complementary.17)

Secondly, there has to be a desire for unity. This unity cannot come about as the fiat of a great power or one of the members. It has to be based on consent of all parties.

Thirdly, there has to be a desire for diversity. Cultural nationalism can play here a decisive part.

Fourthly, the feeling of equality has to prevail among the participating groups. There can be no racial supremacy presupposed (e.g., Slavism, Magyarism, Germanism). Furthermore, there must be mutual trust among the members desiring the union.

Fifthly, there should be no *basic* economic, social, political or cultural difference among the parts. An extremely poor member can hardly federate with a rich one, a democratic with a feudal society, or an illiterate with a highly cultured group.

Sixthly, there must be a sense of regional solidarity cemented by a common aim.

Seventhly, the kind of Democracy, which is not based on the Jacobinic idea that all intermediary groups and associations standing between the sovereign individual and the sovereign state are intrinsically bad and illegal, but a Democracy where the corporate entities have wide, autonomous powers and exercise quasi-governmental functions. Gross calls it "Inner federalism" and it has a rich tradition in Germany manifested in the Guilds, *Staende* and *Genossenschaften* which strongly influenced East Central Europe.18)

As we see from these preconditions, federalism is not connfined to the political sphere of the state. It becomes, more or less, a general basis for human organization in a racially, religiously and nationally heterogeneous area.

In the course of applying these generalizations to the problems of federalism in the Middle Zone, we have to keep in mind the fact that federalism can act in two directions: There can be a centrifugally acting federalism, its direction is away from the center in order to achieve diversity in unity by taking away power from the general government to strengthen the parts. Centripetal federalism strives, on the other hand, to unite separate entities without sacrificing the autonomy of the members.

In different times, we find both trends working in the Middle Zone. During the Austro-Hungarian Monarchy, federalism had a centrifugal tendency. After the creation of the national states in this area, the direction of federalism is centripetal. As a result, the federalist plans during the Monarchy differ in many respects from those formulated after the fall of the Habsburg Empire. But one similarity should be emphasized: Federalism was always the creed of the progressive, revolutionary elements, and centralization, whether within the Habsburg Monarchy or the national states, was always the aim of the reactionaries. Even the leaders of the national revolutions in 1848-49 ended up as advocates of federalism.

Federalism in this area first had to work together with nationalism, but after the Second World War excessive nationalism became its greatest enemy. "Its beginning can be traced to the divergence between the traditional, and still semifeudal, political unit on the one hand, and the units emphasized by the nineteenth and twentieth century nationalism on the other. The historical unit was multi-national. If these units were to be preserved, and the national principle recognized at the same time, a federation of national units was supposed to be created".(19) But, unfortunately, federation never materialized in this area. Its main obstacles were national vanity, vested interest, political immaturity and intellectual aridity. To quote Lang: "deferred hopes, missed opportunities, but unwearied purpose is the substance of our tale ... In this region, as in all Europe, the federal cycle ... is one of aspiring hopes, ineffectiveness, catastrophe, and renewed hope with a heightened tension of urgency."(20)

D. The Middle Zone

East of Germany and west of Russia lies a troubled area consisting of small states, most of them dominated by a foreign power, where democracy, freedom and peace were seldom experienced in its turbulent history and where the causes of the two last wars originated. Close to one-hundred million people live in this area and they speak Lithuanian, Estonian, Latvian, Polish, Ukrainian, Ruthenian, Czech, Slovak, German, Hungarian, Rumanian, Croatian, Slovenian, Serbian, and Bulgarian language. There are few territories where groups are homogeneous. In most cases, they are mixed together, members of the same group can be isolated from each other by other groups, as the Szekler Magyars and Transylvanian Germans are. Consequently, there are and there were no racially just borders because no national border could include all nationalities of one group, without including members of another language group.

A statistical survey will show the dilemma of this area more clearly:

1937 Country	Km.² Territory	Population	Percentage of the leading nationality
Czechoslovakia	140,508	15,263,399	50.8%
Hungary (1937)	93,086	9,038,189	97.0%
Hungary (1910)		20,886,000(21)	54.5% (22)
Yugoslavia	247,542	15,400,177	41.7% Serb
			23.5% Croat
Bulgaria	103,146	6,319,200	91 %
Rumania	295,049	19,646,151	85.7%
Poland	388,634	34,596,000	90 % (23)

The problem of a satisfactory solution in this area became acute after the decline of feudalism and with the beginning of nationalism in the 18th and 19th centuries. Until that time national groups lived under rulers, who were very often not even a member of the dominant race. For example, the Polish King and Transylvanian Prince Báthory was from 1571 to 1581 a Magyar. The greatest Hungarian kings were from the House of Anjou, Charles Robert (1307-1342) and his son Louis the Great (1342-1382), and even the "national" kings were the offsprings of such mixed royal marriages so that it would be hard to say that the Jagellos, Podebrads or even the Habsburgs represented only one national group.

The emergence of nationalism worked as a strong centrifugal force against the existing larger Empire units. These empire units within or extending into the Middle Zone were Russia, which dominated the Baltic nations and part of Poland, and the Habsburg empire.

To cope with the forces of nationalism and other centrifugal forces as different religion, historical background, etc., two methods were used: One was increasing centralism and the denial of rights to the minority groups. The other was an attempt to create national states with more or less success, climaxing in the brutal expulsion of dominated minorities. The first method was used by the Empire units, the second was tried after the first and second world wars. The third method, peaceful federation, based on democratic self-government was never tried in practice in the Middle Zone, despite a sequence of plans, attempts and half-solutions.

F. Vanishing Political, Economic, Cultural and Social Differences

Between the two wars, the East Central European countries had a great variety of political and social systems. Albania, Bulgaria, Yugoslavia and Rumania were monarchies. Hungary, Austria and Poland were a mixture of semi-democratic parliamentary system and autocracy. Czechoslovakia was a democracy. In Hungary and to some extent in Poland, the semifeudal, great-landowning classes had considerable power. In the other countries, the land reforms broke the power of this class. There was also a striking difference in the cultural levels of these peoples.

Under Communist rule great changes took place. These changes equalized the East European satellites to a large degree politically, culturally, economically and socially. North of Greece, up to the Scandinavian countries, the political form of government is republican everywhere. The so-called satellite countries are under foreign rule, which even Austria had experienced, to a certain extent in her Eastern province up to 1955. There is little doubt that all captive nations desire freedom from foreign rule, and it seems that most people of this area desire a free, democratic form of government.(24)

On orders from Moscow, all satellite governments initiated sweeping land reforms. They are all similar except the initial reform in Czechoslovakia which "was totally different in cause, aim and scope."(25) In Hungary the reform abolished all holding over 100 yokes (acres). About 642.000 poor peasant families received small farming estates.(26)

Bulgaria hardly needed any land reform, the average size of a Bulgarian farm before the war being only five hectars. Bulgaria with its "land-reform" started immediately collectivizing agriculture.(27) The Polish land reform was similar to that of the Hungarian. In Rumania all private holdings over fifty hectares were wiped out. The new allotments were not to exceed five hectares.(28)

The basic land reform of 1945 in Czechoslovakia, according to Shepherd "was not an agricultural revolution as such, but an extension of the racial and political offensive launched in every sector against the Sudeten German and Hungarian minorities."(29) It was entitled by one Czech authority "the national purge of Czech land ownership".(30) Its national tendency was best illustrated in Decree No. 12 of June 21st, 1945, issued by the Benes Government.(31) The second Land Bill was more in line with the satellite reforms which in 1947 limited private landholding to fifty hectares.

The achievements of East European land reforms seem rather insignificant today, when after many years of ruthless drives the greatest part of the arable land is collectivized. But the Hungarian Revolution showed that in case of the overthrow of the Communist regime, though the kolkhozes were immediately dissolved, no one challenged the right of the small farmer to his post-landreform holdings. The industrial and trade situation is also rather similar in all satellite countries.(32)

On the cultural field, illiteracy is one of the basic measuring rods. The following table shows that although there were still large differences among the illiteracy rates of the East European countries, these differences were diminishing.

Country	Illiteracy rates in percentage	
	1937	1949
Czechoslovakia	4.1%	—
Hungary	9.6%	6.0%
Poland	23.0%	6.1%
Rumania	.	23.0%
Yugoslavia	45.0% (33)	25.0% (34)

The school system in the satellite countries has been standardized. There is a eight year general or elementary school, a four year secondary or technical school and four years of university or technical college.(35)

There is another interesting cultural phenomenon in the satellite countries. A spectacular rise occurred both in the number of East European books translated into each other's languages and in the ethnic minority language publications.

In 1933 there were no East European translations in Rumania or Hungary. Only one Czech book was translated into Hungarian and published in Czechoslovakia (Karel Capek, *Beszélgetések Masaryk Tamással*, Mukacevo, 1933).(36)

In 1935

Rumania		Czechoslovakia		Hungary
Rumanian language book translated into Hungarian	1	Czech language book translated into Hungarian	2	No translations from East Central European languages
Hungarian translated into Rumanian	1	Hungarian translated into Czech	none(37)	

This chart illustrates, on the cultural scene, the enmity which was prevailing among most of the Danubian nations towards each other. In Hungary, publishers did not handle Rumanian, Serb, or Czech books and the public was not interested in them. On the other hand, for the three million Hungarians living outside the border of Hungary, the succession states published merely 3 books.

This kind of cultural chauvinism changed after Soviet domination, as the following charts will show.

In 1956

Translated from	Number of Books into Hungarian	Number of Books into Czech	into Rumanian
Serbian	4	2	1
Polish	5	16	3
Czech	10	—	2
Rumanian	4	—	—
Bulgarian	2	3	4
Slovak	1	16	—
Hungarian	—	9	13

In Rumania the same year there were:

     26 German
     75 Hungarian
     12 Serbian   language publications

In Czechoslovakia:

     19 Hungarian
     6 German   language publications[38]

In 1958

Translated from	Number of Books into Hungarian	Number of Books into Czech	into Rumanian
Czech	9	—	6
Serbian	6	2	1
Polish	5	10	5
Rumanian	3	2	—
Hungarian	—	5	18
Bulgarian	1	—	—

In Rumania the same year:

     47 Hungarian
     7 Serbian   language books were published

In Czechoslovakia: ·

     18 Hungarian   language books were published[39]

1959 figures are available from Hungary only.

Language translated from	Into Hungarian No. of Books	Combined Circulation
Czech	16	101,300
Rumanian	6	56,900
Serb and Croatian	4	38,500
Polish	7	82,100[40]

It should be noted, that the first two charts include all books translated in the respective countries. The last three charts include only the literary works.

The Communist emphasis of classless society, the persecution of the former leading classes, the admission policies in the institutions of higher learning, made the social stratification in all satellite countries similar. Except for the hatred against the Communist "New Class" there is little or no class antagonism left in East Europe.

The peoples of this area have one common enemy, the Soviet Union, and if there is some lack of brotherly love among the East European nations, the fellowship of common bondage is undoubtedly present. The best evidence for this fellowship is the Hungarian Revolution in 1956, when the people of Hungary, liberated from the Communist Russian bondage, chose freely the path leading to an eventual free federation of Danubian nations. The unpopular Communist puppet governments, on the other hand, lapsed into chauvinism and used it as a weapon to silence and kill the real desires of the East European peoples.

G. The Ideas of Federalism in the Hungarian Revolution.

The Hungarian Revolution of 1956 is important for this study because it was the first opportunity, in a long time, for a Danubian nation to speak out freely, to express its desires, opinions and formulate its goals. Although there were only a few days of freedom in Hungary, public opinion was surprisingly active. Student and worker committees and other political councils were formed together with political parties. In most cases these committees and councils, which were more active than the parties, were elected or appointed by the politically more active element, or as in the case of the National Council of County Vas, and many others they "were formed from representatives of the former coalition parties," obviously drawing their authority from the last free election in 1945, or in some cases the quasi free election in 1947.(41) There the Peoples Democratic Party appealed "to the country as a whole, and primarily to those 800,000 constituents who voted for us in 1947 despite terror and election fraud."(42)

The parties, national councils and committees first formulated their demands and programs and these were supposed to be, according to unanimous agreement, laid before the people which would decide as soon as possible, in a free election. These demands and programs, because of their similarity, can be regarded as the true expression of public opinion. Do they prove the proposition that the Danubian nations desire a closer cooperation? That there is little or no chauvinism? That the emotional precondition for federation is present? As far as Hungary is concerned the proof is convincing. Hugh Seton-Watson even claims that the behaviour of Hungary's neighbors is also a proof for this new friendliness of Danubian nations.[43]

The first mentioning of a federal solution in East Europe comes from the joint meeting of the Student's Parliament of Miskolc on October 26, 1956. Among their 18 demands, number eight states: "Our country should become a member of the Danubian Federation proposed by Kossuth."[44] These demands were broadcasted from Budapest through Radio Free Kossuth.

The Veszprém county Revolutionary National Council issued a proclamation in which point 4 demands:

The Hungarian Government should turn more attention to Hungarians living outside the Hungarian border and should get in contact with these minorities. The Foreign Policy Committee of the Parliament should initiate the reconsideration of the Warsaw Pact and should propose the formation of a Danubian Confederation.[45]

Radio Free Miskolc on October 30, sent this appeal to Hungary's neighbors:

Slovaks! Rumanians! Serbians! Blood is flowing from our wounds and you are silent. We are fighting for liberty and you call us Fascists ... We see that you too are groaning under the yoke we wish to throw off ... We are fighting for you too, for peace, for Socialist truth, for the guarantee of free development of our peoples. Help us in our fight![46]

The *Magyar Szabadság*, a newly published newspaper, on November 1, 1956 wrote a first page editorial emphasizing the need for cooperation with other East European nations.

The most important basis of our foreign policy must become the friendship and cooperation with the neighboring small nations. The lack of our independence hindered this, although the close alliance of the Danubian nations already has been Kossuth's idea. Yes, Hungary, from now on, has to work for the establishment of Kossuth's great legacy, the confederation of the Danubian peoples. This must be the most important demand of our foreign policy because only this way can the small nations, living in this area, permanently safeguard their independence.[47]

The Council of Free Trade-Unions had the following published in its official paper:

As of today we are no longer the tool of a colonialism disguised as socialism, nor a figure on the chess-board of some conqueror or other ...

We are extending a friendly hand towards all peoples—to our neighbor, neutral Austria, and to free Yugoslavia which remains outside any blocs, towards Rumania, Czechoslovakia and the people of the Soviet Union, we hope that their Governments will understand our little nation's thirst for freedom and national life . . .(48)

On the third of November, Free Radio Kossuth reported that the following gift consignments arrived in Budapest by air in recent days: "20 plane-loads from Poland, 26 plane-loads from Vienna, 9 plane-loads from Switzerland, 7 from East Germany, 2 from Bulgaria, 2 from Czechoslovakia and 1 each from Rumania, Yugoslavia and Belgium."(49)

Cardinal Mindszenty in his broadcast the same day said:

We . . . desire to live in friendship and in mutual respect with the great American United States, and the mighty Russian Empire alike, in good neighborly relationship with Prague, Bucharest, Warsaw and Belgrad. In this regard I must mention that for the brotherly understanding in our present suffering every Hungarian has embraced Austria to his heart.(50)

Radio Miskolc and Nyiregyháza sent the following message in Slovakian and Rumanian languages.

Rumanian and Slovak brothers! We are bleeding and you are silent? We are fighting for freedom and you call us Fascists? . . . We are not fighting for irredentism, we proclaim friendship. When we visited you this year you welcomed us with friendship. We saw that you were suffering from the same thing we are now trying to get rid of. Now, to serve foreign interests they want to incite you against us. They lie and slander us . . . When we are talking about a confederation, we want friendship! . . . For us, brotherly nations, we want free development in a neutral political system . . .(51)

The reaction of the other captive nations to the Hungarian events in 1956 gives little indication of their true feelings. The official Communist press, with the exception of Poland and Yugoslavia, echoes the Moscow line and describes the revolution as a reactionary plot of former landowners and aristocrats, incited by Western capitalists to overthrow the People's Democracy of Hungary. But, the *New York Times* reports that in Rumania "protest demonstrations" broke out among "Hungarian-speaking and Rumanian-speaking students." Also "Factory workers and railway employees . . . were known to have expressed open dissatisfaction."(52)

There were several messages of sympathy and friendship from Poland. Even the official press did not come out openly against the revolt. *Trybuna Ludu* wrote the following on October 28:

Many of us are asking ourselves the dramatic question: How has it come about that under the conditions of people's rule a considerable part of the Hungarian people has come out armed in opposition? ... Although, as usually happens ... irresponsible and in some case reactionary elements joined in action, they do not constitute the backbone of such long-lasting and intense struggles. The answer to the question posed should not be sought in a simplified version about "alien agencies" nor in looking for counter-revolution at every step ...(53)

Or, as M. Bielicki wrote in *Po Prostu:* "the whole nation is on the side of the insurgents ... and on the other the Stalinist faction of the Government and the AVO."(54)

Hugh Seton-Watson, professor of Russian History at the University of London sums up the attitude of Hungary's neighbors:

The neighboring small nations did not fight against Hungary in 1956 as they had done in 1848-49 and in 1919. Certainly the Hungarians gave them no excuse, for during these weeks there was no sign of nationalist claims against Slovaks, Serbs or Rumanians. On the contrary, repeated appeals for friendship and help were heard. An unconfirmed report states that the Soviet leaders asked the Rumanian government to send forces against Hungary and that it refused on the ground that it could not count on the obedience of its army. Student demonstrations took place in some Rumanian cities, both in Transylvania and in the Old Kingdom, and it seems there was some unrest among workers in Bucharest. The Yugoslav government expressed sympathy for Nagy in the first days, then justified the second Soviet intervention. In Czechoslovakia there was no sign of activity. At least these countries did not join in the repression.(55)

During the Hungarian Revolution, one does not find any utterances of revisionism or demonstrations of hatred against the other Middle Zone people. This is surprising, because the three million Hungarians living outside the border of this country constitute a fact which normally could cause great bitterness. This lack of hostility can be attributed to the growing spirit of reconciliation among the peoples of this area. It is not important whom to credit for this new spirit.

The long and unhappy story of federalist aspirations in East Central Europe seems to have several implications. It indicates, for example, that a political system, just by appearing theoretically the best solution has no guarantee for its successful establishment. There must be circumstances, conditions, rational and irrational factors, sociological, economic, and other forces present, which would make a certain political solution inevitable and successful. There seems to be convincing proof that in this case the heart of the matter is not legal or constitutional technique, but the pattern of given conditions. During the Habsburg rule the pattern of given conditions did not promote the success of a federal solution. This was the age of growing nationalism, the belief in racial supremacy. Cultural differences were overpowering among the diverse nationalities. The social structure of the different nationalities caused enmity between ethnic groups, and, finally, the democratic basis was not present. What little democracy was introduced, under Joseph II, was developed along the Jacobin, centralistic lines, detrimental to federalism.

The nation-states, after the First World War, established a variety of political systems. This was one of the greatest obstructions to unity. Tremendous hatred was whipped up by the unfortunate peace settlements which punished and rewarded nations regardless of the consequences. As a result, nationalism degenerated into ugly chauvinism, and irredentism emerged. Regional solidarity was turned into regional enmity. New conflicts grew with the number of new states and the small East Central European nations had "their weapons pointing and eyes fixed on one other..." There was little or no desire for unity as a result of chauvinistic propaganda and hatred campaigns launched against each other.

After the conclusion of the Second World War, despite the efforts of several groups and individuals, the Nation-state system was re-established. The Soviet Union was against any kind of federal solution which *would have endangered her divide et impera* policies and E. Benes, the most influential Middle Zone exile politician, was advocating the homogeneous nation-state solution. This solution, borrowing from Nazi ideology, advocated collective punishment of "guilty" nationalities. E. Benes, who had the ear of Western leaders became the errand boy of Stalin in order to achieve the homogeneous Czechoslovakia, creating thereby a renewed feeling of hatred and revenge in East Central Europe, paying for it with Carpathian-Ruthenia, which he cynically delivered to the Soviet Union, completely disregarding the desires and wishes of the population of that land.

After the Iron Curtain fell and the nations of East Central Europe found themselves in a common prison, the pattern of conditions changed. The aggressive nationalism of these peoples turned against the common enemy. The seemed to develop understanding and even tolerance to each other. This was fostered by the nationality laws forced upon them by Soviet Communism. Common fate and common suffering started to wash out the greater differences among ethnic and national groups. In the early days of the people's democracies, ethnic minorities sought refuge in the Communist Party against persecutions. The Communist nationality policy, at this stage of development, was rather tolerant. It allowed the national minorities their more or less nominal national identity, the use of their own language, the development of their own culture, under leaders, who cooperated with the regime. Of course, the freedoms of local autonomy and administration could go only as far as the Party permitted it, but the fact is that chauvinism has become a term of disapprobation and the "brotherhood of Socialist Peoples" is an often repeated slogan.

The most convincing empirical evidence of the lack of chauvinism seemed to be the rather surprising statements of the Hungarian Revolutionary Committees and Councils and Russia's failure to incite Hungary's neighbors against that rebelling country.

The revolutionary pronouncements also showed that there was a desire for unity, at least as far as Hungary was concerned, and it also indicated that a new feeling of equality has developed among the peoples kept in common bondage.

The equalizing effect on the social, political, cultural and economic life under Soviet domination and the Communist system in East Central Europe seems obvious. When and if the land and waterways, the energy supply network, the systems of economic cooperation and productive specialization will be integrated to a high degree, when the industries, agriculture and other productive factors will be interwoven and linked together among the Middle Zone countries, regional solidarity will not be just a desire, but a necessity, an inescapable fact, an ideal precondition for federation.

Today, the practicality of a federal solution seems more clear than ever to the people in this part of Europe. These obvious practical values could be summarized the following way:

1.) The advantage of bigness to small nations, politically meaning more security against foreign attack and domination, economically the blessings of a large free market area.

2.) More effective safeguards for the liberty of the individual and the group (nationality, religion, regional interest).

3.) The advantage of peace over national antagonism.

4.) The advantage of a free, democratic society, based on consent and collective purpose.

These values and advantages, which already have been so well formulated by Madison, Jay and Hamilton in the Federalist Papers are more clear to the East Central European peoples, because they have behind them the sad experience of centralized, nonvoluntary union, the chaos of the nation-state system and the yoke of foreign domination.

(1) Hobbes, **Leviathan,** Part I, p. 115.
(2) **Ibid,** p. 116.
(3) Felix Gross, **Crossroads of two Continents,** p. 2.

(4) **Ibid,** p. 1.

(5) K. C. Wheare, **Federal Government,** p. 11.

(6) W. Garner, **Political Science and Government,** p. 280.

(7) Freeman, **History of Federal Gov.,** pp. 2-3.

(8) Lufer Posener, **Bundestaat und Staatenbund,** p. 15.

(9) D. G. Karve, **Federations,** p. 9.

(10) Reginald D. Lang, "European Federalism" in E. Gross, **European Ideologies,** pp. 960-965.

(11) Sobei Mogi, **The Problem of Federalism,** p. 1111.

(12) **Ibid,** p. 1111.

(13) Kaegi "Selbsbestimmung und Mitverantwortung", **Schweizer Monatshefte,** Heft 8, November 1959, p. 687.

(14) **Encyclopedia of the Social Sciences,** p. 169.

(15) **Ibid.**

(16) K. C. Wheare, **op. cit.,** p. 15.

(17) Lang, **op. cit.,** p. 963.

(18) F. Gross, **op. cit.,** pp. 44-45.

(19) Rudolf Schlesinger, **Federalism in Central and Eastern Europe,** p. 3.

(20) Lang, **op. cit.,** pp. 978-988.

(21) Hungary including Croatia, Slavonia.

(22) Hungary excluding Croatia, Slavonia.

(23) In 1957 after changes in border and the forceful expulsion of millions of non-Polish inhabitants. (Sources: Felix Gross, **Crossroads of Two Continents,** p. 5-6. A. Suha, **Economic Problems of Eastern Europe and Federalism,** p. 110 ff.).

(24) See G. Shepherd, **Russia's Danubian Empire,** M. Lasky, (ed) **The Hungarian Revolution,** J. Galbraith, **Journey to Poland and Yugoslavia,** Edmund Stillman (ed.), **Bitter Harvest: The Intellectual Revolt Behind the Iron Curtain,** R. Byrnes, **East Central Europe Under the Communists;** Center for International Studies, **Cohesive Forces, Tensions and Instabilities in the European Satellites,** H. Seton-Watson, **The East European Revolution,** etc.

(25) Shepherd, **op. cit.,** p. 146.

(26) **Ibid.,** p. 147.

(27) **Ibid.,** p. 153.

(28) **Ibid.,** p. 155.

(29) **Ibid.,** p. 158.

(30) J. Kotatko, **Land Reform in Czechoslovakia.**

(31) **Ibid.,** p. 159.

(32) "What is Left of Private Enterprise?" **East Europe,** Febr. 1959, pp. 18-31.

(33) **Statistical Yearbook,** United Nations, 1957.

(34) US Department of Commerce, **The Population of Hungary,** p. 79.

(35) US Dept. of Commerce, **Population of Poland,** p. 80.

US Dept. of Commerce, **Population of Hungary,** p. 85.

US Dept. of Commerce, **Population of Czechoslovakia,** p. 27.

(36) League of Nations, **Index Translationum,** No. 10, Oct. 1934.

(37) League of Nations, **Index Translationum,** No. 17, Oct. 1936.

(38) UNESCO, **Index Translationum,** for 1956, No. 9, 1958.

(39) UNESCO, **Index Translationum,** Vol. 11, 1960.

(40) **Magyar Statisztikai Zsebkönyv,** 1960, p. 178.

(41) Broadcast of Radio Free Györ, as quoted in Lasky, **op. cit.,** p. 114.

(42) **Free Radio Kossuth,** November 1, 1956, quoted **Ibid.,** p. 172.

(43) Lasky, **op. cit.,** p. 22.

(44) **Ibid.,** p. 90.

(45) "Rádiók Üzenete", **Nemzetőr,** Oct. 15, 1960, p. 4.

(46) Lasky, **op. cit.,** p. 147.

(47) Nemzetör, **op. cit.,** p. 4.

(48) **Népakarat,** Nov. 2 ,quoted in Lasky, **op. cit.,** p. 204.

(49) **Ibid.,** p. 218.

(50) **Ibid.,** p. 216.

(51) Nemzetőr, **op. cit.,** p. 4.

(52) W. Hangen, **The New York Times,** 3 Nov. 1956.

(53) Lasky, **op. cit.,** p. 134.

(54) **Ibid.,** p. 88.

(55) Hugh Seton-Watson, an Introduction to Lasky, **Ibid.,** p. 23.

NATIONALISM VS. FEDERALISM
IN HISTORICAL PERSPECTIVE

FRANCIS S. WAGNER

IT IS a widely accepted view that nationalism has played an epoch-making role only since and through the eighteenth-century French Revolution. The application of this view makes it very simple to explain the genesis of ancient and medieval political formations of a multinational character by supposing that the centrifugal forces of nationalism were completely unknown prior to the French Revolution. Needless to say, this theory proves to be false if pre-Revolution times are historically scrutinized. It is a well-documented fact that though the main stream of ancient and medieval life most of the time did not involve the phenomena of nationalism, national (racial) differences, in one or another form, worked persistently beneath the surface. This can be fairly well illustrated in the founding and downfall of the Macedonian world empire. When Philip II defeated the Athenians at Chaeronea in 338 B.C., he incorporated Greece, excepting never-conquered Sparta, into the League of Corinth. Representation of its cities in the Synhedrion (Council) was accorded by population and district. Nations outside Greece were encouraged to join the Federation. Philip's son, Alexander the Great, preferred even more than his father, Greek solidarity to city patriotism and dreamt of spreading Greek culture through the Orient in the wake of his triumphal armies. Alexander and his advisers, recognizing the national and racial entity of the peoples conquered, readily adapted themselves to Oriental customs in all respects in order to win their hearts. But the conquerors made a serious miscalculation by underrating the depth of Oriental culture and its impact upon the masses. Therefore, after the sudden death of the Master of the World, during the short-lived reign of his successors, the Diadochi, the empire fell into its original ethnic ingredients and, after a while, quite contrary to the conquerors' expectation, Oriental cults started pouring into Europe, including the concept of the divine right of kings, along the same lines of communication which Alexander's invincible troops opened up.

The history of the vast, nomadic world also has some lessons for the observer which can be drawn from its peculiar power politics.

Despite the tremendous might of politico-military formations organized by the nomadic tribes in the steppe regions of Southeastern Europe and Asia, military strength alone proved incapable of controlling the life of those multitribal states in time of crisis. On such occasions, due to the lack of a widespread and deep-rooted common heritage, these political bodies underwent essential changes or even disintegrated. The example of Tartar, Mongolian and other tribes demonstrates that with the downfall of the leading tribe or the death of the chieftain (khan) the empire crumbles. The Orkhon inscriptions of old Turkish and Chinese writings indeed convincingly reveal this political philosophy of the loosely organized tribal groups when their absolute ruler dies. His death is described by the Orkhon inscriptions as if the whole empire had ceased to exist. Evidently, under such circumstances there was no other possible ground for political and social creations than the absolute power of the chieftain. It cannot be overemphasized that the political structure of the nomadic world was so loosely woven that territorial and organizational, as well as population changes occurred frequently there and, depending upon the radius of the centralized leadership, new and new ethnic groups were compelled to join the "federation", while others were able to secede from it.

Ethnically colorful Europe, and especially its heart, the Danube Valley, has not essentially changed its facade since the late Middle Ages. It was and has been a conglomeration of nations. Before continuing our investigation into these complex ethnic conditions, a very basic difference between the Western and Eastern course of development should be pointed out. In Western Europe, historical conditions made possible the evolution of more or less uniform nations while this unification process totally failed in Central and Eastern Europe. Yet the political leadership of the Central and Eastern European nations tried hard to materialize unification programs even in the twentieth century in order to reshape their countries in line with the Western pattern. This anachronistic approach was responsible for incessant power struggles between the so-called state-forming nations and its national minorities. The situation was fairly complicated by the far-reaching consequences of the Tartar and Turkish yoke and the antagonism was also heightened by religious motives.

As I have mentioned previously, the ethnic map of these territories has always been variegated. Several ethnic groups inhabited each and every state in the Danube area, the overwhelming majority being under foreign rule. The latter made coexistence in certain respects even more explosive. This frictional situation could not subside for centuries since the prevailing socioeconomic foundation did not allow the migration of social classes within the nation. Due to this static state of conceptions of power politics, the latter meaning domination. The two world wars exhausted and weakened Europe biologically and social classes, national minorities, even within towns or villages, have dwelt in their voluntarily chosen "ghettos" almost up to the present. There are virtually very few localities in this mixed area whose early history did not mirror this conglomerate character.

In addition, the European concept of state-church ties has also left its mark on the life of intergroup relations. At the beginning this somewhat helped promote coexistence among ethnic groups. But in modern times it became one of the chief obstacles in the way towards rapprochement, especially when the struggling groups differed in faith. And in a later stage of development, the once so peaceful relationship between religious and political elements terminated partly because the old-fashioned monarchies were incapable of coping with the problems of growing social and economic crises. It should always be noted that in the Danube area this striving for social and economic betterment was organically connected with certain language and literary efforts as well as some church factors boosting the growth of mass nationalism. It can be said that these historic features still belong among the main characteristics of mass movements in the socialist countries. Primary sources can undoubtedly prove that these politically motivated language and literary movements in their origin are, in certain respects, of an autochtonous nature, outside influences being capable only of hastening or modifying their otherwise independent course. This occurred, for instance in Hungary, in 1671, well before modern revolutionary times, when a contemporary source, without any apparent external interference, revealed the inner dynamics of nationalism which has remained essentialy unchanged from its very beginnings: "I wish that God granted the glorious and joyous day when Hungary will speak one language and the entire nation will be united again in the one true faith. . . and adore one God for ever."[1] This short quotation delineates the so peculiar symbiosis of religious and nationalist elements in which nationalism has triumphed absolutely over faith, thus reducing to a minimum degree the role of morality in the nationality struggles. The quotation also indicates clearly that the concept of modern nationalism, already in its initial stage, was tightly interwoven with contradictory principles which later contributed to the disintegration of multinational states.

It is not surprising in the least that in all future nationality troubles the language question, in one form or another, played a unique role. Evidently, its core was already ripe at the outset of the 18th century and only the old social and economic order had to be changed to launch the language-based nationalist mass movement. The language movement, with its highly emotional dynamics and the socioeconomic conditions of changing feudalism, aided reduction of the so-called "Gens Hungarica", which heretofore politically comprised all existing nations within historical Hungary, to its natural and individual elements—the Magyar and numerous non-Magyar nations.

This rapid process of disintegration was greatly stimulated by the Western theory of nationality. This "one language-one nation-one state" concept in general corresponded to the interests of the great homogeneous national states of Western Europe. But this concept and its German practice tragically destroyed the very foundations of any future intergroup collaborations in the multinational states of the Danube Valley. Simultaneously, such concepts as "Deutschungar", and the short-lived "böhmischer Landespatriotismus" also lost their historical significance.

Emperor Joseph II was captivated by the ideas of the Western theory.in this spirit, in 1784, he issued his infamous decree on forceful Germanization by means of language, stating that Latin, heretofore used in Hungary, was no longer suitable for official transactions and must be supplanted by German. At first all the nations of Hungary reacted vehemently against the Germanization decree, defending the constitutional rights of *lingua patria* (Latin) against *lingua monarchica* (German). But a few years later, all these nations started promoting their own vernacular. The 1784 Germanization order and the later centralization policy of the Imperial Court were primarily directed against the Magyar nation, because the Magyars were politically more independent than any other non-German nation and, therefore, repre- sented a greater menace to the realization of the idea of *Gesamt- monarchie*. Chancellor Prince Kaunitz of Austria, as early as 1791, formulated the guiding principle of how to administer a multina- tional state: "The more apparent and well considered the attempts at securing the unity of Hungary, Transylvania and the Illyrian nation, are the more recommended and necessary is the principle of *Divide et impera*."(2)

The political renaissance of mother tongues greatly changed the situation and became a significant factor in nationalist awakening. Josef Dobrovsky at a solemn session of the Czech Society of Sciences in Prague, on September 25, 1791, in the presence of Emperor Leopold II himself, delivered an address on the right of usage of the Czech lan- guage and took a cautious but firm stand against any form of German- ization.(3) Dobrovsky's stand, a mixture of loyalty towards the Habsburg dynasty, Slavophilism and well-concealed Germanophobia, impressed not only the Czech but several other non-German nations. Its effect was so universal that even the philologically oriented Josef Jungmann school distinctly expressed its objective stating that "there are as many nations as languages; there are as many countries as languages."(4) In line with this universal trend, István Kultsár, of Hungary, made an early attempt to summarize the goals of this new form of nationalism: "Only that country can be happy and powerful whose population has a national character. The Magyar nation is first in this country concerning its historical rights, first in numbers, first in the culture of its native tongue ... the name Magyar is so glorious, so ancient and famous, and its reign on this blessed soil has been so glorious during a thousand years' period that every nation holds it a special glory to become a Magyar patriot."(5)

Parallelism between the Czech, Hungarian and all other developments can be clearly demonstrated. Naturally, there were some deviations from the general pattern due to the initial phase of the emerging new national consciousness and its changing spiritual as well as material interests. For example, until the early 1830s, which marks the beginning of a more or less organized Magyarization, the Rumanians rather felt that the Slavs and not the Hungarians were their chief enemies. This was because their Eastern Orthodox Church was administered by the Serbian hierarchy using the Cyrillic alphabet which had no respect for the formation of the Rumanian literary language and culture based upon folk traditions. These Serbo-Rumanian-Hungarian relations contributed to some extent to the enthusiastic reception of the reform achievements of Stephen Széchenyi among the Rumanians in Hungary and Transylvania. And the Magyarization campaign as well as Louis Kossuth's quite chauvinistic articles in *Pesti Hirlap* were also favorably greeted by the Rumanians, for they were primarily directed against the Slavs of Hungary.

The Croatian-Hungarian collaboration seemed to be a continuation of their tranquil life so characteristic of the Middle Ages. Josephinism, the common enemy of both nobilities, brought the leading figures of the two nations so close together that Nicholas Skerlecz, a Croat leader en route to the 1790/91 Diet, asserted publicly that "unbreakable ties joined Croatia to Hungary." But somewhat later during the session of the same Diet, delegates of the two countries clashed on certain main points which were to regulate the practice of religion and language and henceforth no real and lasting compromise was possible between them.(6)

The consistent long-term application of the divide and rule principle by the Vienna Court in dealing with the complex problems of administering the multinational monarchy backfired from the very start. Having disastrous consequences for both the cause of peaceful coexistence and loyalty to the dynasty, this double-faced imperial policy was fast recognized by all parties after the 1848/49 Revolution. Even prior to the Revolution this duplicity was realized by several outstanding nationality leaders, among them Jan Kollar and Ljudevit Gaj, who were simultaneously in the service of Vienna and some foreign powers, the latter working also for Tsarist Russia's secret service.(7) T. G. Masaryk, without having access to relevant documents, clearly analyzed that situation when pointing out that "Croats and Slovaks because of the insincerity of Vienna let themselves be used as instruments of reaction in the name of the Slavic idea."(8)

Presumably the insincerity of the Vienna Court contributed much to the impatient political philosophy and practice of L. Kossuth who may have been coerced by circumstances to make efforts to reconcile such opposite poles as liberalism and chauvinistic nationalism in counteracting the duplicity of the central government. Recently published archival sources unanimously indicate that this double-dealing attitude of the Vienna Government was an organic part of the prelude to the 1848/49 Revolution, a real war of races.

In the second half of the past century, the fast-developing nationality and unity movements came to the fore. Historians, political scientists and other experts focused their research on the past and present events of interracial relations. Fact-finding summaries of events pertinent to the French and German-dominated spheres were the products of their investigations. Several theories and doctrines were drawn from actual development to justify the past and present and to chart the roads of the future. It is interesting to note that these teachings were of vital importance up to the end of World War II.

Towards the turn of the last century, the French concept of the nation as represented by Ernest Renan(9) partly relied upon medieval heritage and refused to acknowledge language and national (racial) origin as basic criteria of the nation. Accordingly, the nation is a spiritual and historical reality, and the moral and cultural attitude of individuals should be the determinants of their nationality. One of the chief means of implementing this theory was plebiscite. This French concept had only slight effect on the German sphere of influence.

Central and Eastern Europe on the whole were affected with the German nationality policies. The historic rivalry between the Germans and the Slavs precluded them from making any positive steps towards normalizing their relations. Thus even such liberal-minded professors as Rotteck and Welcker in their *Staatslexikon* (publ. since 1834) expounded belief in the application of the one-nation one-state principle as healthy and suitable for ethnically mixed areas of Central and Eastern Europe as well. They elaborated that Germanization of the Czechlands and Magyarization of Upper Hungary (Slovakia) should be completed with the view of separating the Northern and Southern Slavs by the area's two "chief nations", the Germans and the Hungarians, to prevent the Russian occupation of the Danube Valley. Apparently, this train of thought led directly to the philosophy of the Austro-Hungarian Compromise of 1867. The afore-mentioned views were shared by the distinguished historian Heinrich von Treitschke *(Politik)* and other pre-eminent authorities of that age, such as, Ludwig Gumplowicz,(10) and Paul de Lagarde.(11) Their viewpoints were thoroughly interwoven with the Bismarckian politics and achievements. These well-trained specialists almost unanimously declared the existence of small nations ridiculous, their rights nil, and the expediency of their assimilation or liquidation in order to create a German Central and Eastern Europe. Through the

Bismarckian practice of their theories, the nationality problem was put on the agenda of important foreign policy issues and has remained so up to the present.

So the nationality question entered the arena of world issues. As a subject of international disputes, the question was not judged objectively, but as a part of propaganda machinery by the maneuvering rival great powers. In this struggle neither Great Britain nor any other European power viewed or treated the situations on ethical grounds. They were all fundamentally interested in throwing the nationality problem as an obstruction in the paths of German, Russian or other imperialisms. They have never regarded the fate of smaller nations seriously. In this respect let us refer to the history of the Poles and the Czechoslovaks who in the time of their crises were not even consulted. Obviously, since the Bismarckian times the question of national minorities, and indirectly the cause of federalism, have become an integral part of the fast-changing foreign policy constellations. The memoirs of T. G. Masaryk, Eduard Benes, Albert Apponyi, Winston Churchill, Charles de Gaulle, Robert Murphy and others can fully prove the soundness of this thesis. The importance of foreign policy factors does not necessarily mean, that the smaller nations have been free of certain innate defects. When the Hungarians were in power, they were inclined to commit precisely the same mistake which was later repeated by others. This hereditary disease has been the forceful execution of the political unity (rather oneness) of ethnically different groups. The main intention of the 1867 Austro-Hungarian Compromise was to create two ruling nations in the Danube area.

A year later, Law No. 44 of 1868 on the equality of the nationalities stemmed also from the basic idea of the Compromise, when its preamble solemnly declared the indivisibility of the so-called Hungarian "political nation", which legal term repudiated the existence of national minorities as individual nations. For this reason, Law No. 44 of 1868 could not promote the cause of equality among different nations and, therefore, was mistitled since the Nationality Law safeguarded only certain rights of using the minority languages.(12)

It cannot be overstressed that exactly the same mistake was and has been made by the inter- and post-bellum non-Hungarian regimes. These new regimes have also insisted upon the forceful implementation of the one nation-one state idea historically so inappropriate to the the ethnically mixed conditions. The architects of the new regimes misapplied Woodrow Wilson's points of self-determination, then the only remedy for curing the old, historic disease. Wilson had good ideas, but his era was unable to devise adequate plans for their realization. Then consequentially, Germans and Hungarians, the state-forming nations prior to 1918, were demoted to minority groups, while others, previously in minority status, rose to leadership. In this new situation the old, historic problem of coexistence under nonhomogeneous ethnic conditions has remained unsolved. I think this is the essence of the present-day situation which has been developing at least from the end of the eighteenth century.

Reflecting on the circumstances under which our life in the past decades has developed, we should make a quite depressing diagnosis. Namely, that an apparent breakdown has occurred in morals which has greatly but unfavorably influenced interrelationships. This downward trend in morality, as well as the nineteenth-century doctrines already dealt with, were responsible in part for the stand taken by political leaderships in the heart of Europe before and during the Second World War. These leaderships flagrantly disregarded all the constructive teachings and warnings of the past by flinging open the door to the Race Age whose institutions were so irrelevant to historical conditions. Temporarily during the postwar period, the Soviet-fabricated regimes prolonged the policies of racial prejudices through application of the principle of collective responsibility towards certain nations. Their legislations evinced little, if any, difference from that of the Nazi regimes. But from about 1948 these regimes have changed their course to class warfare, thereby excluding large groups from the nations.

Retaining in our minds the commonly known fact that Soviet theory and its workings clash day by day with the vital interests of oppressed peoples, let us now glance at the nucleus of the Soviet system. This is Lenin's dogma, according to which all mankind is inevitably progressing towards its ultimate destiny, the classless Communist society where all nations of the world are melted into a uniform, new race.(13) Evidently, Lenin's prophecy is as utopian a scheme for the eradication of nationalism as was a Russian linguist Marr's once popular theory that the conversion of tsarist Russia into a proletarian country would result in an entirely new, heretofore unknown, proletarian Russian language. In the early fifties, Stalin's authority was needed to expose and refute the falsity of that statement.

Lenin's dogmatic views and their practice have never been received sympathetically by the peoples through the Soviet orbit. This is because they have witnessed innumerable startling revelations about the true meaning of the Leninist nationality policy whose Janus-faced character was masterly depicted by Frederick C. Barghoorn(14) as follows: "Moscow believes, or pretends to believe, that communism will inherit the earth. It holds out to mankind the vision of the harmonious society without coercion and inequality. But Soviet Messianism justifies a plan for a Russian communist world organized and directed from Moscow." This Moscow-centered Pan-Sovietism is a hotbed of present-day desertions to the flag of national communism.(15)

If the reader now summarizes for himself the history of nationalism versus federalism, he will perhaps see that lasting and sincere cooperation among the various nationalities can be secured only through universal respect of individual freedoms. He will most certainly see the American concept of freedom as it was envisioned one hundred years ago by József Eötvös, a great Hungarian statesman who, when analyzing the structure of a multinational monarchy, concluded: "The Habsburg dynasty had a great mission . . . If the Empire could have been organized on the basis of freedom . . . a great alliance would have developed in Central Europe . . . which would differ from America only in the fact that not the President, but the Emperor would be the head of state."(16) A few years later, in 1870, Karel Sabina, a higly-esteemed executive committee member of the Czech Democratic Society, delivered a keynote address in which he reprehended Austrian absolutism and demanded that the Dual Monarchy be reorganized in line with the American pattern: "I think it would be better to transfer all American ideas to Bohemia, and to materialize the American concept of freedom in Bohemia. It would be better to transfer America to Bohemia, instead of transferring our people to America."(17)

The reform thinkers of Central Europe were convinced that America set an example of equality to all nations. They even dreamed about a United States of Central Europe modeled on the ideals of America. Among them the greatest, Stephen Széchenyi, also inspired by the American concept of personal freedoms, laid down the foundation for a federative system by emphasizing that morals should be in indissoluble symbiosis with patriotism. In his famous academic address(18) the guiding principle for regulating the coexistence of different nations was determined by these biblical words: "Do not do that to others which you would not accept wholeheartedly from others." Széchenyi's lifework on the nationality (racial) issues has always been favorably discussed by his critics regardless of their origin or political credo, but the most grandiose monument was erected by Charles Dickens, who, in his *Journal* commemorated the tenth anniversary of Széchenyi's death, saying: "One last and most important particular remains to be mentioned, in which Széchenyi's opinions remain to this day far in advance of those of his countrymen—far in advance of the opinions which still prevail in England respecting the treatment of alien races."(19)

The prophets of the currently-so-fashionable federalism, if following the path of our historical heritage, will realize that a morally well-founded freedom concept is a prerequisite of forming federations in which the peaceful coexistence of ethnically different groups is lastingly insured.

1) Különböző vallásoknak egy idvösséges hitben... megegyezése. Pozsony 1671. Cf. Fritz Valjavec, Der Deutsche Kultureinfluss im nahen Südosten. Unter Berücksichtung Ungarns. I. München, Verlag Max Schick, 1940, 428.

2) Walter Friedrich, Die österreichische Zentralverwaltung. II. Abteilung. Bd. I, Halbband 2, Teil 1. "Die Zeit Josephs II und Leopolds II" (Veröfentlichungen der Kommission für neuere Geschichte Österreichs, 35 (Wien: 1950), p. 82.

3) Ueber die Ergebenheit und Anhanglichkeit der Slawischen Völker an das Erzhaus Oesterreich. Prag. 1791.

4) Kolik jazyku tolik národu, kolik jazyku, tolik vlasti" — quotation from Prehled ceskoslovenskych dejin. I. Do roku 1848 (Praha, 1958), 748.

5) István Kultsár, "A magyar theátrom," Nemzeti Ujjság vagy Hazai s Külföldi Tudósítások, Pest, 1809, 47.

6) Cf. Francis S. Wagner, "Széchenyi and the nationality problem in the Habsburg Empire," Journal of Central European Affairs, vol. 20, no. 3, 1960, 289-311.

7) For details see Grgur Jaksic, "Izvestaj d-ra Ljudevita Gaja o Srbiji (1847)", Srpski knjizevni glasnik, March 1, 1924, 368-377, and Ph.E. Mosely, "A Pan-Slavist Memorandum of Ljudevit Gaj in 1838," The American Historical Review, July 1935, 704-716.

8) T. G. Masaryk, Ceská otázka; snahy a túzby národního obrozeni. Praha, Pokrok, 1908, 80.

9) Ernest Renan, Qú est-ce qu'une nation? 1882.

10) 11) Ludwig Gumplowicz, Das Recht der Nationalitaten und Sprachen in Österreich-Ungarn. Innsbruck, 1879; Paul de Lagarde, Deutsche Schriften, 1878-1881.

12) Cf. Olivér Eöttevényi, Nemzetiségi törvényünk és a kisebbségi szerződések. Pécs, Dunántul Könyvkiadó, 1925, 24. (Miskolci ev. jogakadémia tudományos értekezéseinek tára, 25. sz.), and Iván Nagy, A nemzetiségi törvény 1868: 44 tc. Budapest, 1943, 162.

13) See M. D. Kammari's study in Voprosy Filosofii, vol. 14, no. 4, 1960, dealing with V. 1. Lenin's views on the fundamental laws governing the development of nations. See also J. Stalin, Marksizm i natsional'nyi vopros. Moszkva, 1946.

14) Frederick C. Barghoorn, Soviet Russian Nationalism. New York: Oxford University Press, 1956, 232.

15) Cf. Francis S. Wagner, "National Communism: From Clementis to Tito." Free World Forum, vol. 1, no. 4, 1959, 29-30.

16) J. Eötvös, Naplójegyzetek-gondolatok, 1864-1868.

17) See Národní Listy, Prague, July 2, 1870.

18) A Magyar Tudós Társaság Évkönyvei, VI, 1840-1842. Buda, 1845, 55-89.

19) The Great Magyar," from All The Year Around, a Weekly Journal conducted by Charles Dickens. April, 1870, 7-8.

CENTRAL EUROPEAN FEDERATION
INCLUDING SWITZERLAND

GYULA TASSONYI

TO restore liberty to the Central European nations and to eliminate the Iron Curtain no longer suffice. Their independence and neutrality should be internationally guaranteed. This goal, however, can be obtained only by uniting these nations in a neutral *federation of states*, or confederation of states.

The *nucleus* of such a federation would — as I see it — consist of the following Central European states: Austria, Switzerland, the two parts of Chechoslovakia: Bohemia and Slovakia, Poland and Hungary. Here I would like to point out that none of the later four have ever been "East European" countries as they are now so frequently referred to, quite erroneously. Both the international and neutral status of the federation would be enhanced by the inclusion of neutral Austria and Switzerland, both highly respected by the East and West. By her entrance, Austria would again belong to her natural economic area to which she has been committed through the centuries. It would enhance her prosperity, culture and prestige in the West.

Switzerland would have unparalleled investment opportunities. Her need for cheaper manpower would be met and the political weight of the country would be much greater than in the European Economic Community where it has a tendency to be overshadowed by the great powers. During the period of transition her excellent militia would help maintain order, protect life and property.

Such a federation, having the status of a great but neutral power, would eventually bring stability to this restless part of Europe. It would end forever the present open or secret rivalry by the outside great powers within the buffer zone. Such a Central European Federation of States may seem new and bold but it is natural because it serves the interests of all the nations in this critical area where two world wars have erupted. This is another reason for neutralizing the whole area in the interest of humanity.

Short- or long-range solutions

It has always been difficult to distinguish between short- and long-range interests. Both, individuals and nations, pursue short-range interests, usually because they are pressing, offering quick but often illusory rewards. Such short-range, short-sighted objectives are often the cause of great personal, as well as national and international tragedies. Following the Second World War, it was the short-range interest of Russia to realize the old dream of the Czars to extend her frontiers to the Adriatic Sea and the Balkans, to dominate as many nations of Europe as her military and political power enabled her to.

The long-range and true interest of Russia would have been to break with the hated imperialistic Czarist policy and bring liberation to the oppressed countries of Eastern and Central Europe. Instead, she merely replaced German with Russian domination. Her long-range interests would have been to observe international agreements and use her influence for a cultural drive and economic cooperation. Stalin, the Red Czar, however, believed he could maintain the same cruel oppression in Europe as he did in Russia. His successors made a similar error when the overthrew the Hungarian revolution in 1956. They damaged their prestige and forfeited the leadership of the Communist countries by taking such dubious steps. The Soviet Union is, as a consequence, not only an economic impasse but also political in a crisis, having no reliable friends and having the German and Central European situation still unresolved at a time when her prestige in China and Indonesia, and a great part of Africa as well is at low ebb and her hopes have backfired.

Bringing liberty to the nations of Central Europe and the creation of a neutral Central European Federation of States would transform about 55 to 100 million unhappy Central European individuals into satisfied members of their nations who would be ready to support the newly established federal order and its neutrality. This area would be ready to defend its liberty on every side. It would mean greater security for Russia, Germany and France than the atomic bomb and the "force de frappe" which is unthinkable in modern Europe. Central Europe would be a neutral zone having no nuclear weapons. (An extended Rapacky plan with regard to the more recent treaty banning nuclear proliferation.) When the outside powers finally acknowledge the necessity for filling the vacuum,, existing since the dissolution of the Austro-Hungarian Monarchy, and consent to the establishment of a Federation of States to form a neutral buffer zone, the solution will follow. The difficulties in accomplishing this must not be underestimated. The composition of the federation, international agreements, regulation of the federation and its constitution must be well planned.

Austria

Following the dissolution of the Austro-Hungarian Monarchy, Austria was the "sick man" of Europe. Since losing her natural resources, she had to fight for her very existence. After the First World War, fear of union between Austria and Germany prompted the Western nations to support Austria through huge loans. Today the danger is nonexistent, at least not to a degree that would warrant financial intervention. However, after the boom that came as a result of concluding the State Treaty in 1955, the disadvantages of Austria's isolation became increasingly evident. For Austria, the return to a natural, Danubian economic and political unity would bring many advantages, whereas the union with Germany, either economically or politically would not be without great danger to the world and all the interested nations. Austria's neighbors and Russia are sensitive to any attempt on her part to join a Western European federation or the Common Market with its possible political consequences.

Switzerland

The membership of Switzerland presents more difficulties. The obstacles are not so much economic as emotional and historical. Coming as a refugee from a Danubian country under Communist rule to "capitalistic" Switzerland, I have pursued with great sympathy and interest the grave psychic crisis triggered by the speed of modern industrial developments that are transforming the seemingly conservative Alpine confederation. Until now, the majority of the population has not grasped the fact that Switzerland's traditional, privileged isolation that she has managed to maintain through two world wars can no longer be held. By the social transformation, Switzerland has undergone, her outstanding leaders have made this country a socially balanced, wealthy and free community of three nations. Visible signs of the social transformation are the introduction of the 5-day workweek, adjustment of old-age pensions, social insurance, collective labor contracts and many other reforms. This small country has demonstrated that social benefits can be achieved without nationalization of industry and bureaucratization of the economic life.

In the Danubian countries, Stalinism discredited Marxist Communism. A class war ideology strange to the people, which overextended the influence of the State into private life — to the churches, literature and economic production. In fact, individuals are confronted in their everyday life with the monolithic power of State bureaucracy. It is the State which does not deliver water taps, which sells offals of poor quality in the butcher shops, cheats the consumer in State-owned stores regarding the quality and quantity of goods sold. Socialism, which ought to have been the driving force of the system, degenerated into an omnipotent Marxist bureaucracy. At present, economic experiments are taking place in the Communist countries as to how to liberalize their over-centralized State system. Both, Switzerland and Austria could serve as examples to the other members of the Central European Federation in their way of life, forestry, horticulture, sanitation, home ownership and thrift.

As a member of the Central European Federation of States, Switzerland would obviously bring benefits to all. But would the average Swiss citizens see benefits for themselves? It can hardly be assumed at this time. The preparation and education for such a step would have to take place in the psychological, economic and political spheres.

Although Switzerland belongs geographically to Central Europe, she is Western in mentality. As do others in the West, many Swiss citizens consider the nations beyond the Elbe and Leitha inferior. It must be said that they did not associate this sense of inferiority with the Austro-Hungarian Monarchy. Conditions created by Moscow behind the Iron Curtain may be one cause of the present thinking on the subject. Many emigrants are helping to dispel such ideas. Nevertheless, such attitudes exist and must be reckoned with.

Switzerland has had a very special position in the field of international economics. With her neutrality in two world wars, Switzerland has been able to attract international capital. These billions on which no interest is paid have contributed to the establishment of Swiss industry the dimensions of which surpass the needs of the population. Now, due to changing conditions, this special position is waning. Industry has remained without the necessary number of workers and without marketing areas. By membership in a Central European Federation of States both problems would be solved. Her need for skilled workmen, as well as markets would be met. The Danubian area is in need of high quality industrial products. Swiss industrial enterprises could flourish and good markets would be available for agricultural products.

In the West European Community, Switzerland would be one of the smaller states from the point of view of the Western system of defense. But in a neutral Central European Federation of States, she would occupy a privileged position partly because of her international connections. At present the Danubian states do not possess an independent foreign policy.

Other Participants

It is perhaps hardly necessary to state the motivation for membership of Poland, Hungary and the two parts of Czechoslovakia, etc., in this federation. All have lived in the shadow of a great power posing as their "protector." A plebiscite gauging free public opinion in this area would welcome such a neutral and federal solution with enthusiasm. But this is not enough. An international atmosphere of goodwill toward the idea must be developed. None of the participating members should fear that their own interests would be endangered. What would be the organ for concluding a treaty on behalf of these states that would be a guarantee for all nations concerned? Hardly the present governments that owe their existence to a foreign power. They obviously could not fully represent their countries at an international meeting.

As free elections are not possible, as a transitional step, national councils should be formed consisting of leading members of the last legal parties and add to those non-party representatives selected from independent scholars, artists and other well-known persons. Such councils could choose preliminary governments which in turn would prepare the international treaties. They would organize the first plebiscites and elections. The treaties would be ratified by the newly elected houses of parliament. Apart from the common affairs, the member states would continue to be independent in accord with the wishes of the majority. Even their form of government would not be of great importance. The federation of states must, however, be neutral and guaranteed by international treaty. Especially the United States of America, Germany and the Soviet Union would guarantee the security and neutrality of this new Federation of States. They would, undoubtedly, have a mutual interest to watch that no power interferes with the domestic policy of the states and the federation. The Federation itself would keep its own militia for maintaining order. The Supreme Court of the Central European Federation would decide constitutional issues and complaints in the field of the common affairs of the Federation.

It is important that no outside power should have reason or cause for suspicion of such a neutral federation. These much-suffering states fervently desire to live in peace. After many centuries of domination by others they want only to live their own lives with policies of reconciliation on both the domestic and international level.

Are such hopes realistic? At present the fear of German and Pan-Slav efforts block the way to European solidarity. There is much suspicion on all sides. Undoubtedly, these efforts are still active under the cover of democracy and Communism respectively of two great nations.

The world is beginning to form large units because it is being forced to do so. Great Britain will probably join the Western European Union and thus another great power will come into being. The participation of Great Britain in the Western European Union would balance the opposing forces of France and Germany. Otherwise England would join a World Union of English-speaking countries. Also, a new although neutral power would be created: the Central European Federation of States and would protect and safeguard Russia who would then be free to concentrate on her resources and strengthen her defenses on her East—especially the Chinese border. On the other hand, the United States, for whom the role of world policeman is a heavy financial and moral burden, would be able to devote her strength to the defense of her own continent and disengage herself militarily from the other nuclear power, the Soviet Union. The buffer zone of a neutral Federation of States between Russia and Germany would be benefical to all powers and nations interested in Europe.

EAST CENTRAL EUROPEAN UNITY

JOSEPH GALGANOWICZ

THE idea of European integration—all-European or regional Federation—is not a new one. Numerous attempts were made in the past. All of these were based either on idealistic conceptions or on conceptions of power politics, the latter meaning domination. The two world wars exhausted and weakened Europe biologically and materially. A tremendous progress of technology especially in the field of transportation and armaments, reduced considerably the political and military role of Europe and even challenged her survival as an independent political entity. There is no doubt today that salvation lies in unity. Only a united Europe would be in a position to match the danger which threatens the political, economic, and cultural freedom of the European nations, and to preserve their historical influence in the world. Therefore, we are in favor of an all-European integration—be it a European Union or the United States of Europe— possessing supra-national legislative and executive organs. But we are realistic enough to comprehend that such a far-reaching integration of Europe is quite a remote ideal which can be achieved only gradually. It can be assumed that a regional federation or unions of states bound by common interests and traditions will in all probability emerge in Central and Eastern Europe immediately after their liberation. Problems of common boundaries and economic problems seem best to be solved by a federation. Federalism is certainly an excellent idea, but we must consider with whom to federalize? That is, as I see it, the first basic question. Nations or states which want to federalize should have a common ideological basis. We cannot imagine a federation of nations or states with different ideologies. Can we imagine a federation of a democratic nation with a totalitarian, fascist or communistic nation? These are not merely theoretical questions. We see democratic and totalitarian federations existing around us. The U.S.A. and the U.S.S.R. are examples. We do not yet see a federation of democratic and non-democratic states. But we cannot dismiss the possibility of such a federation. We hear such suggestions from speakers whom we consider fascists. It could happen that, among the federalized nations, democratic from the beginning, one state could fall into fascist or other anti-democratic lines. Such a change of the basic policy of this state would and should mean the disruption of the federation, which can exist only on the basis of a homogeneous political ideology. Another problem is that of a federation between two or more states with national minorities claiming to be united. I think that these questions should be taken into consideration. Another factor which cannot be overlooked is nationalism, which, fortunately, appears to have lost most of its vital force. We realize that in the present situation no state in Europe can perform the functions for which it was originally designed. Standing alone, it can neither feed its people nor defend them. In time of war, national frontiers no longer have any real strategic significance. But we have to admit that the desire to retain national character and independent regional governments would certainly be strong in East Central Europe even within the framework of a federation. Yet, this self-determination in East Central Europe might be the consequence of international developments. Then the decision regarding a federation will have to be made by the former captive nations, who now live and dwell under circumstances determined by the Soviet Union. These circumstances—cultural, political and economic—should not be overlooked. In light of the possibility of a federation we must neither overestimate nor underestimate the similarities of the oppressed conditions and the political and economic institutions of the captive East Central European nations. I believe that these factors, along with others, work more toward federation than toward separation. I recall that Imre Nagy wrote among others: "Alone, relying on themselves, not one of the small nations along the Danube will be able to withstand the common danger threatening them." This truth applies to each of the East Central European countries. But their union will only be possible if these people will be wise and brave enough to abandon their old-fashioned nationalism; if they will be able to make liberal concessions to each other; if they will be able to fill their national sentiments with progressive values. While the concept of federation itself is more and more accepted, the territory to be included is not quite so well-defined for those who think about the future arrangements of East Central Europe. The question of territory depends on a series of permanent as well as temporary factors. In answer to the question of the ideal geographical limits of an East Central European federation, I believe that the larger the territory to be included, the more realistic the solution.

In conclusion: for the time being it is not practical to ponder which states should and which should not join an East Central European federation. It must depend very much on the dates and circumstances of their liberation. In fact, the East Central European federation, as a unit, should be the extension of the West and not the beginning of the East. If further intercontinental federations should be established, the East Central European federation should belong to the Atlantic federation and not to an East Eurasian one.

COVENANT OF THE PEOPLES IN THE CARPATHIAN AND DANUBIAN BASINS

EUGENE PADÁNYI-GULYÁS

"To everything there is a season, and a time to every purpose under the heaven: a time to break down, and a time to build up; a time to cast away stones, and a time to gather stones together."　　　Ecclesiastes, 3

"A state without the means of change is without the menas of its conservation."　　·　Edmund Burke

I

IN searching for future conditions for a peaceful and happy symbiosis[1] of the peoples in the Carpathian and Danubian Basin we first have to evaluate the bond that ties all the inhabitants of this region to their Creator and which makes them cooperate in his plan as they were taught by Christ.

The resources upon which economy and power are based—such as coal, iron, oil, uranium and gold, as well as the number of populace—enjoy such high regard in our day that is seems unrealistic to attribute any importance to the relationship between man and his Creator within the framework of a political study. It is, however, a fact that the history of this region has been much more strongly influenced by this relationship than by anything else. Venceslas, Stephen and several of his descendants have gained the respect of their people, as saints of their churches. John Huss was burned at the stake because of his faith. Prince Apafy like Joshua, had offered himself and his household for the service of the Lord; and in his land, in Transylvania, freedom of religion was guaranteed by law, for the first time in history. The freedom fight of Rákóczi in 1703-1711 was fought by Hungarian, German, Ruthenian, Slovak and Rumanian insurgents under flags bearing the inscription "pro Deo et Libertate." Croatian and Austrian troops under the leadership of Nicholas Zrinyi and Frater Capistran, along with Hungarians, died in their battles against the Turks with "God" and "Jesus" on their lips. All these, the peoples of this region considered more important than those natural resources which were otherwise at their disposal. That the situation evolved the way it did is to be attributed to the teaching of Christ. The various interpretations of these throughout the centuries, and the intellectual battles resulting from them, prove that these peoples, amidst all hardships, always considered themselves the tools of their Creator in accomplishing their tasks in their historic workshop. Their poets, writers and preachers gave expression from time to time to an unmistakable awareness of their calling. We do not think that this belongs only to the past. Gunsmoke was still hovering over the barricades when the Hungarian workers of Csepel, in October, 1956, demanded freedom of education and religious instruction for their children. The desire to discover the laws of the Creator has not ceased but has become deeper among these peoples.

Such recent ramifications of the Mediterranean-based Christian culture as those of our contemporaries Pierre Teilhard de Chardin and Julian Huxley who raised socioligy from futile experimentation into the ranks of a true science, raise new hope that the peoples of the Danube Region who have always responded vigorously to contemporary intellectual movements will start a new Golden Age through a modern interpretation of the two thousand year old Christian truths. If, for instance, it were possible to accept as a basic tenet that no people desires to further itself at the expense of another—and this was expressed by more than one emigrant[2])—then an example of the practical political application of the Second Commandment would be achieved. The consequences of this can easily be seen. The spirit of solidarity would lead the way, instead of deportation, forced displace ment of populations, genocide, destruction of historical monuments and falsification of history, and instead of jealousy, envy, hatred and revenge, the contructive forces of cooperation and magnanimity would restore all the destruction witnessed and suffered by all peoples during the last decades.

The other basis of their symbiosis—and this is still within the spiritual realm—consists of the unity of the civilization of this region. This is easily noticed if we compare this area, for instance, with that to the east of the Carpathians. The literacy, educational, communications and legal systems, social institutions, the traditions of commerce, the refreshing impact of the influx of ideas from the continent's historical movements such as the Renaissance and the Reformation can be traced and found to be different from the characteristics of the areas east of the Carpathians. The standard of living is generally similar within this area and remarkably higher in comparison to the regions east of the Carpathians.

It is obvious this civilization could hardly have become so homogeneous, without the aid of its geographical unity. One glance at a geophysical map that is free of present political boundaries will explain the unprejudiced scientific opinion according to which the Carpathian Basin with the immediately connected Danubian Valley regions is one of the most ideal geographical entities in the world. Those who neglect or belittle the significance of these circumstances do not give good service to the cause of future symbiosis because this God-given geographical unity is one of the most highly prized possessions of these peoples. Even the advance of technology does not reduce the significance of the Carpathians that encircle this area and affect its climate, commerce and defense. The rivers and their valleys do not create boundaries, but a network of life streams giving direction to a whole system of movements of civilization. The urbanization, the balance between industry and agriculture and the distribution of commercial and cultural centers is the product of the developing and directing work of centuries. The best proof of this is the growing individuailty of certain areas which has become common knowledge. Without letting ourselves stray into sentimental areas—whose sociological significance, however, is not to be underestimated, and admitting that emotions can be stony political facts—it is worth while to recall what prestige the almost endless list of products from the Lipto-cheese to the Kecsmemét peaches enjoyed, and in some cases still enjoy, which through the natural interchange of goods have become accepted as popular assets within the whole region.[3] It is inconceivable to the sober mind, how the Czech textile industry could be promoted by excluding the Hungarian market and by making all Hungarians mistrustful towards anything coming from Prague. The swine husbandry of Serbia and Bácska and its relationship to the Austrian and Hungarian markets was a constant subject of agricultural debate during the first quarter of the century. It is not likely that the consumption within Yugoslavia ever replaced these excluded markets. It is not our object to penetrate into the details of production, distribution and foreign trade. We merely wish to state that those tendencies, which contrary to rational thought, dissolved the commercial unity of this region and complicated it by creating an unnatural development of ill-planned new industry, ill-conceived traffic regulations and artificially established price controls; are all diametrically opposed to contemporary efforts in world economy, the aim of which is the planned joining of larger producing and consuming areas and emancipation and increase of their trade and exchange by doing away with customs barriers. In this evolving new world, the peoples of the Carpathian and Danube Basin regions can hardly afford the luxury of mutual isolationism. The restoration of broken ties would probably cause fewer headaches and require the settling of less significant disagreements than the coal regions of the Ruhr, the Saar region, the Benelux, the Common Market or the Cyprus problems, and these are all of the past.

It is unnecessary to take much time to discuss the dangers to this area from the outside. Even the weakening Austro-Hungarian empire was able to maintain a fifty-year-long period of peace through its united defense which successfully resisted all aggressions. As soon as this united defense ceased in the wake of discord among the respective nations, the whole region became easy prey first to German National Socialists and then to Russian Communist aggrandizement. The bitter experiences still remind us of the bloody reality of those catastrophic mistakes of which millions of innocents became victims. Still, we have to mention briefly, that those military and economic advantages which certain groups of this region enjoyed through the temporary domination of Pan-Germanism and Pan-Slavism are hardly proportionate to the sacrifices which they had to make in losing their independence. Our Slovak neighbors have repeatedly reproached the Czechs, publicly, as have the Croatians the Serbians because of their disappointment over their expectations of Slavic brotherhood. That the founders of Czechoslovakia have never considered the wants of the Ruthenians was proven characteristically when Benes himself threw all of the Carpathian Ruthenians—together with the Hungarian and German populace—to the Soviets in 1945. At that time, 27 years after the proclamation of the Wilson Doctrine, it was not popular any more to speak of self-determination—a fact which does not lessen at all the monstrosity of this notorious example of political horse-trade performed by unconscientious politicians, dealing with the lives of innocent peoples.

Hindsight is easier than foresight—yet the former is not without value. All peoples may accept the words of one of the Rumanian immigrants:[4] "We have been blind. Our lack of foresight, determination and bravery drove us first into the arms of Hitler's Germany and then of Stalin's Russia." If the Austrians, Hungarians, Rumanians, Croatians, Serbians, Ruthenians and Czechs had, in 1937, in place of questionable speculations, thought fast, entered into an alliance and announced that they would, in case of conflict among the major powers, follow a course of mutual neutrality, and their willingness to defend their neutrality with arms; furthermore, even if they had announced this in 1939 without Austrians and Czechs who had already lost their independence—the history of the last decades of this region would have been shaped differently and the horrors of World War II would have been reduced.

Although we have to trust that the feasibility of solving the conflicts between the major powers by war is becoming more and more questionable, we should not forget that which happened yesterday can still happen tomorrow. What we passed up in 1937 and 1939, we have to compensate for as soon as the power to decide is in our hands. No major power or international guarantee exists which would make the combined defense of our own peace and security superfluous. One of the most solid foundations for the happy and peaceful symbiosis of those peoples is the necessity of their common defense against mutually threatening external dangers.

The awareness of the danger of outside attack finds itself rooted in deep historical layers. The peoples of this region all experienced together the Turkish threat in the 15th-17th centuries which was troubling all Europe and which was stopped here at the expense of a century and a half of occupation of a major part of the region. It was under Islamic pressure that significant groups of our peoples north and west of the Balkans established ties with one another. And it was due to the many lives lost during the Turkish wars that resettlement followed in the opposite direction, sending a part of the German population as settlers from west to east. This sequence of partly involuntary and partly planned movement of population colored and blended the anthropological features of this region into what they are today. Complicated as it was, the ethnographic character of the region created a thorny problem for scholars. Although significant islands quite clearly reserved their characteristics, generally, they are pretty well fused. The part of the population which belonged to the middle and upper strata of education—which could study their ancestry with some interest—could rarely brag of being of pure strain. Many of those bearing well-sounding Hungarian names were held as small children on the knees of grandparents bearing German, Serbian, Croatian, etc., names. We shall not even guess what these other names contained on their own background. Bearers of pure German names could often point to more Hungarian ancestors than the other way around. All this mixing continued through the centuries without any planned effort or organized restraint and without noticable detriment. The distant observer can hardly shake off the impression that the historic experiences of their common fate formed the background for this process. Not much was said about it. It was natural. It was not restricted to the memories of catastrophes. Not long ago one of the representatives of the Slovak people referred to "the joy which we had in common in 1848."5) It is a fact, however, that the warning: "The Tartars are coming" has been passed down from mothers to children for six centuries after the Mongolian invasion in this region. It was their descendants who threw in 1956 "Molotov cocktails" at the Soviet tanks to seal with new blood, new sacrifices, and with the memories of new catastrophes, the common fate of future generations.

II

The functions of the Covenant

It is an historical fact that in the last ten centuries only the Hungarians were able to maintain a stable and permanent constitutional system in this region. This has been a sore point with the Slovak and Croatian peoples who lived in this region and were more or less organized even before the Hungarians established their home there in 896 A.D. under the leadership of Árpád. Whereupon the Hungarians recall the realm of Attila which extended over this territory until 453 A.D. and with whom the Hungarians claim relationship and whose descendants, the Szeklers, have been permanent residents of Transylvania ever since. Such arguments and proofs of priority lose their importance in view of the historical vistas opened by modern research. Placing the region in this perspective, it would be difficult for any of its peoples to mistake themselves for "the chosen people." The earliest remains of the Homo Mousteriensis[6]) of the Ice Age were found in the Subalyuk and Krapina caves. Since the earliest findings of human life within the Carpathian Basin, there have been discovered on Mount Avas a pastoral people called the Protocampigniens; then, after the Mediterranean and the Homo Nordicus types, the findings of the Copper, Bronze and Iron Ages all prove that within this region in very early times there developed a cultural center which due to the conditions created by the relative isolation of the basin was able to attain certain independence and develop new human values. These are the words of historians, not of the politicians. Their foundation consists of such facts which could hardly be influenced by political consideration. But if we seek, today, a brief but correct definition of the real function of the peoples of the Carpathian and Danubian Basins, we could hardly find one better than this: They want to preserve their independence resulting from their relative geographical and ethnic seclusion, so that they can create new human values, and add new colors to life evolving on our globe.

This function is in complete harmony with the law of evolution. All such political and sociological movements which hinder or stop the independence and the development of new human values in this region are antievolutionary and, therefore, cannot be lasting. Regardless of the color or symbol of the political interests which attempt to rob the people of this region from the achievement of their function as indicated by science and historical facts, they must with united strength rise against them if they do not want to perish.

Viewed from this angle, functional disorders must arise if a given political system—though maintaining the geographical unity of this region—hinders the individual development of its ethnic elements. Trouble is also created if the ethnic development of relatively large groups of the respective people is assured, but the region itself is subdivided by artificial political boundaries, which increases the number of minority groups and hinders their development. The ethnic map of the Carpathian Basin and similar areas of mixed populace cannot in truth be drawn up by covering certain areas by particular colors signifying nationalities. Any such map would necessarily be untruthful. Finally, trouble is paramount if the geographical unity of the region is disrupted, the free development of the ethnic groups is hindered and, on top of it, the whole disjointed and upset area is forced to serve the interests of outside powers.

The history of the past four or five generations produced clinical examples of the above functional disorders and the results developed accordingly: in place of progress there has been decline; in place of happiness, misery reigns over the entire area.

Until this trouble is eliminated, the Carpathian and Danubian Basins cannot fulfill their function. The unity of this region has to be reestablished and the free functioning of its ethnic energies must be guaranteed by a new covenant. The ethnic and linguistic differences are not a hindrance, but an advantage; for if they are permitted to develop in peace and in free competition, they will promote evolutionary humanism.[7] As a result, new human values will come forth. The advantages of this mutual influence have repeatedly occurred in history But our duty is not only the ennobling of the human values of this region but also showing good examples for our unsettled globe, which has similar problems in many places. The so-called "big powers" often hinder development[8] because of their selfish interests and because they are able to defend these interests with their overpowering strength, even at the expense of the goals of humanity. The period of international politics based on the so-called "balance of power" and on colonization is over. It is impossible to bring back the days of Ghengis Khan, Attila, Alexander the Great, the various Caesars, emperors, "Führers" and dictators. The unrelenting forces of the rapid societal and technological development of the world today doom to failure all experiments aimed at dominating the world ideologically, economically or militarily. Oppression and exploitation become senseless and are replaced by solidarity and cooperation for the common human goals. Those world powers which at present feel capable of fulfilling their wants at all costs are understandably less inclined to accept the theory of solidarity and cooperation in the false belief that they cannot receive, only give. However, such international political applications of the give-and-take theory are also outdated. The states that solve the problems of ethnically mixed population by means of federation, though not significant in numbers, offer more valuable aid by their example to solve world problems than those nations operating strictly through power. The balancing role of the healthy, vigorous and respected middle powers is striking and the experienced people of the Carpathian Basin are definitely lacking in those world forums in which at present, the extremists' voices are so overpowering and aggressiveness often squeezes out inexperience and naiveté.

Historical research[8] has also determined that the Carpathian Basin had developed into a station for the migration from Asia Minor across the Balkans to the North during the Bronze Age. At the end of the Neolithic Age the traces of migration from north to south were discovered through which the first Greek tribes arrived from somewhere in Central Europe to the Balkans. From a central location that developed in this region spread far to the north and south Europe's richest bronze art, sending knives, daggers, swords, helmets, richly ornamented jewelry and dishes through its commerce even into Italy. The jewelry of princes and kings were made of gold from the rich mines of this region. During the Iron Age, around 1200 B.C., the first Pre-Scythian horseback riders settled in the Big and Little Plains of Hungary and the Viennese Basin bringing with them a mobile equestrian, nomadic culture developed in the East. At the same time, the mountain shepherds of the Caucasians settled in the Highlands. The archaeologists are confronted with the same findings of this period in Italy as in the Carpathian Basin, from where at this time the Dorians are being pushed to the south to destroy the Mycenalan culture of the Bronze Age and, through their later descendants, someday to build Rome. Along with the Scythians of the East, the Celts of the West also arrived in the Basin. When the Roman Empire conquered Pannonia, it found Illyr, Celtic, Sarmatic, Jazig and Germanic peoples in peaceful coexistence pursuing their trades. The following ten centuries are recorded as the history of Hungary, but it also includes the fact that this country until recently protected the Saxons who lived in Transylvania as a nation. When the wheel of fate turned, Transylvania became the bridge through which the new Rumanian state entered into the Western community.[9] Being a part of Hungary for ten centuries did not force the Slovak or Croatian people to lose their ethnic individualities or their ambition for national independence. What advantages each of the nationalities had within Hungary is still to be examined and written in an unbiased era. Today's observer of political events can merely state that had this region been patterned after modern American democracy only for one century, it would hardly have been possible for any of the nationalities to preserve their individual language or national culture. Neither Joseph II, nor Chancellor Metternich can be blamed if the populace of the whole region did not become German speaking. Vienna did her best. The "camarilla" is not responsible for the failure.

The function of the Carpathian Basin remains basically the same as that taught by history: the highway of peoples and migrations; the bridge between East and West, North and South; the international trading post; the ancient center of commerce. It is the meeting place of ideological trends, first to be reached by the Renaissance and early by the Reformation whose followers lived there in freedom alongside Roman Catholic and Eastern Orthodox followers of Christ. These peoples react to the ideas of the American and French revolutions in the same way that iron filings do to a magnet. The experimentation of the social revolution which began in the 19th century caused this area to be regarded as its constant proving ground which it remains to this day. George Washington's cavalry was organized by a Hungarian Hussar colonel and the civilization of the United States was built with the help of millions of immigrants from this region. Their grateful descendants were first to raise a statue to George Washington in a foreign country[10] and the name of Woodrow Wilson was not less known to these school children than to those in the United States. The principle of peoples' self-determination smashes historical boundaries even though never really put into practice by plebiscites and the peoples of this region express their enthusiasm together and suffer together with all the enthusiastic and suffering peoples of this troubled world which has shrunk due to today's means of communication and transportation. Those human values that came about in the relative seclusion of this region have now been tempered in the forges of two world wars and the persecutions following them. Under the blows of the hammers of the Slavs of the East and the Germans of the West a kind of man whose historical workshop is the Carpathian and Danube Basin was forged.

Viewed from a distance, however, it becomes clear that even iron will melt if the flame is hot enough. If the people of this region wish to remain useful members of the human community they will have to reach that period of peaceful creativity and constructive cooperation without which the more fortunate Western civilizations could never have developed and become strong. The tendency of the Slavs and Germans to aspire to power through racial theories may be restrained by growing international order. But it is left to the peoples of the Basin to break these waves by united efforts and build sturdy dykes in the interest of their own well-being and world peace.

The fulfillment of the functions indicated by the past and present obliges us to reach urgent conclusions and deeds.

III

The preparation of the Covenant.

Along with the rising nationalism of the peoples of the Basin during the past hundred years there has been a rise of such theories that would eliminate and substitute the role of a Hungary as it existed at the turn of the century. Crown Prince Ferdinand and his Cabinet, the "Camarilla" had wanted to pulverize the ethnic elements of the Austro-Hungarian monarchy so that from the gravel and sand of the peoples and with the cement of his imagined central power a triple monarchy of Austrians, Hungarians and Slavs could be built. His tragic death in 1914 put an end to these plans. Kossuth and Balcescu wrote of a Danubian Confederation and several others followed after them with variations of a federative solution.[11] At the end of World War I, however, those forces won out which had only one desire, the destruction of the Monarchy at all costs—"Detruisez l'Autriche-Hongrie"—

even if by that the autonomy and independence of the whole region were destroyed. Indeed, just that occurred.

This article does not attempt to list the growing number of plans for this region, much less to suggest new ones. We do not doubt the usefulness of such theories. But, since the last word in this respect belongs to the nations involved, and since it is hoped that they will be able to use their prerogative to decide for themselves, it seems more timely and useful to take into account those steps which can be taken by the emigrants and with which we can approach the great common goal, a future covenant of the peoples of the Carpathian and Danube Basins.

Such rapid changes have come about in the thinking of mankind and the scientific and technological discoveries dictate such unprecedented tempo that the rate of obsolescence of our political concepts and notions is enormous. Even concepts that were current during World War II are now outdated. Our whole ideological vocabulary has changed. The super-nationalistic drives, heated by racial prejudices, have lost their meaning in this new world and are restricted rather to the so-called under-developed countries. Where are those days in which it was possible to seduce certain peoples of the Basin and of the world at large with false theories of racial superiority? The German and Slav experiments in this respect brought such terror and bloodshed to this area as to disprove those who promote such unscientific ideas. Who would still believe the theories of Rosenberg; or the stories of Palacky, Safarik and Kollár about the "brotherly humanism of peace-loving Slavs" after all that happened?[12]) And who would dare to claim after the October 1956 Hungarian Freedom Fight that the descendants of Kossuth are a people of "aristocratic class rule" and "despotic suppression"? Prof. Seaton-Watson wrote in the London Times: (16 March 1960 "Although Hungarians were often quoted in the past in England as a people of extremists composed of feudal landlords and slaves who also served Hitler,—the facts in 1956 have shown that Hungarians were among the first who, for a short time, destroyed a totalitarian regime, whilst the Czechs were standing applauding loudly with self-satisfaction and malicious joy the brutal subjugation of Hungary by Soviet forces." We all had a chance to learn that among the numbers of any race or nationality there are base and worthless individuals just as there are outstanding personalities. The peoples are merely the soil from which individuals and leaders of outstanding creativity can grow and the only thing we can do is to create more fertile soil out of national cultures so that a greater number of outstanding people may arise. The proportion of these in comparison with the masses, their respect and acceptance into leadership positions is the only positive proof of quality and the only profit to all of mankind. To enter into noble contests with one another in this respect; to revere others' values in place of destroying, liquidating and deporting each other; to work to our utmost for human progress;—this seems to be the only sensible possibility for the securing of our future. Europe's most powerful nations are seeking survival through greater cooperation, eliminating tariffs, and creating common markets. While they are wiping out visa regulations, accepting each other's currency and organizing for their mutual defense, the peoples of the Basin cannot start their new life after liberation with such methods as separation and isolation which already proved detrimental a half century ago. Our regression even so far is catastrophic. Just consider that during the time of Stephen Széchenyi, the Hungarians opened the Iron Gate[13] for the development of the same region which a hundred years later human stupidity and wickedness is trying to lock up from progress by means of an Iron Curtain. The era from Iron Gate to Iron Curtain has come to a close. The time has arrived to open new gates.

Therefore, we suggest that as soon as circumstances allow, the interested nations should without delay send their representatives to conferences by the following Central European commissions:

1.) CER (Central European Railway)
2.) CEW (Central European Waterway)
3.) CEA (Central European Airway) .
4.) CEH (Central European Highway)
5.) CEC (Central European Culture)
6.) CEE (Central European Economy)
7.) CED (Central European Defense)

The purpose of the above commissions is to render urgent proposals for the common administration of the region's railways, waterways, airways, highways, electric power or other natural resources; economic, educational and cultural coordination and defense until the cooperation of the peoples of the Basin arrives at some legal form.[14]

The formation of a legal organization is a job requiring careful preparation and can be done more easily if the above commissions assure smooth operation in the interim. Life does not stop, and the smooth operation of the various means of transportation along with unified upkeep and improvement of the same would aid the return to normal while the population can freely travel wherever it wishes.

None of these purely practical provisions, nor a blueprint for unified economy can be detrimental to a future political agreement, but will probably facilitate its formation. The production and distribution of electricity, natural gas, wood, steel, aluminum and foodstuff can be achieved much more successfully on the basis of synchronized plans than separately.

The peoples of this region will have to face the complicated task of supervising their existing international trade agreements and the resulting advantages and obligations. Without a doubt, it would be easier for them to arbitrate through joint organizations in which they would have equal representation, than they would on their own. Without such an organization, lack of information, jealousy, and foreign interests could shortchange their common interests. Their revaluation and utilization of ties with the East and West could not be achieved without wasteful duplication of efforts if each of the individual peoples attempted to do it alone.

The friendly atmosphere will depend largely on what kind of history text-books will be used in the schools throughout the region. The Committee for Central European Culture has to make suggestions in this respect.

The preservation of internal order demands immediate united action. The handling of the masses of people returning from concentration camps, emigration, deportation and prisons could lead to such a chaos as to impair seriously the healing process of the region. Revenge and retribution could get so far out of hand that the true culprits could easily hide in the jungle of mismanagement and the innocent would suffer in their place. The bringing together of all the law enforcement agencies of this region would be to the peoples' great advantage. It would be the duty of the Central European Defense not only to issue adequate orders but also to enforce them by organizing sufficient military and police forces.

The commissions should be obliged to perform their duties within a month and should hold their meetings for this purpose in the various major cities of the region. The work of these commissions would also serve the purpose of reacquainting the representatives of the various nations with each other's homes. The mayors of the various cities would certainly accept the responsibilities connected with the honor that would make them the hosts of the Commissions.

After making the first proposals, the Commissions would become permanent delegations to utilize the experiences gained by their work. In all probability the region would have to provide for an increased interest in foreign tourism, which hardly can be efficiently managed without CER, CEW and CEA. Not only will the region have to smoothly adapt its general traffic system to the international network; its modern policy will have to make travelling attractive. If this is the case concerning foreign tourists, it is but elementary that free, unhindered travelling should be granted for its own people. Individuals living in the region should be able to travel as they please from Brusztura to Bratislava, from Vinga to Vienna, from Trieste to Trencin and from Csikszereda to Cirkvenica.

The generation that rightly or wrongly saw its future in the creating of new boundaries, in the developing of discord and in mutual jealousy and mistrust, is partly on the way out, or already departed from the political scene. Those who were able to retain some elasticity of thought and flexibility of judgment can hardly do better than offer experiences to the aid of the new generation which, due to its drastically new experiences, is capable of new resolutions and new solutions. And this is necessary, since in the course of conferences by the above, very hastily sketched Commissions, numerous interesting problems will arise and will test the good will, sincerity, solidarity, talent and imagination of the various representatives. We must hope that they will stand up to these trials.

The exchange of currency at every thousand miles would become cumbersome enough to suggest the idea of common currency in the minds of the convening representatives. Churchill once dreamed up a European coin bearing, on one side, the emblem of the individual nation and, on the other, the common emblem of the united participants. Quite a task for numismatists. Furthermore, what an interesting assignment it would be for the planners to design a flag that contains miniatures of all the flags of the Basin and the proper size and colors of the nation in which the flag actually is being displayed, fluttering in the wind blowing from the Carpathians to the Lowlands and from the Adriatic Sea to the mountains ... the wind that blows over fences and boundaries regardless of how they are changed by the people below.

It is not at all impossible that in the friendly atmosphere developing at the conferences of the preparatory and permanent Commissions, the thought may occur to replace the senselessly destroyed marble monument by Fadrusz in Bratislava. How many bitter feelings would be allayed by such a gesture. Of course, the original monument can never be reconstructed. A copy would not help. It is altogether questionable whether a statue of Maria Theresa is fitting today on that square. But if we consider that she was not only a queen, but a woman and mother as well, then the insult to her memory would remind us of all the terrible insults endured by the innocent women and mothers of this region. Then, in our imagination, there grows a snow white marble statue, sculptured by the descendants of Fadrusz and dedicated to the memory of the women and mothers who suffered in the Carpathian Basin in our time.

There are unlimited artistic possibilities in the creation of monuments that would help to hang a veil of regret and forgiveness over the bloody memories in the minds of those who, in a cleansed atmosphere are so inclined. Novisad, Zalatna, Nagyenyed are a few of such possible places. The Hungarians would probably gladly replace the statue that was erected through foreign pressure on the top of the Gellért Hill so that it should express the new spirit of solidarity and hope of the recovering, reconciled peoples.

Are all these plans merely a dream? Possibly. Let us not forget, however, that such are the dreams of forty, seventy, or who knows how many millions of people, and history teaches us that it is dangerous to forget the dreams and wishes of millions.

Planning is necessary. Nothing is more natural to the architect than the fact, that the houses representing the fortunes of families started out as a few pieces of paper. We have come to accept these scraps and plans turning into reality and creating satisfaction and happiness for the owners. The experienced architect also accepts the fact that during the construction, changes of his plan may occur without any detrimental effect to the creation as a whole. Indeed, some of the changes are beneficial. It will then be understandable that those outlines suggested for the peaceful and happy future of the Danube region are presented in good faith and in the hope that the reaction will be favorable. It is the hope of the author that there will be a few representatives of each of the interested peoples who will agree with these preliminary plans and will—perhaps in the form of a common declaration—suggest and urge the delegation of those Commissions necessary for a trial period. After all, we have to take a step in some direction from our present stand. No doubt, that it is simpler—in place of the difficult task of creating new federations or permanent political systems of any form—if we give our estranged peoples a relatively brief, perhaps a few years long interim, during which they can experiment with the advantages and the possible difficulties of living and working together. A similar commission for a transition period lasting four or five years was suggested by the Belgian Foreign Minister, Mr. Henry Spaak, for a proposed European political union. Of the two possibilities, one is that this experiment would be a failure. In this case, not even the best organized legal systems could help.

The second possibility, however, is that the peoples would enjoy their freedom to travel in an expanded region, and the realization that they could sell their goods to more customers and enjoy the greater variety of opportunities and a more colorful way of life. They would not wish to exchange these advantages for isolation, envy and strife. The job of our statesmen would become very simple under these circumstances.

The whole problem is, after all, rather simple: the peoples of the region want to live in peace and happiness at long last. If their peaceful progress does not agree with certain political theories, the peoples might still get along. But without the peace and happiness of the region, all political ideologies lose their right to exist.

The peace and happiness of the region must represent the peace and happiness of all the peoples living in it. If even one of them is unhappy, the peace of all of them is endangered. Thus, without reference to historic merits or prerogatives, we have to accept simply as *conditio sine qua non* that lasting order in the Danube region is inconcievable without the satisfaction of all the peoples scattered through the whole area. Just a glance at the unstable conditions in the Basin since World War I makes it clear that this requirement has been ignored. We hope that these mistakes form the end of a long line of past mistakes and that we have reached the threshold of new initiatives leading toward lasting, undisturbed peace and welfare for all.

1) The word "symbiosis" is borrowed from biology and is used instead of "coexistence" because of the ill ring of the latter.

2) "The Common Roof" by Franyo Tiso (Nemzetőr, Nov. 1, 1960, p. 4.)

3) Some more items on the list: Pozsony "kifli"; Viennese steak and fashion; hogs from the Bácska; Transylvanian "fatányéros" and apple; folk art of Kalotaszeg, Mezőkövesd, Sárköz, Toroczkó, Lugos; Szekel cabbage and gulyás; Küküllő, Tokaj, Mecsek and Pannonhalma wines; Kassa ham; Czech glassware; Debrecen Bacon; the high protein wheat of the Tisza and Alföld regions; Szeged paprika; Késmárk linen and worsted; Torda "pogácsa." ...

4) Dr. Stan Jonescu: "Danubian Confederation" (Nemzetőr) X. 15, 1960).

5) Dr. T. Galvanek: "Letter to the Editor of Nemzetőr" (Jan. 1, 1961, p. 6).

6) Alexander Gallus: "History of the Carpathian Basin from the oldest times to the Romans" (Kossuth Publishing Co., Textbooks Series, No. 3).

7) The expression "evolutionary humanism" is borrowed from Julian Huxley and is used in the sense as he used it in his "Religion without Revelation."

8) Alexander Gallus, Op. cit.

9) J. Zathureczky: "Transylvanian Christmas" (Nemzetőr, 1960. Dec.).

10) In the City Park of Budapest.

11) See more details in "Federalist Aspirations in East Central Europe" by Edmund I. Lazar. (Published in the present volume.)

12) With reference to the nationality problem and its relation to Pan-Slavism see Francis S. Wagner: "Széchenyi and the nationality problem in the Habsburg empire" (Journal of Central European Affairs, Vol. XX, No. 3, Oct. 1960).

13) Iron Gate is the name of the narrows along the southern part of the Danube, which was made navigable for larger vessels in the 19th century.

14) The problem of the future reorganization of the economy of the whole region is dealt with in more details in the biannual report of the World Federation of Hungarian Engineers and Architects, 1958-59, 12 R.A. Clericy, Avon, S & M, France.

A SAFEGUARD OF PEACE IN EAST CENTRAL EUROPE

Old Problems in New Circumstances

FERENC KOSZORUS

FREEDOM and economic welfare are closely associated with national security induced by powerful self-defense, and the reverse is also true.

Historical events since 1933, followed by the Second World War and its consequences showed: the European balance of power destroyed after the First World War has not been recreated at anytime since.

Clemenceau's foreign policy during 1918-20 tried to create security by force, but it definitely upset the balance of power, with the result that the climate of world politics during the following fifteen years became more uncertain than it was at anytime before. Many small ultranationalist states fabricated upon the ruins of the Austro-Hungarian Monarchy—for some centuries a traditional pivot of the balance of power in Central Europe—were unable to exert an influence toward keeping the balance and promoting security. These new small states with their conflicting interests were too weak and offered an inviting challenge to the powerful aggressors, Hitler and Stalin. The Western Powers, on the other hand, could not permanently nurse the small states, and such a policy would have meant world war within the shortest space of time. Without adequate assistance, these small states proved unable to defend themselves.

In our time, evolution points to the formation of large economic and political units. And it is evident, that after the birth of the idea of the federation of West European states, it would be imperative to unite many small nations in East Central Europe to form a powerful political, economic and military unit within the framework of a European United States. Such a Federation would guarantee peaceful symbiosis, freedom, economic prosperity in countries which in the past decades had been fighting each other; it would be able to defend itself, and by so doing it would contribute to the maintenance of world peace.

Based upon the above aims, we will deal with the military aspects which must be considered as imperative, even before the first steps are taken toward the suggested solution. The political, military and economic problems at the summit are closely interrelated, and it is quite impossible to speak of one problem without referring to the others. It would be a fatal mistake to build first ·a political ground-work for a Federation and at the same time to neglect the military aspect, without which political problems could hardly be solved.

The fundamental basis of this Federation will consist of the geographical and economic conditions of the territories inhabited by many small nations. For organization of such a Federation, the constitution of the former Austro-Hungarian Monarchy, of the United States of America, and also of the West German Republic, could serve as useful examples.

As prospective member states of a Central European Federation, because of their geographical position, the following states could be considered: Poland, Bohemia, Moravia, Slovakia, Hungary, Sub-Carpathia, Transylvania, Rumania, Serbia, Croatia, Slovenia, Bosnia, Herzegovina, Dalmatia and Montenegro.

This would result in a union from 13 to 15 small countries with almost as many languages as countries; and this is not an easy problem if we consider that within the boundaries of each member state their own language must be unconditionally guaranteed. In this case, we cannot count upon factors prevailing in America, which helped merge various early British, French, Spanish, Dutch and German settlers resulting in one official language for the United States. In modern times we know of only one country which consisted of so many small, multilingual nations: this was the Austro-Hungarian Monarchy.

What was that force that kept together the nations of this Empire for more than three centuries? It was first of all, the person of the Emperor and his officers. This fact was universally recognized. It was also realized, that many small nations were living a comparatively happy life within its boundaries, speaking their own languages, living in perfect security, enjoying wealth, cultural progress and civilized life as members of a powerful, large Empire.

We have to utilize these same cohesive component forces and adapt them in the democratic spirit of our times. Condensed into one sentence: the leading principle is complete equality of rights and duties within a large Federation; for member states, as well as for individuals under the leadership of a strong central power, based upon democracy and morality.

In addition to the general terms herein and above outlined; the practical raison d'etre and endurance of the suggested Federation depends also on other spiritual and material components. It is imperative, above all, to set the constitutional and organizational groundwork in such a way that it should strengthen, in every respect, the unity within the state, and should not weaken it during critical periods and vital tests.

The prosperity and endurance of states depend partly upon the political talents of their citizens and partly upon their economic resources. The first factor is the *inborn* intelligence of the people; the second is the volume of natural resources and economic wealth. We, soldiers, consider these two, spiritual and economic factors as equally and vitally important. In the Carpathian-Danubian Basin, in this battlefield of East and West, the Huns—in power and strength superior to the Hungarians—were unable to keep this territory for longer than six decades and the Avars ruled there only for 130 years. The Hungarians, however, kept their country for over a thousand years. The geographical conditions were the same all the time, yet the spiritual factors were different.

The ability of a people or a nation to form a state and preserve it is founded upon inborn intelligence, patriotic self-discipline and self-sacrificing spirit of the individuals. This is the source for a firm moral, resolute, farseeing leadership at the highest level. The common spiritual quality of the community has its roots in culture, philosophy, aims, traditions, ideals and education.

Selection of the member states of the Federation should give priority to the people who have given proof of their state-forming abilities. It is imperative that the spiritual qualities of the member states within the Federation should be in harmony with each other; they should not be divergent and by no means stubbornly antagonistic, for instead of serving and promoting the interests of the state, the antagonistic forces would be spending their strength in internal struggles. This—in case of war— would certainly result in the fall of the Federation.

From a military point of view, it is necessary that the Federation should be formed on the ground of voluntary decisions of the member states and their individual citizens. This self-determination should be based upon the realization that it is better and safer for them to live in freedom in a federation, than to be left alone to their uncertain fate, misery and possible destruction as individual small nations. Needless to say, that a federation, based upon voluntary and harmonious cooperation of its component forces, is more powerful than any state ruled by force alone.

History reveals, that there are indications showing the good will for cooperation, and mutual assistance of the previously mentioned small nations. Most of them lived in friendship during long centuries, often assisting each other unselfishly, as e.g., during the centuries of the Ottoman rule. For 600 years the Polish-Hungarian friendship brilliantly braved the tests even during Hitler's rule.

All these facts considered, it is probable, that the friendly nations now, as contractual parties with equal rights, would be glad to hold once again each other's hands in the interest of their mutual security and welfare. This unity of friendly nations within a Federation will be the core of a magnet, which could draw other neighbors of good will into the union. It will not be obligatory to join.

The affairs of the Federation should be handled by a strong Federal government, responsible to the Federal President and to the Federal Parliament. As the capital of the Federation, Kraków or Budapest could be chosen. The latter would be a preferable choice from a military point of view.

The leadership of the armed forces shall be a federal concern. The president of the federation should be the supreme commander of the federal armed forces. It is his duty to appoint, promote or dismiss military commanders from the rank of commander of a battalion or regiment up to that of the highest ranks. Complying with this duty, he should rely upon proposals made by the chief of staff. The president will have to sanction stratagems submitted by the chief of staff prepared in cooperation with the minister for national defense and the defense committee of the parliament. The president will also have to sanction other proposals of organizational nature. The president will have to entrust the chief commander of the armed forces with strategic tasks; however, he shall not interfere with the practical military leadership. As supreme commander, the president could bring a charge against the chief commander of the armed forces, or the chief of staff; and he must give his sanction to sentences imposed by competent military tribunal.

The highest military position in the federal armed forces, the chief commander of the armed forces, is subordinate only to the President. He is fully responsible for the training and discipline of the armed forces; and after consultation with the federal foreign and defense ministers, together with his deputy, the chief of staff, will prepare the stratagems. These stratagems will then be discussed in the defense committee of the federal parliament. After this, the final proposal will be submitted to the federal president. The chief commander of the federal armed forces must inform the federal government, in peace time, about the strength and preparedness of the armed forces; and, in war, about the military operations. If the Parliament's view concurs with that of the chief of the armed forces, then requests by the Government will be carried out by the chief commander. In case of divergent views, the decision is in the hands of the federal president.

The official language of the supreme command, and of units down to the divisions should be the official language of the Federation. The language of command within other military formations (battalion, regiment), should be the language of the member state which supplies the formation.

Member states should have their own police force, equipped with medium-range weapons. Organization and strength of the police force will have to be determined by the federal government. Discipline and service will have to be directed and supervised by the inspector of police, who is directly subordinate to the federal home secretary. The inspector has the necessary disciplinary and command powers.

It will be necessary to introduce severe legislation to guarantee the unity of the Federation. A permanent mixed organization consisting of civilian and military members, and belonging to the Staff of the Federal President should be established. Its duty would be to watch over the necessary legislation and initiate pertinent investigations concerning federal security. Upon order by the president, the federal parliament, the government, or the chief commander of the Armed Forces, investigations could be initiated against anybody. Depending on the result of such investigations, the attorney general could prosecute any person for high treason, either before a federal court or a military tribunal. The absolute majority of the federal parliament could impeach the president for the same crime.

Many instructive warnings are to be found in the so-called "Peace Treaties" at the end of the first and the second world wars. Decisions concerning the boundaries, based upon force, will have to be avoided. The Polish, German and Russian boundaries deserve careful considerations and, in case of difficulties, a plebiscite should be held. Admission of Austrians and Czechs into the Federation requires careful negotiations. Common historical, cultural, geographical and economic factors, mentioned previously, make the admission of Austria very desirable. However, one has to ponder how long will Austria's neighbor, Germany, abstain from demanding such a large German-speaking territory. In the case of the Czechs, the Polish-Czech and the Hungarian-Czech antagonism is a well-known fact. This reached its climax during the First World War when Benes demanded Russian influence over Central Europe in 1915. This attitude of the Czechs has not changed much since then, and this would not promote the fundamental aims of the Federation.

If approximately 75% of the suggested nations would join, the total population of the Federation would reach 75-80 million people. This would assure that as a major power, the Federation would be able to defend itself and perpetuate its existence. If we take only men from 20 to 35 years of age for compulsory military service in case of war, and, of these only 60% were accepted; within ten years this would make up a total of 6 million trained soldiers. That means more than 100 divisions. Beside this, there would be enough manpower left for the Air Force and the Navy, and also for the higher military formations such as the Army Corps, and the Supreme Command. It is evident, that especially in the beginning, building up the armed forces will show slow progress due to the lack of professional officers. However, after surmounting the initial difficulties, in about 15 years, there would be 100 combat-ready divisions which, compared to the armed forces of other major powers, would be of similar strength, and a powerful deterrent to any aggressor.

As to the economic considerations, the most important requirement is that the Federation should be self-supporting. In this respect the outlook seems to be quite promising.

It is commonly known that the contour of boundaries of a country can make its defense easy or difficult. The latter is the case with our Federation. (See the sketch) Its horizontal planimetric disadvantages, however, will be kept in balance by the vertical formations along the eastern borders for a successful defense. All geographical points considered, the projected Federation would fulfill an important role in keeping the balance between the East and the West. The history of past centuries has proven that these geographical factors helped the nations of this region resist aggressors.

Military-geographical theory and historical experience have proven that the area of the Carpathian Mountains is blocking the main strategic directions from East to West and vice versa. It is a blocking line from a defensive point of view, because it lies along the Southern edge of the power zone. But it is important also because from this fortress successful strategic side attacks can stop and destroy any aggressive powers trying to transgress the Polish plains either northward or westward.

The line of the Carpathians runs practically in a semicircle, defending the Mid-Danube Basin. The wooded, very steep high mountains are passable only through the roads forming bottlenecks, and so comparatively small forces are able to stop and repulse very large enemy forces, as the attacks of the Petcheneg tribe against Europe in the 11th century were stopped and crushed. The same fate awaited the Mongol hordes of the Great Khan in the 13th century. With the help of the Carpathians in the North-East and the East, overwhelming Russian attacks were stopped by the Hungarian forces between March and October, 1944. The small and poorly armed Hungarian 1st Army repulsed the Russian attacks until the Rumanians at the Southern Carpathian passes opened the way for them and let the Russians attack from the rear.

These historical facts prove that this region greatly assisted the defense of Central and Western Europe through centuries. The most recent experiences teach us that the Carpathian Danube Basin, with its surrounding mountains, should be undivided and included as such in the suggested Federation. Any division of this natural line of defense would make this powerful fortress lose its strategic importance.

In summing up our short survey, and considering its historical background, we have to come to the conclusion that a Federation, as suggested, would be desirable. But its realization, however, though not impossible, will not be easy. It is never easy to unite heterogeneous peoples into one powerful organization, even if they are not multilingual. One should not forget the lesson of the American Civil War in 1861-1865. And the difficulties to be encountered with multilingual peoples are best demonstrated by the disintegration of the Austro-Hungarian Monarchy after World War I, when the dissolution started in Bohemia, with a small nation always favored by the Austrian emperors and backed by the West. Another example of the difficulties is the repeated fight of the Hungarians for their independence in the 18th and 19th centuries which also had deep-rooted reasons.

The final conclusion of our deliberations is that a Federation of the nations of East Central Europe is a difficult, but worthwhile project. And from a military viewpoint it may be a real safeguard of peace in Europe. The solution of the old problem in new circumstances will be the test probe of statesmanship, and the proof of the maturity of the respective peoples. They must see clearly their future dangers and eliminate with objectivity and goodwill the obstacles toward unity.

MISSED OPPORTUNITIES FOR FEDERALIZATION

BÉLA PADÁNYI-GULYÁS

THE great French revolution and the revolutions erupting in its wake ended feudalism in Europe. This historic development became advantageous to every country which was predominantly homogeneous linguistically: members of the same nationality acquired equal rights and became the powerful components of those political and economic functions which were previously handled only by the privileged few. Thus the potential of a whole nation was enhanced.

The same historic development also shook the foundations of such multinational countries as the Habsburg Empire, which kept in political and economic unity that vast territory in Central Europe extending from the Carpathian Mountains to the Alps, and from the river Elbe down to the Adriatic Sea. The Habsburg Empire was the product of a still vital and virulent feudalism. Both the Hungarian and the Czechs crowns were acquired by the Habsburgs by royal marriage, which was a legal ground for change of sovereignty in a feudal system. They took possession of Milano with Lomdardy and of Venice with the Istrian Peninsula on the grounds of similar marital contracts. The revolutions overthrowing feudalism destroyed the very power that kept the empire together. The forces of nationalism released by the fundamental social changes were acting like centrifugal forces in the case of the multinational Habsburg empire, and they were working on its final disintegration.

It may perhaps be asked: was the disintegration unavoidable? Was it a must? Or was there a possible way for the component nationalities to find a new political and economic synthesis to replace the bonds of feudalism?—a synthesis which is more and more accepted and necessary today as far as Central European peoples are concerned.

Searching for an answer to the above question one has to admit that the political history of the last century can only be viewed as a series of missed opportunities.

☆ ☆ ☆

Neither in the Reform Era in Hungary in the beginning of the 19th century nor at the time of the revolutions in the middle of the same century, had the Habsburg dynasty an emperor or a statesman of vision with respect to the historic events to come. An unpardonable mistake of Prince Metternich, mastermind of the policy of the Habsburg Empire, was his obstinate efforts to prolong the spirit of the Holy Alliance, which was dead even when it started. Blinded by his stubborn prejudices, he was unable to see that neither the platform of the Reform Era nor that of the first Hungarian responsible* government of 1848 had ever aimed at disengagement from the bonds of the empire. The lawful authority of the Habsburgs was never questioned. The Hungarian nation saw the legality of the 1848 government in the fact that the King gave his sanction to the corpus of the 1848 legislation. Had the Emperor not broken his own pledge, the Hungarian fight for freedom would perhaps not have started at all. But after the King declared "rebels" the members of the same cabinet he had solemnly appointed, and after he ordered the Croat Ban Jellasich to attack with his military forces the new Hungarian system, there was nothing left for the Hungarian nation but a war of self-defense.

Before this happened there was a good possibility for the Empire to transform itself into a federation of constitutionally independent nations with the dynasty in their midst, as happened in the British Isles in the form of the United Kingdom. Had there been a broad-minded imperial policy or politician in the time when Hungary achieved her new Constitution, there would have been no reason why the same status should be denied to Bohemia and Croatia; simultaneously the Poles in Galicia could have developed their own land with Kraków as their national capital; and the multinational territory of Transylvania with her quite special historic traditions and her already existing self-government granted by an imperial diploma, could also have resisted against the popular demands of March 15, 1848; and defending her political unity rather than accepting the Union with Hungary as the motherland, she might have changed as well her outdated Hungarian-Szekler-Saxon feudal form of government to a Hungarian-Rumanian-Saxon unity. Who knows, in the case of Transylvania, what better future could have come for those unfortunate peoples who today are facing the worst ordeal of their history.

While blaming the fatal historic negligence of the imperial leadership in the 19th century, it cannot be denied that the political maturity of the different nationalities was also lacking. The remarkable progress made by the Hungarian nation from the beginning of the Reform Era to the final achievement of a parliamentary government in 1848 had no parallel in Austria, in Bohemia, or in Croatia. Their development from a feudal to a national statehood was much slower. This fact was proved when the nearly simultaneous revolutions in Vienna and in Prague could not incite the Austrian and the Czech nations as a whole. They did not resist the brute forces of the Emperor, as the Hungarians did. The Croats in fact failed to start any action whatsoever toward social reforms.

This lack of a synchronized progress enabled the reactionary imperial leadership to take the worst possible course: to apply the principle of *divide and rule*. The peoples of the Empire were allowed and even encouraged to play a game against each other. Ironically, that immoral policy finally dug the grave of the Habsburg Empire.

The hatred was characteristic and prevailed for a long period, almost up to the present.[1]

The national leaders, excellent as they were otherwise, could not rise above the tragic prejudices. Kossuth, for instance, could arrive at his realistic consideration of a Danubian Federation only in exile.[2] Had he proclaimed it while still the leader of the Hungarian nation, the freedom fight of 1849 perhaps would not have been doomed to a tragic failure in its isolation. The 1867 Compromise (of Austro-Hungarian) whose chief architect was Ferenc Deák meant the starting point of a new historic development, but it offered a solution only for the Hungarian problem rather than for the reorganization of the Empire as a whole. The Emperor could not have resisted against such a proposition at that time when the wounds of his lost wars were still sore. Thus the Compromise of 1867 remained one of the missed opportunities to recreate the dual (Austro-Hungarian) Monarchy at least as a triangular (Austro-Hungarian-Czech) Empire.

If we have critized Ferenc Deák—whose wisdom and political strategy granted him a place among the major European statesmen—more criticism is due to Tomás Masaryk, the noted Czech statesman, for his negligence and lack of foresight. He knew quite well that the chauvinism was aimed at the destruction of the Austro-Hungarian Empire, without regard to its historic and cultural traditions and to the interests of the rest of the nations of the Empire. This meant not only the disregard of the interests of the Germans and the Hungarians, but also those of the Poles, the Slovaks, and the Ruthenians, peoples with equally rich traditions. Similarly, the Croats thoroughly misunderstood their historical and geopolitical assets when they joined a Southern Slav union, namely, Yugoslavia. It may safely be said that the years following World War I represent another examples of the missed opportunities, for there was a good possibility to establish a reliable new system to replace the Habsburg Empire, to create a federation for a loyal and peaceful cooperation of the respective Central European nations.[3]

It is generally admitted today that the Little Entente could never play a positive role in the area. This was most clearly demonstrated at the time of Hitler. Instead of bringing together their own forces, in the atmosphere of distrust, the members of the Little Entente preferred to base their defense on the sanctions granted by the Great Powers.

It is not the purpose of this study to investigate the complicated ideological and political relations existing between the two world wars. Nor does it try to review and judge who made the greater mistake in Hungary: those who expected the correction of all the injustices of the Trianon "Treaty" from an Axis victory or those who hoped that the Soviet "liberation" might bring peace for the Central European nations. We only wish to state two facts: first in the historic cataclysm of the first half of the 20th century, all these nations became suffering victims; secondly, no political trend succeeded in trying to establish a federation of these peoples, which would have granted them peace and security.4) The fact that the nations of Central Europe did not recognize their common destiny prior to or during World War II, cannot be considered as the single cause of all the changes following the war. We are not entitled to expect more wisdom from the political leaders of Czechoslovakia, Hungary or Rumania, than from the signatories of the Yalta Pact, in which nearly half of Europe with independent nations of more than a hundred million population, was given over to the Soviet Union. For Stalin, it was only a matter of time to degrade these occupied countries to the position of Soviet colonies, with no possibility of organized resistance against their aggressor.

We think that no one in the free world would believe that the Czechs, Rumanians, Hungarians, Slovaks, or others whose names are almost forgotten in the West became Communists by conviction and joined voluntarily the Soviet Bloc. Also, though not common knowledge, it is known by many in the West that the hurriedly formed Communist parties lost in the first elections held in the countries under the Soviet occupation. In Hungary only 17% of the representatives in the National Assembly were Communists. In this early time of the Soviet domination, with Communists in the minority in Czechoslovakia, in Hungary, and in Rumania, the anti-Communist political forces were increasing. If only in the three captive nations mentioned above, their common destiny had been recognized, and if they could have organized their joint national resistance, the process of Soviet colonization would have been much more difficult. On the contrary, this colonization was made quite easy in the atmosphere of the old antagonisms among the Central European nations.5) Utilizing the opportunities of that miserable era, Czech and Slovak, chauvinism laid new claims to getting additional territories from Hungary—which had already been mutilated in 1920—and started the forcible deportation of the Hungarian nationalities from Slovakia. At the same time, Czechoslovakia gave over to the Soviets the whole territory of Sub-Carpathia, with all its Ruthenian, German and Magyar populations, without any negotiation or any request for a plebiscite.6) In Transylvania persecution and suppression of the Magyars started.

Soviet propaganda in the meantime tried to make others believe that the quarrels of the Central European nations could be solved only at the "ideological level", i.e., only the Communist international-ism is able to provide for a reasonable synthesis in this multilingual region. The same propaganda earmarked as "chauvinism" and sup-pressed mercilessly every trend toward national independence or toward the formation of ony kind of blocs which might have helped some groups to obtain independence. (Soviet-Yugoslav animosity started in 1948 with regard to the possibility of the formation of a Balkan Bloc.)

What really happened was that the Soviet Union accepted and applied the same immoral policy once used by the reactionary Austrian Empire: secretly stirring the antagonisms between the Central European nations; hindering their contact;[7] not tolerating the development of any ideology recognizing their common destiny and keeping each of them in perfect dependence on Moscow. This became quite clear during the revolutions[8] of 1956 in Poland and in Hungary, where these events kindled national freedom fights as had happened in 1848. A historic opportunity of this caliber offered far-reaching possibilities for all Central European peoples to regain their independence, furthermore, to rearrange all Central Europe—provided that a consciousness of the common goals and of their common destiny could have worked as a political force.

As a witness and participant of the Budapest Freedom Fight, this writer can determine, on the ground of his personal experience that during their life-or-death struggle, the Hungarians had more hope in a possible simultaneous uprisings in Czechoslovakia or in Rumania, than in any help from America, or from the United Nations. Anyone witnessing the events in Hungary knows—what was carefully kept secret, and officially denied by the Communist press—that Ruthenians, Slovaks, and, Ukrainians as well, came over, illegally, to Hungary to participate in the October Freedom Fight.[9] The control of the Slo-vakian boundary became loose because of the sympathetic feelings demonstrated by the Slovak people. And, after being defeated, Hun-garian freedom fighters took refuge in, and received help from Slovakia. Nor has the fact of the participation of partizans of Yugo-slav origin, mainly Croats, who were fighting together with the Hungarians to the end, been ever admitted officially.

All this proves that a common destiny was sensed, if only sporadically, by the peoples beyond the frontiers of Hungary. The Czech, Slovak and Rumanian peoples did not join the Hungarian rev-olution. This can be explained partly by the perfidious and quick Soviet propaganda which claimed that the Hungarian Freedom Fight was aiming at "revisionist" national goals and would develop into aggressive acts against Czechoslovakia and Rumania in order to defend the Hungarian minorities in those countries. This Soviet propaganda was absolutely without foundation. Among several official and unofficial Hungarian statements and demands, there was not a single one alluding to aggression. The contrary is true. The Soviet propaganda, however, succeeded not only in preventing anti-Communist uprisings in Czechoslovakia and Rumania, but also in offering excuses for the old Stalinist factions in both countries, helping them to keep the reins of government in spite of the fact that the Communist Party in Poland, and even in the Soviet Union, took into account the possibility of further "de-Stalinization".[10]

With all this, we arrived at the most recent opportunity which was missed, and which surpassed all previous missed opportunities both in scale and in importance. Thus, the cause of the freedom and self-determination of the Central European peoples was dropped from the agenda, and the rebuilding of a new Central Europe was postponed for an uncertain period of time. The opportunity was not utilized by the Central European nations to regain the initiative in shaping their own future by mutual understanding and cooperation independent of the bargaining great powers.

---

* "Responsible Government" means responsible to an elected Parliament. Governments before 1848 were responsible only to the King.

1) Political struggles in this region prior to the 19th century had not these characteristics. The Dózsa-revolution, the struggles of Bocskai and Rákóczi for religious freedom and national independence, show no signs of hatred between nationalities. As for the latter, it is a fact, that some of Rákóczi's most enthusiastic "kuruc" fighters were Ruthenians.

2) See B. Talbot Kardos, "From Kossuth's unknown federalist papers". Publ. in this volume.

3) "Britain has ... always held it to be her interest that this area, Central Europe, should be held by a Power or Powers strong enough to maintain its own real independence, but not strong enough itself to be aggressive." — C. A. Macartney, "Britain and Eastern Europe," published in this volume.

4) At this point it would be a mistake not to mention some attempts made for a Central European reconciliation, even though they never attained practical results, nor did they represent the policy of any responsible government. Such was the speech of Miklós Horthy at Mohács in 1926, suggesting mutual understanding between Yugoslavia and Hungary; the discernment of Tomás Masaryk in his older age, in favor of a partial revision of the boundaries dividing Czechoslovakia and Hungary, the plan of Tibor Eckhardt, a leader of one of the major oppositional parties in Hungary, to deter the Hitlerian danger, and, finally, the Hungaro-Yugoslav Treaty of mutual friendship and nonaggression pact in 1940, initiated by Minister President Pál Teleki, who sacrificed his life soon after the Treaty collapsed, when German troops marched through Hungary to attack Yugoslavia.

5) Even old Czech and Hungarian emigrants, who collaborated in the exile during World War II, became hostile toward each other. "In Prague I was received with icy coldness... What was even more painful was the fact that the Czechs had succumbed to the same excessive chauvinism against which we had once so passionately fought in Hungary." (George Faludy: **My happy days in hell. An European Autobiography**, pp. 199-200.)

6) See **Hungarians in Czechoslovakia** (New York, 1959, p. 58.)

7) There was a period when it was easier to go from behind the Iron Curtain to the West, than to travel from one "satellite" country to another.

8) The word "revolution" is used very emphatically because both uprisings were real revolutions of the people against the Moscow regime, which grew stiff in its dogmatism.

9) The fact that Soviet military units, stationed in Hungary even prior to the uprising, showed sympathy toward the freedom fight and later joined it was also testified by eyewitnesses.

10) The "de-Stalinization" in Czechoslovakia and Rumania started long after the suppression of the Hungarian revolution.

SLOVAKIA AND THE INTEGRATION PLANS
OF CENTRAL EUROPE

JOSEPH M. KIRSCHBAUM

AT THE END of the First World War President Woodrow Wilson assumed that the universal recognition of the right of national self-determination would bring progress and co-operation to Europe and especially to East Central Europe about which he was concerned in his known Fourteen Points. And there is no doubt that it was a solid basis, providing the principle had been applied consistently and not only to the victors of the First World War, and providing also that those who were privileged would have recognized that there was a correlation of rights and obligations—especially an obligation to respect the rights of other peoples or nationalities.

Instead of a consistent application of the principle of self-determination, there was, however, in East Central Europe a tendency to build national states in an area where during several centuries nationalities and etchnic groups lived intermingled. Some peoples and their leading politicians even identified the ideals and interests of one people with the interests of a State which was necessarily and historically multinational.

As a result, the solution which was given to this area in 1919 was unjust and detrimental to millions of human beings who were persecuted and became second class citizens because of their ethnic origin or because of their desire to develop their respective mother tongues or cultures. The settlement could not eliminate the difficulties. The settlement found itself obliged to make concessions against the ethnic principle in favor of economic, administrative and strategic considerations; in certain cases even in favor of historical considerations, while in others it admitted that the people concerned were not ripe for independence. The nations which were losers by the changes introduced in 1919 naturally struggled against that settlement.

Thus an organization which was supposed to solve national problems and put an end to century-long struggles for national rights brought about discontent to half of the peoples of Central Europe and prevented peaceful co-operation among all of them. As years passed, hatred of those who oppressed instead of governing was increasing. This led to the crisis of democracy and in the final analysis, hastened the disintegration of the Versailles Order. Looking for a new organization of Central Europe became a matter of necessity and of logical conclusion.

Plans for integration of Central Europe were, therefore, revived during the Second World War. Milan Hodza in his work, "Federation in Central Europe,"[1] General Sikorski in his agreement with the Czech politicians,[2] several Hungarian diplomats, as well as certain Slovak politicians in Sweden, Switzerland and the Vatican[3] advocated the only reasonable solution of Central European problems: the integration of the area between Germany and Russia on a federative basis. Milan Hodza was especially explicit in advocating the idea of a federation[4] which, since 1848, was in one form or another advanced and favored by representatives of all the peoples who had inhabited the area between Germany and Russia for centuries.[5]

But the dynamic Soviet Union, which became more imperialistic than Russia had been at any time under any Czar, destroyed in its brutal Drang nach Westen all the plans and dreams of Central European politicians and diplomats who wished to integrate Central Europe as an area of free and democratically governed peoples. A new colonial rule was imposed upon Central Europe, and expulsions and transfers of populations accompanied by inhuman suffering and crimes against humanity made the problems of this area more complex and more dangerous than ever for Europe and the world at large. We cannot but agree with the well-known British expert on Central Europe, C. A. Macartney, who in 1942 warned that "a powerful and aggressive state which robs the East European nations of their independence also threatens the safety of the world, since it remains, as it always has been, dangerous to the world if any one Great Power, or two or three Great Powers acting in permanent collusion (if such a thing is possible), acquire a complete and monopolistic control of this area. The more powerful the state aiming at such control, the heavier the yoke which it imposes on the Danubian peoples if it succeeds, and also the greater the peril to the world."[6]

The Great Power, which by force and by violation of agreements and pledges imposed the brutal communist rule upon the peoples of Central Europe, prevented the East Central European countries from combining their forces and economies to their advantage. There are, nevertheless, in the present situation also several features which could be regarded as being potentially able to make it easier for any future federative organization of Central Europe to function after its liberation from Soviet colonial rule.

By brutal force and disregard for human dignity and feelings the Soviet Union, with the help of Communist regimes, brought Central

Europe to a common denominator in the fields of economy, culture and social structure and exacted similar development from all peoples of that area. Despite the fact that Central Europe had for centuries developed under the same rule and had been influenced by the same political doctrines and Western cultural currents there were great differences among the various Central European peoples in their economic and educational standards, social structure, and industrialization and political systems, all of which would have made any democratic federation a mosaic hard to keep together and govern successfully. By mercilessly destroying the upper classes and bourgeoisie, by nationalization and expropriation, by murder and coercion, the puppet governments of the Soviet satellites eradicated differences and integrated Central Europe in their own way.

No doubt the peoples of Central Europe paid a very high price in blood, suffering and degradation, but plans for a federation of Central Europe will never have a better outlook for success than they will have after that area is freed from Soviet rule and Communist systems.

Such plans become more realistic and appear more realizable than ever before for other reasons as well, but the above should not be overlooked or underestimated. The present trend in Western Europe towards the successful integration of countries like France and Germany suggest that neither the differences and memories of past quarrels and clashes, nor all the attempts at assimilation and persecution should stand in the way of making Central Europe a commonwealth of harmoniously co-operating peoples.

Slovakia's Stand and Place in Central Europe

Today there is perhaps no need to argue that Slovaks are not merely one of the "historic" peoples of Central Europe, but also the people who attained the same level of cultural and political maturity as the other peoples of East Central Europe. Milan Hodza, who for decades supported the Czech tendencies towards amalgamation of Slovaks and Czechs, reversed his stand and at the beginning of the Second World War advocated self-rule for Slovakia stating that "long before World War II Slovakia had reached if not passed the Central European civilization level."[7] And according to C. A. Macartney, Slovak nationalism became a new factor in Central European politics which could not be overlooked.[8]

At the end of the Second World War even such adversaries of Slovak national aspirations as Dr. E. Benes bowed for a short time before these realities and the restoration of Czechoslokavia proceeded according to the principle of a "State combining the two separate nations of Czechs and Slovaks" and the Slovak National Council was accepted as the "rightful representative of the individual Slovak nation" and "bearer of sovereign right on Slovak territory."[9]

There is perhaps no need to prove by statistics enumerating all the various oppressions to which Slovakia was subjected between 1918-1938 or from 1945 on that Slovaks were and remained one of the most dissatisfied peoples of Central Europe to whom the right of self-determination was denied. In 1945 they were robbed even of that limited independence which was tolerated in Slovakia by the Third Reich which, at least formally, peoples of Yugoslavia enjoy under the present Communist system.

The true position of Slovakia in pre-war Czechoslovakia was adroitly camouflaged by clever Czech propaganda and the voice of Slovaks in the free world is often silenced today by politicians who were an obedient tool of Communist and Soviet expansion but who denounce Slovaks as former allies of Germany and, therefore, unfit for the rights which the majority of Germans have been enjoying for more than a decade since the end of the War.

Nevertheless, many observers became acquainted with the true situation in Slovakia and with the aspirations of the majority of Slovaks, as well as with Slovak opposition to the present order and to the regime of 1918-1938.[10] In 1939 Slovaks expressed their stand by proclaiming independence, which did not happen because they were forced to do it, contrary to the false assertions by adversaries of Slovakia's aspirations for independence. Slovaks had no reasons to defend either Czechoslovakia or the political order in Central Europe which denied them not only many fundamental rights but tried to deprive them even of their existence and name.

This opposition to the present status quo which stems either from ideological or political reasons is a matter of principle for all politically mature Slovaks. And news about Slovakia's resistance penetrated not only the Iron Curtain but also the media of information in the free world which are influenced by the adversaries of Slovak aspirations for freedom and independence.

It can therefore be assumed that Slovakia will be a natural and reliable ally of anybody who will seriously try to upset the present situation in Central Europe, a situation which is oppressive for Slovaks not only because of its Communist system and Soviet domination, but also because Slovakia is ruled again from Prague, a fact resented even by Slovak Communists. And we can safely assume also that the system which the majority of Slovaks would advocate if free expression were allowed in Slovakia, and which has constantly been advocated by Slovak politicians in exile, is a Central European Federation: a federation of free peoples on equal political footing in which due respect would be given to cultural, ethnic and linguistic peculiarities, national rights, and traditions, and which would warrant stability and economic prosperity.

This assertion is in no basic contradiction with the aspirations of

Slovaks (or those of any other Central European people) for national independence and self-determination, a hope shared with the majority of Slovaks in the free world. The principle of self-determination is not necessarily one of disintegration. The political right of national self-determination can be reconciled with the exigencies of economic interdependence and security. Peoples may "determine" themselves into larger units as readily as they can into smaller ones, says E. H. Carr.[11] There is no doubt that the individual wants to see the people or group of which he is a member free and independent. But it is also true that he wants to belong to a group large and powerful enough to play a significant role in a wider community.

Once a broader economic and military framework is securely established, there is no limit to the number or to the functions of the smaller national units of self-government which may be built up within it. And there are examples to prove that in a federation the natural and ineradicable desire of the human group for self-determination in the conduct of its affairs can be given the fullest scope and expression.

The conception of fully sovereign nation-states which sprang from nineteenth-century political philosophy cannot, in our age, be applied to East Central Europe without doing injustice to millions of human beings and neglecting the security and economic welfare of all the inhabitants of that area. This became clear to Slovak politicians, and several of them expressed it either in their works or political activities. Conscious of the dangers to which Central Europe has been exposed from the neighboring Great Powers on the one hand, and equally conscious of the evolving economic and political independence of the European peoples on the other hand, the Slovaks are guided in the present struggle by no narrow nationalism or resentments, nor do they wish to recreate the past. The vision of their free and independent Slovakia takes into consideration European, and especially Central European, problems and interests, and it is on a wide European basis that they look for a guarantee of their freedom, national independence and security.

Yet, we must stress that more than anything it will be a solution of national aspirations in the sense of self-determination which will decide "en fin de compte" about the coming into existence and functioning of a democratic Central European Federation.[12]

As many objective observers of Central Europe have agreed, it was not the principle of self-determination which can be held responsible for the troubles we have witnessed in Central Europe between the wars. Th troubles in Central Europe were caused by:

1.) the inconsistency with which the principle of self-determination was applied

2.) the failure to recognize that the principle was a variable one requiring modification in the light of political and economic conditions and

3.) the fact that the extension given it at Versailles was, as we see now, at variance with the twentieth-century trends of political and economic organization. It caused disintegration of existing economic and political units and favored the creation of incoherent smaller units at a time when strategic and economic factors were demanding integration. And by applying it inconsistently, it left many peoples and nationalities dissatisfied and desiring to change the order which was imposed upon them.

As applied in the peace settlement of 1919, the principle of self-determination resulted also in the crisis of democracy in Central Europe and its violation turned ultimately on a moral issue.

The troubles became even worse because they arose out of the violation of the principle of self-determination by those peoples who tried to build a national state in traditionally and historically multi-national areas and out of identification of the ideals of the people —even if it presented less than 50% of the population of the state— with the interests of the state.

Eighteen years of Soviet colonial rule over Central Europe proved that Moscow added to the errors and blunders of Versailles a brutal system of political oppression and economic exploitation, solving the problems of national minorities by expelling millions of people instead of granting them rights and correcting previous blunders.

For political observers, as well as for those Slovaks living in the free world who decry Soviet colonial rule and advocate the right to freedom and independence of Central European peoples, a democratic and integrated Central Europe seems, therefore, again the only solution which will simultaneously satisfy the needs of modern economic organization and the urge of human beings to preserve and develop their own cultures, traditions, and national identities.

1) See Milan Hodza, **Federation in Central Europe**, London, 1942.

2) See Joachim Kühl, **Federationsplane im Donauraum und in Ostmitteleuropa**, Südost-Institut, München, 1958.

3) See J. M. Kirschbaum, **Slovakia—Nation at the Crossroads of Central Europe**, New York 1960, Chapter on Federalist tendencies in Slovakia, pp. 75-84 and 223-230, and F. Durcansky's study in **Revue de droit international**, XXII, 1, Geneve, 1944.

4) Wrote Hodza, "War events in Central Europe obviously fully vindicate the idea of a solidly organized future cooperation of all those eight States

which are placed in complete geographic coherence between Russia, Germany and Italy. A federalized Central Europe is one of the absolute necessities of a new post-war order." Op. cit., p. 32.

5) See Rudolf Wierer, **Der Federalismus im Donauraum**, Verlag Böhlau, Graz-Köln, 1960.

6) See C. A. Macartney, **Problems of the Danubian Basin**, London, 1942, p. 122.

7) Cf. M. Hodza, op. cit., pp. 208-209.

8) See, C. A. Macartney, op. cit.

9) See, Wm. Diamond, **Czechoslovakia between East and West** (London, 1947), pp. 2-3.

10) The aspirations and struggle for a new and democratic Slovakia are voiced in dozens of Slovak newspapers in the free world, in the quarterly **Slovakia**, as well as in numerous memoranda of the Slovak National Council Abroad, Slovak League of America, Slovak Liberation Committee, Canadian Slovak League, etc. Since 1946, several members of the U.S. House of Representatives and Senate recorded in the Congressional Record either resolutions or pledges for Slovakia's freedom and independence. (See Part IV, Documents, in the writer's book.) In the Slovak language, the struggle of the Slovaks for independence is comprehensively treated in these books: Dr. F. Durcansky, **Biela Kniha** (White Book), Buenos Aires, 1954, and Dr. J. Kirschbaum, **Naš boj o samostatnost Slovenska** (Our struggle for Slovakia's Independence), Cleveland, Slovensky Ustav, 1958. In French in J. A. Mikus, **La Slovaquie dans le drame de l'Europe** (Paris 1955), etc.

11) See, E. H. Carr, **Conditions of Peace** (New York, 1942).

12) E. H. Carr states that "self-determination might indeed be regarded as implicit in the idea of democracy; for if every man's right is recognized to be consulted about the affairs of the political unit to which he belongs, he may be assured to have an equal right to be consulted about the form and extent of the unit" ... In its triumphal progress national self-determination and democracy went hand in hand." Op. cit., p. 39.

CZECH AND SLOVAK STATESMEN IN FAVOR
OF A CENTRAL EUROPEAN FEDERATION

JOSEPH OSTROVSKY

NOW that the new Czechoslovak leaders have accepted the idea of transforming Czechoslovakia into a federal state, it will be interesting to examine the point of view of outstanding Czech and Slovak politicians both in the past and present.

Tomás and Jan Masaryk wanted a
Central European Federation. New proofs of it.

Mrs. Marcia Davenport, whose husband was one of the founders of *Fortune* magazine, published a book[1]) in which she tells in detail the last weeks of Jan Masaryk before his death. Mrs. Davenport spent many years in Austria and Czechoslovakia, especially Prague, while writing her book on Mozart. During the Second World War when Jan Masaryk was an exile in the USA, Mrs. Davenport became closely acquainted with him. He later served as foreign minister for Czechoslovakia until his suicide or murder. Mrs. Davenport lived in Prague during the 1947/48 Communist takeover, where Jan Masaryk was in almost daily contact with her, sending penciled notes and making other interesting remarks to her about the tragic events in his country. Based on her conversations with the younger Masaryk, we read in Mrs. Davenport's book: "It is true that Thomas Masaryk was influenced by Woodrow Wilson's stubborn insistence on self-determination for all peoples, away from *Masaryk's own original broader concept* of a post-war reorganization of the Habsburg empire into a *democratic confederation of the hitherto subject provinces. The failure to achieve this after the First World War laid Central and Eastern Europe open to Hitler; and Russians obstruction of any similar plan (which was Jan's own best hope) after the Second World War brought about the Communist satellite countries of today.*" (p. 333)

The text implies that Jan Masaryk shared his father's idea of *forming a democratic confederation in the Central European area.* Jan Masaryk's accusation, however, of Wilson's "stubborn insistence of self-determination for all peoples" influenced the older Masaryk to drop his broader concept of a confederation, is false. We know that President Woodrow Wilson demanded, in his message to Congress January 8, 1918, in Point 10: "The peoples of Austria-Hungary whose place among the nations we wish to see safeguarded and assured, should be accorded the freest opportunity of *autonomous development*." In Anglo-Saxon law "autonomous development" does not mean breaking away from an existing system and forming an independent, sovereign national state. This was still more clearly stated by the British Prime Minister Lloyd George who described the war aims of Great Britain before the British Trade Union Congress in January, 1918, as follows: "The allies are fighting against the German government, not against the German people. They *do not wish to destroy Germany or Austria-Hungary.* (Point 4) They want self-government for the subject nationalities of the dual monarchy." "Autonomous development" and "self-government" in the English-American terminology and especially in terms of federalism does not mean breaking up a territory into sovereign independent states.

That Tomás Masaryk was in favor of a Central European federal solution can be easily proved. His English friend, Seton-Watson, knew Masaryk before and during the First World War intimately, and said of Masaryk's political plans at the time: "Masaryk did not despair of an *evolution in a federal direction* what was often called a *monarchical Switzerland.*"2) The same book contains Masaryk's ideas expressed in a letter to Professor Ernest Denis during Masaryk's first escape from Austria-Hungary. "Some days ago I received the first letter of Mr. Masaryk on the problem of Austria-Hungary" — wrote E. Denis to Seton-Watson. "To *establish a confederation sufficiently large,* leaving to every Diet an authority fairly expanded; not to confer on the Central Parliament more power than is necessary for the military and foreign affairs, the railways and the Post. Insofar as it will be forever impossible to follow the ethnographic frontiers exactly, to establish in the constitutional laws absolute guarantees to minorities, complete equality of languages, schools and universities; to eliminate all that could resemble the domination of one race by another; complete religious freedom; freedom of the press and association." (Letter of *Ernest Denis*, French professor of geography, to Seton-Watson , Oct. 31, 1914, p. 52.)

The well-known German biographer, Emil Ludwig, included in his book "Nine Etchings" his conversations with President Masaryk in Prague. Masaryk told his interviewer "his original plan was the *transformation of the monarchy into a federal state* of which the various members would be *autonomous.*" Professor S. Harrison Thompson proves in his book3) that Charles Kramar, the other most outstanding Czech politician who stayed at home and became the first Prime Minister of Czechoslovakia, published articles in French newspapers during the First World War in which he advocated that a "federal union of the Danubian countries should take the place of the Austrian monarchy." All leading statesmen knew at the time that the Czech members of the Austrian Parliament brought a resolution favoring the "transformation of Austria-Hungary into a *League of States*."4) As late as 1918 Tomás Masaryk did not exclude a free federalization of the Danubian nations. In the issue "New Europe" published in Washington, D.C. he wrote: "Should there be federation of the smaller states, there will be federations freely entered upon out of the real needs of these nations, not out of dynastic and imperialistic motives. Federation without freedom is impossible; that must be emphatically stated to those Austrian and other politicians who are promising autonomy and federation."

E. Benes and Clemenceau, not Woodrow Wilson caused the abandonment of federal plans.

Francis Joseph I died November 21, 1916. His successor, Charles sent a letter to his French relative, Prince Sixtus, in January 1917, authorizing him to begin negotiations for a separate peace between Austria-Hungary and the Entente powers. On the 8th of March 1917, Poincaré stated to Prince Sixtus: "I am willing to send the formal peace offer of the monarchy—when received to the English and Russian governments." Because of this proposal a real danger existed for the East European emigrants that they could perhaps never return to their homelands. But subsequent events in 1917 favored the emigrants. The Germans learned of the secret peace offer which had been refuted by the Austrian foreign minizster, Czernin. Clemenceau was so enraged by the whole affair that he made it public thereby discrediting Austria-Hungary and causing the resignation of Czernin. It was then not a difficult task for the young and active collaborator of Masaryk, E. Benes, who worked in Paris, to persuade Clemenceau that it was in the best interest of France to break up the Austro-Hungarian empire into small units.

Benes himself was, in his earlier years, an ardent federalist. He finished his studies in Paris with the publication of his doctoral thesis5) in which his main idea is expressed in the chapter "La Lutte pour l'Autriche Fédérale". In it he gives a sketch of his federal plan which is similar to that of the Austrian Social-Democrat Karl Renner6) who remained faithful to his idea of a Danubian federalism. Benes and his collaborators in France deserted the idea of federalism after 1915 and succeeded in convincing Tomás Masaryk to favor the creation of French-type national centralized states. To allay possible misgivings of President Wilson, the Czech statesmen inserted the following passage in the "Declaration of Independence of Czechoslovakia", made public in the Philadelphia Hall of Independence October 1918: "We believe that the free nations of Central and Eastern Europe may *easily federate* should they find it necessary." In the Pittsburgh agreement signed in the same year with American Slovak leaders, the text speaks of the Slovak "Diet", i.e., legislature which has never been granted to Slovakia in its full sense. This was the cause of the bitter struggle of the Slovak parties, especially Hlinka's Slovak People's Party, with Prague. It caused many crises, e.g. the Tuka affair in 1928, and finally led to the broaking up of the Czechoslovak Republic. (The "independent" Slovak state under Tiso was a typical satellite state —1938-1944.)

Whenever Benes came under pressure he resorted to federalist arguments. For instance, before the Paris Peace Conference in 1919, when he pleaded for a Czechoslovakia that included three million Germans, one million Hungarians, half a million Ruthenians, etc. he promised (Memoir III): "Le régime serait semblable á celui de la Suisse." (Czechoslovakia's government will be like Switzerland's.) Because these promises were never kept, and because Benes, as the most influential politician and later president of his country, stubbornly refused real federalization and even autonomy for the Slovaks and Ruthenians, Czechoslovakia was unable to withstand the storms that followed. In the last moment, before the breaking up of Czechoslovakia, President Benes offered his "Fourth Plan" on September 5, 1938: "The *cantonization* of the whole area with a system similar to *Swiss cantons*". But the offer came too late just as Emperor Charles' plan for the federalization of Austria in October 1918 was too late. Like the Hungarian Lajos Kossuth after 1849, Benes went a second time into exile where he had time to ponder his mistakes and plan ahead. In 1850-51 Kossuth produced his plan for a Danubian confederation.6a) Ex-President E. Benes, in London and the United States in 1939, again turned to plans for federation. In his program of 19397) he wrote: "This harmony and synthesis can probably be established in a new system of a real and effective collective security... That can mean only a new system of international policy, more peaceful, more moderate, and more *acceptable to all nations* but also a *kind of federative reorganization*, first perhaps in certain regions (the *Danubian region*, the Baltic region, the Balkan, or Northern Europe) which, I hope will be extended later to the whole of Europe. There is *no other possibility* if we wish to avoid a repetition of war and crisis in Europe similar to what we have today, every ten or twenty years."

About the same time Pál Teleki, Prime Minister of Hungary, came to the conclusion that a Central European regional federation was the only protection from powerful Germany and Russia.7a) If Teleki had left Hungary for London instead of committing suicide, he would have been able to associate with former President Károlyi, the Czech Benes, the Slovak Hodza, the Polish Sikorsky and others who all were at that time in favor of the federalization of Central Europe. They could present the plan to the Allied Powers. If such a plan had been the condition of the American Lend-Lease assistance to Russia, the post-war arrangements in Postdam, Yalta and Paris would have conformed more to the real interests of the Central European nations.

Between 1940 and 1942 ex-President Benes worked out a plan for a Czechoslovak Polish confederation which he then discussed with General Sikorsky and other Polish statesmen. He elucidated his plan in *Foreign Affairs*, January 1942: "The creation of this new political unit, *Czechoslovak Polish Confederation* can already be considered as an accomplished fact." He continues:

"It might be joined by Austria and Hungary and possibly by Romania. In Central Europe those territories which have associated together most naturally, must be fused into firm blocs. These will be the foundations for more expansive structures ... I should expect that with the passage of time, a natural bridge will be established between the northern and southern confederation in Central Europe— *that is, between the Polish-Czechoslovak group and the Balkan group—and that in this way, we shall take a further logical step toward the consolidation of Europe as an element in some sort of world commonwealth; for without the first, the second seems to me inconceivable. I go further and affirm that without this broad European framework, no regional confederation can be envisaged."*

As seen from this quotation the Czech statesman stood on the principle of federalism as long as the battle of Stalingrad when he unexpectedly dropped it, went to Moscow and made a pact with Stalin and Molotov. He hoped the Red Army would restore the pre-Munich Czechoslovakia under his presidency as a purely Slavic state without the three million Germans,, one million Hungarians, etc. When he returned to Czechoslovakia he announced his Kosice program (1945) which nullified the citizenship of all non-Slavs. After expulsion of the Germans, the Czech and Slovak Stalinists organized a strictly centralized Communist regime which engulfed President Benes himself. The Stalinist era lasted almost twenty years—up to 1968. Has it completely ended?

Other Czech emigrant politicians who had remained in the West, continued to demand a more prudent federal solution for the area. Dr. Josef Cerny, chairman of the Czechoslovak Republican Agrarian Party, which was banned by the Communists after 1945, wrote as follows:

"The party succeeds to the political heritage of Antonin Svehla and Milan Hodza who many years ago had already realized that small nations placed among powerful neighbors can preserve their liberty and independence only if they build up a close political and economic cooperation among themselves ... The peoples of Central and Southeastern Europe, associated in a *federation bloc* of more than ninety million, would be an effective contribution toward the political consolidation of Europe. It would supply a firm foundation for peaceful order in an area which, already for the second time in one decade, has been the scene of brutal aggression against small and middle-sized nations . . .

"A joint effort with other countries is indispensable in order to develop all existing excellent potentialities and in order to turn to best account the rich natural resources of the whole region. Furthermore, a *federalized Central and Southeastern Europe* would be an important step toward the economic integration of Europe. Aiming at this great goal which is paramount in our program, we shall have to seek a way toward the mutual understanding and cooperation of nations; we shall have to remove obstacles, primarily the economic ones; we must overcome the differences existing between nations. We must recognize that a fair minority policy is an effective instrument toward agreement and peace among us.

"The agrarian parties are coming with a far-reaching cultural, economic and social program which is to be their contribution toward the political consolidation of their respective countries, so as to give adequate strength to the nations that are going to form the nucleus for the federalization of Central Europe."

Other groups of Czech politicians like General Prchala and his Czech National Council (seat in London) advocated similar plans for confederation. General Prchala announced: "Insted of reestablishing a united Czechoslovakia we favor Czech lands (Bohemia-Moravia-Silesia) and Slovakia which will be the cornerstone of a *Central European Confederation*. According to this, the Czech and Slovak peoples will, as equal partners, decide about their participation in a *Confederation in Central Europe*."

Federal Plans Proposed by Slovak Statesmen.

Dr. Milan Hodza, Prime Minister of Czechoslovakia between 1935 and 1938, published his book: *Federation of Central Europe* (London, N.Y., 1942) from which highlights were quoted in the *Studies for a New Central Europe* (Series 2, No. 1, pp. 33-41). Unfortunately, Hodza died in 1944 in England, leaving no counterbalance to the changed policies of President Benes. Other Slovak politicians continued their insistence that a Centralized Czechoslovakia is not the true solution for the Czech and Slovak people. Peter Pridavok, one-time editor of the *Slovak* newspaper, official organ of the Slovak People's Party, later chief of the Official Slovak Press Bureau and Secretary-General of the Slovak National Council in London, explained what kind of federalism the Slovaks want:[8]

271

"Why a federation and *what kind of a federation?* The First World War broke up Austro-Hungary so that President Wilson's principle about the self-determination of nations might become effective. New states were formed—states which were only smaller copies of the former Austro-Hungary. A great economic and military unit was broken up and self-determination remained on paper! The dissolution of Austro-Hungary was one of the main causes of the new aggression of Germany toward the East: there was no one to stand in its way, because the small succession states were not on good terms with each other, they were weak internally and so the German Moloch devoured them 'one by one'. They say that men become wiser after a frecas and thus the world statesmen and politicians today see that it will be necessary to restore in some form the union of the nations in the former Austro-Hungarian empire. That must be done in such a way that the principle of self-determination—again formulated in the Atlantic Charter—be respected and that not only on paper but in reality, so that every nation, even the smallest, becomes the master of its own household and at the same time so that a strong barrier be formed against German expansion.

"This can be attained if all the nations living between Germany and Russia, from the Baltic to the Adriatic and the Mediterranean, unite in one *Central European Federation.* In such a *federation* there can even be smaller states than those which originated after the last war, indeed even smaller, e.g. than Slovakia today because even though all these states will manage their own national affairs according to their needs, their foreign policy, defense as well as federal economic policy shall have to be uniform so that with united strength they shall be able to defend themselves against any kind of a new Hitler in the future.

"Could Slovakia be an equal and full-fledged partner of such a *federation?* It not only could be but *must* be. In a *federation*—as is your in America—every state, even the smallest, has equal rights and equal obligations. In our federation there shall be states that are much smaller than our Slovakia. But even these shall enjoy the same rights as the largest and strongest member of the *federation.* The great warring democracies are eminently interested that in this part of Europe where we live there be peace, order and prosperity, otherwise this area shall become the focus of new disturbances and wars. Therefore in their own interest with combined effort they certainly shall see to it that this organization does not collapse. If its foundations are healthy, every member of it will be content. All the nations of Central Europe taught by the bitter present, will most *willingly go into this joint federation.*"

In October 1945 the Central European Club in London issued a warning that nothing short of a federal solution would bring permanent peace to the Central European are. The Statement of Aims[9]) signed by the Slovak Pridavok, the Czech Lev Prchala, and many others, including Poles, Yugoslavs, Hungarians, etc. says:

"The experience of the period between the two wars and of the last few years have taught us that the idea of *federation* of the area, already present in men's minds before the war, will prove to be the best solution for the future. We wish to make it quite clear that this idea is not peculiar to us. Information reaching us constantly from Central Europe shows that the people there are coming to the same conviction and are taking more and more interest in this solution.

"This makes us confident that our conclusions, elaborated eventually in constitutional lines, will be acclaimed by our fellow-countrymen as their own wish and programme as soon as they are allowed to express their will freely. This is our justification for setting them forth in the following statement:

"1.) Central Europe—that is the area between Germany and Russia—forms a natural geographical and economic entity inhabited by a number of medium-sized and smaller nations possessing mutual interests and similar culture, and therefore ought to be organized on the *basis of a federation*. In this way only, Central Europe will cease to be a field of rivalry between the big powers and an area of constant unrest, endangering the peace.

"2.) Within the framework of a *Central European Federation* (in the following paragraphs referred to as the *FEDERATION*), every nation shall have full rights to preserve its individuality, to cultivate and to develop its own culture and to bring up its young generation in this spirit. Every nation shall have the right to organize its religious, political, social and economic life according to the will of its people in conformity with the *Federal Constitution*.

"3.) The *Federation* must be built upon the fundamental constitutional principle of respect for the full rights of the free men. The Central Federal Authority shall take care that these rights are safeguarded and that internal peace based on Christian charity, universal justice and agreed constitutional order is maintained."

The Slovak National Council[10]) addressed a memorandum to Ernest Bevin, English Minister for Foreign Affairs in which the Council pointed out:

"The Slovak people have not been given the opportunity to express their views with regard to the re-establishment of a centralized, unified Czechoslovakia or to elect to its Constituent Assembly such representatives who would voice the true sentiments, aims and aspirations of the Slovak people ... Never, never again a centralized, unified Czechoslovakia! A *new solution must be found* for the problems of Central Europe. The justest solution excogited so far is a *Federation or United States of Central Europe* ... We protest most emphatically, and in advance, against any future "liberation" activities by so-called "Czechoslovaks" ... There is no Czechoslovak nation to liberate. There is a Czech and a Slovak nation."

The Slovak League of America gave voice to similar demands in a volume published in May, 1951:

"The representatives of Central European nations are working for a federation, for a just and democratic arrangement of the region between Russia and Germany. This is in favor of the establishment of an independent Slovakia. The Slovaks at home and in exile are for such a *federation* of which Slovakia would be an integral part. Admitting Czechoslovakia as a unit within such a federation would not be a just and democratic settlement of the problem of Central Europe because the Slovaks would continue to be exploited."

Resurgence of Federalism in Czechoslovakia, 1968.

All the previous warnings and federal plans went unheeded. They were sometimes dropped and forgotten by their own authors who, once in power, acted as if homogeneous national states could be formed in multinational areas. Who would be so bold as to counsel the breaking up of Switzerland into three or four "national states"? But this was done in the Danubian area with the results before our eyes. The errors committeed led to tragedies for millions but finally, true solutions must emerge. After so many tragic experiments the bureaucratic over-centralization of Czechoslovakia under Stalinist political leaders demonstrated *ad ocolus* that without federalism no lasting solution is possible. Realizing this, the Communist Party of Czechoslovakia, under the leadership of Alexander Dubcek decided to change Czechoslovakia into a federal state. The National Assembly brought a similar resolution September 13, 1968.

Political scientists have neglected the study of federalism, and, therefore, there is great danger of not seeing clearly the difference between true federalism and pseudo-federalism. The latter existed, e.g., in Bismarck's Germany, in the Austro-Hungarian Monarchy, today in the Soviet Union, and in several South American federal states dominated by military juntas. True federalism may exist in a small country like Switzerland, present-day Austria, or in a large area like Australia, Canada, the United States. Czechoslovakia may follow the example of present-day Austria which followed the Swiss pattern. If, however, the Czech and Slovak leaders think that instead of one national state, a federation of two national states will solve the problem, especially under the dictatorship of the Communist party, then they are on the way to another form of pseudo-federalism, as was the case with Austria-Hungary under the meddling rule of the emperor. As soon as Slovakia demanded statehood in January 1968 within a federal system, Moravia immediately announced its claim to a similar status which was denied to it. In a truly federal structure, each community, town, district, Land or canton has its autonomy in its own local affairs. Consequently, the Czech and Slovak leaders would do better if they studied the Swiss or present Austrian federal system. A true federalism would perhaps not be possible under the Warsaw Pact. Therefore, the present experiment will mark only a transition. After a period, there will be formed a Common Market of the states between Russia and Germany and a return not only to President Benes' "cantonization plan" of 1938, but the much earlier plan of Tomás Masaryk[12] for a confederation in the neutralized zone of Central Europe.

1) Marcia Davenport: **Too Strong for Fantasy.** A personal record of music, literature and politics in America and Europe over half a century. New York. Charles Scribner's Sons. 1967, pp. 498.

2) Seton-Watson: **Masaryk in England,** Cambridge. 1943, p. 20.

3) S. Harrison Thompson: **Czechoslovakia in European History.** Kingston Press. 1943, p. 390.

4) Tomás G. Masaryk acknowledges in his book **Making of a State** (p. 394): "The Czech Parliamentary Association in Vienna demanded the transformation of Austria-Hungary into a League of States."

5) Benes: **Le Probléme Autrichien et la Question Tchéque.** Paris, 1908, p. 312 (The Austrian Problem and the Czech Question).

6) Renner: **Grundlagen und Entwicklungsziele der Oest. Ung. Monarchie.** Wien, 1908.

6/a) From Kossuth's Unknown Federalist Papers. Publ. in this volume.

7) E. Benes: **Democracy today and tomorrow.** New York, 1939, p. 218.

7/a) Teleki's message to Minister Pelényi in Washington was published in the **Journal of Modern History,** Chicago. June 1964.

8) Peter Pridavok: **A Good Word to Slovaks Worthy of It.** Jednota Press, Middletown, Pa. USA. 1963, p. 16.

9) The Central European Federal Club: **Statement on Aims.** Oct. 12, 1945. London.

10) Memorandum of the **Slovak National Council** in London to Ernest Bevin, Minister for Foreign Affairs, London. March 1948. Signed by Peter Pridavok, chairman.

11) The Slovak League of America: **Slovakia.** Vol. I, No. 1. May 1951.

12) Dan Morgan reported in the **Washington Post,** Sept. 16, 1968 from Prague that the anniversary of Tomás Masaryk's death (Sept. 14, 1937, exactly 51 years after the birth of his son, Jan) passed without official mention—an ominous sign of relegating Masaryk again to silence instead of returning to the ideas of federalism proposed by Tomás and Jan Masaryk.

PRONOUNCEMENTS ON FEDERALISM IN THE DANUBIAN AND CENTRAL EUROPEAN AREA

The Mid-European Research Institúte

MR. ANTHONY EDEN, British minister of foreign affairs and later prime minister states: "It may be that as a result some *closer relationship among the Danubian states* will once again emerge as a stabilizing influence in this part of Europe. This is *not likely to take the old form* but if led with statesmanship could buttress confidence in these precarious lands. The *collapse* of the *Austro-Hungarian Empire* was a *calamity for the peace of Europe.* If the countries that formed it could *one day find some arrangement* that would allow them to work together again in happy association, *how welcome this would be.*" (*New York Times,* Oct. 6, 1950.)

Professor C. A. *Macartney* says in his *"The Danubian Basin"* (Oxford, 1939) about the "Future Possibilities" (last chapter): "For ultimately—the only true solution lies in a *readjustment of the relationship between nationality and State* ... If the Danubian nations have much that divide them, they have also much in common. A *settled and united Danube,* not directed against any outside Power nor the puppet of any, would be infinitely *more satisfactory to all Europe,* including Germany herself, then either the position of to-day (1939) or that of ten years ago" (p. 30-32).

The *American Peace Delegation of 1919* was originally inclined toward federalism. *What Really Happened at Paris. The Story of the Peace Conference, 1918-1919* is the account of the American delegates edited by Col. E. M. *House* and Charles *Seymour* (N. Y. Scribner, 1921). Charles *Seymour,* Yale University professor, chief of the Austro-Hungarian Divison of the American Peace Commission, wrote "The United States and Great Britain *would have been glad to create a federation of the Danubian nationalities* which, without the vices that had led to the fall of the Habsburgs, might have accomplished the economic integration and preserved the political order, so essential of the tranquility and prosperity of Southeastern Europe ... The Conference lacked the right, as well as the power, to impose union upon them."

President Franklin Delano Roosevelt on regional federations and on a *Danubian Federation.*

In the summer of 1941, after Poland, the Baltic, Danubian and Balkan small "national states" fell victim, one following the other to aggressive Germany and Russia, President Roosevelt received Otto von Habsburg in Hyde Park to whom he disclosed some of his ideas concerning the reorganization of the world on a regional, federalist pattern (a fuller text in French, published in *"Federation"* (Paris) Aug.-Sept. 1951, pp. 443-453.):

"The President studied the conditions of a world composed of viable units with with America could trade. To arrive at such a world, he thought of creating semi-economic, semi-political units. These would be the Western Hemisphere, the British Commonwealth, Europe, the USSR, the Middle East, Southeast Asia. Within these spheres custom duties and internal commercial barriers should be abolished, such basic units created which are large enough to give cohesion to the whole, and finally to organize political councils which would harmonize international relations ... The President wanted to base these units on *regional federation—Danubian Federation, Balkan Federation, German Federation*—and on the other States, which like France and Spain form a real unit by themselves, to create a common and Supreme Council."

Karl *Renner*, President of the Austrian Republic, advocated as early as 1906 *"eine demokratische Schweitz im grossen,"* a transformation of Austria-Hungary into a Switzerland on a large scale in his "Grundlagen und Entwicklungsziele der Oest. Ung. Monarchie (Wien. 1906, p. 248). Some of his *"zweidimensionale Föderation"* (Federation with two dimensions) is still useful because he distinguished between the *territorial* federal structure and the *national cultural sphere* (Nationsuniversitaet) which latter should be organized on *personal-individual, not* territorial basis.

In the July 1948 issue of the American quarterly *"Foreign Affairs"* Karl *Renner* explained in an article entitled "Austria, Key for War and Peace" the double mistake of the Paris peace conferences in creating small-scale "national states"; "The other possible course" says Renner, "for the Peace Conference of 1919 would have been to decide that this *well-balanced economic territory with the unified system of money and credit* and *communications* should *remain an entity* ... components not enjoying complete sovereignty would have the highest *possible measure of national autonomy within a federal constitution."*

The Polish minister-president *Sikorsky* presented the federal plan of the London Danubian Club to *President Franklin D. Roosevelt* early in 1943 and Sikorsky sent the following information to emigrant organizations (Sikorsky's letter dated March 9, 1943):

"Concerning the *Central-European Federation,* the Government of the United States of America is of the opinion that the Russian government should be informed of these current plans. No action should be concealed from Moscow."

Somewhat later, on June 1, 1943 the Hungarian emigrant politician

Tibor Eckhardt sent the following message from America to the underground leaders at home:

"*Roosevelt* is in favor of a *Central European Federation. Churchill* considers a larger common *Danubian-Balkan Federation* which necessarily means a looser construction ... Stalin is opposed to federation of any kind."

Count *Pál Teleki*, Hungarian prime minister, in his last days became convinced that nothing short of a Danubian Federation could save the small nations for South Eastern Europe. His last message to his American friends is printed in the volume of *Cornish*, Louis C.: "Transylvania. The Land Beyond the Forest", Philadelphia. 1947, pp. 166-168, and how it was transmitted to America is told in this source as follows:

"Count Paul *Teleki*, Hungarian Prime Minister had been working on plans for *Danubian Federation*, and the night that was to end all his hopes was falling. In those dark days of 1941 he was under the espionage of the German Gestapo, there were a thousand of their agents in Budapest known to the Hungarian police, yet he managed to receive an intimate friend very late at night, and through him he sent the following information to his friends in the United States. (Footnote: So far the author can learn it has not been published before.)

"He foresaw clearly the complete defeat of Nazi Germany, and the European chaos that would result from the war. He believed that no future was conceivable for any of the minor nations in Eastern and Central Europe if they tried to continue to live their isolated national lives. He asked his friends in America to help them establish a federal system, to federate. This alone could secure for them the two major assets of national life: first, political and military security, and, second, economic prosperity. Hungary, he emphasized, stood ready to join in such collaboration, provided it was firmly based on the complete equality of all the members states."

"To the question, which nations should usefully federate, he gave two answers. A *minimum federation* would considerably improve conditions. It would be within the strategic triangle of Europe formed by Budapest, Vienna and Prague. It would combine those nations living in the Carpathian Basin formed by the Carpathian and Sudeten mountains and the Alps. It is a dire mistake, he held, to believe that the peace of Europe can be defended on the Rhine. The Danube, not the Rhine, is the European river. Only by solving the Danubian problem can the peace of Europe be established."

"Desirable as Teleki believed this minimum union to be, he favored a *larger federation*. Besides the nations just mentioned (Hungary including Transylvania, Austria, Czechoslovakia), he believed all the Balkan nations could be wisely joined. He did not fear lowering the Danubian higher price level, social standards, etc, by allowing unhampered Balkan competition. He pointed out that the Balkan peoples—Yugoslavs, Romanians, Bulgarians, have made great and rapid progress since their comparatively recent liberation from Turkish domination. They have developed an intelligent and progressive middle class, intensified their agricultural production, and started successful industrialization. While elimination of all tariff barriers within the proposed federation, Teleki agreed, would involve readjustements and temporary losses, these would be soon compensated by free access to raw materials and a far larger market."

"The greatest, the most important advantage to the member states is the *larger federation*, in Teleki's view, would be their greater security. They would then enjoy in Europe a standing equal with the great powers and they could successfully resist undesirable interferences and intrigues from outside, which in the past have made life intolerable throughout this whole Danubian region. The young nations would be free to develop their energies and talents. The region would show the quickest development in all Europe."

"This is important testimony"—concludes Mr. Cornish his account on Teleki's last political message to his American friends. Later, on p. 185 Mr. Cornish repeats it: *"Count Teleki wanted federation. Dorothy Thompson*, in 1941 supports the statement of others." "I took from Count Teleki's office a monograph which he had written upon the structure of European nations. A distinguished geographer, he was developing a *plan for regional federation*, based upon geographical and economic realities."

John Pelényi, minister of Hungary in Washington between 1933 and 1940 published in the *Journal of Modern History* (Chicago, June 1964) Prime Minister *Teleki's* last messages to him:

"Teleki directed me: Tell the American government that with war approaching all the small states in this part of the world must look for shelter, and the only way to obtain it is *to join in some form of federation*. Tell them that *Hungary is willing and ready to form and join such a federation with her neighbors."* When I asked whether he meant a federation with *all* of Hungary's neighbors, he replied: "Yes, Hungary is ready to join a federation with *all* her neighbors."

"Upon my return to Washington I found in the Department of State only a faint academic interest in these messages" says Mr. Pelényi in his recollections deposited at the Baker Library of Dartmouth College, Hannover (New Hampshire).

Pál Teleki had the intention of leaving Hungary and forming a government in exile in order to work for a new Central Europe on a federal basis. Mr. Pelényi testifies that "In August 1939 during my last leave of absence in Budapest Teleki told me, The memorandum (in which Pelényi advocated forming a Hungarian government in exile) has my closest attention and if the situation envisaged should arise, I myself will dash abroad, provided that I can still get to a plane."

Students of diplomatic history may discuss the problem of what would have happened if Teleki—instead of committing suicide in his crucial dilemma—had left Hungary for London and Washington in order to work with representatives of other East European nations for a Danubian federal union, accepted by the Allied Powers and presented to Stalin as a precondition to Lend-lease aid. The tragic consequences of the years after World War II could have been avoided. Instead of an Iron Curtain and other antagonisms, the Danubian nations would now enjoy peaceful federalism and economic prosperity.

Mr. *Royall Tyler*, an internationally known scholar and financial expert, who represented the Financial Committee of the League of Nations in Hungary during the years between the two world wars, made some inquiries in Budapest, whether a trend exists towards political federation. At that time (1940) false hopes blinded public opinion so much, that he regretfully reported in his memorandum, which he handed over to Mr. Moffatt, chief of the Division of European Affairs in the State Department on March 11, 1940: "Plans for a future federative state of the Danubian region are looked at askance by Hungarians ... They feel they have given proof of their own will to be independent."

History of recent decades has proved sufficiently that real independence of any state in the Danubian area is not possible except within a free federation. See further documents of the negotiations of Mr. Royall Tyler in Switzerland with representatives of the Hungarian government towards the end of World War II in *The Hungarian Quarterly* (New York, 1962. No. 1-2, pp.5-16).

Dr. Stephen *Kertesz*, expert in international law, secretary of the Hungarian Peace Delegation in Paris, 1947, later Minister to Rome and at present professor at the University of Notre Dame, Indiana, proposed the following principles in one of his lectures: "The Danube Valley *calls for its own organization*, which can be built securely only on voluntary collaboration of its independent but complementary national units. Lasting peace in the Danube Valley can only be brought about by a system providing for a *common defense* of the area, *strong enough to repel any outside interference*, and constituting an effective barrier against Germany's and Russia's imperialistic ambitions. At the same time, economic prosperity can only be attained by *eliminating the artificial barriers erected* against the free flow of trade among the complementary national units of the Danubian area.

To insure the security, friendly collaboration, and economic prosperity of all Danubian peoples, bound indissolubly by a common destiny to each other, the following are necessary.

a.) To *organize a Danubian Federation or at least a Danubian Economic Union.* Such federation, or union, would be able to protect and promote the welfare of the Danubian peoples, who will no longer be a burden on the Western World.

b.) Within the Danubian federation the boundaries must lose their *importance,* and should have *rather an administrative character.* Intercourse and communication must be entirely free.

c.) Nevertheless, to eliminate all possible national frictions, the *State boundaries should be drawn according to the wishes of the population concerned,* in *conformity with the principles of President Wilson and of the Atlantic Charter.*

d.) Within the member states of the Danubian Federation a large autonomy should prevail to assure a complete freedom and equality for the so-called island minorities. The *cantonal system of Switzerland could be taken as an example in this respect.*

e.) Apart from the indispensable limitations, imposed by Danubian cooperation, every state must be independent and free to choose its form of democratic government. A totalitarian or antidemocratic system of government, for obvious reasons, cannot be tolerated within the Danubian federation.

f.) A truly international control of the Danube and internationalization of all rivers and canals in the Danubian Valley is considered as indispensable.

g.) The highest organ of the Federation (Union) *could be a Council of Danubian States,* composed of *one representative for each member State.*

h.) A *Permanent Committee for Economics Affairs* has for its principal purpose to work out plans for the promotion of the economic and social welfare of the Danubian peoples, that is, plans for common utilization of natural resources, for developing the agriculture and industries, and particularly for improving the water system of the Danube Basin, and developing irrigation, having in view the improvement brought about in the Tennessee Valley, etc.

i.) An *Inter-Danubian Cultural Committee should revise all textbooks used in the schools of the Danubian countries with the aim of advising* the governments in eliminating from the teaching all inaccurate facts and tendencies detrimental to the true friendship and cooperation of the Danubian nations. This committee should further the spread of ideas of common interest and interdependence of the Danubian peoples, with the aim of promoting friendly relations and mutual understanding. A system of educational, scientific, and cultural exchanges will also be enacted.

j.) Besides the necessary executive organs, a *Danubian Supreme Court* will be erected to settle all differences among the Danubian States.

k.) A general system of European collaboration would promote the success of a Danubian Federation. The *basis of a new European system could be the regional federations or unions.* The integration of these regional entities into a continental organization would be the guarantor of a lasting peace, terminating a long period of senseless wars.

The Danubian Federation accepts the obligation for human rights and fundamental freedoms assumed both in the United Nations Charter and in any further Conventions recommended by the United Nations for the implementation of these primary obligations.

Brutus *Coste,* former Rumanian diplomat published an article in *"Public Opinion Quarterly"* 1951 Winter issue (Princeton University) in which he says among others:

"What they (the Eastern European nations) need, are some lessons on the practical working of a true democracy. The discussion of such problems as that of the reorganization of these nations on a democratic basis; the working of *national and local government in the United States...*" The task of furthering *regional and European solidarity.* "There is today an inarticulate awareness that *purely national solutions cannot protect Eastern Europe* against the recurrence of the tragedy which has been its lot not only in the past of its history. This awareness has to be fostered and made more articulate. Any effort in this direction would bring benefits not only after liberation but would also make for synchronized action when the time for action comes, since it would make people conscious of the strength for over 80 million people who are morally united"... "the *necessity of building a powerful federation* that would assure them a long period of peace in which to develop cultural and economic potentialities; talks on the advantages of joining a European federation when and if such federations should take shape. Such talks would have to stress that an *Eastern European federation will be established* even if Western Europe has not merged by the time. The new approach in the teaching of history can greatly assist such efforts, as would reports on any *plans of federation worked out, in common, by exiles from these lands.*"

Feb. 11, 1951 an important Declaration of Liberation was accepted, signed and solemnly promulgated in Independence Hall, Philadelphia. This "Declaration of the Aims and Principles of Liberation of the Central and East European Peoples" set forth the fundamental Bill of Rights of the peoples concerned and contains the following statements about their federalization:

"The reconstruction of Eastern Europe involves problems of a political, economic and social order beyond the capabilities and powers of nations to resolve separately; the dangers to which they remain exposed have prepared them to seek *salvation through union.* This tendency toward close international collaboration is in harmony with the present order of events: the *federal* principle, signifying *union* in liberty and implying the creation of organic ties, is the most appropriate and sure means of uniting the states; the peoples of the East are resolved to apply this principle to the *regional organization which they envisage;* these same peoples proclaim their right and their desire to take part in a United Europe on a *federal basis,* which they regard as the realization of all their prayers, and in spirit these *continental* and *regional unions* signify further steps along the road to the indispensable organization of the *free world as a whole.*"

"The peoples of Central and Eastern Europe are eager to take their natural place in the great movement of free peoples toward better relationship and closer union. *They are desirous of establishing among themselves strong ties of a federal character* and of joining in the formation of a United Europe. Such a *fraternal federation* must prize and respect the distinctive values of *each nation* for the common good of our European civilization and for the cultural heritage of mankind throughout the world."

Signed by: Dimitar *Matzankiev,* member of the Bulgarian National Council, former member of Parliament; Gen. Alexander *Todorov;* Luben *Vichegorov,* Metropolitan Opera singer, and Kiril Z. *Fournadjiev,* fellow of the Mid-European Studies Center.

Dr. Stefan *Osusky,* former Ambassador to Paris; Václav *Majer,* Dr. Josef *Cerny,* Dr. Jozef *Lettrich* and Dr. Hubert *Ripka,* all former Cabinet members, and Dr. Jan *Papánek,* former Ambassador and chief delegate to the United Nations.

Ferenc *Nagy,* former premier; Tibor *Eckhardt,* former chairman of the Smallholders Party; Zoltán *Pfeiffer,* chairman Hungarian Freedom Party; Charles *Peyer,* chairman, Social Democratic Party; Dr. Béla *Fábián,* former member of Parliament; Msgr. Joseph *Közi-Horváth,* chairman, Christian Democratic movement; and George *Bakács-Bessenyey,* member, Hungarian National Council.

Gen. Nicolae *Radescu,* former Premier; Constantin *Visoianu,* former minister for foreign affairs; Charles A. *Davila,* former Rumanian minister to Washington; Emil *Ghilezan,* former Under-Secretary of State; Brutus *Coste,* former Charge d'Affaires in Washington, and Dr. Augustin *Popa,* former member of Parliament.

Dr. Vladko *Macek,* former vice-premier and chairman of the Croatian Peasant party; Dr. Milan *Gavrilovic,* former ambassador to Moscow, Constantin *Fotic,* former Ambassador to Washington; Dr. Miha *Krek,* former Vice-Premier; Ivan *Mestrovic,* sculptor; Dr. Slobowan *Drashkovic,* member of the Serbian National Central Committee, and Dr. Bogdan *Radica,* history professor, writer, and others.

"Constitutional *Resolution* of the *Central-Eastern European Committee"* adopted on April 16, 1951 in Washington, D.C., USA: "... Whereas the mutual understanding among the nations of Central-

Eastern Europe is an indispensable requirement for the establishment of a system of international unity, democratic process of government, religious and individual freedom and social justice—

Be it resolved by the undersigned democratic representatives of the main popular political movements of the nations of Central-Eastern Europe—

That the *Central-Eastern European Committee* for *planning an organized co-operation* be constituted—

That the Committee *lay the foundations for the unification of the nations of Central-Eastern Enrope into a regional union* as soon as this harmonious co-existence of nations, will be possible and contributing thus to the unity of Europe—

That for the attainment of this aim, the Committee shall institute expert studies and research concerned with the international and national as well as legal, political, economic, social and cultural aspects of the problems connected with the *creation of a Central-Eastern European Federation.'* ...

Signed by George *Assan*, Constantine *Visoianu*, Augustin *Popa* and Iancu *Zissu* (Rumanians), István *Barankovics* and Ferenc *Nagy* (Hungarians), Josef *Cerny* (Czech), Vladko *Macek* (Croat) and Miha *Krek* (Slovene), Milan *Gavrilovic* (Serbian), George M. *Dimitrov* (Bulgarian), Stanislaw *Mikolajczyk*, Karol *Popiel*, Marian *Seyda* (Poles), Adolfs *Blodnieks* (Latvian), Kazys *Pakstas* (Lithuanian), Vaclovas *Sidzikauskas* (Lithuanian).

Full text of the resolution was published in the "Monthly Bulletin of the International Peasant Union" May, 1951, Washington, D.C.

MANIFESTO FOR A DANUBIAN FEDERATION

Béla Bartók, Zoltán Kodály, Endre Ady and other artists, writers and scholars.

Time: Fifty years ago, end of World War I

Place: Budapest, Hungary

Occasion: The disintegration of the Austro-Hungarian Monarchy, homeland of the "brother nations" — Austrians, Croats, Czechs, Hungarians, Rumanians, Ruthenians, Serbs, Slovaks, Slovenes.

"November 3, 1918.

Hungarians are now reorganizing themselves as a nation. Old Hungary has collapsed. Hungarians lie no more on the Procrustes bed of the historic empire of the Habsburgs. We are left alone, separated from other nations. Hungary is on her own, by her own will. From now on our goals are in no conflict with the goals of others. We aren't enemies of anyone. We have no claims on any of our brother nations. We too feel rejuvenated, rising to new life from the ruins of the Monarchy, just like our brother nations. It is a great relief to know that we do not have to support any oppression. The freedom of our fellow nations is a pledge for our own freedom. Who can be free as long as his neighbors aren't free? Let us be free, all of us! Let us live together in peace as free nations should.

But the time is also over for nations to live in rigid isolation. We are all interdependent. The smaller a nation is, the more it is in her interest to be protected geographically and economically against the dangers of isolation. We are now witnessing the birth of many nations. But like individuals, nations are born to live in societies. Hungarians! We have to confederate with our fellow nations! This is our interest, as it is theirs. And this federation should not endanger or restrict the freedom of any of its members, by any other nation. This must be mutually guaranteed and we are ready to grant it just as it must be granted to us. There is not a great state among us. Not a single one of those to be federated has a population over ten million. None of us will endanger the others. And this federation must be made by free choice, based on self-determination according to the Wilsonian principles. Historical boundaries must not hinder self-determination, nor language barriers: there can be more than one state with the same language. And we request that plebiscites be held in each controversial case, controlled by unbiased international authorities. We consider the Czech, Slovak, Polish, Transylvanian Rumanian, southern Slav, Austrian, Austrian German and Ukrainian nations—all those living in the territory of the former Monarchy— as independent nations, equal with Hungarians, to their right of self-determination. They can join the federation or they can stay out, by their free choice. This confederation must me based on the independence of the individual states. Their finances, defense, interior and foreign affairs, or their cultural-educational systems must be their own affair, unless they prefer to act cooperatively. No restrictions shall spoil their free trade, free economic exchange. Traffic and communication must be arranged according to their mutual interests. Any people living in any state as a minority group shall have the right to receive material or spiritual support from their mother state. They can maintain schools of their own in any of the member states; they can help their kinfolk by all means. And there shall be no quarrel about languages. Public authorities must use any language of the member nations according to the expressed wish of citizens from any of the confederate states.

Such a federation would create a society of nations within its framework. Societies in which the existence of moral law cannot be denied by any member. Moral law binds nations as well as individuals. This principle means the very essence of a free confederation. A confederation based on moral law is the best guarantee for free democratic development of the individual states. Where no nation wants mastery over other nations, there cannot be any servitude!

Hungarians! We have spoken out. We have expressed our hearts desire. We request that the National Council contact immediately the national councils of the brother nations to form a federation and to take the first steps necessary towards complete democratic establishment, without delay . . ."

This document was signed by Endre Ady, Mihály Babits, Dezső Kosztolányi, great poets, who started in our century a new epoch in Hungarian literature. Other signers: Béla Bartók and Zoltán Kodály became world famous composers; György Lukács still lives in Budapest, although secluded after 1956; was the author of many books and is the most eminent Marxist esthetician and Moscow-trained theoretician; Eugene Varga later became the greatest authority in economics in the Soviet Union; Rustem Vámbéry was a famous criminal lawyer and Hungarian Minister in Washington in 1948-49; Béla Balázs, Andor Gábor, Lajos Barta and B. Fogarasi were outstanding Communist writers; Marcel Benedek, Aladár Schőpflin, György Bölöny, Sándor Hevesi, Gy. Földessy, as non Communists, have great merits in art criticism, theatre, literature. Lajos Kassák, a social democrat poet, was persecuted under the Rákosi regime, but later rehabilitated. He was also honored by the Communists. All who signed the Manifesto are also acknowledged by the present Hungarian regime and their Manifesto was republished in the review *"Helicon"* (Budapest, no. 1, 1967).

The Manifesto and the proposition of the Hungarians went unheeded. Their ideas, like similar ideas of Slovak and Rumanian federalists, were completely disregarded in a political climate of upsurging ultranationalism and chauvinism at the "peace conference" of 1919. The Manifesto was printed and circulated as a leaflet in Budapest and was later published in Viena (1921) by Oscar Jászi in his booklet "Tárgyalásaim a román nemzeti komitéval" (My Negotiations with the Rumanian National Council). Oscar Jászi was a member of the Hungarian National Council, and he later became a minister in the cabinet. In the United States he was well known among American sociologists. As professor at the Oberlin University, he published his main work "The Dissolution of the Habsburg Monarchy" (Chicago, 1929).

III

THE NATIONALITY
QUESTION

PSEUDO-NATIONAL STATES OR REAL NATIONAL IDENTITIES IN CENTRAL EUROPE

ALEXANDER GALLUS

> ... Diex peut bien permettre á des eaux
> insensées—de perdre des vaisseaux, mais non
> pas des pensées.
>
> (Alfred de Vigny)
>
> God may rightly allow the dumb Ocean to
> destroy ships, but not Ideas.

IT IS a necessity of life to revise from time to time the semantic contents of our tools of thinking, of our notions and ideas.

During the strong central administration of the absolute monarchies of the 17th century in Europe, the strongest ethnic element of the state progressively assimilated all ethnic enclaves within the boundaries of its area of influence, and thus created the idea of the centralized national state: one language, one administration, one absolute ruler and one religion.

As a consequence, the "minorities" fought a losing battle against the dominant power for an independent language, religion and privileges. France and Spain having reached the final stage of concentration in the 18th century, the question of frontiers and safety of the state-territory became the central core of their strategic thinking. Territory and frontier-lines became important from the point of view of political dominance and military defense. Occupying new territory means also the expansion of central rule, with all its efforts for unification.

In Central Europe a more archaic situation prevailed. The Medieval State was built on correlation and not on central uniformity. The local privileges of cities, barons, settlers were jealously guarded and the unity of the realm depended on personal loyalty to a ruler. The state conserved a certain fluidity, as the boundaries were easily altered by marriages, contracts, inheritance or changes in loyalty. This medieval order of local privileges preserved within the Central European Medieval Hungarian Kingdom of the Árpáds the ethnic identity of the Croats, Slovaks, Rumanians, Ruthenians and Germans, to mention only the largest groups, whereas in Western Europe the equivalents of these culturally and racially inbreeding ethnic units (Catalans, Bretons, Burgundians, etc.) became successfully assimilated. When the medieval state in Central Europe was attacked by the Turks, communication with the West was interrupted and the whole process of 17th-18th century political development in the Western States stopped at the borders of the Ottoman Empire. Osman rule preserved the medieval situation inasmuch as no central pressure for a unified language, religion, education, etc., in Central Europe, was exerted. After liberation from the Osman rule, all the different ethnic units emerged again, only to find themselves now subjected to aggressive actions, stemming from the contemporary ideal of the centralized national state.

The Hungarians, who defended their national identity against the centralized administration of the Habsburg emperors, kept under the cover of the Hungarian State, or even "Nation" ("Nemzet"), as opposite to "People" ("Nép"), the many ethnic units of the Carpathian Basin, who had preserved their ethnic unity under the Medieval Hungarian Kingdom and under Osman Rule: Croats, Slovenes, Ruthenians, Serbs, Rumanians, Germans. During the Hungarian national revival before 1848, and after 1867, a considerable part of the German middle class in the cities was assimilated. But when after 1867, the Hungarian Central Government belatedly stepped up centralization according to current Western ideals of the "National State," it, of course, caused immense trouble and could not succeed with other nationalities because it attempted to achieve the impossible. The later war cry, however, in and after 1918, of "Hungarian oppression" was more than surprising as it was raised partly by representatives of Western centralized national states, who in the not too distant past had done the same thing, and had done it successfully.

But the big difference was in the *time factor*. A process which succeeded in the 17th-18th centuries, could no more be repeated and defended in the 20th century. History and human ideals change.

It was not only the Hungarian statesmen who acted in an anachronistic manner in Central Europe between 1867 and 1914. Learning nothing from the Hungarian failure to establish central national administration; Czechs, Serbs, Rumanians nursed also dreams of national centralization after 1918. The leaders of the new states, created by the victorious Western Powers, attempted to organize their own states according to the same principles of central national administration and assimilation which had been condemned by Western war propaganda in 1918.

The political leaders of Czechoslovakia tried to build up a new centrally administered national state based on the Czech elements and reacted with hostility when Slovaks, Ruthenians, Germans, Hungarians struggled for maintaining their own national and ethnic identity. The same was attempted by the dictatorship of King Alexander in Serbia (Yugoslavia) for the benefit of the Serb element; the situation being highlighted by two emotional killings: the Serbs killing the Croatian national leader, Radic and the Croats retaliating by killing King Alexander. The ensuing diplomatic stir in the League of Nations only showed that the Western leaders did not have the slightest understanding of the tensions in Central Europe. In the same way the Rumanians attempted and still attempt to build up a centralized state based on the administration of the privileged Rumanian element.

These tendencies resulted everywhere in a disregard for "minority rights" as formulated in the Peace Treaties after 1918.

The same tendencies culminated in incredible cruelties inflicted on minority ethnic units, amounting to genocide, during and after the Second World War: death camps, shooting of prisoners of war, confiscation of property, expatriation, mass trials, etc.

By now it should be sufficiently clear, that the Western ideal of a centralized national state, which necessarily leads to the penalizing of minority groups, is completely inadequate, and that it cannot assure lasting peace and humane conditions in Central Europe.

But is there any alternative?

These problems and our groping for a satisfactory solution should especially be understood in Great Britain, where human relations developed differently from that of Western Europe. Great Britain is the result of political solutions, aiming at coexistence, rather than assimilation. It seems that the English were never numerous enough to press for full centralization. Now a similar situation exists in Central Europe. There is no single dominant nation in Central Europe, only outside of it. But instead of trying to eliminate each others as in Central Europe, the different ethnic units in the British Isles arrived at a synthesis, not without armed conflict, however.

The vexed question of Ireland was solved after the First World War by granting her total independence.

The Welsh joined England early in the Middle Ages, but preserved their language and separate religion. Scotland after a long and cruel conflict was offered and accepted a political union by "common consent," which was ratified in both parliaments. The Act of Union preserved the local legal system, a separate religion, their own banking system and an autochtonous language where the inhabitants themselves have not abandoned them.

Why then should world opinion tacitly support a situation in Central Europe which still remains opposed to a humane regulation of the same problems which seem to have been satisfactorily solved in Great Britain?

A new Central Europe can only be reconstructed by discarding the ideal of the centralized national state, and by accepting, as a regulating force, those instincts of national identity which during centuries in Central Europe succeeded in asserting themselves, in spite of so many attempts to the contrary, thus proving their vitality. These instinctive forces emanate from peoples and not from states. A state is a conscious organization with boundaries, legal system and central administration. A people, on the other hand, is not a conscious construction. Its cohesion is biologic and not administrative; it is an interesting community with an accumulation of uniform creative, and behavioristic tradition (culture). It does not have solidified boundaries. The flow of its settlements and family units interpenetrates with other flows within a geographic territory.

If we acknowledge the "people" (the "nationality" or "ethnic unit") as the basic unit to be preserved in Central Europe, or better said as *the basic value to be safeguarded,* then our notions of "state," "state boundaries," and "state organization," must be reshaped and we shall discard the ideal of the "centralized national state."

For a people or ethnic unit, state boundaries are nonexistent. Members of the "Hungarian People" presently live in Hungary, Czechoslovakia, Yugoslavia, Rumania, the U.S.S.R., Austria, and all over the world.

The first problem thus to be solved in Central Europe is the restoration of free intercommunication, cultural unity and information between members of the same ethnic unit, or people, wherever they live. "Frontiers" must remain nonexistent in relation to communication between members of the same ethnic unit. The notion of "national minority" must disappear and the strife and struggle for state boundaries must become completely irrelevant. Administrative units with boundaries would, of course, still exist, but they would exist under the ideal conditions of a new federated system as envisaged by the opinions and plans presented in this volume.

The practical solutions for coexistence in Central Europe must create a modus vivendi, which makes it possible that the actual site of a particular human group's abode, within or outside the main body of a dense settlement of a particular nationality, is irrelevant, because the full enjoyment of national identity (and not only "individual freedom") remains ensured everywhere within the larger area of the federated territory.

What really does matter is the frontier line of the federated territory itself, because the frontiers of the federated territory are real inter-ethnic pressure zones, with different ways of life, history, culture and tradition on both sides of the line. Thus they are organic and natural. They divide Central and Eastern Europe from Western state organizations, immediate neighbors, who have built up successfully a centralized national structure, and thus from our point of view exist on another level of organization, not applicable in Central Europe.

It is important for historians and politicians alike to perceive that *the periods of influence of this alien complex of ideas of organization have been and are the ultimate cause of the deep disturbances in Central Europe.*

A new solution in Central Europe must mean a final departing from foreign categories of thinking and the embracing of a train of political thought more congenial to Central European history and to the working of their own minds.

The peoples of Central Europe know that it is not in their power to make this an immediate reality, but I would like to remind the reader once again of De Vigny's prophetic words:

> Le vrai Dieu, le Dieu fort, est le Dieu des idéees
>
> . . . . .
>
> Jetons l'oeuvre á la mer, la mer des multitudes.
> Dieu le prendra du doigt pour le conduir au port.
>
> The real God, the strong God, is the God of ideas ... Let us then toss our work to the ocean of the multitudes. God will take it on his palm to guide it into port.

SOCIO-LINGUISTICS FOR A JUST PEACE
IN THE DANUBIAN BASIN

ADAM MAKKAI

1. *Introductory Remarks*

THE present paper is, by necessity, programmatic and not a report on research in progress. This, however, does not mean that there is no socio-linguistic information available to Western scholars on the Danubian Basin. Quite to the contrary. But in most instances the information is "frozen" on the academic level of dialect descriptions, aspects of regional pronunciations, etc., and the scholars to whom the information is available do not possess the practical power of recommendation to the local governments to correct injustices or to shape the government policy on education. Published data on population concentration of ethnic minorities are subject to doubt as to their accuracy. The Western scholar's main problem approaching the socio-linguistic problem of the Danubian Basin, then, is this: 1.) How should one proceed with the basic field work of gathering correct information on the census of minorities; 2.) and to what practical use can one put this valuable information?

2. *Linguistically Diverse Areas versus Linguistically Troubled Areas in the World: A Brief Survey*

An important point must be made at the outset: Linguistic diversity need not necessarily mean political unrest, and conversely: Political unrest can frequently be artificially instigated by deliberate exploitation of the language issue. It is the present writer's conviction that multilingual areas, or languages in contact correlated with ethnic diversity do not, by themselves, necessarily result in oppressive antidemocratic societies, whereas the opposite is frequently true: Oppressive, antidemocratic societies can create political issues out of ethnic and linguistic diversity. In order to illustrate this point let us take a look at the following "linguistically diverse" cultures in order to attempt to find some correlation between the ethnic-linguistic composition and the social-political structure of the countries concerned.

2.1 The United States

It is a common joke that in New York City one hears more foreign languages spoken in the streets than English. The USA is truly a country of immigrants; there is probably no country in the world whose major languages are not spoken by some group of people in America. Add the large number of indigenous Indian tongues spoken on the reservations and the socio-linguistic problem of the black ghetto areas, and the picture becomes quite bewildering. Nevertheless, the USA has, so far, not had any language-riots. (Race-riots, yes, but that is another matter.) Nor is it likely that foreign accents, dialectically marked accents, or, in certain areas, a total lack of fluency in English should ever add to any "potential disruption" of the United States. I very seriously doubt that black Americans will ever demand that Swahili or Yoruba be set aside for them as their separate official language, just as European immigrants have never demanded that Spanish, German, French, Dutch, Polish, Rumanian, Hungarian, or Czech be given any official status in the United States. The reason: After all is said, English remains the main medium of communication that, eventually, everyone embraces by free will, and not because otherwise they would perish. The unifying force of English, then, is one of seduction via economic and social advantages rather than one of coercion. Because of a definite desire on the part of black-ghetto inhabitants not to identify themselves with the white middle class, Negro dialects of American English are studied and described with considerable scientific rigor and thoroughness, and teachers of English in ghetto areas receive linguistic training in dialectal bilingualism.[1] Far from being oppressive, American universities and the scholarly community make concentrated efforts to accommodate and make known to the public the linguistic behavior and resultant needs of minority groups throughout the country.

2.2 The Soviet Union

Whereas the United States assimilates its immigrants by social-economic seduction, i.e., "democratically", the Soviet Union superimposes in a dictatorial way Russian as the official language on a vast number of formerly independent nations ranging from the Baltic States of Estonia, Lithuania, Latvia, through annexed portions of Finland, Hungary, and Poland, to the ancient Asiatic cultures of Tadzhikistan, Turkestan, and so on. A large number of indigenous tribes also survive in Siberia, the Caucasus range, and around the Ural mountains, some belonging to the Finno-Ugrian family of languages, some to the Altaic, and some still scientifically unclassified. Compulsory education, however, is in Russian, with minor concessions made to local cultures concerning local cultural affairs. The Georgian Stalin and the Ukrainian Khrushchev both ruled the USSR in Russian and showed particular ruthlessness in the political administration of their respective homelands within the Soviet Empire. The Soviet Union, then, is at present, for reasons entirely different than those of the United States, also—with the exception of the Ukraine—not a "linguistically troubled country", but merely a "linguistically diverse" multinational area where the human cultural tragedy of the annexed nations is legally, at least for the present, a Russian "Soviet internal affair", which nobody (including the United Nations) can do anything about.

2.3 Canada

We tend to think of Canada as rather similar to the United States; i.e., a country of vast territorial expanse and economic affluence. On the other hand, Canada, too, is subject to political upheavals closely connected with "linguistic diversity". The case in point is the French separatist movement of the Province of Québec which keeps erupting periodically. Montréal is, in fact, a North American micro-Switzerland, one of the most "Europeanized" cities on the Continent. Canada's particular socio-linguistic problems arise from the fact that it is perhaps the only major country in the world (with the possible exception of India) where linguistic diversity has frequently led to political upheavals on a mass scale precisely because the rebelling minorities had the freedom to do so. This observation forces one to reach the paradoxical conclusion: Active, linguistically instigated uprising may be the symptoms of healthy, vigorous and essentially democratic societies, whereas apparent tranquility in the face of linguistic diversity without violent conflagrations may be the symptom of an autocracy. Canada in others words, may be a "linguistically troubled area" vis-á-vis the "peaceful" Soviet Union, but it is "healthy" trouble that may eventually be solved by democratic means. The USSR is merely "linguistically diverse" and outwardly peaceful, but this is an unnatural state of affairs which must, eventually, lead to an atrophying of the indigenous cultures incorporated in the Soviet Super State. Whether the common sense of Canadians will ultimately prevail or secessionism continues, remains one of the question marks scarring the face of that beautiful land.

2.4 India

A special book could be written on the history of linguistically aggravated racial-religious bloodshed on the entire subcontinent. The separatist movement of the area of Madras (with a much darker, Dravidian Tamil-speaking population) keeps erupting time and again raising the spectre of massacres that occurred after the assassination of Gandhi in 1948 when Moslems and Hindus annihilated each other by the hundreds of thousands resulting in the establishment of East and West Pakistan independent of India. The late Prime Minister Nehru consistently spoke English whenever he made a tour of the various states, always with an interpreter at his side. Despite the medieval conditions still prevailing throughout the larger portions of India, it is also the only democrary on the Continent, in the Western sense of the word. All differences in climate, history and character notwithstanding, this very fact establishes a major resemblance between Canada and India. Both countries are simultaneously linguistically diverse *and* troubled, but they both also have a chance to resolve their problems internally (i.e., without foreign intervention) and essentially in accordance with the principles of democracy.

2.5 Ceylon

The island-republic of Ceylon had some serious trouble in the past. The Singhalese majority (all Buddhists) who are fairer in color tend to oppress the darker, mostly Roman Catholic Tamils, who speak a non-Indo-European language of the Dravidian family. The Malaysian model would be the ideal one for them to emulate.

2.6 Malaysia

The present writer lived in Malaysia (Kuala Lumpur) from September 1963 until September 1964, just when the Federation first came into being. The country is racially and linguistically quite complex. Malay and English were joint official languages until September 1967,[2]) with native Malays barely in the majority.[3])

On the Peninsula itself we find Chinese, speaking Cantonese, Mandarin, Hakka, Amoy, and Foochoow; Northern Indians speaking Punjabi and Marathi, also some Gujarati speakers; Southern Indians speaking Tamil, Telugu, and Malayalam. Peninsular Malay itself comes in several distinct dialects, in addition to which on the Peninsula we find indigenous aboriginal tribes whose languages have not yet been fully described, let alone classified, one of the better known ones being Temiar. Europeans speaking English, Dutch, French, etc., cluster in larger business cities.

On the island of Borneo, in Sarawak and Brunei, the original inhabitants speak related Malayo-Polynesian languages, but Malay has to be learned in school. Riots have been known to occur primarily between the Malays and Chinese both for politico-economic as well as for racial and linguistic reasons.

Even after the loss of Singapore Malaysia has remained a solvent country. The government exerts a mild, but constant pressure on all of its citizens to learn the now sole official language, Malay. Each year they have a "National Language Month" and each morning from 8 A.M. to 9 A.M. Radio Malaysia broadcasts a language lesson both for beginners and for advanced students. The program is called "Learn A New Word A Day". It enjoys great success. The government maintains a special institute called the *Dewan Bahasa Dan Pustaka* whose job is the promotion of the *Bahasa Kebangsaan* (national language) *through the capitalist device of the profit-incentive*. Government employees can take more and more advanced language examinations in Malay, and receive increases in salary according to their proficiency. In the meantime the Malaysian television broadcasts its daily news in four major languages: Malay, English, Chinese, and Tamil. The rights of each minority are rather well respected.

2.7 Africa

This continent alone has produced more new independent nations in our century than the rest of the world produced in the past five hundred years. The linguistic problems of Africa are just now beginning to be realized and will probably become the subject of elaborate future research programs in many a leading university throughout the Western world. But merely to touch the surface: Description, standardization, usage regulation, education, designating of the role of temporary *post-European linguae francae* are merely the overture to the enormous tasks that lie ahead for scientific linguistics of the twenty-first century.

3. *The Paradoxical Situation of Eastern Europe*

The foregoing note on "linguistically diverse versus linguistically troubled areas" serves but one purpose here: To show that *most (if not all)) linguistically troubled areas of the world are relatively young in terms of independent statehood with a reasonable chance to work out their problems according to the democratic tradition.* The student of Eastern European affairs can, therefore, take consolation from the fact that it is not Eastern Europe alone where linguistic-cultural barriers enhance and aggravate the frequently artificial political ones. For example, India has suffered much greater losses fired by religious-racial-linguistic fanaticism than did Rumania, Czechoslovakia, or Hungary.

The problem as I see it, lies elsewhere.

The Serbo-Croatian, Czech, Slovak, Ukrainian, Polish, Bulgarian, Slovenian, and Russian languages can all be traced back via Old Church Slavic and Proto-Balto-Slavic to Proto-Indo-European, and assigning one thousand years of attestable separate existence to each of these languages on the average is perfectly reasonable. Rumanian, clearly a Romance language with Slavic loan elements in its vocabulary, may be said to be as old as Hungarian, the only non-Indo-European language in the area concerned.

Scientifically proven to belong to the Finno-Ugric family of languages, Hungarian (or Magyar) was clearly the intruder between the years 895-896 A.D., when the Magyar tribes entered the Carpathian Basin from today's Western Russia, driving a wedge between the Northern and Southern Slavic languages.[4)]

Surrounded by German, Slavic, and perhaps Rumanian speakers, Hungarian (as a language) has nevertheless endured for one thousand one hundred and fifty years until today. The point of this article is not either to justify or to condemn the presence of the non-Indo-European Hungarian speech island in its Indo-European surroundings. It is a *fait accompli* just as the historical existence of Germany, Austria, or Switzerland. Nor would it be in place here to eulogize Hungarian contributions to Western civilization beginning with the Turkish wars of the 16th century through Louis Kossuth's 19th century concept of a Danubian Federation, the music of Bartók and Kodály, and the revolution of 1956. All this is, strictly speaking, irrelevant here, as is the circuitous and never-ending argument as to "who was the oppressor against whom in the Austro-Hungarian Monarchy?" Our present endeavor is to examine the East European situation *objectively, from without,* basing our examination of the area on the scientific methods of socio-linguistics couched in the political tradition of the great Western democracies. Before we proceed, however, with our proposals for a socio-linguistic solution to the minority problem in Eastern Europe, we must take a brief look at the countries concerned one by one.

4. The Problems of the Satellites

4.1 Yugoslavia

East of Austria, Yugoslavia is the least tyrannical state today in Europe. By constitution a Federal Republic, Yugoslavia has been the least unsuccessful in solving its internal minority problems. Yugoslav citizens speak several dialects of Serbian, Croatian, and Macedonian, and have additional minority groups of Italians, Turks, and Greeks. Larger cities in the northern part of the country are heavily populated by Hungarians. Novi Sad, for instance, has a relatively active and viable Hungarian cultural life with magazine and book publishing somewhat freer and more independent of political considerations than the still semi-Stalinist book publishing in Budapest. Works of a novelist such as Lajos Zilahy, who lives in New York, for instance, may be published in Novi Sad, but not in Budapest! (This, of course, does not mean that all classical or modern Hungarian authors, living in the West, could be published in Yugoslavia.) A striking paradox, indeed! And yet the relations of Serbia, later Yugoslavia and Hungary were anything but peaceful during the past one hundred years; World War I started in Sarajevo and border-raids and massacres originating on both sides during both world wars are well-documented and only too well remembered. Why is the linguistic diversity of Yugoslavia nevertheless not of the tragic, but of the more colorful, reassuring type? Because President Tito's leadership is less chauvinist and revanche-minded than that of other Iron Curtain countries; because Yugoslavia is separated geographically from the Soviet Union by other neighboring countries and because it has an extensive seacoast; because the Tito régime keeps an open border, which means that the Yugoslav worker may earn his living in Italy and send his money home, can buy a Fiat in Milan and drive it home to Belgrade. Yet, of course, not everything is well. The multinational country with many religions is extremely poor in certain areas and a great deal of economic reform needs to be enacted in connection with further steps toward democracy, before true linguistic equality can exist.

4.2 Czechoslovakia

The end of World War I brought with it the dissolution of the Austro-Hungarian Monarchy.[5] As a result hundreds of Slovak and Hungarian villages kept changing masters during the past decades. Most cities and villages, in this area have two, sometimes three names, as, for instance, Kosice-Kassa-Kaschau, Bratislava-Pozsony-Pressburg, etc. It cannot be the job of a socio-linguistic paper to argue history. What one inescapably notices, however, is that the linguistic diversity of the Eastern European arena is inextricably interwoven with the politics of the area, where the politics is essentially different from the situation in the Far East. In Asia (outside the Soviet Union and China) it is within essentially democratically organized states that minority rebellions feeding on language grievances occur, whereas in Eastern Europe linguistically troubled areas arise as the residue of border struggles between linguistically and culturally well-established older nations. In the Far East language rebellions are fostered by a search for self-identity, while in Eastern Europe it is revanchism, irredentism, and chauvinism that cause constant friction between neighbors. I don't think any historian or statistician will ever be able to come up with a satisfactory answer as to who is "guiltier", say, between the Czechoslovaks and the Magyars. The answer is that human stupidity and narrow-mindedness are the guilty parties. The Czechs deported thousands of Hungarians after World War II, while due to a temporary benefit derived from the Stalinist "socialist constitution", Hungarians in Rumania actually enjoyed, for a very brief period, a certain amount of "cultural autonomy".

A few months before the writing of this paper Czechoslovakia seemed to be on the move toward a Yugoslav-style reorganization of the national minority problem. The "friendship treaty" between Dubcek and Kádár certainly could have worked for the mutual benefit of both countries. Dubcek, himself a Slovak, and thus the member of a minority group, could certainly have become more tolerant toward Hungarian writers and intellectuals in Bratislava-Pozsony, than his Stalinist predecessor, Novotny. Recent hopes for a genuine reconciliation of the two nations instead of a superficial rubber stamping of meaningless treaties between puppet commissars have been brutally shattered by the August 1968 Soviet intervention in the internal affairs of Czechoslovakia. Dubcek's reform-minded leadership understood the need for democratization of the national minority problem and, as far as they were able to, they tried to rise to the occasion. Once again the Soviet tanks that rolled through the streets of Budapest in

1956 have raped a defenseless country thereby preventing both Hungarians and Czechoslovaks from working out their mutual problems in a spirit of friendship. Nobody can predict at this time how and when these two countries will ever be able to come to a mutual understanding of real issues so long as they are both Soviet satellites.

4.3 Hungary

This former partner of the ill-fated Monarchy has all but completely lost its minorities.[6] There remain ·a few villages on the eastern border where there are Rumanians. The Hungarian government is bending backwards doubly and triply to woo and accommodate their every desire. They have high schools, newspapers; they are, in fact, a privileged minority. German-speaking Swabians have dwelt in various parts of Hungary since the early Middle Ages and have never been really oppressed; as a matter of fact during Hitler's days of the infamous "Volksbund" they were very much on top either as members of the "Arrow Cross Party", or as German soldiers. They, too, have today their German language newspapers and schools iñ the appropriate regions. The number of Czechs, Serbians, etc., on the territory of today's Hungary is minute. So we simply cannot realistically speak of a minority problem in Hungary. The impartial Western observer, then, must sadly conclude that in the second half of the twentieth century Hungarians are the major victims of Eastern Europe's politically agitated linguistic diversity which arose in the wake of the First and Second World Wars.

4.4 Rumania

The sorest spot of all in this regard is Rumania (Table I). With approximately 2.5 million Hungarians[7] (Rumanian statistics acknowledge only 1.8 million; they are aided by the fact that many frightened Hungarians—especially if they happen to be intermarried—would rather rumanianize their names and declare themselves Rumanian; thus many a *Bodor* became *Bodorescu*, etc.). Rumania, otherwise a clever, congenial nation with a hospitable Latin temperament, has been the least successful in coping with the minority problem in a democratic and relaxed spirit. There are, of course, the usual "justifications" of fear of Hungarian chauvinism (no wonder that there *are* Hungarians, even in the United States, who would like to see the borders rearranged between the two countries). West erners are frequently amused by what goes on between Hungarians and Rumanians: they have engaged in a futile and romantic battle of "who is more *ancient* than the other?" First, the Rumanians invented the untenable Daco-Roman hypothesis, flatly claiming to be the descendants of Romulus and Remus. Outraged Hungarians retaliated and claimed that being the offspring of Attila the Hun, father of the Szeklers, they are in fact the true heirs of Transylvania. Now that this hotly debated piece of real estate once again is in Rumanian hands,[8]) more than a fair share of archaeological discoveries is all too rapidly labelled as Rumanian-Latin, whether it belonged to the Avars, Huns, or Scythians. Thus, quite apart from any potential scientific value of this currently fashionable hypothesis, embittered Magyars have anxiously retaliated and are promoting, both in Transylvania, and in the United States, the theory of their Sumerian ancestry.[9]) Be this as it may, it is actually irrelevant to the synchronic issues at stake.

NATIONAL COMPOSITION OF RUMANIA 1910-1966 [9a])

Census:	1910	1920	1930	1948	1956	1966 March 15
			in thousands			
Rumanians	10,524	13,186	11,360	13,597	15,080	16,781
Hungarians	1,823	1,362	1,553	1,500	1,654	1,603
Germans	829	593	636	344	395	377
Ukrainians	1,032	576	117	116	113	
Bulgarians	340	261	64	13	13	
Turks	222	174	43	29	14	
Slovaks, Czechs	25	32	47	25	25	
Yugoslavians	66	53	47	43	43	
Tartars	32	35	43	20	21	
Gypsies	126	133	90	80	67	
Jews	820	873	452	150	146	
TOTAL	15,723	17,641	14,218	16,500	17,489	19,105

NATIONAL COMPOSITION OF RUMANIA IN PERCENTAGES
1910-1966

Census:	1910	1920	1930	1948	1956	1966 March 15
Rumanians	67.0	71.9	71.9	85.7	86.2	87.8
Hungarians	11.6	9.1	7.9	9.4	9.4	8.4
Germans	5.3	4.5	4.1	2.2	2.2	2.0
Jews	5.2	4.9	3.1	0.9	0.8	1.8
Others	10.9	9.6	13.0	1.8	1.4	
TOTAL	100.0	100.0	100.0	100.0	100.0	100.0

LOSS AND GAIN OF THE NATIONALITIES IN RUMANIA
BETWEEN 1910-1966
Increase (+)   Decrease (—) in their percentages

Census between	1910-1920	1930-1966	1910-1966
Rumanians	+4.9	+15.9	+20.8
Hungarians	—2.5	—0.5	—3.2
Germans	—0.8	—2.1	—3.3
Jews	—0.3	—2.2	—4.4

The question we must ask is that if Hungarians could have their schools and University under Peter Groza immediately after World War II, why can the same not be done under Maurer and Ceausescu, especially when the latter have so successfully moved away from total Soviet enslavement? Cluj-Kolozsvár-Klausenburg, one of the most prominent Hungarian cultural centers and far older than Budapest, is certainly entitled to a Hungarian University. Nevertheless in 1962 Hungarians "voluntarily demanded" that their University be taken away from them and named Babes-Bolyai, instead of just Bolyai. Their well-argued "reasons" were, of course, that one could not do much with a Hungarian diploma. But why can a physician not cure pneumonia and polio with a Hungarian diploma? These diseases strike Rumanians and Magyars alike, or do they also *talk*? A certain misled stratum of Rumanian society still feels it necessary to discriminate against Hungarians due to revanchism[10]) and some kind of deep-seated insecurity rooted in the fact that they actually know that Transylvania is merely administered by them due to the changing fortunes of world power politics. Yet *on a deeper, human level*, there is no reason why the two nations could not get along with one another like the nations in Switzerland. After all, their vital interests are identical: They need industry, education, more money, free elections, better trade and cultural contacts with the West, and increasingly more freedom from the Soviets. The Kremlin, of course, fears these common needs of the two nations very much, and deliberately uses their mutual distrust of one another to its own political ends, based on the Machiavellian concept of "divide and conquer". Should Bucharest go too far in pursuing an independent foreign policy course, Moscow can always blackmail the Rumanian leadership by arousing the Hungarians. Thus, understandably, the Rumanian Communist Party spends most of its newly won "freedom" on gradually erasing the Hungarian minority within Rumania, while it is not too late. Re-districting and internal deportation are the infamous methods used to achieve this end. These are accompanied by the constant, milder pressures of under-employment, failing of students who opt to take a University examination in Hungarain instead of Rumanian, discourtesy in shops toward Hungarian-speaking customers.

5. Outline of a Proposed Solution:
How Can Socio-Linguistics Help?

The "helvetization" of East Central Europe is no idle hypothesis invented by American intellectuals. It is, in fact, the only viable alternative to more bitterness, more injustice, continuing revanchism. The pendulum of irredentism must be stopped once and for all. In order to achieve lasting peace in the Danubian Basin, *the United States and Western influence must help bring democracy to this part of Europe, the Yalta Agreement and the status quo notwithstanding.*

The historian of 2150 may be able to look back upon our century and remark that while four-fifths of mankind emerged from slavery during this century, one fifth, once independent and free, subscribed to being dominated by others. Such a conclusion would be far from cynical and unfounded; it would be all too sadly correct. But it does not have to happen that way. We have thirty-two years to go before the century is out, just enough time for a generation of neo-humanists to grow up and put to practice the principle of tolerance, first advocated by one of the greatest political thinkers of all times, Montesquieu, who in his *L'esprit des lois* first outlined the current American practice known as "the separation of powers". The responsibility of the United States towards Europe is simply enormous and cannot be overemphasized. In an age of civil rights and interventionary wars in the Far East, Europe, still stunned by the blows of World War II, gradually begins to look towards independence. President Charles De Gaulle's France has successfully emancipated his country from American patronage; the Yugoslavs under Tito have, for all practical purposes, torn themselves away from the clutches of the Kremlin, and Rumania has being pursuing a relatively independent foreign policy course.

Hungary today is no longer the same Stalinist prison it was before the tragic uprising of 1956, and there is reason to hope that Czechoslovakia, too, despite the Soviet military intervention, will not return to hard-line Stalinism.

The American role in Rumania is particularly important. Rumania wants American aid in using nuclear power, and building oil refineries. The science of linguistics has received extraordinary stimulus and growth in the United States in the 20th century, and socio-linguistics, American style, could be one of America's greatest contributions yet to a lasting peace in Europe. We map the ghetto and the slum dialects; write grammars of languages spoken in the Amazon jungle, maintain a Summer Institute of Linguistics, a Linguistic Society of America, the American Bible Society with its manifold linguistic projects. America has made considerable advances in the fields of machine translation and computational linguistics as well as in general linguistic theory, and Indo-European studies. Hundreds of graduate students leave leading American universities each year with advanced degrees in linguistics. An impartial group of American scholars trained in socio-linguistics could found, lead, and supervise specially trained research committees, perhaps backed by UNESCO. In what follows I will present a brief outline of some of the basic steps to be taken by such socio-linguistically trained research committees in the Danubian Basin:

(1) All concerned countries in the Danubian Basin would be invited to send a representative committee of linguists to an international summit conference. Being linguists and not politicians, they would vow total impartiality and would seek to approach the multi-

lingual problem of the Danubian Basin from the human angle rather than the political-étatistic one. In other words: They would adopt the ideological platform that their discussions are not about *borders*, but about *life*. Thus in a pre-federation stage of "United Central Europe" the "summit" would decide that it will turn its multi-lingual areas into research areas instead of disaster areas.

(2) The summit conference would divide the Danubian Basin into multi-lingual research areas based on accurate and truthful population statistics. Joint committees of the mixed national groups concerned would then conduct socio-linguistic investigations and would proceed to make specific recommendations to each local government concerned, indicating what needs to be done in the sphere of equal opportunity in elementary, high school, and university education in the local language of each specific area; what the needs and resources of teaching personnel and jobs are in relation to the local population statistics. Thus, in Bratislava-Pozsony-Pressburg a joint committee of Slovaks, Hungarians, Austrians, and relatively disinterested Rumanians trained in socio-linguistics, would record the number of speakers of each dialect, outline their educational background, the number of their children; they would indicate the parents' desire as to w h a t l a n g u a g e t h e y w i s h t h e i r c h i l d r e n t o b e e d u - c a t e d in. Likewise, in Cluj-Kolozsvár-Klausenburg, a committee of Rumanian, Hungarian, Saxon, Czech, Slovak, and Serb, Croat, Slovene ethno-linguists would conduct similar field-work and make concrete recommendations to the Rumanian government. In turn, the Rumanian government would have the right to inspect all Rumanian groups in all other countries concerned, and if it finds the educational and employment facilities lacking may make b i n d i n g c o u n t e r - r e c o m m e n d a t i o n s to the Hungarian, Bulgarian, Slovak, etc., authorities.

6. Conclusion

Socio-linguistic research proceeds much as census-taking, and is, accordingly, a Janus-faced activity. In the present context this means that one of its faces is definitely political with certain sociological goals in mind, but on the other hand, from the point of view of the science of linguistics proper, such studies would be extremely valuable also. They would reveal what happens to the phonology, morphology, syntax, and lexicon of *languages in contact*[11]) when the contact is one of political pressure and social inequality, in contrast to Switzerland or the United States. The results of such investigations could reveal whether or not there is a significant difference in the respective developments of the politically favored and the politically disfavored language; whether languages in contact affect each other similarly or differently depending on favorable or unfavorable political circumstances. The rate of change of vocabulary could be calculated for languages in contact under peaceful democratic circumstances, and in "linguistically troubled areas", then, the precise nature and effect of the political factor could be correlated with the findings which are generally valid about languages in contact without aggravating political circumstances. Such investigations might reveal, for instance, that languages tend to be more conservative when they are in contact with other languages under adverse political circumstances, because the group under pressure desires to maintain its identity much more acutely than an unthreatened minority.

The feasibility of such research is by no means beyond our technical capabilities: The tape recorder, the computer, the voting-machine could all be usefully put to work. The time is certainly ripe. Will we able to rise to the occasion?

1) Of considerable significance in this area is the work of Professor William Labov of Columbia University, who worked with a large number of Harlem Negroes and Puerto Ricans. In the Midwest, Professor R. I. McDavid at the University of Chicago is an international authority on American dialectology. The present writer is aware of two M.A. theses being written at the University of Illinois at Chicago Circle both dealing with South Side Negro dialects, one in particular, with the vocabulary of the Blackstone Rangers.

2) Both Malaya and Singapore are former British colonies and thus, even after independence, English was retained as a joint official language for a predetermined period.

3) See the Encyclopaedia Britannica **Book of the Year**, 1968, under **Malaysia**, for the events of 1967.

The tragic Malay-Chinese conflict of Spring 1969 could, if things turn out for the worse, amount to an end of democracy in Malaysia, yet it is not impossible that the country will once again be able to find its social balance characteristic of the years from when the present description of linguistic diversity in Malaysia was taken. Whatever the present situation or the future, therefore, "The Malaysian Model" remains a reality; if nothing else as a historic record of a fine experiment.

4) The Northern and the Southern Slavic languages were not clearly separated before the Hungarian conquest. The present Slovakia was populated by the Slavs of Prince Svatopluk whom the warriors of Chief Árpád subjugated and with whom the Magyars intermarried. For Slavic loan words in Hungarian see Kniezsa's **Szláv jövevényszavak a magyarban** (Slavic Loan words in Hungarian), Budapest, MTA, 1952.

5) See the excellent article by F. O. Miksche in this book.

6) The population of Hungary in 1967 (Encyclopedia Britannica, 1968 Yearbook, p. 401) amounted to 10,196,926, 97% of whom were Hungarian, 2.2% German, and only 0.8% other nationalities.

7) The statistical table of Rumania's national composition between the years 1910-1966 was compiled by the Mid-European Research Inst.

8) Transylvania was returned to Hungarian rule for only a little more than three years during Worl War II by the second Vienna Award. This was indeed tragic. Thus the Hungarians received what was rightfully theirs from the wrong benefactor: Despite Governor Horthy's attempts to liquidate the war, just when Rumania managed to declare war on Germany in the fall of 1944, after a tragic coup d'état by the Hungarian Fascist Arrow Cross Party, Hungary became the last faithful ally of Nazi Germany. Thus, when it came to the border decisions, Stalin as well as some of his Western allies favored Rumania and forced Hungary to accept the ethnically unjustifiable Trianon Treaty borders giving all Transylvania to Rumania.

9) The present writer is primarily a descriptive linguist and thus wishes to disavow any vested interest for or against the Sumerian-Hungarian hypothesis. Interested readers are directed to the interesting but highly controversial writings of Ida Bobula, especially **The origin of the Hungarian Nation,** American Hungarian Literary Guild, Gainsville, Florida; Viktor Padányi's **Dentumagyaria,** Editorial Transylvania, Buenos Aires, Argentina, 1956; but also to Géza Bárczi's **A magyar nyelv életrajza** (The History of Hungarian Language) Budapest, 1963, which treats the history of Hungarian language from the standard Finno-Ugric point of view.

9a) SOURCES: For **1930-1956: Anuarul Statistic** (Statistical Yearbook of Rumania) Bucuresti. 1965, pp. 74-75, for the present-day territory of the country. **1948** figures for the same territory: **Populatia Rep. Populare la 25 Jan. 1948. Probleme Economice.** No. 2. Martie 1948. Bucuresti. **1910 and 1921** figures are for the larger territory of Rumania between the two world wars: D. B. **Vasiliu: Situatia demografica a Romaniei.** Cluj. 1925, p. 69: N. **Istrate: La statistique des nationalités.** Bul. Geogr. 1930: W. **Winkler:** Statistisches Handbuch der europaischen Nationalltaten. Wien. 1931, p. 228: E. **Jakabffy's** Erdély statisztikája. Lugos. 1923, p. 31 (for 1910); **1966** figures are preliminary figures as published in Rumanian and Transylvanian newspapers of Sept. 1966. Before 1918, Rumania was much smaller and had a population of only 9,234,920. In the Table, the 1910 census figures of the newly acquired territories were added to those of the old territory.

10) Even though the Trianon Treaty after World War I was ethnically unjustifiable in giving Transylvania to Rumania, a generation of Rumanians grew up between the two world wars who felt that it was unjust that it be given to Hungary while an essentially unjust and criminal war was being waged in Europe. The bitterness of these Rumanians may have been greatly aggravated by the perfectly understandable zeal of the Hungarians who were only too eager to move into Transylvania with their armies, even though this worked against their interest in the long run.

11) A famous book by the title **Languages in Contact** was written by the late Uriel Weinreich, professor of linguistics at Columbia University in 1953 and has been regarded as a classic on the subject ever since.

CULTURAL PLURALISM AND THE STUDY OF COMPLEX SOCIETIES IN ANTHROPOLOGY.

ALEXANDER GALLUS

> "The dogma that public issues are beyond the interest or competence of those who study and teach about man is myopic and sterile professionalism and a fear of commitment which is both irresponsible and irrevelant."
>
> (Berreman, 1968, p. 391)

IN modern anthropology there is mounting awareness of shift towards new subject matters. The rapid development of new national states in the area of former colonial territories, has created a new situation in which the term "primitive" has acquired derogatory meaning. (Hsu, 1964; Clearhout, 1965).

Peoples which around the turn of the century still lived under traditional and more simple ("primordial") conditions, have moved out of their heritage and are in the process of adapting themselves to prevalent forms of a technologic civilization, which after the Second World War developed into a global stage.

"Acculturation" becoming inevitable, the traditional subject matter of anthropology, the study of "primitive peoples," (or peoples still living under "natural" conditions, = "Naturvölker"), became either impossible or obsolete ,and anachronistic.

A new approach towards understanding man and towards a systematisation of his behavior, had to be found. Especially in America a vivid reaction to the new situation can be observed. In America the traditionally maintained broad, synthetic approach towards anthropology as a study of man and of his behavior in general, has been redefined. A spirited discussion about a "holistic", or a "compartmentalized" approach to anthropology took place in recent years (Marshall and Thompson, 1967; MacLachlan, Marshall and Thompson, 1968; Hultkranz, 1968). The emblem of "Current Anthropology, A World Journal of the Sciences of Man," sees anthropology as the sum of the following specific disciplines: Prehistory, Archeology, Linguistics, Folklore, Ethnology, Social Anthropology and Physical Anthropology. This holistic approach is coupled with a scrupulous concern about scientific objectivity, to the extent of consciously avoiding personal and nationalistic bias. (Embres, 1950; Haring, 1951; Macquet, 1964; Gjessing, 1968; Nurge, 1968).

Redefinition of a holistic approach makes it possible to embrace the study of phenomena, which are characteristic for the new, global phase of human history: acculturation, the interaction and integration of human ethnic units within a larger society, the nature of "complex societies", or in other words the nature and structure of larger human administrative and political organizations, which embrace a certain number of subcultures and ethnic groups.

Recent discussions have shown, that "complex societies" have already long ago elicited interest, only, no attempts have been made to conceptualize the specific nature of this study. Papers followed the personal inclinations of researchers, who have occupied themselves with some detailed aspects of the structure of human behavior within the confined sphere of a particular society.

A large literature exists on "acculturation", "culture change", "culture growth" and "culture contacts", with attempts towards generalizations in these particular fields and the formulation of "models", which apparently is a modern expression for "working hypothesis".

These studies created an awareness for the importance of limitations in the spheres of human contacts and understanding, which limitations have their source in restrictions caused by traditional ways of thinking, and in the compulsive force of culturally ingrained forms of behavior (including institutions and organizations). These limitations often lead to difficulties in communication between human groups, a low level of tolerance and understanding and a breakdown of cooperation.

A general review like this, cannot even in the slightest way give adequate references to the scientific trends, which exist in this field, but let us note the conceptualization of "cultural drift" (Sapir, 1921; Herskovits, 1948; Eggan, 1941, 1963).

"Cultural drift" means day by day small variations, whose continued accumulation results in long range directional changes in the character and form of human social life. It is the progressive summation of minor variations in accordance with preexisting tendencies. Contact with other modes of behavior, which may lead to acceptance of foreign influences (acculturation) or to resistance against change, seem often explicable in terms of this "drift", which represents the organic and specific flexibility of the cultural life of a human group. According to this "model", only those values and traits are assimilated, which lay in the direction of the organic process of change (its potential and its possibilities) within a particular human group.

Cultural development ("drift") of a particular human group thus depends on basic traits of human behavior, which must have been operative at the time of the formation of this group and which is equivalent to the history of cultural change. The already consummated process of change, with its accumulated results stored in tradition, language, institutions etc., determines the future direction, constancy and limitations of the "drift", and thus determines the latitude of acceptable influences. This "drift", of course, cannot be constructed as an absolute determinant. It appears as a determinant of limitations within which free choice can take place.

Already Spengler in his "Untergang des Abendlandes" made it clear, that it is much nearer to reality to conceptualize so-called "influences" in a positive way, that is, to understand them as a positive activity ("choice"), as an "acceptance" of new values, because they fit into the established pattern of a particular group. Thus *influence" does not depend so much on the originator, but much more on acceptance, which is a positive and not passive activity.

It clearly follows from such conceptualisation ("model") that human cooperation and the building up of a more complex human society cannot be achieved by contact alone and will be absolutely hopeless when existing different cultural trends are overcome by administrative means and force alone.

The uniqueness of cultural behavior, its persistence in cultural drift, tradition and institutions, and the specifc limitations which exist for the acceptance and assimilation of foreign values, will be shortly referred to in the following with the Aristotelean term "Entelechia" (= specific "form of being" of a human group, its individuality or "essence").

The above "model" makes it possible to understand, how ethnic "Entelechia" (national groups) persists through centuries of alien domination, without leading to higher forms of organizational unity, but leading to immediate segregation, when historic opportunity arises. (Examples are legion: rebirth of the Irish Republic in our times, the strong Entelechia of the Scottish people, the nationhood of the Jews, the Finns, the Baltic peoples, and finally the emergence into nationhood of ethnic groups after the end of colonial unification.)

It seems clear that lasting human organizations, which extend over geographic areas larger than the homeland of an ethnic unit, can only be built upon acceptance and never against it, short of genocide.

G. P. Murdoc has noted as characteristics of "drift", in connection with the evolution of social organizations, the following: "... limitation in the possibilities of change, a strain towards consistency, shifts from one to another relatively stable equilibrium, compensatory internal readjustments, *resistance against any influence from diffusion, that is not in accord with the drift ...*" (Italics mine) — (Quoted in Eggan, 1963, p. 348).

Kröber, 1952, in a most important conceptualization, stated that drift can be understood as a "momentum quality". The performance of a culturally patterned activity appears to carry with it implications for its own change, which is by no means altogether random. Forms in general as D'Arcy Thompson has shown, have "momentum qualities".

They might even be "cultural orthogenesis within particular limited scopes, that is *the direction of at least some culture change is more predetermined by earlier forms of the culture*, than caused by environmental stress and individual variability." (Italics mine) — (Quoted by Eggan, 1963, p. 348).

It seems clear then that we are faced with the presence of flexible human social units, which ,when regarded in a historical perspective (that is in the process of change), show the quality of a specific and consistent "drift" or momentum.

It seems further clear that the ideals of modern global society tend towards peaceful organization of the globe and not towards the application of force, according to dogmatic preconceptions, as in the past. In such a historical situation then, the modern trend towards applied anthropology becomes especially meaningful.

It can be rightfully asked that in the present situation of awareness in which anthropologists have advanced to meaningful conceptualizations, why should these conceptions not play an important role in the formulation of practical policies, which need a deepened understanding of the "Entelechia" of human social units?

This question is now asked with increasing urgency in anthropologic literature (Reyes and Medina, 1963, p. 320; Bunzel and Parsons, 1964.)

The need for insight and understanding for the planning of human relations, cannot be enough emphasized today, and the results of a methodical and disinterested scientific approach are not only ready to be applied in international policy decisions, but their application is absolutely necessary.

As an aftermath of a recent meeting of U.S.A. Anthropologists in 1962, it was suggested that anthropologists should analyze "conflict resolution mechanisms in a variety of societies, to emphasize the complexity of non-technical determinants of conflict". It was voiced that "anthropologists stand for cultural pluralism; they are against imposing the cultural ideals of any one political bloc on the rest of mankind." They devoted much time "to outlining anthropological research that could provide insights or useful information for problems of peace and international stability".

Work on three levels was suggested: 1. Basic research on the nature of war and peace and the socio-cultural process involved in conflict and conflict resolution. 2. Research on immediate problems of international and internal tension. 3. Strategies for improving communication and extending anthropological influence on world affairs.

It was recommended to study: "social change with attention to the conditions under which social integration takes place. Relevant areas of study would be the *development of confederacies* and nation states in the past." To study "current situations of culture contact and the *readjustment and new syntheses involved in the integration of units* and the abolition of war between social components."

Attention should be directed towards "intercultural relations in a world of nations. The apparent paradox that a relationship exists between increased communication and *interdependence,* and the growth of national consciousness and hostility should be examined in the light of larger concepts of cultural process."

Anthropologists stated: "We must anticipate the *emergence of completely new institutional structures.* The study of the implications of these changes in the light of general theories of culture change is a proper field for anthropological research..." "Anthropologists possess certain skills, as well as conceptual tools, and a considerable body of knowledge, that are relevant to the problems of world peace." (Italics mine). (Bunzel and Parsons, 1964).

It is pathetic to observe with what prehistoric (in the sense of being outdated and thus completely inadequate) methods, was the reorganization of Central Europe attempted after the end of the First World War. It has been pointed out already by contemporary analysts how the statesmen at that time were still influenced by conceptions of power politics. (Gallus, 1966). Organization of human life in that part of the world has been attempted along the lines of preconceived ideas of strategy, aimed at the military and economic defence of a situation which was deemed advantageous, for those, who won the war, and which strategy caused the withdrawal of the United States from the Peace Treaties.

For sure, thus was the way, how treaties were negotiated in human history, after victorious wars, in the past.

But only few observers realized the necessities of a new human situation, the dawn of the breakthrough of human existence into a global stage, in which the strategies and endeavours of the past were no more adequate. Only after the logical consequences of the post-1918 treaties became evident, only then began consciencious statesmen and political historians, formulate the need for new concepts to be formed and applied in human relations and international politics.

These new concepts are only able to emerge in an objective and scientific atmosphere, and thus the ideal statesman of today and in the future is envisaged as a person of mature and broad intellect, whose decisions are influenced by an adequate body of facts about the behavior of human groups, and about their "Entelechic" limitations. Propositions relating to human organization, cooperation and coexistence must in the future depend on *what is acceptable (as established on the ground of objective, scientific enquiries) to all the*

314

groups concerned, and not on what seems desirable from the egotistic point of view of a potentially dominant power.

It is typical for the human and scientific situation around 1918 that the anthropologic concept of "Cultural Pluralism", which could have helped to understand the human scene in Central Europe, was apparently first developed only in 1939, by J. S. Furneval, in connection with an analysis of the former colonial territory of the Netherlands Indies (Furneval, 1939). He noticed, (it sounds incredible that anthropologists should have avoided so long to generalize on this subject) how different "cultures" lived side by side without much mingling and observed that "Nationalism within a plural society is itself a disruptive force, tending to shatter and not to consolidate its social order." (Quoted, Despres, 1968, p. 11). Steward, (in discussion, Despres, 1968, pp. 21-22) also remarks that Indian cultures in the U.S.A. were first viewed by American anthropologists as "ethnic minorities within the United States", only in the mid thirties. It can be noted that there is still reluctance in Australia, e. i., in regard to the aborigines as an "ethnic minority", with the status of an independent human social unit!

Furneval's trend of thought (which, let us confess, to us Central Europeans, seems to be rather commonplace truth) was since used by political scientists for the analysis and explanation of the situation in now independent, former colonial areas, (Almond and Coleman, Ed. 1960; Smith and Kuper, Ed. 1960; Despres, 1968), a situation which led to political and ethnic catastrophes in many parts of the world.

"Plural Societies" according to Despres, 1968, following Smith, 1960, are societies in which *"groups living within a political unit have very different systems of . . . basic institutions".* (Italics mine). In a plural society the cultural plurality of the society corresponds to its social plurality: the culturally distinct units of a plural society are its "cultural sections". Generally these "cultural sections" are "historically deep-rooted" and highly exclusive in the sense that each displays and area of common life-form, beyond which relationships with the larger, encompassing society, of which they form part, are only segmental, governed mainly by economic and political structures (Despres, 1968, pp. 11-12).

There are several interesting features in this text. First: how is it that so many anthropologists have failed to notice the frequently "ethnic" or "tribal" character of the "cultural sections" in question? It is the ethnic aspect which turns these "cultural sections" into so-called "minorities" in respect to another ethnic group, the dominant partner in the organization of a plural society.

These ethnic groups can be regarded as covered up "tribal societies" of anthropologic interest, which on the level of their rural settlement-areas remain strictly intermarrying gene-pools, often preserving characteristic regional physical features. They maintain distinct tradition (folk-lore, "traditional norms", religion), language, organized and spontaneuos social and behavioristic habits (Siverts: "conceptual and valuational systems", quoted in Despres, 1968, p. 21). They are still near a stage of natural units where "shared meanings and values are homogeneous and a wide range of different activities are carried on in terms of uniform structure" (Despres, 1968, p. 12).

In Central Europe these primeval groups interpenetrate in their habitats but do not mingle substantially with each other. (Matl, 1963). This still primordially ethnocentred life is overstratified but never extinguished by an administrative level of a more sophisticated social structure. At the present stage of social organization in Central Europe, "Western European Type" national states are forced onto the area, every small state having been constructed by the Peace Treaties in such a way, that one dominant ethnic group retains the possession of state administration, the other groups remaining "minorities" (Gallus, 1967-68).

That this must lead to mutual oppression and unnecessary deprivation and human suffering, should be clear by now to every historian and rationally thinking human.

As the aim of a future reorganization must be the elimination of the "Western Type" national state; the elimination of "minority" status; and the substitution of a more realistic model of state organization: further scientific approach must rest on the study of the ethnic groups themselves, and on the study of the best way of solving the coexistence of these groups, who all have a different emotive-reactive matrix, embodied in their past history, entelechia and tradition, *which they want to preserve.*

The second outstanding feature of the Despres-Smith treatment of plural societies is the strange fact, that none of the authors so far mentioned by us and quoted by them, has ever thought to cast a glance on Central Europe. They had acumen enough to recognize problems and difficulties in Africa and Asia, where the formation of new states was hindered by ethnic (tribal) rivalries and wars (called "cultural units" by Despres, 1968, but "tribal" or "ethnic" groups by Cohen in his comments on Despres paper, Despres, 1968, p. 18). Gjessing, 1968, p. 402, approvingly quotes the findings of an Anthropologic Conference (Bunzel and Parsons, 1964) that one of the major areas on which anthropologists might contribute to the solution of world problems, is the study of emerging nations, of the non-western world. Apparently anthropology is still struggling with its traditional focus of interest in "non-western" peoples!

If conceptualization would have been developed on the lines of "ethnic" groups or units, or "minorities", instead of "cultural sections", a large array of phenomena could have lent itself to generalization from Ireland and Scotland, through Bretagne and Central Europe, to Ukraine and Georgia and Transylvania or to the Arab-Israeli war and tribal warfare in the Congo and Nigeria.

Thus it must be pointed out that the problem treated in this essay is not confined to Central Europe, but it is a world-wide phenomenon, which becomes especially acute when viewed in the light of world-organization and world-peace.

If then a solution can be worked out and applied successfully in Central Europe (as it has worked in Switzerland) such a successful solution will have its repercussions and applicability on a world-wide scale.

Conceptualisation and analysis thus cannot rest on the idea of "cultural sections" alone, because the eruptive dynamism and persevering ability of these groups cannot be understood on such a simple basis. A scientific discipline whose conceptualisations should clearly have relevance in this respect for the scholar, is "Ethnology", as we shall see lather.

This leads to a third pecularity of Despres' theory or "model". Despres talks of "functional integration" "on the societal level" which holds together the different "cultural sections". But how this "functional integration" works, remains rather obscure. "A minimum core of shared values" is mentioned, which when absent, the "integration of society" can only be maintained by force, and apparently for many anthropologists the only society which is maintained by force seems to be exclusively "colonial society". (Despres, 1968, p. 12).

Thus in concentrating on "colonial society" the theory neglects the role of integrating force in the structure of the so-called "national states". Whereas a proper analysis of power-structures in the administration of the modern centralized states would have directly led again to the discovery of the problems of "plural society" under the surface of "national states" in Central Europe and elsewhere.

This omission is the more strange as the theories of Nadel, 1957, have already pointed into the right direction. (Nadel, 1957, pp. 114-127, quoted by Despres, 1968, p. 8). According to Nadel, a systematic theory of "social structure'" can be deducted from two "criteria of relevance":

1. The *differential command* that one actor has over the actions of others.

2. The *differential command* that actors have over existing benefits or resources.

Despres comments: "In short Nadel concludes that *power relationships* are the essence of social structure in formal terms." In Nadel's words: "Society has no single structure, and the many structures which it contains are neither logically nor empirically articulated". What actually has structure is the "Polity" (i. e. the State).

If we accept Nadel's distinction, then we can state, that a new organization in Central Europe, must have the aim to build a "Polity", so that the struggle for dominance between groups can be controlled. Such a control can be achieved in many ways. It is, however, maintained here that a solution in terms of the "National State" *is destructive on the long run*. The maintenance of single national states in Central Europe, needs a large amount of power organization, which gives "differential command" over "existing benefits and resources and "over the actions of others", to one ethnic group only, which appears as the state-building factor in every single state. This need for power, leads to the need of support from foreign powers and results in imperialistic control over the whole area by a foreign state, with the exploitation of local resources (economic and human) for the benefit of the organizing foreign state.

Thus the organization of "Polity" in Central Europe must be in future built on the consent and coexistence of the different ethnic groups themselves (the unit of administration being the ethnic group).

The anthropologic concept of "Plural Society" or of "Cultural Plurality" must be regarded as a specific variant of the more general and comprehensive phenomenon of our modern, so-called "Complex Society", where the existence of "subcultures" (industrial city, country town, rural village society, age groups, professional groups, religious communities, social strata etc.) is further complicated by the survival of ethnic entelechias ("nationalities") within the administrative system of the state. A large amount of detail has been in the past accumulated by anthropologists on "Complex Society" and the ground has been fairly laid for an understanding of "cultural" (i. e. ethnic) plurality. (Mitchell, 1960, Eisenstadt, 1961; Depres, 1968; Banton, 1966; and further literature quoted by these authors).

Further analysis must lead to a situation where the questions of ethnic minorities will be lifted out from the realm of administrative, strategic and legalistic thinking (minority "rights", "rights" of self-determination), and will be solved with reference to anthropologic insights into human behavior, or in other words will be solved on *humanistic grounds* only.

It must be admitted that back in 1918, the mental tools of Anthropology and of the Social Sciences in general, were not yet elaborate and clear enough in this field. We can safely assert that conceptualisation about the nature of the interaction of human ethnic groups and in general the nature and psychology of these groups, has been primitive or nonexistent, even a generation ago, but a breakthrough of rational and scientific thinking and an objective solution should be available by now, for a settlement, which does not need physical force and constant foreign intervention for its maintenance.

The neglect of an objective and scientific analysis of problems of coexistence of different ethnic groups within the same administrative unit, is astonishing, but it might be due to the prevalence of traditional ideas about "state sovereignty" until the end of the Second World War. It must have been felt as undue interference with "internal problems" of a state, if e. i. an American postgraduate student with a state grant, would have visited, say, Rumania, with the aim to inquire into aspects of the Hungarian minority there, or would have arrived in Hungary, to study the life and status of the German minority or perhaps of the Gypsy population. This practical field study would have been impossible in many instances. On the other hand much of the available descriptive and statistical material is suspect to machination by interested parties ("propaganda"), which in itself appears, of course, as proper subject of anthropologic study. Berreman, 1968, has rather forcefully suggested, that the pressure of state interests ("governmental, military and corporate elite") inhibits free scientific inquiry into all aspects of human behavior. Or as Gjessing, 1968, says (p. 399): "the social sciences are to a fairly great degree dependent on the socio-political values of the establishment".

These difficulties, though not yet overcome, have diminished since. Scientific disciplines themselves are parts of trends within human history. (Gjessing, 1968, pp. 397-99; Moses, 1969).

The science of Ethnography, whose adept study "the folk component of their own cultural heritage" (Hofer, 1968, p. 311), began as an offshoot of the romantic movement (Herder, Grimm), which drew its inspiration from the ideal of national culture of the monolithic state. Thus their efforts linked up with the "centralized, Western Type National State" (Gallus, 1967-68), or in other words with the ideal of one ethnic entelechia, which enforces dominance within rigid state boundaries. As a necessary corollary, the concept of "minorities" has been developed, who were supposed to be safeguarded by so-called "minority rights", which, however, were seldom put into operation, as "assimilation" of the minority ethnic groups was a desirable aim. The whole situation was supported by the presence of an officially fostered fixation or idiosyncrasy in the minds of the leading class of the dominant ethnic group, to the effect, that they are in possession of specific human values. These values were regarded as representing human progress in the area, and to be more valuable than those of the other ethnic groups.

Thus dominance within an area and its state boundaries was built up on specific conceptualizations of: "vocation", "talents" (e.i. "talent for organization"), inborn "leadership" etc. which all added up to the necessity of rendering special service to the area under dominance, which no other nationality could fulfill. All this racionalized or else mysticized the simple fact of dominance of one ethnic group over the others. The National State has created initial euphoria, but on the long run, *it became the most traumatic experience in Central Europe.*

Today the differences between Ethnography (the study of one's own people) and Ethnology (the study of foreign people) have lost significance and meaningfulness when regarded in the light of emerging universalistic trends in modern Anthropology. We thus might define the comprehensive study of "Pluralistic Society" as the development of Ethnography towards *"Comparative Ethnography",* where especially the underlying common human behavioristic elements are analysed and an objective aspect of mutual tolerance can be gained.

Comparative or "crosscultural" ethnographic analysis can be regarded as a modern equivalent of both, Ethnology and Ethnography, which appear today anachronistic in their "paradigmatic" (Despres, 1968, p. 6) limitations.

Most of the conceptualizations quoted by Janowitz (1963), who also analyzes Nadel, 1957, appears of significance in this respect. Human social structure is made up of a variety of social structures with a great variety of potential and real conflict situations. We have already quoted Nadel's view (1957), that within social organizations, differential command exists over one another's actions and over existing benefits or resources. The stability of such a situation rested in the past and still rest in many areas upon ideas of sovereignty and organized power.

Dobzhansky (1963, p. 138) has strongly and rightly emphasized the role of conscious and intelligent (rational) willpower in influencing the direction of human development, which is not "foreordained or immutable". "Man and man alone has it within his capabilities to refuse to accept the evolutionary direction of blind forces of nature as his inexorable fate. Man may be able to understand, to control and to guide his evolution."

In our era of growing consciousness (Nurge, 1968, p. 422: "Increased self-awareness"), in which many hitherto unconsciously regulated, or rather subconsciously acting processes become conscious and rationally approachable (conception, influence on mental processes through drugs or psychoanalytic treatment, the analysis of so-called "ethnocentrism" in anthropologic field-work and method of researchers, definition of the so-called "cultural bias", the dragging into consciousness of everything hidden before, see the copious literature on sex etc.) in this era, it seems legitimate to overcome instinctive and emotionally biased ethnocentric behavior, through rational and scientific insight, and to arrive through rational and objective inquiry at rationally based solutions of hitherto unsolved problems of coexistence and mutual tolerance.

Natural selection operates in a mechanical way by assuring the survival of those spontaneous variants which as a matter of fact contain an optimal array of physical and behavioristic features, best suited to a particular environment. ("Adaptation").

Human adaptation has already for several thousand years followed a path, which favored selection not so much for fitness within a natural environment (the main difficulties here have been long ago overcome), but *fitness within an artificial environment*, that is: natural environment modified by cultural activity.

Dobzhansky, 1963, p. 147, called this new man-made environment "socio-cultural" environment.

Survival of human groups within this highly competitive, artificially created human environment, was largely determined in the past by wars, and the requirements of power politics. The "winning of wars" depended in the last two world wars on the possession of raw materials, the development of engineering, the development of the sciences and the number of combatants. It is possible to see the present "population explosion" as a biologic adaptive response to this ever-increasing need for competitive potential, which a large populace undoubtedly possesses. This competitive potential is consciously emphasized by nationalism, or patriotic anxiety about birth rate as compared with that of surrounding nations. Dobzhansky, 1963, p. 148, sees in "reproductive fitness" the measure of fitness of a genotype, in relation to its environment.

If we want to lead mankind into a new global phase of existence this "competitive" character of the artificially modified natural environment, must consciously be changed. Human behavior must be based on "coexistence" and "cooperation" in order to liberate the energies and resources, which hitherto have been bound by, and annihilated in competitive behavior. Considerable resources could then be employed for the creation of a non-competitive human milieu. Of course, aggressive competitiveness is a human instinct, *or in other words a human adaptive trait*, which has evolved through many hundreds of thousands of years. But being an adaptive trait *it depends on a milieu, in which this trait is an advantage*. If by an effort of consciously applied will-power we can change this milieu into one, in which "aggressive competitiveness" is no more an advantage, the possibility for selection for other behavioristic traits arises, at least in the field of international relations and intergroup behavior. A shrewed observer might perhaps point out, how aggressive statesmen of the old type have lost popularity in recent history (Sukarno, De Gaulle, Johnson), and how wars in foreign territories ("aggressive wars") elicit spontaneous resistance and sympathy for the attacked (Vietnam, Czechoslovakia).

The prevailing trend in human evolution is towards increasingly conscious, rational control of human relations, which in the past have been governed by behavioristic traits which have evolved as adaptation to a form of artificial human environment, which was based on competitiveness.

Emphasizing the rationality of this trend, we again must come back to the importance in the present world situation, of "scientific enquiry" as a guide. To quote Dobzhansky (1963, p. 148): "**Natural** selection is the sole known mechanism, *outside of human contrivance*, which can translate the challenges of the environment into adaptive alterations of the organisms, responding to these challenges." "It is in other words the biological regulatory mechanism which makes possible the feedback relation between the genotype and the environment, the relation which is the basis of adaptive evolution". "Man if he chooses *may introduce his purpose into his evolution.*" "He may choose *to direct his evolution towards the attainment of the purposes, which he regards as good.*" "The ultimate function of anthropology is no less than *to provide the knowledge requisite for the guidance of human evolution.*" (Italics by me.)

Thus we can see a modern movement towards a *functional role* of anthropology. It shows an essential transformation in the attitude of scientists towards society. Academic detachment of scholarly investigation is by no means imperilled by the new trend. Objectivity is still needed to discover "truth". And unless the insight into human behavior does not reflect the true working of the human mind, social organization cannot be influenced, as a false notion of matter cannot lead to the right manipulation of matter. Thus the very essence of the new trend depends on the most rigidly objective treatment of the subject matter, as far as it is humanly possible. (Gjessing, 1968, pp. 399-400, emphasizes the recognition even of "our unconscious motivations" to attain at objective truth in the human behavioristic sciences.)

Gough, 1968, p. 406, in an enumeration of modern goals for anthropologic research, has mentioned "comparative studies of modern inter-societal political and economic dominance which would help us to define and refine such concepts as imperialism, neo-colonialism etc. How, for example, does Russian power over one or another of the East European countries compare with that of the United States over certain Latin American or Southeast Asian countries with respect to such variables as *military coercion, the disposal of the subordinate society's economic surplus* and the relations between political elites. How does Chinese control over Tibet compare historically, structurally and functionally with Indian control over Kashmir, Hyderabad or the Naga Hills, and what have been the effects of these controls on the class structures, economic productivity, and local political institutions of these regions?"

It has been further pointed out by Cohen, 1968, pp. 410-11, that in ultimate analysis such concerns of functional anthropology stem from a "commitment to humanism" of the scholar himself, who is by conscience bound to use his knowledge and insights for the benefit of mankind. This commitment is a "moral commitment of man as an ethical being", and thus "applied anthropology" becomes "applied ethics". It is the "ethics of humanism" and such values as "service of mankind", leading the scientists by means of essentially moral experiences towards a definition of a range of *"acceptable goals"*, which "exclude those goals, which seem to him clearly wrong." This attitude leads to moral decisions in concrete situations. (Italics mine.)

The *Studies for a New Central Europe* has steadily developed towards an ideal of the application of objective scientific research in order to arrive at a practical and workable solution of the problem of the coexistence and cooperation of ethnic groups within a larger administrative area in Central Europe, which would eliminate "aggressive competitiveness" within that area. Our *Review* offers its pages to anthropologists, political scientists, and sociologists, who want to contribute to functional ("applied") anthropology in the area of this Review's particular interest: Central Europe (The "concrete situation" of Cohen). They can even regard it as a test-case, an experiment of great importance, whether the rational phase of global human evolution, as diagnosed above, really exists?

Almond G. A. and J. S. Coleman, ed. **The politics of developing areas.** Princeton University Press. 1960

Banton M., ed. **The Social Anthropology of Complex Societies.** Association of Social Anthropologist of the Commonwealth Monographs. No. 4. London, Tavestock Publications, 1966.

Berreman G. D. **Is Anthropology Alive? Social Responsibility in Social Anthropology.** In: Social Responsibilities Symposium. Current Anthropology. Vol. 9, Nó. 5, 1968, pp. 391-396.

Bunzel R. R. L. and A. Parsons, with comments by M. Mead and R. Metraux. "Report on Regional Conferences." **Current Anthropology.** Vol. 5, No. 5, 1964, pp. 430, 437-442.

Claerhout G. H. "The Concept of Primitive; Applied to Art." **Current Anthropology.** Vol. 6, No. 4, 1965, pp. 432-438.

Cohen E. "Comments to Berreman, Gjessing and Gough: Social Responsibilities Symposium." **Current Anthropology.** Vol. 9, No. 5, 1968, pp. 410-411.

Despres L. "Anthropological Theory, Cultural Pluralism and the Study of Complex Society," **Current Anthropology.** Vol. 9, No. 1, 1968, pp. 3-16.

Dobzhansky Th. "Anthropology and the Natural Sciences — The Problem of Human Evolution," **Current Anthropology.** Vol. 4, No. 2, 1963, pp. 138,

146-48. (See also Th. Dobzhansky, **The Biological Basis of Human Freedom.** Columbia Paperback Edition, 1960.)

Eggan F. "Some Aspects of Culture Change — The Northern Philippines," **American Anthropologist.** Vol. 43, No. 1, 1941, pp. 11-18.

Eggan F. "Cultural Drift and Social Change," **Current Anthropology.** Vol. 4, No. 4, 1963, pp. 347-355.

Eisenstadt S. N. "Anthropological Studies of Complex Societies." **Current Anthropology.** Vol. 2, No. 2, 1961, pp. 201-22.

Embre J. T. "A note on ethnocentrism in Anthropology," **American Anthropologist.** Vol. 52, 1950, pp. 430-32.

Fortes M. and E. E. Evans Pritchard. **African political systems.** London, Oxford University Press, 1940.

Furneval J. S. **Netherland India, a study of plural economy.** London, Cambridge University Press, 1939.

Gallus A. "Forgotten Sentiments." **Studies for a New Central Europe.** Vol. 1, No. 4, 1966, pp. 67-73.

Gallus A. "Pseudo-National States or Real National Identities in Central Europe," **Studies for a New Central Europe.** Series 2, No. 1, 1967-68, pp. 15-19.

Gjessing G. "The Social Responsibility of the Social Scientist." In: Social Responsibilities Symposium. **Current Anthropology.** Vol. 9, No. 5, 1968, pp. 397-402.

Gough K. "New Proposals for Anthropologists." In: Social Responsibilities Symposium. **Current Anthropology.** Vol. 9, No. 5, pp. 403-07.

Haring D. G. "Ethnocentric Anthropologists," **American Anthropologist.** Vol. 53, 1951, pp. 135-37.

Herskovits M. **Mand and his works; The Science of Cultural Anthropology.** New York, 1948.

Hofer T. "Anthropologists and Native Ethnographers in Central European Villages; Comparative Notes on the Professional Personality of Two Disciplines," **Current Anthropology.** Vol. 9, No. 4, 1968, pp. 311-15.

Hsu F. L. K. "Rethinking the Concept 'Primitive'," **Current Anthropology.** Vol. 5, No. 3, 1964, pp. 169-78. (See also: **Current Anthropology,** Vol. 7, No. 2, 1966, pp. 196-7.)

Hultkranz A. "The Aims of Anthropology: A Scandinavian Point of View." **Current Anthropology.** Vol. 9, No. 4, 1968, pp. 289-310.

Ishida E. et al. "European versus American Anthropology," **Current Anthropology.** Vol. 6, No. 3, 1965, pp. 303-18.

Janowitz J. "Anthropology and the Social Sciences," **Current Anthropology.** Vol. 4, No. 2, 1963, pp. 139, 149-154.

Kroeber A. L. and C. Kluckhohn. "Culture, A Critical Review of Concepts and Definitions; Papers of the Peabody Museum of American Archaeology and Ethnology." Harvard University. Vol. XLVII, No. 1. Cambridge, 1952.

MacLachlan B. B., D. S. Marshall and L. Thompson. "On Anthropology: General and Unified," **Current Anthropology.** Vol. 9, No. 4, 1968, pp. 331-32.

Maquet J. J. "Objectivity in Anthropology," **Current Anthropology.** Vol. 5, No. 1, 1964, pp. 47-55.

Marshall D. S. "General Anthropology; Strategy for a Human Science," **Current Anthropology.** Vol. 8, No. 1/2, 1967, pp. 61-66.

Matl J. "Ideas of an Austrian on the Coexistence of Nations in the Danubian and Carpathian Basins," **Studies for a New Central Europe.** Vol. 1, No. 1, 1963, pp. 28-33.

Mitchell J. C. **Tribalism and the Plural Society.** Oxford University Press, 1960.

Moses J. A. "The Crisis in West German Historiography: Origins and Trends," **Historical Studies.** University of Melbourne. Australia. Vol. 13, No. 52, 1969, pp. 445-59.

Nadel S. F. **The Theory of Social Structure.** New York, 1957.

Nurge E. "Comments to Berreman, Gjessing and Gough: Social Responsibilities Symposium," **Current Anthropology.** Vol. 9, No. 5, 1968, pp. 422-3.

Reyes F. and A. Medina. "On Anthropological Studies of Complex Societies," **Current Anthropology.** Vol. 4, No. 3, 1963, pp. 319-20.

Sapir E. **Language.** New York, 1921.

Smith M. G. "Social and Cultural Pluralism." In: Social and Cultural Pluralism in the Caribbean. **Annals of the New York Academy of Sciences.** Los Angeles. University of California, 1960, pp. 763-77.

Smith M. G. and L. Kuper, ed. **Pluralism in Africa.** Los Angeles. University of California Press, 1960.

Thompson L. "Steps Toward a Unified Anthropology." **Current Anthropology.** Vol. 8, No. 1/2, 1967, pp. 67-77.

THE HUNGARIAN MINORITY PROBLEM
IN RUMANIA

International Commission of Jurists

FROM the eleventh century until 1918, Transylvania,* a region of some 23,300 square miles, or some 40,700 if the larger area including Maramures, Crisana and the Banat is included, came in one way or another under Hungarian rule. In 1918, it was ceded to Rumania as a region then consisting of some five and a quarter million, of whom half a million were German, one and a half million Magyar and the remainder Rumanian. There is a bitter and bloody history of national tensions. The region now comprises one of the most important national and linguistic minorities in Eastern Europe and provides an absorbing case study on the treatment of minorities in a Communist People's Republic. The total Hungarian population of Rumania, according to the 1956 census, was approximately 9.1%.

The detection of discrimination in most countries is a difficult process which does not appear from the *ipsissima verba* of legislation and it is difficult to pin down administrative practice as discriminatory unless the group discriminated against is expressly designated. It is usually a simpler process to examine legislation and practice to see what is missing from the point of view of the rights of a group in question. In a Communist State the denial of freedom to any particular group must be examined in te context of the entire social and political outlook of the State, since many rights and freedoms as understood in liberal democracies are denied to the whole population. If it be that a particular group resists the process of socialization more vigorously than another, it is not easy to see the line between discrimination against that group and the employment of greater force to deal with greater resistance. These facets of a Communist State have been much in evidence in the past and it is against this background that the minority question in Transylvania has to be considered. The experience of the Chinese People's Republic, with the peculiar blend of Communism and chauvinism on the part of the ethnic majority, viz, the Great Hans, towards the Tibetans was, for example, admitted by the Chinese themselves. Again, discrimination exists in the Communist ideology itself, but is part of the general doctrine that social progress is to be achieved through the strengthening of the proletariat, which requires for its accomplishment the strengthening of class-consciousness among the people. This has nothing to do with discrimination against a national, ethnic, religious or linguistic group.

A further obstacle to a fully documented study of minority problems in Transylvania is the absence of sufficient reliable data. In a Communist society the public ventilation of grievances at the political level is severely restricted and silence extends also to minorities with a grievance.

The Peace Treaty and the Constitution of 1952

The Peace Treaty concluded between the Allied Powers and Rumania in 1947, stipulates in Part II (Political Clauses), Section I, Art. 3 that

1) *Rumania shall take the steps necessary to secure to all persons under Rumanian jurisdiction, without distinction as to race, sex, language or religion, the enjoyment of human rights and fundamental freedoms, including freedom of expression, of press and publication, of religious worship, of political opinion and of public meeting.*

2.) *Rumania further undertakes that the laws in force in Rumania shall not, either in their content or in their application, discriminate or entail any discrimination between persons of Rumanian nationality on the ground of their race, sex, language or religion, whether in reference to their persons, property, business, professional or financial interests, status, political or civil rights or any other matter.*

Thus, the wording of the Peace Treaty clearly excludes discrimination against minorities and it is of little consequence whether the Hungarians in Transylvania are to be regarded as an ethnic, i.e., racial group, since their language alone is sufficient to bring them within this protection.

Particularly striking, both with reference to the Peace Treaty and in comparison with the Constitutions of most other People's Democracies, are the provisions of Article 82 of the Rumanian Constitution of 1952. This Article provides that all the national groups in the territory of the Rumanian People's Republic are entitled to use their respective languages and to have at all levels establishments of public education in which instruction is given in their mother tongue and further provides that the spoken and written language used by administrative and judicial authorities in districts where a national group other than Rumanian is in the majority should be the language of this national group; civil servants in such areas should be appointed from among members of this majority group, or if from other groups, it is necessary that they speak the language of the majority. Article 84 follows the lines of the Soviet Constitution in recognizing not only the separation of Church and State but also the exclusion of the Church from education. No religious community may have its own educational establishments, but theological schools may train people to carry out their part in religious services. In two other Articles the Constitution deals with the rights of national minorities. In Article 17, which lists the duties of the Rumanian State, there is a duty owed by the state to protect national minorities and especially their culture, which ought to be socialistic in its content and national in its form. Article 81 goes into the realm of enforceable legal sanctions protecting minorities and within the general framework of provisions concerning equality before the law it is provided that any kind of chauvinistic persecution of non-Rumanian national minorities or any kind of propaganda calculated to bring about such persecution is a criminal offence.

It should be noted that only the cultural rights of minorities are mentioned and Article 17 designates the Rumanian State as unitary, independent and sovereign, thus excluding any form of federation, such as, e.g., the Soviet Union or the United States. In this respect, restricting minority rights to cultural matters and protection from persecution shows little advance from the position of national minorities in the former Kingdom of Rumania between the two World Wars. How far the cultural rights of the large Hungarian minority in Transylvania are respected will now be considered.

Administrative Measures

Foremost among these is the redemarcation of regions and cities, thereby fragmenting the Hungarian population in such a way as either to reduce their majority or to convert it into a minority. The Hungarian Autonomous Province was created in 1952 by Articles 19 and 20 of the Constitution of that year. The total population of this Province was, according to the 1956 census, composed of 77.3% Hungarians, 20.1% Rumanians, 0.4% Germans, 0.4% Jews and 1.5% Gypsies. In December 1960 a governmental decree modified the boundaries of the Hungarian Autonomous Province. Its whole southern part, which was predominantly Hungarian, was attached to Stalin Province, which has now of course been renamed and is known as Brasova. In place of this, several districts with an overwhelming Rumanian majority were joined to it from the southwest. This boundary adjustment reduced the Hungarian population by approximately 82,000 and increased the Rumanian population by approximately 131,000 out of a total population of just over half a million. The official reasons were to facilitate commmunications and administration, but the new name given to the freshly demarcated province echoes the real fact of the situation, viz., the substantial dilution of its Hungarian character. The Province was no longer called the Hungarian Autonomous Province but the Mures-Hungarian Autonomous Province, after the River Mures.

The process of dilution was carried still further, though by less obvious methods, by the drive towards industrialization. The region adjacent to Hungary already had the highest rate of industrialization in the country but the programme aimed at an overall stepping up, for the border regions of Transylvania as well as for the rest of the country. In a Socialist economy not only does industrialization mean the growth of the urban proletariat, but it also means the creation of a large industrial bureaucracy. In the process of stepping up the industrialization of industrial Transylvania, large numbers of civil servants, administrative staff, industrial bureaucrats and workers of Rumanian nationality swelled the Rumanian population in the regions neighboring Hungary. In this case it is difficult to speak of a failure to respect the rights of the Hungarian minority. Industrialization with its consequent internal migration is a common enough feature of many societies. Where, however, there is an influx of a minority group and an exodus of a majority group the consequences for the culture of the majority group are important enough if the matter stops there. Many young Hungarians are obliged to leave Transylvania in search of work in the territories to the south and south-east of Transylvania, which are known as Old Rumania. And, it should be observed, the matter does not remain there, as will be shown later in this article.

There is another technique which frequently conceals *de facto* discrimination beneath a facade of general applicability. Whether or not the famous Law No. 261 of April 4, 1945, and Decree No. 12 of August 13, 1945, did in fact discriminate against Hungarians, its provisions certainly weighed very heavily on Hungarians who had Rumanian citizenship. This Law provided that all persons who served in military or para-military organizations of a state having been at war with Rumania lost their Rumanian citizenship. Decree No. 12 fixed the operative date for such service as after August 22,1944. For practical purposes this meant that the Hungarian minority would lose their Rumanian citizenship. The circumstances were that Rumania joined the Allies against the Axis Powers in 1944, whilst Hungary was under German occupation and on the Axis side until the end of the war in May 1945. The northern and predominantly Hungarian part of Transylvania was given back to Hungary in 1940 by the Germans and Italians and under the Hungarian regime of Horthy all adult males were obliged to enlist for military service and youth were required to join young people's para-military organizations. Through these circumstances few Hungarians escaped the threat of losing their nationality. It was provided that joining the Communist Party would save them from losing it.

Discrimination in the Cultural Field

The steps taken by the Rumanian authorities to weaken Hungarian culture are again in some cases mixed with what might be merely part of general Communist policy. Thus, for example, both Catholic and Protestant churches were deprived of their schools; this in itself was merely part of the normal materialistic and secular policy of a Communist State and as such, although it struck a particularly severe blow at Hungarian culture, it was not discriminatory. But there was also a widescale destruction of centuries-old Hungarian private or public archives and libraries, and the devastation of old Hungarian castles to provide stone material for new buildings. Vital links with the past were thereby wiped out.

Until 1958, a large-scale educational system, from the primary to the university level, flourished in Hungarian. Since then, however, the situation has changed rapidly. The number of Hungarian primary schools is steadily dwindling and a decree now in force authorizes only the eldest of a family's children to study in a Hungarian-language school. At the level of higher education the Rumanian authorities introduced a system of "parallel sections". This meant that in such an institution a parallel Rumanian curriculum with Chairs held by Rumanians was introduced. When this cuckoo in the nest was big enough it took over the whole nest and the Hungarian section disappeared. Another method which helped in cutting down instruction in the Hungarian language was for the student body and the teaching staff of the institutions concerned to announce that for practical considerations and in accordance with their desire to perfect themselves in "the beloved Rumanian mother-tongue" they had decided to combine with a Rumanian-language institution, or in the case of a bi-lingual institution to go over entirely to Rumanian. This process was carried so far that even student hostels felt its impact. Those for Hungarians became for mixed nationalities and Hungarian students asked to share a room with a Rumanian in order to perfect their knowledge of Rumanian. At the present time the Medical School in the capital of the Mures-Hungarian Autonomous Province is undergoing "parallelization". For Hungarian academic establishments there is now a limited admissions quota. In 1958, the Hungarian University in Cluj, Bolyai University, fused with the Rumanian University of Babes. The fusion was marked by the suicide of three of the professors at Bolyai University.

Odd facets of this process could in isolation be laudable. For example, it is an excellent language training to share a room with someone speaking a different language, but the whole pattern of cutting down Hungarian-language instruction in an area which is or was so Hungarian that it was part of Hungary for almost 900 years cannot be reconciled with respect to the constitutional rights of the

Hungarian minority and is by no means explicable as part of the normal process of shaping a Communist society. For centuries Hungarian culture and tradition have taken deep root and survived the vicissitudes of fortune, both kindly and outrageous. It is difficult to conceive that a people so deeply rooted in its culture would itself clamour for the destruction of that culture by absorption into the Rumanian mainstream.

A further instrument for the dilution of the Hungarian majority in Transylvania is the resettlement of Rumania refugees coming from Bessarabia. Their reintegration into Rumanian economic and social life has taken place mainly in Transylvania, where they constitute a large part of the labor force in the industrial development from the western belt neighboring Hungary to the heart of the Mures-Hungarian Autonomous Province, and they are settled mostly in cities where the proportion of the Hungarian population is still high, e.g., in Cluj, the capital of Transylvania.

The Rumanian National Statistical Office carried out a census in 1956 and it was emphasized that the civil servants carrying out the census were obliged to call attention in each case to the basic difference between nationality, i.e., ethnic origin, and mother-tongue. All persons registered had to state to which national ethnic group they belonged. The distinction between national group and mother-tongue and the obligation to state before officials one's national group drive a wedge between a people and its culture and this indeed is reflected in the figures given by the census. For every thousand people of declared Hungarian origin there were one thousand and forty-two giving Hungarian as their mother-tongue. It is difficult to believe that Hungarian, difficult and almost unrelated to other languages, is the mother-tongue of any but Hungarians, and yet 4.2% of the Hungarian minority group shrank from stating that they were Hungarian. The reasonable conclusion to be drawn from this is that in their eyes it was better not to declare oneself to be Hungarian. The more innocent explanation of gross inefficiency in the compilation of the census would seem to be negatived by the deliberate distinction drawn by officialdom where no real distinction exists.

Too many individual items which could be capable of other explanations than discrimination if taken singly point unmistakably when viewed as a whole towards a pattern of conduct. In short, as far as the Hungarian people in Rumania are concerned, they appear in the give and take of living together to lose on both the swings and the roundabouts. When this happens to a minority group it is difficult to resist the conclusion that they are being subjected to discrimination.

(Bulletin of the International Commission of Jurists, No. 17, December 1963, p. 35-41.)

THE HUNGARIAN MINORITY PROBLEM IN TRANSYLVANIA

A Letter from the Federalist Union of
European Nationalities (FUEN)

General Secretariate
Rolighed - Rungsted Kyst - Danmark, Tel. Hoersholm 629
2nd of November 1964
Ref. No. 1-11-14-64

To His Excellency,
Ion Gheorghe Maurer
President of the Ministerial Council of the
Rumanian People's Republic
Bukarest, Rumania

Your Excellency,

properly documented reports, which were submitted to the 14th Regensburg Congress of the FUEN between 11th and 14th of June 1964, caused the September 27/29 session of the Central Committee of the FUEN in Andorra to entrust me with the task of calling your attention to the serious situation of the Hungarian minority in your Republic.

Above Congress established that the legal statutes of the Hungarian national minority are not satisfactory for the maintenance of its peculiar national existence, as its permitted minority organizations are subdued to the central powers of the Rumanian majority, and depend upon their measures without appeal. The Hungarian minority of 1,700,000 persons has no political representation of its own, either.

The Congress and the Central Committee of the FUEN express their disappointment over the policy your Government and the Rumanian Workers' Party pursue with the apparent purpose of denationalising the Hungarian minority. This policy has in the recent years reached the extent of an intellectual genocide against this ethnical group, which is subject to discrimination in all fields of life.

The FUEN regards this policy as incompatible with the principle laid down in Article 21 of the Rumanian Constitution.

The Congress of the Central Committe of the FUEN beg to call your Government's attention to the fact, that the internationally recognized rights of national minorities—may we point to Article Two of the UNO General Statement on Human Rights, dated 10th of December 1948—refers first of all to the free use of the mother tongue in public education, in culture, in history and in all fields concerning national civilization, and they also refer to the free preservation of the nation's past and present spiritual inheritance. The Congress and the Central Committee regret, therefore, the oppression of these rights and the Rumanisation of Transylvania, and inherited and ancient country of the Hungarian minority.

The Hungarian minority in the Rumanian People's Republic has no facilities whatsoever to defend itself against discrimination and denationalization, it has no representation of any kind in the political life of the Rumanian People's Republic. It cannot ask for protection from any international authority, nor from the Government of the Hungarian People's Republic, its ethnical sister-land. With special emphasis I request Your Excellence to instruct your Government to consider what measures should be passed to save in time the cultural life and the language of this national minority, which is a loyal and integrated part of the Rumanian People's Republic, bears great European traditions, highly estimated by all European states.

I beg Your Excellency to accept the expression of my highest regard

SVEND JOHANNSEN
President

POVL SKADEGARD
Gen. Secretary

(A copy of this Note has been sent to Mr. János Kádár, then President of the Ministerial Council of the Hungarian People's Republic, as well.)

THE SITUATION OF HUNGARIANS
IN TRANSYLVANIA AND RUMANIA

Memorandum of the American Transylvanian Federation

"WHAT SHALL BE DONE TO HELP THE OPPRESSED HUNGARIANS IN TRANSYLVANIA AND RUMANIA."

The so-called Trianon Peace Treaty, forced upon Hungary on June 4, 1920, gave Transylvania—which was part of Hungary for 1,000 years—to Rumania, placing 1,750,000 Hungarians and 500,000 Germans under Rumanian sovereignty.

The rights of the Hungarians and Germans in Transylvania were guaranteed by the Paris Treaty of December 19, 1919, concluded between the Allied Powers and Rumania. The execution of the sections concerning the treatment of minorities left much to be desired up to 1940, while the whole of Transylvania belonged to Rumania.

In August 1940, the Vienna Arbitration which was requested by Rumania, returned to Hungary the northern half of Transylvania. Following the Second World War, the Allied Powers in the peace treaties with Hungary and Rumania placed this area again under Rumanian sovereignty. The rights of the Hungarian and German populations were guaranteed by the 1947 Paris Peace Treaty with Rumania in the following:

"Treaty of Peace with Rumania by Allied and Associated Powers."
Part I. *Frontiers.* Article 2. "The frontier between Rumania and Hungary as it existed on January 1938, is hereby restored."
Part II. *Political clauses. Section I. Art. 3.*
"1.) Rumania shall take all measures necessary to secure to all persons under Rumanian jurisdiction,, without distinction as to race, sex, language, or religion, the enjoyment of *human rights* and of the fundamental *freedoms;* including freedom of expression, of press and publication, of religious worship, of political opinion and of public meeting.

2.) Rumania further undertakes that the laws in force in Rumania shall not, either in their content or in their application, discriminate or entail discrimination between persons of Rumanian nationality on the ground of their race, sex, language or religion, whether in reference to their persons, property,, business, professional or financial interests, status, political or civil rights or any other matter."

The United Nations Resolution of December 1948 on Human Rights defined exactly the general and unalienable human rights.

On the basis of these international guarantes we request the safeguarding of human and minority rights of Hungarians in Transylvania:

1.) Rumania must grant local autonomy to regions inhabited by Hungarian majorities and restore the original Hungarian Autonomous Region comprising the four "Sekel" counties.

All officials assigned to regions populated by non-Rumanians should belong to the local majority or at least be fluent in speaking and writing the language of the respective local majority.

2.) Free and uninhibited use of the mother tongues of all minorities in all walks of life, including administration and judicial procedures, stores and factories, collective farms and co-operative organizations, railroads and post offices.

3.) Education in the mother tongue. The teaching staff of minority schools should belong to the respective ethnic groups, excepting instructors of Rumanian and possibly Russian languages.

The former independence of Hungarian schools presently incorporated into Rumanian institutions shall be restored under Hungarian teachers. The Hungarian Bolyai University of Cluj and the College of Medicine and Pharmacy at Targu-Mures shall be restored in their independent and Hungarian character.

Freedom of religious practices in minority languages, theological education and assignment of priests, ministers, and rabbis by their churches and synagogues without interference by the Rumanian authorities.

4.) Preservation of Hungarian cultural institutions and organizations. These should be under the direction of ethnic Hungarians and should employ Hungarians only.

The libraries and archives of Hungarian cultural and educational institutions which were expropriated and presently are in danger of slow destruction must be promptly restored to their rightful owners.

Existing or future cultural agreements should also cover the minorities, and student exchange programs should include persons from the minorities according to population ratios. The selection of students, doctors, and scientists should be left to the discretion of the corresponding minority institutions.

THE NATIONALITY PROBLEM IN
CZECHOSLOVAKIA AFTER WORLD WAR II

FRANCIS S. WAGNER

THERE were sweeping political, socioeconomic, cultural as well as foreign policy changes in East Central Europe between 1918 and 1945. But the most critical question of this region since the late Middle Ages has remained unsolved. No political system has ever succeeded in organizing a lasting and peaceful co-operation among the various ethnic groups. I think their basic approaches failed because of their refusal to recognize the ethnically distinct entity of smaller nations and to apply the principle of self-determination.

More or less the same old mistakes were committed by the Marxist-Leninist nationality policy in all of the Soviet bloc countries after the February 1945 Yalta agreement which acknowledged de facto spheres of influence whereby the Kremlin was given a free hand in Eastern Europe and in a part of Central Europe, including Czechoslovakia.

The theory and application of the Marxist-Leninist-Stalinist nationality policy were based on the Kosicky vládny program (Kosice Government Program) of April 5, 1945, as a result of the Moscow negotiations held in March 1945.[1] The Kosice Government Program was the cornerstone of the post-1945 political system. Because of this and from the point of view of the nationality question it was of utmost importance. Without a detailed analysis of the Kosice Program, the nationality policy of the Prague regime cannot be fully understood.

Foremost, the nationality policy of the Kosice Program made a very sharp distinction between Slavic (Czech and Slovak), and non-Slavic (German and Hungarian) nations. Some antecedents of this distinction far in advance of the Kosice platform clearly indicated that the forthcoming Republic would make serious efforts to eliminate the non-Slavic ethnic groups. Jan Sverma was one of those who months before had determined the guidelines for the Kremlin-controlled Czech and Slovak Communists. J. Sverma, in his October 3, 1944 address to the Slovenská národna rada (Slovak National

Council), among others, said:[2] "The new (Czechoslovak) Republic cannot be founded on the basis of artificial ties, agreements, but as a brotherly Republic of three Slavic nations: the Czechs, Slovaks and Carpathian Ukrainians. In this Republic, Czechs will be the masters of the Czech lands, Slovaks of Slovakia, and Carpathian Ukrainians of Carpathian Ukraine." At that time, Jan Sverma did not yet know that the new Republic would consist of only two state-forming nations: the Czechs and Slovaks because the Carpathian Ukraine would, similar to the Baltic states, be incorporated into the Soviet Union. The incorporation of the Carpathian Ukraine (Podkarpatská Rus; Kárpátalja) into the USSR was already a topic at a Moscow meeting of Czech and Slovak Communists (Klement Gottwald, Václav Kopecky, Ladislav Novomesky, J. Való, E. Fris) in the first half of December 1944. According to the report of V. Kopecky, himself a participant at the meeting, the presiding Georgi Dimitrov, former secretary general of the Comintern, then head of the division of foreign affairs of the Central Committee of the Communist Party of the Soviet Union, expressed his convictions concerning the Carpathian Ukraine that the will of the Ukrainian people must be respected and that the mass movement of Carpathian Ukrainians should not be hindered.[3]

In a stenograpically recorded dialogue with Compton Mackenzie which took place between July 1943, and May 1944, President Benes, while in exile, voluntarily offered Carpathian Ukraine and Eastern Poland to the USSR by saying:[4] "We are content that they should join the present Ukraine." Very characteristically, and completely in line with the Yalta spirit, the Western powers had no objection to the incorporation of the Carpathian Ukraine into the USSR in June 1945. The attitude of the Western powers has changed considerably between the wars and in order to prove this let us refer to T. G. Masaryk's remarks[5] about the 1919 peace treaty negotiations on the Carpathian Ukraine: "Our allies, the Western powers, would not wish to see Russians on the southern side of the Carpathian Mountains. Russia's defeat enabled us to incorporate the Carpathian Ukraine into Czechoslovakia."

Now, it seems clear why the Soviet Union has always so enthusiastically supported the creation of a "national state" in the newly founded Czechoslovak Republic. Even at the 1947 Paris peace treaty negotiations she was the only one of the great powers to do so.[6]

The nationality policy of the Kosice Government Program aimed at eliminating all the non-Slavic minorities in order to create a national state, was proclaimed in the new Constitution promulgated May 9, 1948. According to the Declaration[7] of this Constitution: "We have decided now that our liberated State shall be a national state, rid of all hostile elements, living in brotherly harmony with the family of Slav States and in friendship with all peace-loving nations of the world." (§ 9) The same objective is expressed in one of the basic articles of the Constitution:8) "The Czechoslovak Republic is a unitary State of two Slav nations possessing equal rights, the Czechs and the Slovaks." (Article II/1)

The new nationality policy was carried out generally by the Czechoslovak and in Slovakia by the Slovak Communist party. It is based upon heretofore unpublished documents written by key figures of the Communist Party of Czechoslovakia, such as Klement Gottwald, Bohumir Smeral, Jan Sverma, and Václav Kopecky, while in exile in Moscow. They formulated the guiding principles of the Kosice Government Program, and even drafted the most significant chapters of the Program. It is interesting to note that, for instance, Václav Kopecky drafted chapters 4 on foreign policy, 6 on the national rights of the Slovaks, and 9 dealing with the status of the Germans and Hungarians in postwar Czechoslovakia.9)

In order to camouflage the intentions of the forthcoming combined efforts for Sovietization and Slavification, the Stalinist Communist leadership and its bourgeois fellow travellers invented and applied the theory of collective guilt in relation to the role that the national minorities supposedly played in destroying the pre-Munich Republic. They argued that both minority groups should be held responsible for the creation of the foreign policy constellation which culminated in the Munich four-power agreement of 1938.10)

President Benes quickly and affirmatively responded to the idea of collective responsibility all the more because his policy concerning the peaceful coexistence of different ethnic minorities had never been sincere. He made an all-important statement11) about the implementation of the Kosice Program in his brief stay in Bratislava en route from Kosice to Prague: "After this war there will be no minority rights in the spirit of the old system which began after the First World War. After punishing all the delinquents who committed crimes against the state, the overwhelming majority of the Germans and Hungarians must leave Czechoslovakia. This is our resolute standpoint ... Our people cannot live with the Germans and Hungarians in our fatherland."

Dr. Gustáv Husák, the most talented and highly influential leader of the Communist Party of Slovakia in the immediate postwar years and now in the Dubcek-regime, readily shared President Benes' views by saying:12) "The past seven tormenting years have changed our opinion and the opinion of the majority of the world on the minority politics. This is the fourth lesson we are drawing from the fall of 1938, a lesson pointing to the historic crime of the Hungarian and German minorities in the destruction of the Republic of Czechoslovakia, a lesson showing the sufferings of the population of Czechoslovakia, a lesson on the inevitability of expelling and exchanging the minority populations in the interest of the European peace and the peaceful coexistence of the nations."

1945 through 1948 was the first period of the implementation of the Kosice Government Program. Its principal error was to convert a multinational state into a national one by means of force. Although there was dualism in the restored legislative, executive and judicial functions, significant divergences showed: on the one hand, in Bohemia, Moravia and Silesia and, on the other, in Slovakia. But there was perfect harmony between Prague's centralism and Slovakia's local organs in the way they dealt with minority policies. The presidential constitutional decree No. 33/1945 (August 2, 1945) revoked the Czechoslovak citizenship of all Hungarians (then about 600,000) and of all Germans (then around 3,000,000) on the peculiar grounds that they all were enemies of the newly founded Republic. Subsequently, hundreds of discriminatory laws and statutes reminiscent of the Nuremberg legislation were issued by the president, the central organs, as well as the local administration which completely outlawed both minorities. Living under such inhumane conditions, the German ethnic group had absolutely no possibility for any means of legal defense. Their properties were confiscated and almost the whole ethnic group expelled. The situation of the Germans became more serious when in July, 1945, their expulsion from Czechoslovakia was authorized by the Allied and Associated Powers at Potsdam. The Potsdam conference did not authorize the transfer of the Hungarian population from Czechoslovakia but, due to the increasing Soviet and Czechoslovak pressures, the Budapest government was compelled to conclude an agreement with Czechoslovakia on the population exchange which was signed on February 27, 1946. The sole democratic and human aspect of this Agreement was that it allowed the Hungarian government to set up its diplomatic missions in Czechoslovakia for the purpose of rendering legal aid to that portion of the Hungarian minority which was designated by the Prague government for transfer to Hungary. Without this legal aid and intervention the Hungarian ethnic minority would have been de jure and de facto in the same situation in which the defenseless Germans[13] found themselves.

Between 1945 and 1949, there were two turning points in the course of the development of the Kosice Government Program,—first, the May 26, 1946 general elections in Czechoslovakia when the Communist Party obtained a relative majority: 43.25% in Bohemia, 34.46% in Moravia and Silesia, and 30.48% in Slovakia, while in Soviet-occupied Hungary, in November 1945, the Communist Party received only 17% of all of the votes. The comparatively small proportion of votes cast for the Communists in Hungary strengthened Czechoslovakia's position within the Soviet bloc in its fight against the Hungarian minority. Secondly, a secret agreement was reached on the basis of the *status quo* in the summer of 1948 by the Communist Party of Czechoslovakia and the Hungarian Working People's (Communist) Party on the Hungarian minority problem. The chief obstacles to the friendship and mutual assistance pact concluded between the two countries in April 1949 were thus eliminated.

Beginning in the second half of October 1948, first in Bratislava, then elsewhere, Czechoslovak citizenship has been gradually regranted to the members of the Hungarian minority, a positive step on the road toward normalization. Undoubtedly, since then the position of the Hungarian ethnic group has improved.

As a consequence of the racially biased policies, far-reaching quantitative changes have occurred on the ethnic map of Czechoslovakia. From a statistical point of view, Czechoslovakia, beginning in 1945, lost its prewar multinational character—from 1948 onwards, 94% of its population consisted of Czechs and Slovaks, and only 6% of minority groups, while in the pre-Munich Republic the minorities constituted 36% of the whole population.[14]

As a direct result of the implementation of the nationality policy of the Kosice Government Program, the German ethnic group comprising several million virtually disappeared and the Hungarian minority suffered significant losses between 1945 and 1948.[15]

On the threshold of the Stalinist era, Czechoslovakia once more experienced the worst type of national chauvinism stemming this time from the confused ideology of the February 1948 coup d'état. Once again, though for a very brief period, a combination of nationalism and class warfare with a sharp racial overtone flared up. This evidently downward trend of morality captured the thinking of the political leadership in the heart of Europe before and during the Second World War. This new political leadership flagrantly disregarded all the constructive teachings and warnings of the past by flinging open the door to Racism so detrimental in Central Europe. In this postwar period, the Stalinist regimes prolonged the policies of racial prejudices through the application of collective responsibility toward certain nations. Their "laws" evinced little, if any, differences from those of the Nazi regime. Due to this racially biased attitude, 70% of the total number (8055) of war criminals convicted in Slovakia on the grounds of the so-called Retribucny dekret[16] was of Hungarian ethnic origin, although, in 1945, the Hungarian ethnic minority constituted only 18% of Slovakia's population and the Hungarian ethnic group did not support the Nazi regime more strongly than the Slovaks. It is of importance to recognize this Stalinist "proletarian racism" as having been for years—since the inauguration of the Kosicky vládny program (Kosice Government Program)—the main feature of the nationality policies. This proletarian racism was contemporaneously recognized even by an influential, prolific Slovak Communist author, A. Kalina, who in his article, "Slováci, Novoslováci, Reslováci",

340

readily acknowledged the presence of racism in Czechoslovakia's Moscow-directed nationality policies by saying:[17] "Our situation is as follows: whether or not we are willing to acknowledge the existence of our racial laws, their existence is proven by practice." This statement is all the more important because it was published in a Communist weekly organ founded, owned and edited by Dr. Gustáv Husák. But it should be emphasized that from about the middle of 1948, the regime changed its course to general class warfare thereby excluding large groups from the Czech and Slovak nations. Among all the nations of the country, the Czechs were affected most adversely by this new national policy because they had the best-developed and largest bourgeoisie which was en bloc excluded from the concept of the "proletarian nation." Theoretically, a proletarian nation could be composed of the following three layers only: industrial workers, working peasantry, and progressive intelligentsia. Starting with the February 1948 events, this social policy was energetically implemented in order to liquidate any remnants of bourgeois nationalism. As a result an entirely new social stratification, the proletarian nation, emerged.

SOCIAL COMPOSITION OF THE CZECHOSLOVAK SOCIETY[18]
(in 1000)

Year	Industrial Workers	%	Other Employees	%	Coop. Farmers	%	Other Producers	%	Small Farmers	%	Free Occupat.	%	Capi- talists	%
1950	6,950	56.4	2,028	16.4	20	0.0			2,500	20.3	470	3.8	378	3.1
1961	7,738	56.3	3,834	27.9	1,466	10.6	164	1.2	484	3.5	60	0.5		
1965	8,201	58.1	4,122	29.2	1,218	8.6	161	1.2	351	2.5	54	0.4		

Keeping in mind the rigid Soviet theory of nationality and its application which is in conflict with the vital interests of oppressed peoples, let us now look at the essence of the Soviet concept. According to Lenin's dogma, all mankind is inevitably progressing towards its ultimate destiny, the classless Communist society where all nations of the world are melted into a uniform, new proletarian race.[19] Evidently, Lenin's prophecy is as utopian a scheme for the eradication of nationalism (and of nations) as was the Russian linguist. Marr's once popular theory that the conversion of tsarist Russia into a proletarian country would necessarily result in an entirely new, heretofore unknown, proletarian Russian language. In the early fifties, Stalin's authority was needed to expose and refute the falsity of that statement.

It is interesting to note that Czechoslovakia's socioeconomic development since the late fifties sharply disproved the applicability of Lenin's theorem. Despite the "proletarian nature" of the social composition of the country's population, the age-long nationality problem has reappeared and the Communist leadership has been forced to meet the challenge by promulgating the 1960 Constitution which—quite contrary to the 1948 Constitution—did acknowledge the existence and positive role of ethnic minorities. This new, socialist Constitution appears to contain ambiguous elements. On the one hand, its Chapter Two Article 20 (2) proclaimes[20] that "The equality of all citizens without regard to nationality and race shall be guaranteed." In addition to this, Article 25 of the 1960 Constitution declares that "The State shall ensure citizens of Hungarian, Ukrainian and Polish nationality every opportunity and all means for education in their mother tongue and for their cultural development." (p. 59) The Constitution does not contain any positive guarantees. In regard to the *above-stated minority* rights the 1960 socialist Constitution is seemingly nothing but a return to the bourgeois concept of cultural rights with the exception that it was not granted universally because the German minority was implicitly denied this "privilege". On the other hand, the 1960 Constitution negated any autonomy still enjoyed by the Slovaks as a result of the 1945 Kosice platform. This socialist Constitution eliminated virtually all the legislative functions of the Slovenská národna rada (Slovak National Council) and abolished the all-important institution of the Sbor povereníkov (Board of Commissioners), thus Slovakia and the Slovaks again came under the administration of the Prague centralism so reminiscent of the pre-Munich Republic.

The present socialist Constitution does not acknowledge the Slovaks de facto as an ethnically distinct nation. The 1960 Constitution recreated the same familiar source of nationality struggles for self-determination which were such characteristic features of the Slovak past under both the Hungarian or Czech domination prior to the Second World War. And the Novotny regime tore open the old scars of the Slovaks. It can safely be said that there has been no striking difference between the Benes and Novotny concepts of the Slovak nation because both concepts were deeply rooted in the same source: power politics in the service of centralism.[21] Neither was willing to recognize the political entity of the ethnically distinct Slovak nation and to act accordingly. They did not so much as allow some kind of cultural autonomy for the Slovaks, though Vladimír Clementis, a Slovak statesman and intellectual, decades earlier proved that not only Slovak separatists but also Communists fought for the idea of self-determination. On June 4, 1935, in his address at the Prague Parliament, Clementis[22] made these remarks: "We Slovak Communists are firmly for our national self-determination which we are about to realize in brotherly link with the proletariat of all nations of the state."

Up to now, the Dubcek regime has reached in its liberalization trend the farthest point of any political systems—except Switzerland and maybe a few other countries—in its acknowledgment of the ethnically and politically distinct entity of the nation by applying the principle of federalization and self-determination.[23] This is, most likely, the highest achievement of the Czech and Slovak intelligentsia which has been solidly united behind the democratization process. This reform movement made indeed an unbelievably big step forward by promising to re-establish the minority rights and putting emphasis on the political representation of national minorities, Germans included. According to two experts on nationalism of the Dubcek regime, J. Zvara and J. Sindelka:[24] "Political representation of national minorities is a serious problem. It should be the minimum requirement to create state secretariats in the central government as well as in the Czech and the Slovak governments; also, parliamentary committees and various commissions in both the state and party organs. Present cultural associations are not the best possible forms of political representation of national minorities."

On the eve of the implementation of these plans, the Warsaw Pact troops began occupying Czechoslovakia on August 20, 1968 thereby reintroducing the centuries-old principle of divide and rule in the political activities of Eastern and Central Europe. Now the Kremlin has little hope of rekindling ideological enthusiasm among the Czech, Slovak and other Communists because the masses, especially in Czechoslovakia, have displayed continuing stubborn and near-unanimous resistance to Soviet aims. In this situation when no lasting *modus vivendi* appears to be shaping up between Prague and Moscow, the Kremlin is being forced to atomize any massive resistance cropping up anywhere in the Soviet orbit. For this purpose the nationality problem can be used as a weapon by the Kremlin. The Slovaks against the Czechs, and the large Hungarian ethnic minority in Transylvania and even in Vojvodina against Rumania or Yugoslavia if these countries are not willing to yield to Soviet pressure. An indication that the time has become ripe for applying *divide et impera* tactics may be the assumption of a key role by Dr. Gustáv Husák, an experienced Slovak opportunist known for his anti-Czech and anti-Semitic views. The divisive role designated for Dr. Husák is all the more likely because his loyalty to the Soviet Union is the only feature of his personality which has never changed and has never been questioned since his first major political task assigned to him in conjunction with the Slovak National Uprising against the German troops in August 1944. Undoubtedly, Dr. Husák is well equipped to execute the new, as of yet partly known dictates of the USSR. Already in the spring of 1945 he eloquently expressed his unchanging views[25] of the Soviet Union: "Let no one be mistaken in one thing: no one and nothing can change the Eastern orientation of the Slovak nation, and its Slavic and Sovietophil conception."

I am fully cognizant that I cannot analyze in greater detail the complex conditions of the nationality question in Czechoslovakia with a view to making comments on the unforeseeable future due to the present brutal Soviet intervention. But one thing seems to be sure. It is truly admirable how the Czech and the Slovak nations have recently carried the banner of their democratic traditions by which they became united against Soviet objectives. Moreover, it seems to be evident that in this true mass resistance the teachings of T. G. Masaryk on democracy as a political expression of humanism as well as his resolute anti-Bolshevik and anti-Marxist views are being reflected. This mass feeling may indicate that the traditional Russo-Czech cordial friendship has collapsed.

The reform thinkers of Central Europe, similar to the present-day Czech and Slovak cultural elite, have always been convinced that the peaceful co-existence of ethnically different groups can be lastingly insured only within the framework of federations based upon a morally strongly rooted concept of freedom. The current experience in Czechoslovakia and elsewhere in the Soviet sphere has demonstrated that the masses are prepared for and longing for such a solution. Now the only prerequisite for its fulfillment would be the neutralization of this much-tried region from any outside influence stemming from the power politics of East-West relations.

Washington, D.C. September 20, 1968.

1) Cf. Chapter "Moskovské rokovania" (Moscow Negotiations) in Gustáv Husák's monograph **Svedectvo o Slovenskom národnom povstaní.** Bratislava, Vydavateľstvo politickej literatury, 1964. See also Zdenek Fierlinger, **Ve službách CSR.** II. Prague, 1948. Both authors participated in the Moscow negotiations and rightly emphasize in their books that the program of the Communist Party of Czechoslovakia was on the Moscow agenda which included the most essential points of the Kosice Government Program including the new concept of the Czecho-Slovak relationship as well as the idea of population transfer.

2) G. Husák, **Op. cit.,** 522.

3) G. Husák, **Opt. cit.,** 539.

4) C. Mackenzie, **Dr. Benes.** London: George G. Harrap & Co., 1946, 290.

5) T. G. Masaryk, **Světová revoluce.** Prague, 1925, 301.

6) See Dalibor M. Krno, **Jednali jsme mir s Madarskem.** Prague, Orbis, 1947, 317. D. Krno emphatically stated that the USSR was the only great power which fully supported the objectives and methods of the Prague government to solve the Hungarian and German minority questions.

7-8) **The Constitution of the Czechoslovak Republic; Constitutional Act of May 9th, 1948.** Prague, Czechoslovak Ministry of Information, 1948.

9) Cf. Bohuslav Lastovicka's article "Vznik a vyznam Kosického vládniho programu," **Ceskoslovensky Casopis Historicky,** vol. 8, no. 4, 1960, 449-471.

10) Jozef Jablonicky, **Slovensko na prelome; Zápas o vitazstvo národnej a demokratickej revolucie na Slovensku.** Bratislava, Vydavateľstvo politickej literatury, 1965, 401.

11) Cas, Bratislava, vol. 2, no. 19, May 12, 1945.

12) G. Husák "Poucenia z jesene 1938," Nové Slovo, vol. 2, no. 20, October 12, 1945, 1-3.

13) For a more detailed review of the de jure and de facto situation of national minorities in post-1945 Czechoslovakia see Francis S. Wagner's study entitled "Hungarians in Czechoslovakia 1945-1949", a part of a collective work, Hungarians in Czechoslovakia. New York: Research Institute for Minority Studies, 1959, 11-37; Samuel Cambel, Revolucny rok 1945. Bratislava, 1965; Konfiskace, správa a prevod neprátelského majetku. Prague, 1947; E. Benes, Sest let v exilu, and his Pameti; Precan, Slovenské národne povstanie — Dokumenty, etc., and Kálmán Janics' extensive book review "Két történelmi tanulmány a szlovákiai magyar kérdésről," Irodalmi Szemle, Bratislava, vol. 11, no. 5, 1968, 439-454.

14) Rudé Právo, Prague, August 16, 1968, 5.

15) Cf. "Nationalities in Czechoslovakia, 1950-1965" in Statistická rocenka Republiky Ceskoslovenské, 1966. Prague, 1966, 77.

16) Cf. Dr. Julius Viktory's official report published in Pravda, Bratislava, March 20, 1948.

17) A. Kalina, "Slováci, Novoslováci, Reslováci," Nové Slovo, vol. 3, Nos. 32-33, 1946, 20.

18) Statisticka rocenka Republiky Ceskoslovenské, 1966. Prague, 1966, 92.

19) M. D. Kammari, "V. I. Lenin ob osnovnykh zakonomernostiakh natsional'nogo razvitiia," Voprosy Filosofii, Moscow, no. 4, 1960. See also Francis S. Wagner "Nationalism vs. Federalism in Historical Perspective," publ. in this book, and Frederick C. Barghoorn, Soviet Russian Nationalism, New York: Oxford University Press, 1956, 232, and J. V. Stalin, Marksizm i natsional'nyi vopros. Moscow, 1946.

20) The Constitution of the Czechoslovak Socialist Republic. Prague, Orbis, 1960, 57.

21) See E. Benes, Masarykovo pojetí ideje národni a problém jednoty ceskoslovenské. Bratislava, 1935, 22. See also Karol Sidor, Slovenská politika no pode prazského snemu 1918-1938. Bratislava, 1943.

22) Francis S. Wagner, "National Communism: From Clementis to Tito," Free World Forum, vol. 1, no. 4, 1959, 30, and K. Sidor, Op. cit.

23) The plenary session of the Czechoslovak government held August 13, 1968, approved the guidelines of the federalization of Czechoslovakia (by creating the Czech lands and Slovakia for this purpose), as well as the minority rights for all nationalities, including the Germans, for the first time since the war. See a CTK news report in Rudé Právo, Prague, August 16, 1968, I.

24) Juraj Zvara and Jan Sindelka, "Zijeme v jedné zemi; Národnostní mensiny a jejich práva," Rudé Právo, Prague, August 16, 1968, 5.

25) Dr. Gustáv Husák, "Z Bystrice do Bratislavy," Nové Slovo, vol. 2, no. 1, June 1, 1945, 1. See also G. Husák, "O pomere Cechov a Slovákov," Nové Slovo, vol. 3, no. 11, 1946, 1-3.

THE CHANGING IMAGE OF T. G. MASARYK
BETWEEN 1945 AND 1968

FRANCIS S. WAGNER

UP to the end of the Second World War, the portrayal of the founder of the Republic was conspicuously uniform. President Masaryk (1850-1937), especially in Czech and Slovak writings, was highly esteemed as a statesman and a world-renowned philosopher of humanism who possessed morally unique personal characteristics. Regardless of their differing political viewpoints, this positive approach has overwhelmingly been shared by such leading Masaryk-scholars as Frantisek Krejci, Emánuel Rádl, J. L. Hromádka, Josef Král, J. B. Kozák, Josef Tvrdy, V. K. Skrach, I. A. Bláha, Karel Capek, Zdenek Nejedly, St. K. Neumann, F. X. Salda, Jindrich Kohn, Emil Utitz, and J. L. Fischer. This image survived even the most hectic days of the Communist coup d'état of February 1948, when all non-Marxist phenomena of pre-Munich Czechoslovakia were vehemently denounced. The prestige of the late President ran so high that even Communist leader Klement Gottwald, as the newly elected president of CSR, made a pilgrimage to Masaryk's resting place at Lány after the Putsch to insure, at least symbolically, the legal continuation between the first and the post-1948 republics.

Quite parallel with the Kremlin-dictated Bolshevization of the Communist Party of Czechoslovakia, a series of monographs, articles and commemorative items have appeared since the early fifties representing a sharp turn in the heretofore basicly affirmative Masaryk-interpretation. As an aftermath of the February 1948 Putsch, Václav Kopecky, a high-ranking Party figure, criticized Masaryk's views on Communism.[1]

On the basis of the late President's anti-Marxist views, Václav Král denounced Masaryk's "counterrevolutionary" and "anti-Soviet" policy during the Great October Socialist Revolution (1917-1921) and afterwards.[2]

Following the Soviet pattern, Czech and Slovak Communist sources on the basis of a one-sidedly selected and misinterpreted collection of documents, reiterated that Masaryk conducted a policy contrary to the interests of the nation and the people.[3]

Foreign expert Jiri Hájek sought to minimize the role President Woodrow Wilson played in the establishment of Czechoslovakia,[4] and thereby added a new color to the Masaryk picture by portraying him as an agent of Western, chiefly U.S., imperialism.

The downgrading of T. G. Masaryk became a policy during the years of the Siroky-Novotny regime up to January 1968. This was all the more so because Masaryk was a sharp critic of the Russian spirit permeating tsarist and Bolshevik times alike and a very successful opponent of the philosophy of Marxism-Leninism. Therefore, Julius Dolansky, also an influential Party leader, bitterly attacked Masaryk for his activities in Russia prior to the Revolution of October 1917.[5]

Mikhail A. Silin, a leading Soviet expert on Czechoslovakian affairs who after the February Putsch of 1948 became Soviet ambassador to Prague, reviewed with more hostility than anyone before the theory and workings of bourgeois politics in Czechoslovakia. According to Silin, the pre-Munich state with its anti-Soviet tendencies under the influence of T. G. Masaryk was a hotbed of reactionary forces, which caused the Republic to lose its significance completely for progressive mankind.[6]

Since January, 1968, the Dubcek reform movement has made a breakthrough in several segments of public life which, in turn, has created a more or less objective Masaryk portrait. The reform movement revaluated the country's historical past on the basis of its progressive traditions. Thus, the regime necessarily designated an honorable role for T. G. Masaryk by placing him among the greatest personalities of the past such as Jan Hus, Petr Helcicky, J. A. Comenius, Frantisek Palacky, Karel Havlicek-Borovsky, Bozena Nemcová and P. O. Hviezdoslav. Milan Machovec's book[7] mirrors the Masaryk portrait as reproduced by the Dubcek regime. The author, an internationally famed scholar (b. 23 Aug. 1925), has been associated since 1953 with the Faculty of Philosophy at Charles University in Prague as head of the Seminar on Religion and Atheism. Though he also found fault with Masaryk's theses on the philosophy of human existence as well as his bourgeois theory of politics, Machovec at the same time objectively showed Masaryk as an outstanding ethical philosopher whose humanism was of lasting nature and acknowledged his excellence in leading his nation's struggle for independence. Thus, Dr. Machovec has essentially returned to the positive standpoint of pre-1945 Masaryk scholars. In summary, Dr. Machovec said: "Masaryk will have an honorable place among the non-socialist and relatively 'leftist' politicians of the twentieth century in the company of such men as Roosevelt, Gandhi and similar ones." (p. 12)

It is evident also from our survey of the changing portrait of T. G. Masaryk that his life and works should be scrutinized more objectively in order to depict the whole man. A thorough, objective research ought to be done on his multi-faceted scholarly works and political activities. Understandably then, this scholarly investigation should in no way be dependent upon the chameleon-like political situation. Undoubtedly, the central theme of such an inquiry should be Masaryk's political philosophy and ethics. Though Masaryk failed to apply consistently the federative system as a far-reaching practical solution for the centuries-old problems of small nations, and though his views on the nationality question were not entirely free of errors, he nonetheless attained the highest peak in political philosophy of our times. And this is attributable to the fact that his freedom-based ethics necessarily constituted an organic part of his philosophy according to which democracy was the political expression of humanity. This innate synthesis of politics and morality in Masaryk's mind captured the interests of thinkers in the Czechoslovak reform movement of 1968 and led to the revaluation of the Masaryk problem. But they are still far from understanding Masaryk who ended his memoirs with the sentence: "Jesus, not Caesar, is the true meaning of history and democracy".

1) V. Kopecky, T. G. Masaryk a komunisté. Prague, Kulturne propagaeni oddeleni sekretariátu UV KSC, 1960. 31 p.

2) V. Král, O Masarykove a Benesove kontrarevolucni protisovetské politice. 1st ed. Prague, Státni nak. pol. lit., 1953. 234 p. Published also in Russian entitled O kontrrevoliutsionnoi i antisovetskoi politike Masaryka i Benesha. Moscow, Izd-vo inostrannoi lit-ry, 1955.

3) Dokumenty o protilidové a protinárodni politice T. G. Masaryka. 2d ed. Prague, Orbis, 1953. 269 p.

4) Jiri S. Hájek, Wilsonovská legenda v dejinách CSR. 1st ed. Prague, Státni nakl. pol. lit., 1953. 217 p.

5) J. Dolansky, Masaryk a Rusko predrevolucni. 1st ed. Prague, Nakl. Ceskoslovenské akademie ved, 1959. 322 p.

6) M. A. Silin, Kritika burzhuaznoi ideologii i pobeda marksizma-leninizma v Chekhoslovakii. Moscow, 1960. 212 p.

7) M. Machovec, Tomás G. Masaryk; Studie s ukázkami z Masarykovych spisu. 1st ed. Prague, Svobodné slovo, 1968. 261 p. (Odkazy pokrokovych osobnosti nasi minulosti. Sv. 24)

IV

ECONOMIC PROBLEMS

MICRO- OR MACRO-ECONOMICS*) OF THE CENTRAL EUROPEAN NATIONS

RICHARD K. BARTONIEK

THE West European nations now realize that a Common Market of several nations is necessary in order to raise their standards of living, competitive strength and to apply successfully modern production methods. Practically speaking, the Soviet Union is also a Common Market. East of the Carpathians there are no internal customs lines; no tariffs; one currency exists; unhindered facilities for long distance transport; and similar trade methods prevail. Thus the Soviet Union expects to reach the living standards of other "common markets" like the U.S.A., Canada, Australia and Western Europe. The economic future of the next decades belongs to such common markets. Their political form should be federalism or true "confederation" within which Macro-Economics can be practiced. Lacking this Common Market organization, small nations are and will continue to be at a great disadvantage in international competition while their standard of living remains at a low level.

Will not the multinational area between Western Europe and the Soviet Union be permitted to develop its own Common Market? How long will this area remain in its economic straight jacket of miserable micro-étatism which is so obvious to Central European visitors.

A real precedent for a multinational Central European Common Market

The area of the Habsburg Monarchy up to World War I formed practically the nucleus of a Common Market. It had an excellent silver-gold currency, freedom of movement for men and goods without customs barriers at state frontiers, no passport and visa obligations. Although its political structure was outmoded, from an economic and historical-geographical viewpoint, the area formed a natural unit joined together by the Danube and its numerous tributaries. There were rich natural resources[1] of iron ore, coal and oil deposits, natural gas, water energy, vast forests and fertile lowlands.

With the exception of cotton and tropical plants, agriculture could produce all the foodstuffs and textiles for a population of 50 to 100 million. Moreover, its economic institutions were not unfavorable to growth and development. The internal customs barriers had long since been abolished; long distance transportation and communication were unhindered. Under such favorable conditions some 47,000 km long railways were built between 1867 and 1913. (See map)[2] The map shows how much better developed the railroad system was within the Austro-Hungarian "Common Market" area than to the South and East: Rumania, the Balkans and the Ukraine. The length of navigable rivers exceeded 11,000 km. In fact, plans were already under way to connect the Danube river system with the Elbe and the Rhine rivers. The monetary system was so exemplary that the American dollar was named after the famous Austrian Thaler.[3] Before the outbreak of World War I, in my childhood, gold coins of ten and twenty crowns were in common circulation. The credit system, public finances, taxes, cooperation between complementary regions were well developed, and administrative and statistical methods had reached a comparatively high level.

Economic fragmentation after World War I

After 1919, the well-built railway system of the Danubian area (see map) was splintered by the boundaries of the newly created small states. The main arteries of communication, e.g., between Vienna and Budapest, Vienna and Triest, Budapest and Fiume, crossed so many frontiers that transportation and travelling were paralyzed. Several thousand kilometers of solidly built railroads and highways became overgrown and unused. Not only tariff walls were erected between the Succession States but bitter tariff wars frequently erupted. Formalities of customs declarations, export and import licenses became so complicated that perishable foodstuffs could not profitably be shipped from Hungary to Vienna and Bohemia. Moreover, the trade in manufactured goods and raw materials fell off to a large extent.

In 1913, Austro-Hungarian post offices handled 125 million parcels and 65 million money orders. Because of the new state frontiers and export-import license requirements, the number of parcels mailed dropped to one sixth, money to one third—of which the majority were inland. The international credit and money transfer system broke down almost completely.[4] Old public debts were divided between the Succession States but never paid; each new state created its own currency (one worse than the other); bank notes were printed without reserves to back them up, nullified and withdrawn several times. Inflation between 1920 and 1925 reached unprecedented levels; in consequence, savings dwindled, life and other

MAP 3

RAILWAY AND ROAD SYSTEMS OF THE DANUBIAN AREA

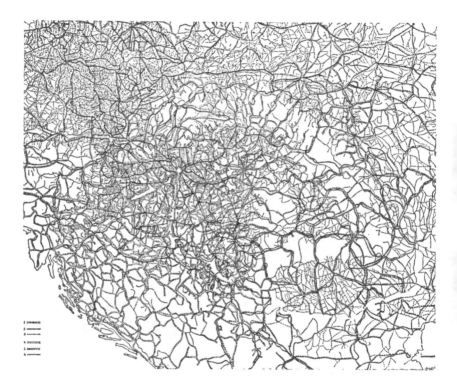

1. Double track railroads.
2. Single track railroads.
3. Narrow gauge railroads.
4. First class highways.
5. Second class roads.
6. Third class roads.

insurance policies became a farce. Direct money transfer from one place to even a neighboring town in another state could not be accomplished without costly and time consuming procedures through the National Bank systems. In Zürich, the national currency units of the Danubian states were quoted below two cents.[5] The balance of payments[6] between 1920 and 1937 deteriorated so much that heavy foreign debts were incurred which aggravated the situation. In the thirties, the economic crisis further dislodged the price system and trade balances. Several prominent economists, e.g., the Hungarian banker, Elemér Hantos, elaborated detailed proposals to improve the monetary, communication, trade and financial systems of the Central European states (See his "Mitteleuropa" books). The Stresa Conference in 1932,[7] the Tardieu and Hodza plans in the thirties tried unsuccessfully to improve the basically erroneous economic system of micro-étatism.

Then intensive pressure and interference were brought to bear by Germany, Italy and finally by the Soviet Union. Beside the payment of heavy war damages and requirements of the armies in the years 1944-1948, the small Danubian countries were obliged to start reconstruction from scratch.

A period of experimentation after 1945

A straight jacket, an étatistic kind of micro-economic was formally re-established under the eye of the Red Army. But even after the Communist takeover of the East European countries, the isolation and estrangement between neighboring countries increased for a period of about fifteen years from 1947 to 1962. During this decade there was scant intercourse over state frontiers with the exception of party and government officials or delegations, and collective groups of visitors. Family members separated by frontiers could not visit although physically they were perhaps only ten or twenty kilometers apart. After 1948 the Yugoslav frontier was completely closed toward the neighboring states, the whole area being sealed off toward the West by an Iron Curtain. Such measures so effectively cut off travel and trade, that one could only dream of a trip from Budapest to Vienna, Ungvár-Uzhorod to Kosice-Kassa or Kolozsvár-Cluj to Zagreb or Prague—which before 1918 had been such a simple journey. Most people gave up after unsuccessful attempts to get passports and visas. International trade was and continues to be strictly bilateral, a continuation of the rigid bilateral quota trade system in existence before 1944. All trade is now done exclusively by one Communist state bureaucracy with another state bureaucracy. Each export or import item is considered individually within quota agreements by a series of offices and the two National Banks. Pressures are exerted on all sides, premiums given or denied amounting to

250-400 per cent above the official rate of exchange. Dumping in exports is practized systematically by all Communist states.

All East European Communist currencies, including the rubel, are nonconvertible paper currencies for domestic use only. They are not negotiable abroad and cannot be legally taken out of the country. There is a certain official exchange rate but beside this other multiple exchange rates exist for different purposes.[8] E.g., traveling from Vienna to Czechoslovakia, the official rate as given in guidebooks, is seven korunas to the dollar. But over a certain amount the traveler receives 14 and even 28 korunas to the dollar and the black market pays about 40 korunas. In commercial transactions the National Bank grants all sorts of premiums and deducts special surcharges according to the individual case. All this makes foreign trade a purely political and bureaucratic affair.

In Communist satellite countries, domestic prices have also two or three levels having very little relation to the cost of production. For example, in Hungary and Rumania, corn is usually more expensive than wheat while bread is cheaper than wheat, etc. The difference is paid by the State and usually collected from indirect taxes. Every three to five years a complete and arbitrarily fixed overhauling of the chaotic and rigid price system is arranged and a "new economic policy" announced which quickly degenerates into another official blunder and makes calculations uncertain. Within the Moscow led COMECON, the terms of trade between the USSR and individual Communist countries, are kept secret. But those who have access to these figures have found them slanted heavily in favor of the Soviet Union—the stronger party to the bargain. The Communist bloc has made great efforts for many years to establish its own "Socialist international price system" independent of the fluctuations of world markets but it has never succeeded and has been forced to return to price calculations based on world prices and the American dollar. In 1962/63, the Soviet Union and its satellites organized an International Bank for Clearing purposes (MBES = Mezhdunarodny Bank Ekonomicheskogo Sotrudnyichestva) which tried to operate with a "transferable clearing rubel." But, because the rubel has no international value, the Poles and others demanded the balance paid in gold which was refused by the Russians.[9]

A brighter future:
an independent Central European Common Market possible

More than twenty experimental years have elapsed since 1945 and fifty years since 1918, but the economic life in Central Europe is still very abnormal, micro-economic and over-bureaucratic. In 1912, a writer like Franz Kafka, or a poet like Rilke could have walked to the railway station in Prague, bought a ticket to Budapest, Paris,

Rome or London. They could have traveled without a passport to any European country, remain to study as long as their means allowed. Before 1915 an Hungarian engineer, a Czech scholar like Masaryk, a Rumanian lawyer from Transylvania, a businessman from Zagreb or Brünn did not require permission or passport to travel or stay abroad. But now?

Since 1962 most Communist regimes have relaxed somewhat the travel restrictions between their countries although remaining restricted for noncommunist countries. Yet in this respect it is still far from the no passport, no visa, no currency, no restrictions of the Common Market era before 1915. Today's tourist in the Danubian countries is under constant administrative control. He is required to show his passport, have five or six visas that he pays for, declare his currencies of so many denominations and produce other official papers. He must report to the police whenever he stays over a few days. On the other hand, returning to Vienna no one demands presentation of his currencies and statements about his plans, etc. In some respects, however, even free Austria and Switzerland have not yet returned to normalcy. Their own territories are too small for modern industries; their foreign trade is hampered by tariffs and other trade restrictions of other states. Now they are pressed between the East and West. Because they are neutral they cannot join the Western Common Market without causing political crisis.

The solution is a Common Market comprising all the small nations between Germany and Russia, neither isolated nor antagonistic to them. It is possible for two or three common markets to exist side by side in friendship and as good neighbors like Canada and the United States. As the West European Common Market evolved over a period of years so would the economic community of small nations in a neutralized Central European zone develop gradually. Finally, there would be not only a customs union but also a fully coordinated single monetary system. It may be noted that the Soviet Union introduced a currency unit nominally not very different from the American dollar (1 rubel = $1.10). Should not the other six or seven Central European currencies have the same basic unit and have a common Federal Board of National Banks? All bank notes would be federal Central European currency bank notes printed on one side with texts in the languages of all participating nations while on the other side, the text of the issuing and guaranteeing member state would be printed. They could, however, circulate freely in the entire area of the Common Market. Such a coordinated currency system would make possible the development of a single price system throughout the area within five to ten years. Because the production costs and prices would be easily compared, in the absence of internal tariffs—long-distance transport of goods and products would be advantageous and easy. Now that Central European countries have been industrialized, the antiquated communication system needs modernization, i.e., roads, trucks for long-distance hauling of perishable agricultural products, airlines, etc.; also, the use of water energy, bauxite, natural gas, etc., resources, navigable rivers, etc. need drastic improvement possible only within a Central European Common Market.[10]

*) The terms micro- and macro- economics are not used in the sense as Communist and some Western economists use them. Micro- and macro do not refer to enterprises but to States.

1) See the 24 volumes of **Die Österreichisch-Ungarische Monarchie in Wort und Bild.** Vienna 1886-1902.

2) E. Radisich: Dunatáj — **The Danubian Region.** Budapest. 1946, vol. II, p. 130.

3) In Bohemia, the valley of Saint Joachim was very rich in silver (at present its rich uranium mines are worked for the USSR). The famous silver Joachimsthaler was coined here since the 15th century. Well received the world over this Austrian Thaler became the ancestor of the American Dollar.

4) Leonhardt Compass. **Finanzielles Jahrbuch.** Band: Österreich; Ungarn; Yugoslavien, Rumanien, Tschechoslowakei, etc. Wien (Yearly publication on finances).

5) **Royal Institute of International Affairs,** South Eastern Europe. A political and economic survey. London 1939.

6) **League of Nations:** Balance of Payments, 1920-1937; **League of Nations:** International Trade Statistics, 1920-1938.

7) **League of Nations.** Report by the Stresa Conference for economic restoration of Central and Eastern Europe. Geneva 1932.

8) See the description of multiple rates of all East European paper currencies in the authentic **Pick's Currency Yearbook,** New York. (Last volume 1965/66.)

9) Early 1967 the Comecon countries held a conference in Budapest on their almost unsolvable present price, trade and currency problems.

10) Interesting ideas in this field may be found in the lecture of Dr. Joseph Klaus, Austrian Chancellor, given in Budapest, May 3, 1967 on "An active policy of international relations in the Danubian Valley" published in the **New Hungarian Quarterly.** Budapest. 1967, no. 27, pp. 3-9. In the same issue Tibor Pethő, a political commentator, favors "Modern forms of cooperation in the Danube Valley." pp. 10-17. See also the Budapest report of David Binder "Hungary Pursues a New Policy, Stressing Danube Cooperation" **(New York Times,** Oct. 2, 1967).

COOPERATIVES:

PROBLEMS AND SOLUTIONS

GEORGE KELER

BESIDES the Secret Police and the Communist party, cooperatives are probably among the most hated institutions behind the Iron Curtain, at least as far as the rural population is concerned. This applies first of all to the so called "Producers Cooperatives," the collective farms known in the free world under their Russian name "Kolkhos." For many years, the governments of the communist-dominated countries of Central and Eastern Europe have used every means of enticement and coercion in order to persuade the farmers to give up their independence and join such producers' cooperatives, handing over their land, animals, and farming equipment to them. The results of these endeavors depended entirely on the measure of the coercion applied and, accordingly, the extent to which collectivization has been carried through varies considerably among countries. It is nearly one hundred per cent in Hungary, Rumania, and Bulgaria, much less in Czechoslovakia and Eastern Germany, and the least in Poland where many of the collective farms were dissolved by the members after the thaw in 1956. The same happened, of course, also in Hungary during and after the October uprising, but there, not only the formerly existing collective farms were soon restored, but even the still independent farmers were subjected to increased pressure with the above-mentioned result.

In the communist countries both the producers cooperatives and the independent farmers, as far as there still exist any, are under the obligation of selling the greater part of their products to the government at prices fixed by the authorities. These products have to be handed over to the so-called "Farmers' Cooperatives"—multi-purpose cooperative societies whose other tasks are to supply the rural population with all kinds of goods and to further the activities of the producers' cooperatives. As there are no private traders, commodity distribution in the countryside is the monopoly of these cooperatives and the rural population depends entirely on them even for the supply of its most essential life needs.

Commodity distribution in the towns and the industrial areas is a state-monopoly and, as far as I am informed, Eastern Germany is the only communist country where there consumers' cooperatives in towns still exist, while in the other countries they have been dissolved and their shops have been taken over by the government. This, of course, was accomplished under "strictly democratic" forms, like in Budapest where about 100 of the more than 120,000 members of the local society attended the general meeting which unanimously voted for its dissolution. No mention at all was made of the assets of the society, and it was only natural that they became government property.

One category of cooperatives to be found in all the communist countries, both in the towns and in the countryside, are the cooperatives of handicraftsmen. Practically all craftsmen, with the exception of village barbers and cobblers, had to join these societies and hand oved to them their machines and tools. Here the procedure was extremely simple, as those who refused were cut off from all supplies of raw materials and had no other choice than to give up resistance. Even though there exists evereywhere an extensive black market in materials stolen by the workers from the factories, it is too risky to rely entirely on this source of supply, although it does serve as an indispensable supplement to meager allocations by the authorities.

There are also other kinds of cooperatives, such as those of the lawyers and solicitors. They portion out the cases among the members whose fees are paid in to a common pool out of which each member draws a salary fixed by the Board of the Society.

According to the Indian Constitution, the country is to be transformed into a "Cooperative Commonwealth" based on the high ideals of mutual aid and unselfish work for the common welfare of the people. To a superficial observer it may appear that the communist countries have reached this ideal stage but, unfortunately enough, the real state of things is very different. The difference between genuine cooperatives and those behind the Iron Curtain is exactly the same as between democracy and a peoples' democracy. On the paper, the constitution of the communist cooperatives is fully in keeping with the famous Rochdale principles but, as we have seen, membership is far from voluntary. Besides, and this is perhaps the most fundamental difference, the election of the functionaries of the cooperatives, just like the parliamentary elections, takes place on the basis of one single list of candidates nominated by the almighty Party. As a matter of principle, the elections are secret and the members have the right to cancel the names of candidates, but in practice very few dare take the risk. Anyway, whatever happens, there is always a majority of about 99.5 per cent.

It is a question of paramount importance to the countries concerned whether after liberation from communist dominance the cooperatives, reorganized on a democratic basis, would be able to fill the vacuum created by the complete suppression of private enterprise, and if so, to what extent? When trying to find an answer to this question I shall depart from agriculture which, in spite of the progressing urbanization of the population, still represents a substantial sector of the economic life of these countries.

One can safely presume that as soon as the peasants will be free to decide about their future their traditional individualism and their aversion to all forms of collectivism will result in a rapid dissolution of most of the "Producers' Cooperatives." On the other hand, the land reforms carried through by the then still semi-democratic governments immediately after the war had brought about the dismemberment of the land into small and often quite uneconomic units, partly because the main purpose of the reform was to satisfy as many people as possible, and also partly because the communists were already strong enough to bring their influence to bear in order to create in this way the prerequisites for future collectivization. Besides, as a result of urbanization and the insufferable working conditions in the "producers cooperatives," there is in the countryside a rapidly increasing lack of manpower, especially as far as the younger generation is concerned. The communist governments are making great efforts to make up for this deficiency by gradually replacing manpower by agricultural machines; and even if the supply of machines is still lagging far behind actual need, the mechanization of agriculture is a fact to be taken into consideration when planning for the future.

It is quite probable that most countries will undertake a revision of their abortive land reforms without, however, creating units large enough to allow the use of modern agricultural machines. There are also other installations, such as storage facilities, stables for breeders, milk separators, etc., which no individual small farmer can afford. There must be, therefore, a collective ownership and use of such machines and installations, and this is possible only on a cooperative basis. During the late thirties a certain number of cooperatives were formed in Hungary in order to secure small farmers facilities similar to those enjoyed by bigger landowners. And even if they have been in existence only a few years, the results achieved have been rather promising. I must admit, however, that, while there exist in many countries cooperatives for the joint ownership and use of agricultural machines, the type of cooperatives I am thinking of is relatively new and unproven. In Sweden, e.g., they have attempted encourage the formation of cooperatives of such type by legislative measures, but, as far as I am informed, only very few have been founded and at present only two of them are in function. Although it is true that they do not infringe upon the principle of private ownership they nonetheless involve to a certain extent the surrender of independence by the farmers, and it will therefore certainly need much persuasion to convince them of the advantages of the system.

As I mentioned before, in the Communist-dominated countries the bulk of agricultural products has to be handed over to the multi-purpose village cooperatives which, however, only act as agents of the respective governments. All processing, marketing, and exportation of products is done by state enterprises. In all these countries there existed before the communist takeover cooperative marketing organizations which, in competition with private enterprise, have played an important—in many cases dominant—role in this field. They owned numerous modern processing plants where the products collected by the local societies underwent the necessary treatment before being sold on the home market or abroad. The profits were returned to the farmers in the form of higher prices or patronage refunds.

It is wishful thinking to imagine that once the communist system has been abolished private industry and trade will be able to take over the role of state enterprise in the field of processing and marketing agricultural products. The reorganization of marketing cooperatives capable of operating the processing plants and carrying on the marketing of the products will be, therefore, one of the most urgent tasks.

When, about 80 years ago, the first marketing cooperatives were formed in Denmark, the small local societies not only collected the products from their members but also processed them on the spot. National organizations were set up merely to handle the export of the processed products, such as butter, bacon, etc. The Danish system served as an example for the other Scandinavian countries, and even some countries of Western Europe organized the cooperative marketing of agricultural products on more or less similar lines. In Central Europe, however, processing was mostly the responsibility of the national or regional organizations and the role of the local societies was limited to the collection and delivery of the products. Very often no separate cooperatives were formed for this purpose, but a special department of the local credit or consumers' society was entrusted with the task. Recent technical developments in the field of food processing, transport and storage, and the invention of entirely new processing methods for many products, such as deep-freezing and dry-freezing, have created entirely new conditions for the cooperative processing and marketing of agricultural products and even the Scandinavian cooperatives are increasingly changing over to large-scale processing plants run on a national or regional basis.

The given pattern for the future organization of the processing and marketing of agricultural products in the Communist-dominated countries is, therefore, a number of strong central organizations, each handling the processing and marketing of a certain category of products. They should be linked up in a federation, the task of which would be to safeguard their common interests and to deal with cooperative education and propaganda. From having been the agents of the communist national enterprises, the local multi-purpose societies, reorganized on a truly cooperative basis, should become the agents of the new central organizations for the collection of the products from the farmers. It would also remain the task of these societies to supply the farmers with agricultural equipment, fertilizers, seeds, etc., and even with consumers' goods. One may safely presume that as soon as the freedom of establishment is restored it will not take long before enterprising people will open shops, but this will most probably be the case in towns where it will be easier for them to get the necessary supplies than in the countryside. One must keep in mind that there are no wholesalers left in these countries and it is no doubt a much more difficult problem to rebuild wholesale trade than to start retail shops.

It is very possible, of course, that in all these countries foreign enterprise will play an important role in the reorganization of commodity distribution. In the Western world a revolution is currently taking place in this field, a characteristic feature of which is the increasing interest of powerful financial groups for retail trade. Already, big American and Canadian firms are erecting supermarkets, especially in the countries of the European Common Market where this form of distribution is still in an initial stage of development. Similarly, chain store organizations and department stores are extending their activities to nearly every country of Western Europe. For these groups and organizations a Central and Eastern Europe liberated from communist dominance will mean virgin land and they will not be late in availing themselves of the opportunities for further expansion. But they, too, will, at least in the beginning, concentrate their efforts on the towns and communication centers where, as mentioned before, the only existing form of commodity distribution consists in the state shops. The obvious solution would be to hand these shops over to consumers' cooperative societies formed for this purpose since nowhere would there be people with enough experience and capital to run them. On the other hand, no country would be willing to abandon commodity distribution entirely to foreign enterprise.

In all the Communist-dominated countries the formerly existing cooperative wholesale societies have been dissolved and the multi-purpose village cooperatives receive their supply of goods from the so-called "national enterprises" on the basis of official allotment, a most bureaucratic and inefficient method of distribution. It will be urgently necessary to set up in each country a new cooperative wholesale society in order to secure the supply of goods not only for the multi-purpose village cooperatives but also for the consumers' cooperative societies to be formed in the towns. Considering the complete lack of wholesalers in these countries, it might even prove an incentive to entrust the wholesale societies, as a temporary measure, and their supply of goods to private traders who, of course, should be free to decide whether they want to avail themselves of this possibility or not.

While it is not my intention to enlarge here upon the extremely difficult problem of the restoration of private ownership in the industrial sphere, I would like to mention in this context that, as far as light consumers' industries are concerned, it might be the best solution to let the cooperative wholesale societies operate such factories which, for one reason or other, cannot be handed back to their former owners. If the factories are handed over to the cooperative wholesale societies they will come under—if only indirect—democratic control and will presumably be run in a business-like and efficient way. In all the countries concerned, the cooperative wholesale societies used to operate factories of their own. In Great Britain and in many other countries of Western Europe factories owned by the cooperative wholesalers are often among the leading enterprises of the respective branches of industry.

So far I have only been speaking about the contribution which the cooperatives might be able to make towards the reorganization of agricultural production, the processing and marketing of agricultural products, and the supply of goods to the farmers of the Central and Eastern European countries after their liberation from communist domination. I have purposely left until last the most difficult problem to solve: the problem of agricultural credit. It is generally known that the communist governments have completely destroyed the credit system of these countries. Not only the big commercials banks, but also the mortgage-institutes, the communal and private savings banks, the Post Office savings banks and, of course, the cooperative credit societies, have disappeared. In each of these countries the State Bank is the only source of credit. In order to be able to revert to a freer economy they will be in urgent need of foreign capital and it may be safely presumed that, to begin with, the Western world will be willing to assist them with loans and grants. In the longer run, however, they will have to make every possible effort to further the formation of capital, an endeavor for which the existence of a sound banking system is an inescapable prerequisite.

As far as agriculture is concerned, if the "Producers' Cooperatives"—the "Kolkhoses"—are dissolved and the private ownership of land is restored, many farmers will have neither farm buildings nor houses in which they can live. More fortunate ones will be lacking only animals and equipment, but there will most probably be very few who will not need either long or medium-term credit for some purpose or another. Besides, all of them will certainly need short-term credit for the purchase of fertilizers, seeds, etc. The most urgent needs will no doubt have to be satisfied by means of foreign capital, but this can only be a temporary solution, and later on the farmers will have to rely upon self-help, at least as far as short-term credit is concerned. In all the communist-dominated countries there have been in the past networks of cooperative credit societies with a strong central clearing institute. Experience as well as the example of many other countries shows that this system is best fit to satisfy the requirements of the farmers. A credit society based on the joint responsibility of the local farmers and directed by functionaries elected by them from among themselves offers them greater safety for their savings deposits than an impersonal banking institute and the leaders of the cooperatives. Thanks to their knowledge of the character and standing of their fellow-farmers, the farmers themselves are the best qualified to form a judgment about their credit requirements and their solvency and to control whether the credit is being used for the purpose for which it has been granted. The existence of a central credit institute makes it possible to divert idle funds from one credit society to another where they are better needed. Besides, such a central institute can also obtain deposits and loans from sources outside the farming community and eventually act as an agent of the government for the distribution of state loans to farmers and their cooperatives.

Cooperative credit societies can only grant short-term and, to some extent, medium-term credits, but they are no solution for the problem of long-term credits. For this purpose there existed in these countries, like in many other countries of the world, cooperative mortgage institutes, and it is highly desirable that even in the future the satisfaction of the needs of the farmers for long-term credits should be organized on a cooperative basis since this is the best way to secure their active collaboration and develop their sense of responsibility. To begin with, of course, the contribution of the farmers to the capital of the mortgage institute can only be more or less symbolical and the government will have to supply most of it in the form of loans and guarantees, but here, too, self-help must be the leading principle in the long run.

After the abolition of the communist system in these countries, the craftsmen will be in a position very similar to that of the farmers. They, too, have been forced to join so-called cooperatives and they, too, will be eager to regain their independence. But, even if the cooperatives are dissolved and the machines and tools divided among the members, most of the craftsmen will need credit in order to be able to start on their own again. The purchase of .the necessary raw materials and, for certain categories of them, the sale of the finished products, will also present serious problems. These, of course, are no new problems but have also existed before the communist take-over, and they also exist in the free world. Cooperative methods have been and are being used for their solution in many countries, and even in most of the now communist-dominated countries craftsmen have in the past formed cooperatives for this purpose. It is, there-fore, desirable that instead of dissolving the cooperatives based on compulsion, the craftsmen of Central and Eastern Europe should reorganize them on a voluntary basis. In such a case the activities of most of the societies would probably be restricted to the provision of credit, the supply of raw materials and the sale of the finished products, but there would no doubt also be quite a number of cooper-atives, the members of which would of their own accord prefer to maintain a common workshop in order to use more expensive ma-chines jointly and perhaps even to work on a joint account. As in the case of farmers' cooperatives, central organizations will also have to be set up for the cooperatives of craftsmen in order to serve as clearing centers and to organize the joint purchase of raw materials and the sale of finished products, especially their exports.

It would be a tragic mistake if the countries of Central and Eastern Europe, after having regained their freedom of decision, would revert to the economic nationalism of the years between the two world wars. One must hope that they will form a close economic union which will make it possible for their central cooperative organizations to collaborate to the benefit of their members. A first attempt to establish such collaboration was made about 30 years ago by the leaders of the Hungarian, Rumanian and Yugoslav cooper-ative marketing organizations, but general conditions in those days were not favorable for initiatives of this kind. Close collaboration between cooperative organizations is possible and desirable not only in the marketing of agricultural products but also in the purchase of goods. I am thinking here of the example of the Scandinavian cooperative wholesale societies of Denmark, Finland, Iceland, Nor-way and Sweden, founded in 1916, which, by pooling the purchasing power of the consumers of the five countries, have acquired a unique position on the world market. Their success, of course, is partly due to the similarity of the needs and consumption habits within the region. Conditions are in this respect equally favorable in Central and Eastern Europe. Close collaboration between the cooperatives of the region would in no way preclude intimate relations with other European cooperative organizations but, on the contrary, would strengthen the basis for such relations. Besides the joint purchase of goods certain results have also been achieved within Scandinavia in the form of the rationalization of cooperative production through a division of labor between the cooperative factories of the region. The proposed extension of the European Common Market will create the prerequisites for a similar division of labor between productive enterprises owned by cooperative wholesale societies everywhere in Western Europe. If, as may be hoped, the liberation of Central and Eastern Europe will bring about a further integration of the European economy, nothing would prevent the cooperative organizations of the region to become partners in such a continental partnership.

When reviewing the possibilities cooperation offers for the solution of some of the problems of the transition from the communist system to a system of free economy it was not my intention to draw up the contours of a utopian "Cooperative Commonwealth." Cooperation is not a panacea, and even less is it a socialist alternative to state-directed communism. It is a product of economic liberalism and an indispensable corrective to the abuses of freedom. Cooperatives do not aspire to a monopolistic position and they thrive best in free competition with private enterprise. But the great difficulty of the period of transition will lie precisely in the complete lack of private enterprise in the countries concerned and it is not impossible that until this deficiency can be made up for, the cooperatives will have to play an even more important role than would appear from what has been said previously. This would not be without precedent. For example, during the agricultural crisis of the early thirties, cooperatives had to assume tasks far beyond their original goals, and in certain cases even to exercise monopolistic functions which were contrary to their fundamental principles. On the other hand, a de facto monopoly due to the absolute loyalty of the members to their cooperative organization does not imply an infringement on these principles. Thus, in several Scandinavian countries, as much as 90-95 per cent of the marketable surplus of certain products is handled by cooperatives.

The contribution which cooperatives will be able to make to the solution of the economic problems arising from the abolition of the communist system will, however, ultimately depend on the extent to which people in the countries concerned will understand and follow the true cooperative ideals. In all these countries, cooperation has an old tradition but there are not many left of the generation from the ranks of which the elected functionaries of the societies have been recruited. The members of the present generation only know cooperatives as a means of communist compulsion. There will probably be enough trained staff to do the administrative work which in many respects will not be too different from the work they are doing at present. But it will need considerable effort to educate competent leaders both on the local and national level, and all the assistance the International Cooperative Alliance and cooperative organizations in the Western world will be able and willing to grant to this effect will be most welcome. However, the Hungarian uprising and all the manifestations of the resistance movements in the communist-dominated countries have clearly shown that the years of oppression have not only left the love of freedom in the hearts of the people unaffected but have also fostered in them an unprecedented spirit of solidarity which is bound to make them receptive to the high ideals of cooperation.

Cooperation, as does every human institution, certainly has its limitations, but if one has seen, on the other hand, cooperatives run efficiently by e.g., illiterate natives of Central Africa and Southeast Asia or the oil wells and up-to-date refineries of the farmers' cooperatives of Kansas, or if one knows the history of the successful fight of the Swedish consumers' cooperatives against powerful international trusts and cartels, one may rightly say that the limits for cooperative activities are extremely wide. Today, the cooperative movement is facing the challenge of the very high hopes which, as it appears from the above-mentioned stipulation of the Indian constitution, the developing countries are setting on its capacity of solving their social and economic problems. Let us hope that the day is not too far when it will have to meet the challenge of new possibilities for cooperative action in Central and Eastern Europe. It will be up to men and women of good will to avail themselves of these possibilities in the interest of the people concerned and of humanity in general.

V

APPENDIX

MAPS AND STATISTICAL DATA

THE NUMERICAL STRENGTH AND GROWTH OF THE DANUBIAN NATIONS BETWEEN 1851 AND 1967

IN preparing this statistical survey the *Mid-European Research Institute*, New York, used all official census returns between 1851 and 1960. In 1851 a most comprehensive and relatively "neutral" Austrian conscription of the population[1] of the Habsburg Monarchy took place (see also Map 4). By the "Danubian area" we mean the territories of the typical Danubian states: Austria, Hungary, Czechoslovakia, Rumania, Yugoslavia and Bulgaria. Therefore, besides the former Austro-Hungarian Monarchy (Map 5), the statistical figures also contain the population of the pre-World War I Serbia, Montenegro, Rumania (Regat) and Bulgaria which, in 1851, were not part of the Habsburg Monarchy but were under Turkish domination up to the second half of the 19th century (Map 5). Because a sizable number of Rumanians live in Bessarabia (present Moldavia in the USSR) and in Bukovina (the greater part of which was taken over by the Soviet Union) these provinces are contained in our figures although their inclusion in the Danubian area may be questioned.

In 1851 this multinational Danubian area of 1,029,000 km² contained a population of 38 million which more than doubled to 80 million by 1960—year of the last published census returns (Tables 1-3). When the figures of the population growth are analyzed nation by nation, great differences become evident (Table 2). When Czoernig published the figures of the Austrian conscription, the greater part of the Danubian region was under the authoritarian regime of the Habsburgs and the Balkans were still under Turkish rule (see Map 4). In 1867, the Austro-Hungarian Federal Compromise laid the foundation for the Dual Federal Monarchy which remained unchanged up to 1918. (See Map 5.)

The era between 1918 and 1938 may be called that of the Little Entente or new small states (see Map 6) under the protection of France. The invasion of Hitler began in 1938 and the German National Socialist domination collapsed at the end of the Second World War. After 1945 the USSR dominated the Danubian area with the exception of Austria and, after 1948, Yugoslavia.

Up to the middle of the 19th century many nations (in Tables 1 and 2) were still undeveloped and referred to as "nationalities" with a middle class intelligentsia and city life still embryonic. They now have either statehood or have become "independent" republics, or have some degree of autonomy although heavily overshadowed by the Red Army and the dictatorial power of the Communist party. While the capitals of these Danubian nations have developed, commerce and industry have also had a significant growth. So, by the middle of this century all the Danubian nations have advanced industrially although still far behind the Western nations.

Non-Slavic Nations

Tables 1 and 2 show how the different Danubian nations increased in numerical strength under the various political systems:

Germans: with 7.8 million in the middle of the 19th century were in a dominant position at that time and the most numerous among the Danubian nations. They increased up to 1944 to above 12 million when they fell back with the collapse of Hitlerism as several millions were expelled from the Danubian countries. Their total number in 1945 returned consequently to that of 1851. Now, less than 10 percent of the 7.9 million Danubian Germans live as minorities outside of present Austria.

Hungarians: Although Hungarians suffered great reduction in number during the 160 years under Turkish occupation of their central Lowlands (1526-1686), their recovery was rapid during the 18th and 19th centuries. The 1851 Austrian census found almost 5 million Hungarians in the Carpathian basin living on both sides of the Danube and Tisza rivers. Their number doubled under the fifty year period of the Austro-Hungarian political federation up to 1918. The Trianon Peace Treaty of 1920 allotted more than three million Hungarians to the newly created neighboring states where the census returns showed less favorable figures for Hungarians and other minorities. About 250,000 Hungarians left these lost territories after the First World War and some 308,000 after the Second World War. These increased the number of Hungarians now living in present Hungary to almost 10 million. If more than 3 million now living in neighboring countries are added, their total is 13,250,000—second among Danubian nations whereas they were third in 1851.

Rumanians: With six and one half million in 1851, Rumanians have advanced numerically to become the largest nation in the Danubian area because they have increased to over 19 million—almost three times their number one hundred years ago. Of the 19 million, 2.3 million live in Moldavia, Bessarabia, annexed by the Soviet Union in 1945; 170,000 live in Bukovina also annexed by the USSR; 160,000 are in Yugoslavia and some 16,000 in Hungary.

Jews: Up to 1851 "Jews" included religion and race in the Austrian registration but after 1867 during an era of liberalism, both Austrians and Hungarians registered Jews by religion—"Israelites"— and not by race. Questioners also asked their "Umgangsprache" in Austria and their "mother tongue" in Hungary thereby registering them as Germans, Hungarians, Rumanians, Czechs, etc. But this practice was discontinued after 1920 by the Succession states. Questionnaires then also asked their "nationality" meaning their "ethnic origin" but as few Jews declared for "Jewish nationality", for statistical purposes, the denominational figures better indicate their actual number.

Following the emancipation of the Jews in the middle of the 19th century and the abolishment of the ghetto, their number grew rapidly, not only through natural increase but by heavy immigration from Russia and Poland—the latter being also under Czarist rule. Under the 50 year period of the Austro-Hungarian monarchy, Jews increased as follows:

Jewish Population in Austria-Hungary
(in thousands)

Year	Austria	Hungary
1851	338	369
1869	822	552
1880	1,005	638
1890	1,143	725
1900	1,225	831
1910	1,400	922

In 1851 the number of Jews in the Danubian area was 777,000 which by 1910 had increased to 2.4 million—more than three times the original number. The Jewish population enriched the commercial and intellectual life of the great cities of Vienna, Budapest, and Prague during this period. But after the First World War their total number began to decrease while the genocide of National Socialism after 1938 brought their number down to 380,000—less than half of the 1851 figures.

Slavic Nations

Czechs: The Czechs with almost 4 million in 1851 were the fourth largest nation. They increased to above 9 million, becoming the third largest and industrially the most advanced nation in the Danubian area. If we look to previous decades we find that the Czechs increased their number under the era of the Dual Monarchy faster than the politically dominant Germans. The Czechs increased by 65 percent whereas the Germans increased by only 53 percent between 1851 and 1910. The more rapid increase of the Czechs followed after the First—and especially after the Second World War when the Sudeten Germans were ousted from the Czech lands.

Slovaks: The Slovaks show a comparatively slow increase between 1851 and 1914. This is explained partly by their heavy rate of emigration to America between 1899 and 1914. 310,000 Slovaks emigrated to America during this time. Nevertheless, the Slovaks living in Hungary increased from 1.7 to 2.1 million up to 1910, in the whole Danubian area to 4.2 million till 1967. Their increase therefore exceeds that of the other Slavic nations with the exception of the Croats and Bulgarians.

Rusins (Ruthenes): In tables 1-3 only those Rusins are included who live within the Danubian area—the Carpathian Basin. It seems that their number was erroneously stated in 1851 and again in 1869. The Rusins live mostly on the upper parts of the Carpathian mountains and the 1851 and 1869 conscription figures were mainly estimates. The first individual conscription was taken in 1880, the result of which showed only 353,000 in all of Hungary. Between 1889 and 1910, 58,000 Rusins emigrated to America which explains the slow increase in their number although it is generally known that Rusins had a high birth rate but also a high mortality rate. After the First World War the great majority of Rusins lived in the province of Subcarpathian Ruthenia ("Podkarpatská Rus") in Czechoslovakia. After World War II, the Soviet Union seized and took over this land. Annexed to the Soviet Union under the name "Zakarpatskaya Ukraina", Ukrainians inundated the country. In consequence, the number of Rusins increased to 890,000. The 1959 census showed also an influx of 30,000 Russians plus the Red Army.

Serbs: Somewhat below 4 million in 1851, the Serbs increased fairly evenly up to 1910. During the Balkan wars of 1912-1913 and the First World War, they suffered heavy losses but after 1920 recovery was rapid. According to the latest figures the Serbs now approach 8 million having advanced from fifth place in 1851 to fourth place among the Danubian nations.

Croats: The increase of the Croats was slow before the First World War when 100,295 Croats emigrated to America. But with emigration now stopped the number of Croats has increased, especially after 1920 and has now passed the 4.4 million mark.

Slovenes: With 1.1 million in 1851 the Slovenes, almost all of whom lived within former Austria—now the Republic of Slovenia in Yugoslavia—show the lowest rate of natural increase not only among the Slavs but among all the Danubian nations. The Slovenes increased very slowly from 1.1 million in 1851 to 1.6 million throughout the entire century. They did however reach a comparatively high cultural level.

Bulgarians: Even today a predominantly agricultural nation, the Bulgars more than trippled during this century. From a nation of 2.2 million subjected to Turkish rule they increased to 7 million although some hundred thousand live outside of Bulgaria in Dobrudja and Macedonia, the latter being under hot dispute with Yugoslavia.

Summary: Growth of Slavs and Non-Slavs compared.
New Problems.

If we consider the growth of nations during the Dual Monarchy we see that before 1910 the politically dominant Austro-Germans increased only by 53 percent while the other still predominantly agricultural nations grew more rapidly—the Hungarians by 109, Rumanians by 78, and the Bulgarians by 77 percent. The 209 percent exceptionally high increase of the Jewish population is explained by their high rate of immigration during the era of liberalism when they prospered highly, especially in the capitals and cities. Others— the Slovaks, Croats and Serbs grew more rapidly after the First World War when their emigration stopped and they continued to increase after the Second World War. But in the last decades the increase was caused by state interference at the expense of the drastically reduced Jewish element, the expelled Germans and Hungarians living as minorities.

Table 3 groups the Danubian nations as Slavs and non-Slavs. The totals show that the non-Slavs increased in the Danubian area from 20 million to 38 million while the Slavs increased more rapidly from 15 to 25 million. Among the non-Slav nations the faster growing Rumanians and Hungarians somewhat counterbalanced the radical but politically caused decrease of Germans and Jews. The comparatively fast increase of the southern Slavs partly explains why the grand total of all Slavs increased during this more than one hundred year period by 132 percent while the non-Slavs grew only 92 percent. The rate of increase between 1851 and 1960 follows in their order of growth:

Increase between 1851 and 1960 if 1851 = 100

1.	Bulgarians	303
2.	Rumanians	269
3.	Hungarians	260
4.	Croats	259
5.	Czechs	232
6.	Serbs	212
7.	Slovaks	209
8.	Rusins	183
9.	Slovenes	143
10.	Germans	100
11.	Jews	44

As can be seen, the comparative strength and growth of the Danubian nations were influenced only partly through natural increase. Sometimes political events played a much greater part in these last hundred years. As a rule, however, agricultural populations increased more rapidly as the more rapid growth of the Bulgarians, Rumanians, Hungarians, Croats, Serbs and Slovaks show. Industrialization (see Map 7) slows down the natural increase of the population but political factors may counterbalance this relatively slow, natural increase, e.g., in the case of the Czechs. Population experts may find causes for the relatively faster or slower increase of the population also in the religious composition of the population.

It should be pointed out that the ten or eleven Danubian nations do not have clear ethnic boundaries. The greater portion of each nation lives in an area where it forms 75 percent or more of the population but large territories between those almost purely national areas are inhabited by two or three nations mixed together as majorities and minorities in a peculiar multinational symbiosis. It should be clear therefore that a political form like the Swiss federation would be more natural and appropriate for this multinational Danubian area than the present pseudo-national small states with their pseudo-independence. (See Maps 8 and 9)

The normal life and development of the minorities living in the present so-called "national states" of the Danubian area are not secure. The national composition of whole areas and large towns was changed during the last decades by violent political interference. The dominant nations used expulsion, administrative methods, school systems, expropriation of landed estates and properties, confiscation of the press and cultural institutions to change the composition of the population and increase the majority of the dominant nation at the expense of the minorities. This trend of State interference increased constantly after the era of liberalism closed at the outbreak of World War I.

The climax of violent State interference came after 1939 with National Socialist and, after 1944, under Communist-Stalinist regimes when hundreds of thousands or even millions were expelled, imprisoned, de-nationalized or forced to join the dominant nation. After the thawing of Stalinism, some improvement became evident—first in Yugoslavia after 1948, in Czechoslovakia after 1968 but least in Rumania. Politicians of today should remember that national chauvinism and oppression of minorities caused two political explosions in the Danubian area, first in 1938-40 when the French supported Little Entente system was broken up and after 1944 when German domination of the area was stricken down. Those who now rely on the presence of the Red Army to maintain oppressive policies should understand that oppression based on a foreign power and militarism cannot always continue.

Leading Slavic politicians in particular should be most careful in considering the future of their nation. Table 3 shows that notwithstanding the strong Slavic thrust forward during the last decades, the majority of the Danubian peoples is still non-Slav and this important group of nations occupies the *geographic center of the Danubian area:* Austrians, Hungarians and Rumanians living between the northern and southern Slavs. Instead of national domination and oppression of minorities within pseudo-national states under the protection of the army of a foreign power, an autochtonous solution of the Danubian nations is needed for which international neutralization and federalization, or Helvetization, are the basic principles of a just solution: a new Compromise.

1) Czoernig, Karl von, **Ethnographie der Österreichischen Monarchie,** Wien, 1857, 1-3 vol. Die Verteilung der Völkerstaemme und deren Gruppen in der Oest. Monarchie. Wien. K.K. Direction der Adm. Statistik. 1861. From Czoernig's official statistics the population figures of the north Italian provinces, lost in 1859, were deducted. Galicia, which is not a part of the Danubian area and is presently divided between the Soviet Union and Poland was also excluded.

TABLE 1.

THE DANUBIAN NATIONS FROM 1851 TO 1967.

(in thousands)

Year	Austro-Germans	Hun-garians	Ru-manians	Czechs	Slo-vaks	Rusins	Serbs	Slovenes	Croats	Bulgars	Jews
1851	7,800	4,917	6,474	3,914	1,730	447	3,727	1,127	1,619	2,200	777
In the era of Habsburg Absolutism											
1869	9,781	6,325	7,471	4,800	1,947	469	3,747	1,135	1,764	2,428	1,468
1880	9,963	6,628	7,944	5,213	1,995	353	4,413	1,141	1,942	2,611	1,743
1890	10,362	7,620	8,878	5,508	2,057	379	5,092	1,177	1,968	2,835	2,218
1900	11,307	8,962	10,048	5,995	2,182	424	5,280	1,193	2,117	3,253	2,284
1910	11,987	10,301	11,449	6,476	2,146	464	5,560	1,253	2,277	3,917	2,402
In the era of Austro-Hungarian Dual Monarchy											
1920	11,066	9,828	11,811	6,886	2,211	490	4,617	1,025	3,265	4,367	2,114
1930	11,589	10,722	13,195	7,536	2,546	564	5,267	1,222	3,589	5,190	1,968
1940	12,058	11,397	—	—	—	—	—	—	—	5,703	—
After the peace treaties of 1919/20											
1949/50	7,698	12,074	16,137	8,423	3,372	—	6,621	1,415	3,837	6,200	380
1960	7,829	12,790	17,470	9,111	3,939	808	7,874	1,589	4,340	6,674	348
1967 *	7,864	13,250	19,254	9,235	4,214	890	7,914	1,610	4,420	6,976	345
After the Second World War											

* Estimate based on last census and natural increase of the subsequent years.

TABLE 2.

INCREASE OR DECREASE OF THE DANUBIAN NATIONS BETWEEN 1851 AND 1967

A. NON-SLAVIC NATIONS

Year	Austro-Germans	Hun-garians	Ru-manians	Jews
In the era of Habsburg absolutism 1851 = 1.00				
1851	1.00	1.00	1.00	1.00
In the era of the Austro-Hungarian Dual Monarchy				
1869	1.25	1.28	1.15	1.89
1880	1.28	1.35	1.23	2.24
1890	1.35	1.55	1.29	2.59
1900	1.45	1.82	1.55	2.93
1910	1.53	2.09	1.78	3.09
After the Paris Peace Treaties of 1919/20				
1920	1.42	1.99	1.82	2.72
1930	1.49	2.18	2.19	2.53
1940	1.55	2.32	—	—
After the Second World War				
1948	0.98	2.49	2.46	0.48
1960	1.00	2.60	2.69	0.44
1967 *	1.01	2.69	2.97	0.44

B. SLAVIC NATIONS

	Czechs	Slovaks	Rusins	Serbs	Slovenes	Croats	Bulgars
In the era of Habsburg absolutism 1851 = 1.00							
1851	1.00	1.00	1.00	1.00	1.00	1.00	1.00
In the era of the Austro-Hungarian Dual Monarchy							
1869	1.18	1.12	1.05	1.01	1.01	1.09	1.09
1880	1.33	1.15	0.79	1.19	1.01	1.19	1.18
1890	1.40	1.18	0.85	1.36	1.04	1.21	1.29
1900	1.53	1.26	0.92	1.41	1.06	1.30	1.47
1910	1.65	1.24	1.09	1.49	1.11	1.41	1.77
After the Paris Peace Treaties of 1919/20							
1920	1.75	1.28	1.26	1.23	0.97	2.01	1.98
1930	1.92	1.48	1.28	1.41	1.02	2.19	2.36
1940	—	—	—	—	—	—	—
After the Second World War							
1948	2.12	1.95	—	1.76	1.28	2.36	2.81
1960	2.32	2.09	1.83	2.12	1.43	2.59	3.03
1967 *	2.35	2.44	2.21	2.15	1.43	2.73	3.17

TABLE 3.

INCREASE OF THE DANUBIAN NATIONS IN THE CENTURY
BETWEEN 1851 AND 1960

Year	1851	1960	if 1851 = 1.00
	(in thousands		
A. *Non-Slavic Nations*			
1. Germans	7,800	7,829	1.00
2. Hungarians	4,917	12,790	2.60
3. Jews	777	348	0.44
1 - 3 TOTAL	13,494	20,967	1.55
4. Rumanians	6,474	17,470	2.69
A. TOTAL 1-4, Non-Slavs	19,968	38,437	1,92
B. *Slavic Nations*			
a) *Northern Slavs:*			
5. Czechs	3,914	9,111	2,32
6. Slovaks	1,730	3,939	2.09
7. Rusins	447	808	1.83
5 - 7 TOTAL	6,091	13,858	2.27
b) *Southern Slavs:*			
8. Serbs	3,727	7,874	2.12
9. Croats	1,619	4,340	2.59
10. Slovenes	1,127	1,589	1.43
11. Bulgars	2,200	6,674	3.03
8 - 11 TOTAL	8,673	20,477	2.35
B. TOTAL Slavs. 5 - 11	14,764	34,335	2.32
A and B: ALL THE LARGER NATIONS (1 - 11)	34,732	72,772	2.06
OTHER SMALLER GROUPS and NATIONALITIES	3,648	7,575	2.07
GRAND TOTAL, POPULATION	38,380	80,347	2.09

MAP 4

AUSTRIA—HUNGARY IN 1859 AND BETWEEN 1867-1918

(The Italian provinces were surrendered in 1859)

MAP 5

AUSTRIA—HUNGARY AND BORDERING STATES IN 1914

MAP 6

DISMEMBERMENT OF AUSTRIA—HUNGARY IN 1919-1920

1. Galicia was transferred to Poland.
2. Transylvania (Erdély) and Bukovina were transferred to Romania proper which acquired Bessarabia from Russia and Dobrudja from Bulgaria.
3. The Czech lands with Moravia, Slovakia and Subcarpathia were united as Czechoslovakia.
4. The Kingdom of the Serbs-Croats-Slovenes, later called Yugoslavia, was created by adding several provinces shown North and West of Serbia.

MAP 7

AGRICULTURAL POPULATION IN TRANSITION
IN THE DANUBIAN AREA ABOUT 1930

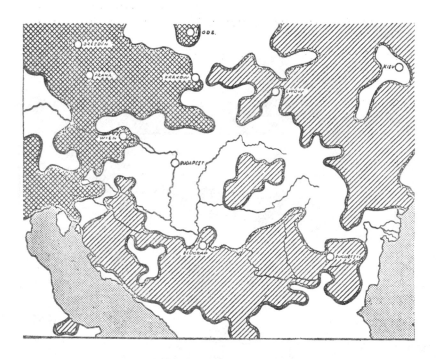

 Agricultural population was more than 80%
of total population.

Industrial population was above 25%
of the total population.

 Agricultural population is less than 80% but industrial
population has not yet reached 25%
of the total population (1930).

MAP 8

MIXED AREAS BETWEEN THE NATIONS IN CENTRAL EUROPE.
AREAS WITH NATIONALITIES IN MAJORITY ABOVE 75 PER CENT (Last pre-war census figures)

1. Hungarians
2. Germans
3. Italians
4. Roumanians
5. Poles
6. Czechs
7. Slovaks
8. Ruthenians
9. Slovenes
10. Croatians
11. Bosnians
12. Serbians
13. Serbians-Bulgarians mixed
14. Bulgarians
15. Albanians
16. Turks
17. No majority

385

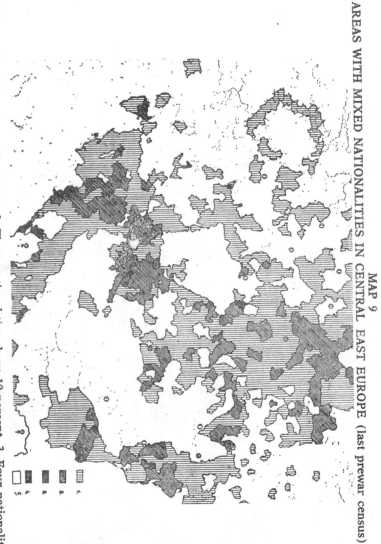

MAP 9

AREAS WITH MIXED NATIONALITIES IN CENTRAL EAST EUROPE (last prewar census)

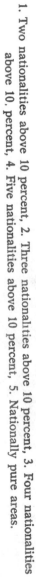

1. Two nationalities above 10 percent, 2. Three nationalities above 10 percent, 3. Four nationalities above 10, percent, 4. Five nationalities above 10 percent, 5. Nationally pure areas.

CHART 1

GROWTH OF THE DANUBIAN NATIONS BETWEEN 1851 AND 1967 BASED ON OFFICIAL CENSUS RETURNS.

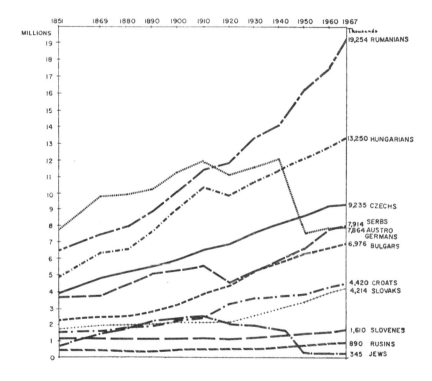

CHART 2

INCREASE OR DECREASE OF THE DANUBIAN NATIONS
BETWEEN 1851 AND 1967
BASED ON THE YEAR 1851.

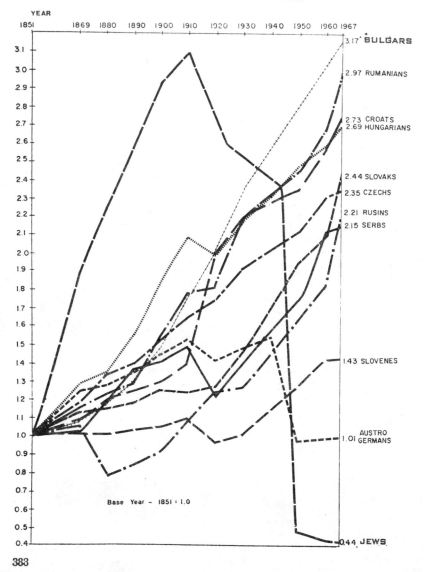

Index

Compiled by *Christina Maria T. Wagner*

DANUBIAN PRESS, INC.
Astor Park, Florida 32002
Price: $8.50